Alexander the Great

Alexander the Great

Coinage, Finances, and Policy

Georges Le Rider

Translated by W. E. Higgins
with a Preface by G. W. Bowersock

American Philosophical Society
Philadelphia • 2007

MEMOIRS
of the
AMERICAN PHILOSOPHICAL SOCIETY
Held at Philadelphia
For Promoting Useful Knowledge
Volume 261

Copyright © 2007 by the American Philosophical Society for its *Memoirs* series.
All rights reserved.

ISBN-13: 978-0-87169-261-0
US ISSN: 0065-9738

Translation of French publication *Alexandre le Grand: Monnaie, Finances et Politique.*

Library of Congress Cataloging-in-Publication Data

Le Rider, Georges.
  [Alexandre le Grand. English]
  Alexander the Great : coinage, finances, and policy / Georges Le Rider ;
translated by W.E. Higgins with a preface by G.W. Bowersock.
    p. cm. — (Memoirs of the American Philosophical Society ; 261)
    Includes bibliographical references and index.
    ISBN 978-0-87169-261-0
    1. Coins, Greek. 2. Alexander, the Great, 356-323 B.C. 3. Money—
Greece—History. I. Higgins, W. E. (William Edward), 1945– II. Title.

CJ405.L413 2008
938'.07—dc22
                                                            2008005172

Contents

Preface xi

Translator's Note xiii

Abbreviations xv

Introduction xvii

Chapter 1 **Coinage with the Name and Types of Alexander: Questions of Classification, Interpretation, and Chronology** 1

Presentation of the Currency with the Name and Types of Alexander: The Works of L. Müller, E. T. Newell, and M. J. Price 2

The Traditional Interpretation of the Coinage with the Name of Alexander and with the Types of Herakles Head and Seated Zeus for Silver, and Athena Head and Nike for Gold 6

The Date of the First Tetradrachms with Herakles Head and Seated Zeus, and the First Gold Staters with Athena Head and Nike 8

Chapter 2 **Alexander and Coinage in Macedonia from October 336 to April 334** 17

The Monetary Situation Philip II Bequeathed in October 336 18

The Financial Organization of the Macedonian Kingdom 20

Macedonian Finances under Alexander from October 336 to April 334   24

Alexander's Coinage in Macedonia from October 336 to April 334   31

The Continued Striking of Coins of Philip II after Alexander's Accession   37

Alexander and the Coinage of Philip II   41

Chapter 3 **Coinage in Macedonia under Antipater from April 334 to June 323   45**

Antipater's Financial Burdens from 334 to 323   45

Antipater and Coinage Production in Macedonia from April 334   50

Reflections on the Chronology of the Silver Coinage Issued by Antipater with Alexander's Name and Types Beginning c. 332   57

M. Thompson on Coinage Production in Alexander's Mints and the Return of Demobilized Soldiers   60

A Critique of the Thompson Thesis   62

Chapter 4 **Alexander and Coinage in Western Asia Minor   73**

Is It Possible to Estimate the Monthly Cost of Alexander's Army during His Stay in Asia Minor?   73

From the Battle of the Granicus to the Capture of Sardis: How Alexander's Financial Situation Evolved (Spring 334)   77

Note on the Revenues of the Great King and Alexander   79

Alexander's Financial Situation during Summer 334   80

Alexander's Monetary Practice in Asia Minor   84

Attribution of a Coinage with the Name and Types of Alexander to Western Asia Minor   85

Chronology of Alexanders Struck in Western Asia Minor in the Years Following the Macedonian Conquest   88

Remarks on the Alexander Drachms of Asia Minor Issued at the End of the Fourth Century and the Beginning of the Third   95

Why Would the First Alexanders from Asia Minor Have Been Struck at a Relatively Late Date? 99

The Currency Used in Asia Minor from 334 to the End of Alexander's Reign 105

Chapter 5 **Alexander and Coinage in Cilicia, Phoenicia, Syria, and Cyprus 111**

Financial and Monetary Questions 112

The Sidon Mint Began Striking Alexander Tetradrachms in 333/332 (October 333 to September 332) 113

Alexander at Tarsus 117

When and Why Alexander Decided to Issue His Own Silver Coinage with the Types of Herakles Head and Seated Zeus 120

Comments on the Types of Alexander's Tetradrachms 123

Alexander and Tyre 125

Beginning and End of Alexanders from Tyre 130

The First Gold Coins of Alexander; Importance of the Capture of Tyre; Role of the Tarsus Mint; General Remarks on the Types 134

Other Coinages of Alexander in Phoenicia, Syria, and Cyprus 139

Some Comments on the Volume of Alexander Issues from Cilicia, Phoenicia, Syria, and Cyprus up to c. 318 143

The Coinages of Cilicia, Phoenicia, Syria, and Cyprus in the Last Two Years of Alexander's Reign (325/324 and 324/323) 149

Alexanders and Local Coinages 152

Chapter 6 **Alexander and Coinage in Egypt 161**

Alexander in Egypt (November 332 to April 331) 162

Egyptian Coinage before 332: C. M. Kraay's Treatment 165

Egyptian Coinage before Alexander: The Proposals of T. V. Buttrey 167

The Syrian Hoard: Additional Data   168

Did Alexander Strike Bronze Coins in Egypt between November 332 and April 331 with His Portrait on the Obverse? Price's Theory   171

P. Debord's Elaboration of Price's Interpretation   173

Comments on the Interpretations of Price and Debord   175

Cleomenes of Naucratis, Master of Egypt from April 331 until the Aftermath of Alexander's Death   179

What Were Cleomenes's Expenses?   182

Cleomenes's Extraordinary Ways to Raise Money   184

Cleomenes and the Grain Trade   185

How to Judge Cleomenes as Financial Manager?   188

The Problem of Currency in Egypt from 332 to 323   191

Cleomenes and the Coinage with the Name and Types of Alexander   192

Would Cleomenes Have Struck Coins Other than Alexanders?   195

What Currency Did Cleomenes Use?   196

Note on the Mint Where the First Egyptian Alexanders Were Struck   197

Chapter 7   **Alexander and Coinage in Babylonia and East of the Tigris   201**

Alexander's Arrival at Babylon   202

Alexander's Decisions at Babylon; Officials of Babylon between 331 and 323   203

I: Babylonian Coinages from 331 to 323   206

Mazaeus's "Lion" Coinage at Babylon and its Posterity   206

Gold Double Darics and Darics (and Possibly Silver Sigloi): Were They Struck in Babylonia during Alexander's Reign?   210

Coinage with the Types of Athens Struck in Babylonia 214

Babylonian Coinage with the Name and Types of Alexander; Newell's Attribution and Price's Objections 219

Arguments in Favor of Newell's Classification 222

The Date of the Alexanders of Groups 1, 2, and 3 224

II: Alexander and Babylonia from 325/324. Antimenes of Rhodes 225

Remarks on Coinage Activity at the Babylonian Mint between 325/324 and Late 317 225

Alexander's Expenditures in Babylon and Babylonia at the End of His Reign 227

Antimenes of Rhodes 228

Alexander's Treasury in 324/323 233

Antimenes and Coinage in the Name of Alexander 238

III: Alexander's Coinage East of the Tigris 240

Mediums of Exchange in the East 240

Alexander's Currency Requirements 240

The Daric: Alexander's Gold Coinage in the East? 243

The Other Coins Alexander Would Have Used in the East 246

IV: A Mysterious Group of Silver Coins: The Coinage Memorializing Alexander's Combat with King Porus in India 247

The "Porus" Decadrachms and Related Tetradrachms 247

Conclusion 253

Notes to Plates 259

Index 271

Preface

This English translation of Georges Le Rider's comprehensive study of the coinage and financial policy of Alexander the Great brings, for the first time, the magisterial scholarship of one of the world's greatest living numismatists before an Anglophone public.

For more than forty years Le Rider has published fundamental studies on the coinages of the ancient Middle East and eastern Mediterranean world, particularly from the time of Philip II (Alexander's father), Alexander himself, and the Seleucid Empire. These include classic books on Susa under the Seleucids and Parthians (1965), the gold and silver coinage of Philip II in Macedonia (1977), and the finances of Philip II (1996). Le Rider's collected papers were published in three large volumes in 1999. His *Alexandre le Grand : Monnaie, Finances et Politique* (2003) that is now appearing in English represents the culmination of a lifetime of reflection on the coinage of Alexander.

Throughout his career Le Rider has demonstrated a rare and unusual ability to combine the meticulous analysis of coins and coin hoards with interpretations that convey the historical significance of the finds. He thereby joins the instincts of a great collector with the passion of a great historian, and this study of Alexander's finances draws the reader over and over again from detailed analysis and scholarly controversy into a compelling evocation of a canny and pragmatic world conqueror.

It is not only Le Rider's gift for seeing the implications of his multitudinous coinage issues that every reader of his works in French will know so well, it is also the uncommon lucidity and simplicity of his presentation of the material. No one could hope to capture the crystalline clarity of his French prose, but by working closely with Le Rider himself and with numismatic specialists, above all Le Rider's friend and collaborator Hyla Troxell, William E. Higgins has created a book worthy of the original. It manages to retain the excitement of a detective investigation that begins with an anecdote handed down by Plutarch and ends by subverting it.

In a rich and varied career Georges Le Rider has taught at both the École Pratique des Hautes Études and the Collège de France. He has also served as Director of the French Institute of Anatolian Studies in Istanbul. From 1975–81 he had the major position of *Administrateur général* of the Bibliothèque Nationale of France. Since 1989 he has been a Member of the Institut de France in the Académie des Inscriptions et Belles Lettres.

Georges Le Rider has been a frequent visitor in the United States, notably at the American Numismatic Society and the Institute for Advanced Study in Princeton. In 1996 he was elected a Foreign Member of the American Philosophical Society, and it is therefore particularly fitting for the Society to be the publisher of his first book in English. The Aristotle Onassis Foundation generously funded the translation through the intercession of Michel Amandry, to whom everyone involved in this project must be grateful.

Glen W. Bowersock
Membre de l'Institut de France
Professor Emeritus
of Ancient History,
Institute for Advanced Study

Translator's Note

I would like to alert the reader to certain features of the following translation.

I have translated the text of the original edition, correcting its occasional errors of citation, and I have updated certain references for the convenience of an English-speaking public. Professor Le Rider has also made several revisions of style and substance, to take account of new material or to reflect his own latest thoughts. I have also translated the other scholars Professor Le Rider quotes, whether in French or another modern language, in the latter instance noting the occurrence. I have sometimes added brief explanatory remarks of my own, identified by the initials WEH, to aid the nonspecialist's understanding. Passages in the original edition, set in smaller type, offering detailed elaboration of the main argument, are here placed in square brackets out of concern for the reader's eyesight.

For the ancient sources, I have employed, without other acknowledgment, the translations of the Loeb Classical Library. I have sometimes provided different published English translations, identified as they occur, in the absence of, or in preference to, a Loeb. Occasionally I have offered my own versions, marked by the initials WEH, or, noting the occurrence, I have modified the translation used to suit contemporary usage better or to make Professor Le Rider's point more clear.

All references to Arrian, unless otherwise indicated, are to that author's *Anabasis*.

I would also like to acknowledge the Bobst Library at New York University and the library at the American Numismatic Society, both of which facilitated my efforts.

I am especially grateful to the indefatigable Hyla A. Troxell for her scholarly and editorial vigilance with the manuscript. Readers from the Press made useful suggestions and sharpened my numismatic usage.

Finally, I would like to thank Professor Le Rider for his prompt, careful, and helpful reading of my drafts and his responses to my queries. It has been a pleasure as well as an honor to work with him on this project.

Abbreviations

Most of the abbreviations used should be readily comprehensible, so I limit this list to the following:

AJN	*American Journal of Numismatics*
BCH	*Bulletin de Correspondance Hellénique*
BMC	*British Museum Catalogue of Greek Coins*
CH	*Coin Hoards*
Demanhur (1923)	E. T. Newell, *Alexander Hoards II. Demanhur, 1905* (Num. Notes and Monographs 19, Amer. Num. Soc., New York, 1923)
ESM	E. T. Newell, *The Coinage of the Eastern Seleucid Mints, from Seleucus I to Antiochus III* (Num. Studies 1, Amer. Num. Soc., New York, 1938)
IGCH	*Inventory of Greek Coin Hoards* (1973)
JHS	*Journal of Hellenic Studies*
NAC	*Numismatica e Antichità Classiche*
NC	*Numismatic Chronicle*
Naissance	G. Le Rider, *La naissance de la monnaie. Pratiques monétaires de l'Orient ancien* (Paris, 2001)
Philippe II	G. Le Rider, *Le monnayage d'argent et d'or de Philippe II frappé en Macédoine de 359 à 294* (Paris, 1977)
Price, *Alexander* (1991)	M. J. Price, *The Coinage in the Name of Alexander The Great and Philip Arrhidaeus* (Zurich-London, 1991)
RBN	*Revue Belge de Numismatique*

REA	*Revue des Etudes Anciennes*
REG	*Revue des Etudes Grecques*
RN	*Revue Numismatique*
Reattribution	E. T. Newell, *Reattribution of Certain Tetradrachms of Alexander the Great* (New York, 1912)
SNG	*Sylloge Nummorum Graecorum*
Troxell, *Alexander* (1997)	H. A. Troxell, *Studies in the Macedonian Coinage of Alexander the Great* (Num. Studies 21, Amer. Num. Soc., New York, 1997)

Introduction

Plutarch, in his treatise *On the Fortune or the Virtue of Alexander*, where he seeks to show that the Macedonian king owed his successes and glory to his moral and intellectual qualities and not to good luck, reports the Conqueror's reflections that his encounter with Diogenes the Cynic inspired (1.10, also *Moralia* 331 E–332 D).

Alexander liked to say, "If I weren't Alexander, I would be Diogenes." Plutarch has him elaborate on this statement as follows: "If it were not my purpose to combine foreign things with Greek, to traverse and civilize every continent, to search out the uttermost parts of land and sea, to push the bounds of Macedonia to the farthest Ocean, and to disseminate and shower the blessings of Greek justice and peace over every nation, I would not be content to sit quietly in the luxury of idle power, but I would emulate the frugality of Diogenes." Alexander continued by observing that, thanks to his victories, Indian philosophers and Diogenes would become aware of each other. If one trusts the reading of three important manuscripts, Alexander supposedly ended his reminiscence on Diogenes with a comment that seizes the attention of every reader interested in monetary matters: "I, also, like Diogenes, must make a new coinage and stamp barbarian currencies with the impress of Greek government."[1]

Everybody knew that Diogenes had been involved with coinage during the first part of his life. A native of Sinope, the great port on the Black

---

1. This translation has retained the version of these three manuscripts: *Parisinus 1957* (end of tenth century), *Parisinus 1671* (1296), and *Parisinus 1675* (dated around 1430). *Parisinus 1671* gives the text Planudes corrected and entrusted to a professional copyist. On the manuscripts of Plutarch, see J. Irigoin, *Histoire du texte des "Oeuvres morales" de Plutarque*, in Vol. 1 of the Universités de France edition, 1987, pp. CCXXVII–CCCX. [The modified Loeb translation given here agrees in its reading of the MS tradition with the "Budé" French translation of C. Froidefond cited by Professor Le Rider (coll. des Universités de France, 1990)—WEH.]

Sea, he had directed that city's mint. The writer Diogenes Laertius, who lived after Plutarch, mentions different versions of what befell him (*Lives of Eminent Philosphers*, 6.2.20-21). On one point they all agree: Diogenes altered the metal of the coins he was in charge of issuing. When found out, he was forced to leave his homeland.

Diogenes Laertius, in describing Diogenes's official misconduct, notably uses the verb *parakharattein*, which can be translated "to manufacture coinage different from the expected coinage, the standard coinage." In effect, Diogenes was regarded as having put into circulation coins that, while being of the city's type, differed from its standard coins because he had illegally modified their metallic quality for his own profit.

Plutarch has Alexander first say that he is going to strike a new coinage (*nomisma parakoptein*); the verb that begins the second part of the sentence, *parakharattein*, is the same word Diogenes Laertius uses, and it was probably the verb people readily used when speaking about Diogenes of Sinope. I am inclined to think, therefore, that Alexander, in this second part of the sentence, was not quitting the monetary context and that he was seeking to say precisely how he would go about creating his new coinage. I prefer this version, which seems logical to me, to one given in two other manuscripts.[2] According to the latter, after having announced his intention to circulate a new coinage, Alexander allegedly expressed a general conclusion by saying that he would go forth to the Hellenization of the barbarian world (*parakharattein* being taken figuratively).

To establish this parallel between the schemes of Diogenes and the design of Alexander, Plutarch had to play on words: the new coinage of Diogenes was fraudulent and profitable to him alone, while that of Alexander was an integral part of a civilizing program. It would replace barbarian currency (initially the Great King's gold darics and silver sigloi), and its types (chosen by Alexander) would promote the good of humanity.

What especially interests me in Plutarch's narrative is how the Greek writer judged that it was only natural for the Macedonian king to plan to impose his own coinage throughout his domain. In the same way, many modern authors, without necessarily sharing Plutarch's grandiose vision, like him imagine that the Conqueror wanted to strike a coinage that might supplant all others and cause their disappearance in the countries where he became master.

What actually happened? To be in a position to evaluate Alexander's attitude towards coinage, it is necessary not only to study the currency issued with his name and types closely and, in particular, to date the differ-

---

2. These two manuscripts are *Barberinianus 182* (end of tenth century) and *Ambrosianus 881* (thirteenth century).

ent series precisely, but also to take most careful account of the monetary, financial, and political realities that characterized each of the regions of the immense Macedonian empire.

That is why, after having presented the coinage bearing Alexander's own types, I will adopt in what follows a geographical arrangement. I will seek to detail and explain the sovereign's conduct of monetary matters, first in Macedonia, then in western Asia Minor, Cilicia, Phoenicia and Syria, in Egypt, Babylonia, and finally in the vast territories situated to the east of the Tigris and the Euphrates.[3]

---

3. The fifth updated edition of P. Briant's *Alexandre le Grand* appeared, in February, 2002, in the series "Que sais-je?", number 622. I recommend it.

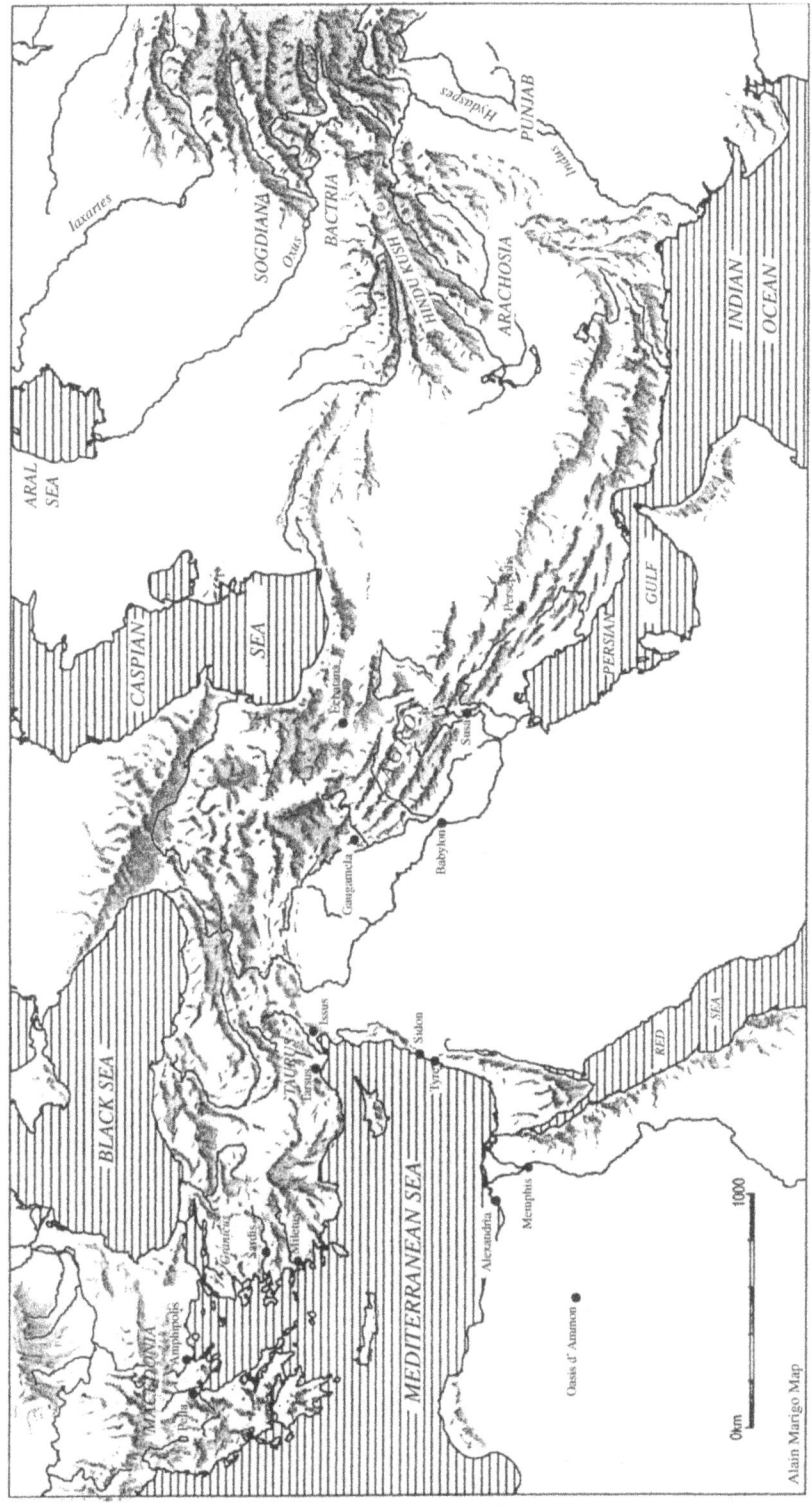

Map 1

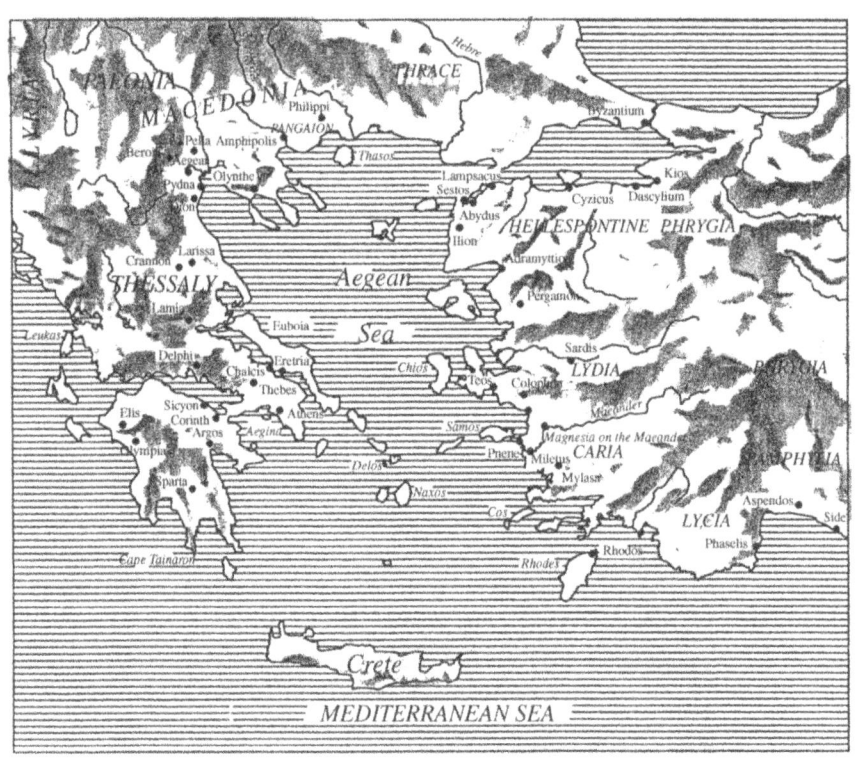

Map 2

Map 3

Map 4

Chapter 1

~

Coinage with the Name and Types of Alexander: Questions of Classification, Interpretation, and Chronology

Ancient authors were never prodigal with information on the financial and monetary measures of the personalities whose great deeds they record for us. The sparse data we possess in this area have an anecdotal character or are bound up with an individual episode. The Greek and Roman historians of Alexander are no exception. To be sure, the stunning career of this uncommon man elicited so many detailed narratives that the amount of financial information about his reign is far from negligible. But, strictly speaking, no ancient text informs us specifically about the coinage of Alexander. It is therefore on the study of the coins themselves, above all, that modern scholars have based their work.

In this first chapter, which will be devoted to presenting the coinage struck with the name and types of the Macedonian king, I will demonstrate that many problems associated with it can be considered settled today but that, despite this progress, numerous uncertainties still remain. As we will see throughout this study, on important points discussion is far from closed.

Alexander, who was born, according to Plutarch (*Alexander* 3.5) in July 356, was a little over twenty years old when he succeeded his father Philip II in October 336.[1] Having consolidated his power in Macedonia,

---

1. Philip II was assassinated at Aigeai, the old Macedonian capital, when he was jointly celebrating major festivals and the marriage of his daughter Cleopatra to Alexander of Epirus. This event used to be dated to summer 336, but it has been shown that it ought rather to be placed in the autumn of the same year, at the start of the month called Dios, which opened the Macedonian calendar and corresponds to our October. For the current state of the issue,

Greece, and the Balkans, he crossed the Hellespont at the start of spring 334 (probably in the first days of April). He carried off three memorable victories over the Great King, Darius III: at the Granicus River (end of May 334), which gave him possession of Asia Minor; Issus (autumn 333), which made him master of Phoenicia, Syria, and Egypt; and Gaugamela (October 1, 331), which marked the end of the Persian Empire. Alexander entered Babylonia and took over Susa, Persepolis, and regions still farther east. He reached India, crossed the Indus, and continued his journey to the most easterly tributary of the Indus, the Hyphasis, whereupon he redirected his route to the west. He died in Babylon on June 10, 323, not quite thirty-three years old.[2]

Presentation of the Currency with the Name and Types of Alexander: The Works of L. Müller, E. T. Newell, and M. J. Price

The coins of Alexander: these words principally call to mind two denominations that numerous publications devoted to the great Conqueror have made familiar to all who are interested in Antiquity. These are the silver tetradrachms with Herakles head and seated Zeus, and the gold staters with Athena head and Nike, the goddess of Victory.

1. On the tetradrachms (pl. 1, 1): the head of Herakles, beardless, wearing a lion skin headdress, appears on the obverse; Zeus, seated, carrying an eagle on his right hand (Zeus is the "eaglebearer") and holding a scepter in his left, appears on the reverse; the usual legend is *Alexandrou* (the Greek genitive case indicating that the coinage is "Alexander's"). These coins,

---

cf. N. G. L. Hammond, "The Regnal Years of Philip and Alexander," *Greek, Roman and Byz. Studies* 33 (1992), pp. 355–73; M. B. Hatzopoulos, "The Oleveni Inscription and the Dates of Philip II's Reign," *Philip, Alexander the Great and the Macedonian Heritage* (Washington, 1982), pp. 38–42, observed that marriages took place, according to an attested custom, during festivals in honor of Zeus Olympios held in the month of Dios and that these are the festivals in question in Diodorus's account (16.91–92). On this dating, year one of Alexander's reign is not the year 337/336, but the year 336/335. Hatzopoulos took up the Oleveni inscription again in *Chiron* 25 (1995), pp. 163–85, where he establishes the date of Philip's accession.

2. A cuneiform astronomical tablet from Babylonia made it possible to establish that Alexander died on June 10 and not June 13, as a less reliable source had led us to suppose: cf. P. Bernard, "Nouvelle contribution de l'épigraphie cunéiforme à l'histoire hellénistique," *BCH* 114 (1990), p. 528. Bernard provides a commentary on tablet 322 of the collection by A. J. Sachs and H. Hunger, *Astronomical Diaries and Related Texts from Babylonia*, Österreichische Akad. der Wissenschaften, Philos.-hist. Klasse, Denkschriften 195 (1988). Similarly, tablet 330 of this collection confirms that the battle of Gaugamela took place on Oct. 1, 331 (Bernard, op. cit., p. 515).

weighing ±17.25 grams, are on the Attic weight standard, well known in the Mediterranean world thanks to the popularity of the fifth- and fourth-century Athenian currency.

Silver drachms with the same types and legend (pl. 3, 11), weighing ±4.30 grams, were likewise struck in appreciable quantities. Other denominations also exist: decadrachms (they are rare: pl. 8, 3), didrachms, hemidrachms (triobols), and smaller fractions; but the tetradrachms and drachms eclipse these denominations in our collections.

We note that some drachms and their fractions issued in Macedonia do not show a seated Zeus on the reverse but an eagle (or, on the diobols, two eagles). These coins are also on the Attic standard.

2. On the gold staters (pl. 1, 2): a head of Athena wearing a Corinthian helmet adorns the obverse; a Nike (Victory), standing and holding a wreath in her right hand and a *stylis* in her left, adorns the reverse (on the *stylis* as a naval emblem, see later in this chapter); as with the tetradrachms, the legend is *Alexandrou* and the weight standard is Attic: ±8.60 grams (a stater having the weight of two drachms).

Other gold denominations are known, but they are relatively rare and were not produced for any length of time: double staters (±17.25 grams), half-staters, quarter- and eighth-staters. The quarters can have a bow and a club as reverse type; the eighths bear a thunderbolt there.

Alexander also struck bronze coins. I merely mention them because I will not be dealing with them in what follows.

There remains a small group of silver tetradrachms in Alexander's name that elicit frequent discussion: the types (head of Zeus/eagle standing on a thunderbolt) and the weight standard (±14 grams) set these coins apart from the others. I will examine them in chapter 2, p. 32 (pl. 1, 12–13).

The first task in studying any coinage is to sort out the classification and chronology of its various issues. In the case of Alexander's tetradrachms with Herakles head and gold staters with Athena head, these problems are particularly complex.

As to classification, it is clear that a number of mints were opened throughout the empire. Scholars, therefore, must divide the known issues into coherent groups and attribute each group to a specific production center. At least in the earliest series, the coins rarely bear an explicit mark that allows identification of the site where they were struck. The symbols and monograms placed on the reverses of the coins generally designate those in charge of the issue, those whom we call, for want of a better expression, "mint magistrates" or "moneyers." Thanks to the insight of numismatists, a fair number of mint attributions have been established that can be taken as definitive. The list of those still doubtful or uncertain, however, remains long. New evidence, we can hope, will gradually bring further clarification.

The chronology of the issues is not always very clear, either. On the one hand, debate continues over the date when the first Herakles-head tetradrachms and Athena-head staters appeared; I shall return to this question presently. Moreover, only rarely can one date precisely the moment when a given mint opened. Finally, Alexander's death in June 323 did not end coinage with his name and types. His immediate successors continued to strike it, and the chronological borderline between the last coins struck during the king's lifetime and the first coins struck posthumously often remains fluid. Furthermore, the dividing line one chooses is not without importance. It is, in fact, around 323 that a sudden increase in the volume of issues is observable: is it because of a decision made by Alexander at the end of his reign? In some cases, do not the currency needs of his successors explain the change in production tempo at a given mint? In short, the explanations proffered vary considerably according to the chronology adopted.

Such was the role and privileged status of Alexander's coinage at the end of the fourth century that, during the third and second centuries, and even down to the beginning of the first, numerous cities produced "Alexanders" (as scholars and collectors commonly designate the coins with the name and types of the Macedonian king). This production consisted primarily of silver tetradrachms, but it also included some issues of gold staters.[3] For this period, attributions are easier to establish because the cities often put explicit marks on their Alexanders: an identifying symbol or, better still, their more or less abbreviated name (occasionally a monogram)—symbol and abbreviated name sometimes appearing jointly on the coins. Dating is less certain; nevertheless, general stylistic evolution and the evidence of hoards furnish good points of reference.

Coinage in the name of Alexander has never ceased, since the nineteenth century, to exercise scholarly ingenuity. I do not wish to write a history of scholarship here, but I cannot pass over in silence the pioneering work of L. Müller, *Numismatique d'Alexandre le Grand, suivie d'une appendice contenant les monnaies de Philippe II et de Philippe III* (Copenhagen, 1855). Müller made the effort to classify Alexander's issues by mint and to arrange them chronologically (the issues struck before June 323 as well as the posthumous issues). He led the way with his often accurate intuitions.

E. T. Newell's work made the decisive leap in this field, and his attributions continue to this day to be taken as standards. His publications dealt

---

3. Also, unless otherwise indicated, the expression "silver Alexanders" designates the tetradrachm, while "gold Alexanders" designates the stater.

especially with the "early" Alexanders (those dating from the fourth and the beginning of the third centuries), but he had an admirable knowledge of the later series, as his classification of his own vast collection (preserved at the American Numismatic Society in New York) testifies. In a book that appeared in 1912, *Reattribution of Certain Tetradrachms of Alexander the Great*,[4] he demonstrated all that systematic research into linkages among obverse dies brought to bear: two tetradrachms struck with the same obverse die sometimes have different marks on the reverse; the fact that they were struck from the same obverse die justifies the conclusion that they came from the same mint. Tying this research to stylistic considerations, Newell was able to establish firm groupings and to distribute them among a definite number of production centers. The publication in 1923 of a vast hoard from Demanhur in the Nile delta, whose 4,826 coins[5] he had catalogued (all tetradrachms), allowed Newell to set forth his conclusions on the classification (sorted by mint and chronology) of silver Alexanders up to about 318; the hoard was buried, in fact, in the second half of 318 (or at the beginning of 317), as the dated tetradrachms from Sidon and Tyre (Ake)[6] it contained show.[7] One can only admire this great numismatist and historian's sure judgment. He employed with equal felicity all that he gleaned from technique and style; he exploited the slightest peculiarities presented by the coins under study, he analyzed the hoards and findspots judiciously, and he showed himself ever alert to respecting historical probability.

M. J. Price, in an important book, *The Coinage in the Name of Alexander the Great and Philip Arrhidaeus* (Zurich/London, 1991),[8] surveyed the Alexander coinage from the fourth to the first century BC. He brought together all the known varieties, so that we now possess a complete list of the issues with the types and name of Alexander that have come down to us as of 1990. Although Price mostly maintained Newell's attributions (which were very often beyond dispute, especially for the Alexanders of the third, second, and first centuries), his critical commentaries are stimulating and

---

4. Hereafter cited as: Newell, *Reattribution*.

5. An investigation by O. H. Zervos has added 1,125 coins to Newell's list: "Additions to the Demanhur Hoard of Alexander Tetradrachms," *NC* 140 (1980), pp. 185–88. The hoard probably contained more than 8,000 tetradrachms, cf. *IGCH* 1664; we note that ten of them, struck in Egypt by Ptolemy, showed on the obverse the head of Alexander wearing an elephant hide headdress (no change on the reverse: seated Zeus and *Alexandrou*).

6. A relatively abundant coinage, classified by Newell as from Ake in Palestine, very probably comes from Tyre: cf. below, chapter 5.

7. Newell's publication is entitled *Alexander Hoards II. Demanhur, 1905*, Num. Notes and Monographs 19 (Amer. Num. Soc., New York, 1923), hereafter cited as: Newell, *Demanhur* (1923).

8. Hereafter cited as: Price, *Alexander* (1991).

allow us to appreciate the level of uncertainty that still exists in the classifications of the coins struck up to the beginning of the third century.

The mention of Philip Arrhidaeus in Price's title requires an explanation. Alexander, who died before the birth of the child his Iranian wife, Roxane, was expecting, had a half-brother, Arrhidaeus, who was feeble-minded but respected because he was the son of Philip II. The royal council, headed by Perdiccas and supported by the cavalry, negotiated a compromise with the Macedonian soldiers of the phalanx, after June 10, 323: Arrhidaeus, whom the soldiers backed, was declared king and took the name Philip (III); if Roxane's child turned out to be a boy, he was to share the throne with Philip III. That is what happened, and the boy was called Alexander, Alexander IV to us. Philip III reigned from the summer of 323 until his death in the autumn of 317. In several mints of the empire, on the coins of Alexander types, the legend *Philippou* occasionally replaced *Alexandrou*: these issues are not to be separated from the coinage in the name of Alexander.

The Traditional Interpretation of the Coinage with the Name of Alexander and with the Types of Herakles Head and Seated Zeus for Silver, and Athena Head and Nike for Gold

Alexander struck this coinage in Macedonia and in a certain number of conquered territories, as numismatists' classifications have shown, and historians have quite naturally seen it as the currency *par excellence* of the empire, whose use, they argue, was widespread and supplanted previously produced coins. Thinking along these lines, they have reasserted the idea Plutarch had, as I noted at the end of the introduction.

D. Schlumberger[9] attributed a definite monetary policy to Alexander, and it is worthwhile, I think, to quote the passage where he has expressed his point of view. His thesis concerns the silver coinage, because that was the currency most commonly used at the time:

> What Alexander wanted to do seems clear. He wanted to give an empire that didn't have one, a silver coinage acceptable everywhere as such, and in doing this to extend the use of silver coinage as currency (and not as bullion) throughout the extent of this empire.
>
> To do this he had to take out of circulation the innumerable coinages from a variety of dates, types, and standards found there. He had to adopt a single weight standard ... and to convert the empire's

---

9. *L'argent grec dans l'empire achéménide*, in R. Curiel and D. Schlumberger, *Trésors monétaires d'Afghanistan* (Mémoires délég. Arch. Française en Afghanistan, 14, 1953), pp. 27–28.

circulation to that of an imperial coinage, marked as such by its types and legend.

All of this, in the brief span allotted Alexander, could be only partially accomplished.

The picture Schlumberger gives of coin circulation in the Persian Empire on the eve of Alexander's conquest requires adjustment. This circulation, as I indicated in an earlier book,[10] was less disorganized than it seems. The silver currency of the Persian sovereign, the siglos with the archer king as type, predominated in that part of the royal territories where coinage was accepted as currency and not as bullion. Schlumberger justly emphasized that the Persian Empire was split in two monetarily. Elsewhere, in the vassal states, the Great King authorized the issuance of local coinages, and this is what explains the great variety of coinage types and weights found in the western regions of the Empire. Moreover, foreign, particularly Athenian, coinages are often present in the fifth- and fourth-century hoards found throughout its expanse. I have commented on this situation in the work just cited, noting both that hoards found within the borders of royal territory must be distinguished from those found in vassal lands, and that Athenian tetradrachms were attractive owing to the added value that this currency obtained in the Mediterranean world. In short, the currency circulating in the Persian Empire was less chaotic than Schlumberger leads us to understand, but it is true that the discretion the Great King accorded his subjects in this matter could not help but entail considerable coinage diversity.

Schlumberger emphasized the brevity (thirteen years) of Alexander's reign, which arguably impeded the effectiveness of his monetary decisions. One may add that the warfare occupying these thirteen years consumed practically all of the Conqueror's energy. Although we must take these two factors into account, it is inappropriate to exaggerate their importance. In principle, it suffices for kings or cities to decree that a given coinage will have sole currency in their territories to cause the rapid disappearance of other coinages from local circulation. In any event, our task is not to reckon what would have happened if Alexander had lived longer and had known a period of peace. Ours is to try to evaluate, in light of the evidence, what occurred during his reign in currency matters.

Several authors have suggested that Alexander decided to create an imperial coinage. Thus, G. Kleiner titled a book, to which I shall have to return, *Alexanders Reichsmünzen*.[11] Although Kleiner considered that the

---

10. *La Naissance de la monnaie. Pratiques monétaires de l'Orient ancien* (Paris, 2001), pp. 165–87; hereafter cited as *Naissance*.

11. This book was published in Berlin in 1949 (Abhandl. Deutschen Akad. Wissensch. zu Berlin, Philos-hist. Klasse, 1947, num. 5); cf. esp. pp. 6–7.

true imperial coinage was the silver currency with Herakles head and Zeus types and the gold currency with Athena head and Nike types, he noted some anomalies: Alexander, he says, issued at Babylon some gold double darics (with the type of the Great King as archer) and silver tetradrachms showing Baaltars (the great god of Tarsus) on one side and a lion on the other. Mazaeus had chosen these types of Baaltars and the lion when he served as a Persian satrap. After he had sided with Alexander, the latter allowed Mazaeus to strike similar coins that continued on after his death in 328. According to Kleiner, these double darics and lion tetradrachms, despite their limited circulation, are also to be regarded as an imperial coinage by which Alexander announced himself as the Great King's successor.

M. Thompson and A. R. Bellinger, in the preface to their 1955 study of a hoard of Alexander drachms,[12] cited Schlumberger's ideas with approval. Nor did they neglect to insist on the diversity of the coinages issued under Alexander in his domain, but their agreement with Schlumberger's analysis shows that they, too, thought that Alexander intended to extend the usage of the Herakles-head tetradrachms and the Athena-head gold staters throughout the empire.

M. J. Price,[13] in turn, in 1991 characterized this coinage as "imperial," putting the word in quotation marks but providing it no further explanation.

Explicitly or implicitly, the authors just mentioned attributed to Alexander what might be called a monetary policy. At some point in his reign (for some, soon after his accession, for others, a little later, after the battle of Issus), he created a silver and gold coinage that allegedly became the imperial currency, the official currency of the empire. Does this interesting vision stand up to factual scrutiny? This is what I propose to elucidate in the following chapters.

The Date of the First Tetradrachms with Herakles Head and Seated Zeus, and the First Gold Staters with Athena Head and Nike

Among the chronological problems still unresolved that I noted above, the dating of the first Alexander tetradrachms with Herakles head and his first staters with Athena head remains the object of sometimes pas-

---

12. "Greek Coins in the Yale Collections, IV: A Hoard of Alexander Drachms," *Yale Class. St.* 14 (1955), pp. 3–45. This study contains a general classification of Alexander drachms and has for a long time remained the standard in this field; it is still worth consulting.

13. Price, *Alexander* (1991), p. 29.

sionate debate. I shall try to present the arguments in the most objective way possible; those supporting my own conviction will be clear.

E. T. Newell's "High" Chronology

The debate on dating the coins in question began in the nineteenth century, but I shall begin with the opinion Newell expressed in 1912.[14] Newell did not ignore several decades' worth of scholarship. "Numismatists," he writes, "seem to have been reluctant to admit that Alexander, on his accession, found the time and opportunity *immediately* [Newell's italics] to supplant his father's coinage by his own." Newell did not see what could have prevented Alexander from striking his own coinage right from the start of his reign: the types, he remarked, perfectly suited the Macedonians as well as the rest of the Greek world, which the young king was going to engage in a war against the Persians. Alexander's gold coins had the same weight as his father Philip's and thus facilitated the continuation. The weight change of the silver tetradrachms, however, which now weighed ±17.25 grams as on the Attic standard, and no longer ±14.45 grams as under Philip, might have required some delay for planning, Newell admitted. But he suggested this reform might, perhaps, have already been planned at the end of Philip's reign, leaving Alexander merely to implement it.

Newell wrote this at the start of his career in 1912, when he was twenty-six. He never changed his opinion about the date of the first silver coins with Herakles head and the first gold coins with Athena head. His authority so prevailed in anything concerning Alexander's coinage, and has remained so pervasive to this day (Newell died prematurely in 1941), that many scholars have confidently adopted his dating.[15] Newell's opinion was all the easier to follow, given that we are accustomed to the idea that a new sovereign is wont to mark his accession by issuing his own coinage. It is a way to make his name known (and his portrait, once the custom arose of placing the royal countenance on the obverse of coins) and to herald a message serving his interests by judiciously chosen types.

The "Low" Chronology of G. Kleiner and O. H. Zervos

Kleiner relaunched the debate with the publication of his monograph *Alexanders Reichsmünzen* in 1949. The book is a little disconcerting, full of interesting ideas but also of questionable assertions, and all set forth without much concern for helping the reader's comprehension. Some years later,

---

14. *Reattribution*, pp. 27–30.
15. I myself, in my *corpus* of the silver and gold coins of Philip II (Paris, 1977), sided with Newell's opinion. In order to reconcile Newell's chronology with my own analysis of the evidence, I assumed that Alexander, at the start of his reign, had produced his own currency concurrently with coins bearing the name and types of Philip.

Zervos, who had worked on the style of the first Alexander tetradrachms, recognized that he agreed with a certain number of Kleiner's analyses, and he decided to publish a commentary on them that would permit him to introduce his own results. Zervos emphasizes that Kleiner wrote "a confusing book" and continues: "What the author clearly needs is an interpreter." He therefore eliminated an entire series of Kleiner's misguided scholarly suggestions and kept to what was essential.[16]

Zervos, for example, set aside the argument Kleiner developed concerning the gold staters that the Roman proconsul T. Quinctius Flamininus struck in Greece.[17] Flamininus, who defeated the Macedonian king, Philip V, at Cynocephalae in 197, declared the freedom of the Greek cities the following year. The gold staters bearing his portrait and name show a Nike on the reverse similar to that on Alexander staters, the only difference being that the goddess holds a palm and not a *stylis*.[18] Flamininus's adoption of Alexander's type indicated, Kleiner wrote, that Alexander's Nike evoked for the Greeks the victory over the Persians and the liberation of the cities of Asia Minor in 334. This meaning would not have been possible, according to Kleiner, if Alexander had chosen this type before 335, the date of his victory over Thebes and sale of the Thebans into slavery.

Zervos also did not mention Kleiner's thoughts on the Herakles head on the obverse of Alexander's silver coins. Herakles, Kleiner said, indisputably enjoyed a special veneration in Macedonia. He was the ancestor of the dynasty, founded by the Argive Temenos, one of Herakles's direct descendants. Several Macedonian kings before Alexander had chosen the Herakles head as a coin type; Philip II had placed it on the obverse of his didrachms, drachms, and small gold coins.

Yet, Kleiner goes on, Alexander seems to have had Achilles as his ideal: he was never without his *Iliad*, which he considered daily nourishment for

---

16. O. H. Zervos, "Notes on a Book by Gerhard Kleiner," *NC* 142 (1982), pp. 166–79. This article is followed by an article of M. J. Price, "Alexander's Reform of the Macedonian Regal Coinage," pp. 180–90. Price, defending an early, or "high," dating, replies to the arguments of Kleiner and Zervos. Both contributions are presented under the title, "Debate: The Earliest Coins of Alexander the Great." I add that A. R. Bellinger, *Essays on the Coinage of Alexander the Great* (Num. Studies 11, New York, 1963), pp. 9–10, provides a quick summary of Kleiner's book.

17. On this frequently discussed coinage, see, for example, M. H. Crawford, *Roman Republican Coinage* (Cambridge, UK ,1974), I, p. 544. Flamininus was the first Roman to place his own portrait on coins (to be precise, his staters were struck in Greece, not in Rome). F. Chamoux, "Un portrait de Flamininus à Delphes," *BCH* 89 (1965), pp. 214–24, has identified a Parian marble head, found in the excavations at Delphi, as a portrait of the Roman proconsul.

18. Flamininus, whose victory over Philip V occurred on land, would not have given the Nike a naval symbol: cf. Kleiner, op. cit., p. 6.

a warrior spirit. Aristotle had given him his personally edited copy of the epic, which Alexander kept locked in a precious casket captured from Darius (and therefore called the "*Iliad* of the casket"). He always had this within reach and before going to bed used to place it underneath his pillow beside his dagger (Plutarch, *Alexander* 8.2 and 26.1; Strabo 13.1.27). At Ilion he paid homage to Achilles's memory (Plutarch, *Alex*.15.8; Arrian 1.12.1). In Kleiner's view, Alexander only became preoccupied with Herakles upon his arrival at Tyre (January 332), when he informed the Tyrians that he wanted to enter their city to offer a sacrifice to Herakles, who had a famous shrine there. When the Tyrians denied him access, and Alexander had begun the siege, Herakles appeared to him in a dream (Arrian 2.15.6; 16; 18.1). When he took the city, Alexander pardoned those who had sought refuge in the shrine of Herakles, and he offered numerous honors to the god (Arrian 2.24.5–6). In light of all this, Kleiner concluded that the head of Herakles could only have appeared on Alexander's coins after the fall of Tyre in July 332. In fact, Kleiner thought that Alexander's imperial coinage began in 331, following the financial reorganization that the Conqueror decided upon in the spring of that year, when he was once again in Tyre, on his way back from Egypt.

It is understandable that Zervos did not take account of such an argument, which not only fails to convince the reader but is also likely to discredit the whole book. As for Achilles and Herakles in particular, Kleiner confused the ideal warrior so special to Alexander and the ancestral tradition to which Alexander belonged. Alexander always held Herakles in high regard. At the end of 336, he reminded the Thessalians of "the ancient kinship from Herakles that united them" (Diodorus 17.4.1, WEH).[19] In 335, on the banks of the Danube (the ancient Ister), he sacrificed to Zeus the Savior, to Herakles, and to the river god (Arrian 1.4.5). When he crossed the Hellespont (April 334), "he set up altars both where he started from Europe and where he landed in Asia to Zeus of Safe Landings, Athena, and Herakles" (Arrian 1.11.7). His piety towards Herakles was unfailing.

Some of Kleiner's arguments were better founded, however, and Zervos drew attention to his stylistic analysis of the type on the reverse of the tetradrachms, the seated, eagle-bearing Zeus. Kleiner wanted to make two points: that the Zeus of Alexander's tetradrachms struck at Tarsus (pl. 1, 1 and 4, 11–12) derived directly from one of the images of Baal appearing on the silver staters that Mazaeus, the Persian satrap, had issued in this city, and, more important, that the Zeus engraved at Tarsus had inspired the Zeus

---

19. According to Justin 11.3.1, he made much of the family tie that united him to those on his mother's side, the descendants of the Aeacids; now, Achilles was an Aeacid, and Alexander certainly cherished this tie with one whom he took as his warrior model. But his connections to Herakles were of a different order.

engraved for the first tetradrachms Alexander struck in Macedonia. The Macedonian silver coins with the name and types of Alexander would therefore have been produced after those of Tarsus. Because Alexander captured Tarsus during the summer of 333, his silver coinage with Herakles head and seated Zeus could not have started before this date.

Zervos considerably enriched Kleiner's stylistic analysis, and he completely approved the idea that the first Macedonian tetradrachms were later than the first from Tarsus. The fact that, initially, the head of Herakles on the Macedonian coins (pl. 1, 6) closely resembles that on the obverse of certain didrachms of Philip II (pl. 1, 5) seemed to him easy to explain: the Macedonian engravers reproduced this type, which they knew well, according to their usual practice. For the new Zeus type, they employed the model from Tarsus, copying it more or less accurately, or omitting details that did not belong to their usual repertoire.

Zervos corrected Kleiner's proposed dating for the first tetradrachms. Kleiner, as we saw, suggested that they were struck after spring 331. Now, an issue of these tetradrachms, produced by the mint at Sidon, is dated to the year one of Sidon (pl. 4, 2), which has been shown to fall in 333/332. Zervos supposes, correctly in my view, that this coinage was inaugurated at Tarsus very probably after the victory at Issus (autumn 333).

For the gold staters with Athena head and Nike (pl. 1, 2), Kleiner conjectured that Athena had become dear to Alexander after his visit to the sanctuary of the goddess at Ilion (April 334): Athena had sent him some favorable omens and had assured him of her support (Diodorus 17.17.6–7). Kleiner added that the *stylis* Nike holds on the reverse is related to the conquest of the sea, effected in 332, at the time Tyre fell. To be clear about the stylis,[20] generally placed on the ship's stern, it was a spar near the top of which was a crossbeam with a small vertical projection at each end (p. 1, 2: the extremities occasionally terminate in a "T"). The crossbeam, sometimes of considerable length, could carry the name of a patron deity (often of Zeus *Sōtēr*, Zeus the Savior) who protected the vessel and who was invoked at the time of battle. The *stylis* had the same meaning for the crew as the flag did for the soldiers of a regiment.

Zervos, in approving Kleiner's contention, supposed as Kleiner did that the types on the gold coins referred especially to Alexander himself and that panhellenic considerations had played only a secondary role in their selection. He furthermore observed that, from a stylistic point of view, the positioning of the types on the silver tetradrachms had influenced the disposition of the types on the obverse and reverse of the gold staters. Kleiner was mistaken, Zervos said, in wanting to date the introduction of the silver

---

20. See J. N. Svoronos, "Stylides, ancres hierae, aphlasta, stoloi, acrostolia, embola, proembola et totems marins," *Journal intern. d'archéologie numism.* 16 (1914), esp. pp. 84–120.

and gold coinage to the same time: the tetradrachms appeared a little after the victory at Issus (autumn 333), the gold staters not before the fall of Tyre (July 332); it was impossible to specify whether in summer 332 or later.

Reassertion of the "High" Chronology: M. J. Price

Price's treatment followed directly upon Zervos's in the 1982 *Numismatic Chronicle*. Price rejected the hypotheses of Kleiner and Zervos and returned to Newell's "high," or early, dating.

Price was convinced that the Zeus engraved on the reverses of Alexander's Macedonian tetradrachms had nothing to do with the Zeus of Tarsus, and that Zeus had appeared on the Macedonian coins soon after the accession of the king in 336. Price tried to show that one or another of the stylistic elements Zervos labeled oriental were found in sundry Greek coinages: in fifth-century Arcadian coinage and in fourth-century coins from Terina and Taranto in southern Italy. He wrote: "In comparing therefore the Zeus of Macedonia with the Baal of Tarsos, I find nothing in the five 'oriental' features which must have originated with the Baal and cannot have been devised independently in the Greek world."

Price emphasized, moreover, that Alexander needed sizeable sums of coined money right after he ascended the throne. Because he was opposed to the idea that Philip II's silver coinage could have continued for a certain time after 336, Price thought that the issuance of Alexander tetradrachms with Alexander's own name and types had necessarily begun immediately after Philip's death.

He insisted as well that the words and deeds by which Alexander had shown his devotion to Zeus and Herakles between 336 and 334 could perfectly well explain the types on these tetradrachms (cf. above).[21] Within this context, it was not surprising that Alexander chose these divinities as coin types. In short, Price concluded, "the reform of the Macedonian coinage that Alexander effected is most intelligible if it took place in 336 BC."[22]

New Arguments Favoring the "Low" Chronology: F. de Callataÿ and H. A. Troxell

F. de Callataÿ, before he published his study,[23] which appeared in the same year as those of Zervos and Price, was aware of the cases they made.

---

21. To the evidence already mentioned, one may add, for Zeus, the stage contests that Alexander organized upon his return from Thebes, at Dion in Macedonia, in honor of Zeus and the Muses, contests that were preceded by magnificent sacrifices in honor of the gods (Diodorus 17.16.3).

22. Price repeated the same ideas in *Alexander* (1991), pp. 27–28.

23. "La date des premiers tétradrachmes de poids attique émis par Alexandre le Grand," *RBN* 128 (1982), pp. 5–25.

His own research, carried out independently, had led him to prefer the late dating. His article showed that Price's comparisons of the Arcadian Zeus with the type of Zeus on the reverse of the tetradrachms were not convincing. He emphasized that while one could doubt the oriental origin of certain stylistic traits that Zervos noted on the first Macedonian tetradrachms, two particular features had nonetheless to be considered as typically oriental: the globular or bell-like bulges on the legs of the chair Zeus sits upon, and the beaded pattern on its horizontal bars as well as on the scepter. The Macedonian engravers presumably copied these two features from the tetradrachms issued at Tarsus in 333/332. These are the stylistic traits, Callataÿ wrote, that provide "the most convincing arguments in favor of the position Zervos defends."

In 1991, using as her source the rich collection of Alexander coins at the American Numismatic Society in New York, H. A. Troxell[24] set forth some even more precise stylistic observations, which, in my opinion, tip the scales in favor of the low or late dating. She examined those Macedonian tetradrachms of Alexander that can be considered the very earliest of the series there (cf., for example, pl. 1, 6 and 2, 4–6), and she focused on three features appearing on the reverse of these coins that are always present on the tetradrachms from Tarsus: the bell-like decoration at the bottom of the legs of Zeus's chair, the "flowering" scepter, and the footstool. It so happens that in Macedonia these three features were carelessly engraved (the footstool, in particular, is awkwardly depicted) and, what is more, they were quickly discontinued, as if they were unassimilated foreign elements. This implies that the Macedonian artisans had an image of Zeus in front of them, some of whose details were not at all familiar. Troxell concluded that the model came from Tarsus and that the Macedonian coinage with the name and types of Alexander did not begin, therefore, before 333/332.

The analyses of Zervos and F. de Callataÿ had led me to prefer the "low" chronology. After Troxell's technical remarks, I am convinced: Alexander's first tetradrachms with the types of Herakles and Zeus were struck at Tarsus, picking up from the silver staters with the type of Baal that the satrap Mazaeus produced there. The sequence that Kleiner proposed must be accepted: the Baal of Mazaeus led to the Alexander Zeus at Tarsus, which was the prototype for the Zeus from Macedonia.

---

24. "Alexander's Earliest Macedonian Silver," in *Mnemata: Papers in Memory of Nancy M. Waggoner*, W. E. Metcalf ed. (Amer. Num. Soc., New York, 1991), pp. 49–61, esp. pp. 56–57. A revised version appears in her *Studies in the Macedonian Coinage of Alexander the Great* (Num. Studies 21, Amer. Num. Soc., New York, 1997), pp. 87–89. This book will hereafter be cited as: Troxell, *Alexander* (1997).

The First Gold Coins of Alexander

If the date of Alexander's first tetradrachms now seems settled satisfactorily, that of the first gold staters still remains uncertain. Zervos, as we saw, thought that the general appearance of the types on the tetradrachms had inspired that on the gold coins' obverses and reverses (pl. 1, 2). The head of Athena facing right, wearing a Corinthian helmet, corresponds, he argues, to the head of Herakles facing right, wearing a lion skin headdress; the Nike standing in three-quarter profile to the left, holding a wreath in her right hand and a *stylis* in her left, echoes the Zeus seated in three-quarter profile to the left, holding an eagle on his right hand and a scepter in his left; the spar of the *stylis* and the shaft of the scepter have the same length. These similarities are not without interest, but they do not constitute compelling arguments.

Scholars have sought to make something of the head of Athena placed on the obverse and of the *stylis* Nike holds. A. R. Bellinger reviewed the opinions expressed up to 1963, the year when his book appeared.[25] Not wanting to repeat what he has said, I will set forth a recent viewpoint from M. J. Price.[26]

Price did not think that the head of Athena was chosen out of respect for Athens;[27] it was only natural, in his opinion, that the goddess of wisdom, victory, and freedom adorn a coinage "designed to provide finance for a military expedition to free the Greeks of Asia Minor." If it was necessary to see a political allusion in this type, he continued, it would probably be a reference to the Athena of Corinth, for that city was the seat of the league whose objective was the fight against the Persians.

According to Price, the stylis on the reverse, a reference to a naval victory, evoked for Greek contemporaries the naval victory over the Persians at Salamis in 480. In his opinion, Alexander was evincing a prudent political sensibility by recalling this great accomplishment, cherished in the memory of all Greeks and symbolizing their maritime supremacy.

As we see, Price refused to relate the stylis to a personal victory of Alexander. Yet such a possibility is not to be ruled out. W. B. Kaiser,[28] in 1986, proposed interpreting this object as an evocation of the Conqueror's successful traversal of the Hellespont in April 334: "The crossing of the Hellespont is the great and successful naval undertaking to which the stylis

---

25. Op. cit., pp. 3–13; cf. his note 12.
26. *Alexander* (1991), pp. 29–30.
27. Athena's helmet is decorated with a serpent, a griffin, a lion-griffin, a sphinx, or a bird; Price observes that the serpent, griffin, and sphinx are found at Athens in relation to Athena, but he is right not to attach any special importance to these motifs.
28. "Alexanders Goldmünzen," *Revue Suisse de Numism.* 65 (1986), pp. 41–57; the cited sentence [Le Rider quotes the original German—WEH] appears on p. 57.

in the Nike's hand alludes." Kleiner, for his part, considered the presence of the stylis as unlikely before the fall of Tyre (July 332). I am inclined to follow this line of thought, and when I deal with Alexander's stay in Cilicia and in Phoenicia, I will try to pinpoint the circumstances that could have prompted the creation of his silver tetradrachms with the types of Herakles head and Zeus, and his gold staters with the types of Athena head and Nike.

For a long time, most historians have readily accepted that Alexander created his great coinage right after his accession. They considered it only natural that a sovereign of this stature had taken care, as soon as he mounted the throne, to issue a currency whose types would reflect his ambitions. E. T. Newell's authority did much to entrench this opinion. The few voices raised against it found no support. It was only at the start of the 1980s that debate grew and began to sow doubt in some minds. Today, the idea has apparently won favor that Alexander did not inaugurate his famous silver coinage until the end of 333 and his gold coinage even later. I certainly defend this chronology, and in the following two chapters I am going to try to show all the consequences that it entails for the Macedonian coinage of the years 336–323.

Chapter 2

Alexander and Coinage in Macedonia from October 336 to April 334

From October 336 to April 334 Alexander spent only a little time in Macedonia.[1] Immediately after Philip II's assassination, he had himself proclaimed king in the theater at Aigeai by the Macedonians gathered there (the great autumn festivals and Cleopatra's wedding to Alexander of Epirus had surely attracted a considerable crowd).[2] He saw, next, to Philip's funeral, and he settled the fate of the accomplices in the murder. Then he left for Thessaly, where he obtained the right to succeed his father as the head of the Thessalian Confederation, which conferred on him the hegemony of Greece by decree. The Amphictyonic Council of Delphi, which he had convened at Thermopylae, also accorded him the hegemony. Having silenced the Athenians and Thebans, he went to Corinth, where he won the support of the Peloponnesian city-states (except for Sparta) and introduced himself before the Council (the "synhedrion") of the Greeks, which we call the "League of Corinth." Like his father, he was named "hegemon," commander of the forces united against the Persians and guarantor of the "common peace" (*koinē eirēnē*) concluded among the Greeks.

Alexander then returned to Macedonia, where the usual royal seat was located at Pella; it must have been near the end of 336. Some troubles arising in the Balkans caused him to undertake a military campaign at the start of spring 335, resulting in the imposition of his authority on the peoples of that region: the Thracians, the Triballoi, the Getai, and the Illyrians

---

1. On the early period of Alexander's reign, see N. G. L. Hammond, *A History of Macedonia* III (Oxford, 1988), pp. 3–17 and 32–35.

2. On this point, see M. B. Hatzopoulos, *Macedonian Institutions Under the Kings* (Meletēmata 22, Athens, 1996), pp. 276–77.

were all rapidly subdued. Alexander then (summer 335) learned of the Theban revolt, fomented by the Persians and occasioned by the false news of his death. He hurried by forced marches and took control of the city (beginning of autumn 335), whose fate was determined by the Council of the League of Corinth. Thebes had effectively broken the "common peace," and Alexander implemented the judgment rendered: the city was destroyed, its people enslaved, its fugitives declared outlaws.

Back in Macedonia, Alexander actively prepared the expedition against the Persians. In 334, at the beginning of spring, probably in the early days of April, he crossed the Hellespont and marched into Asia Minor. He was never to see his homeland again.

Is it possible to shed any light on the stance Alexander adopted in financial and coinage affairs during the eighteen months he spent in Europe from October 336 to April 334? To judge better, it is worth recalling how matters stood at the time of Philip's death.

The Monetary Situation Philip II Bequeathed in October 336

In 336, Philip II was issuing silver and gold coins[3] (and bronze, too, but I will not be commenting on currency in this metal).

1. His silver coins were tetradrachms on the "Macedonian" standard, weighing ±14.45 grams; didrachms (±7.20 grams), drachms (±3.60 grams), and half-drachms (±1.80 grams) had accompanied the tetradrachms at the start of his reign. A little later, the drachm and half-drachm denominations disappeared, to be replaced by a ±2.80 gram coin.

The tetradrachms of the second part of the reign (pl. 1, 7) bear a head of Zeus on the obverse and a nude young horseman (a jockey) on the reverse, whose head is bound by a victor's fillet and whose right hand holds a palm branch; the legend is *Philippou*. The didrachms (pl. 1, 5) bear the head of a beardless Herakles on the obverse and the same jockey as the tetradrachms on the reverse (the horse not strutting). At some point the type of the victorious jockey had replaced that of the mounted king (pl. 1, 8) who advances to the left, raising his hand in a salute (the horse in a strutting gait).

The coins weighing 2.80 grams had different types: on the obverse, a youthful head tied with a fillet; on the reverse, a nude young rider, holding the reins in his two hands, on a rearing horse with leg bent (pl. 1, 9).

---

3. I refer to my book *Le monnayage d'argent et d'or de Philippe II frappé en Macédoine* (Paris, 1977) hereafter cited as: *Philippe II* (1977); also to the conspectus I have published more recently, *Monnayage et finances de Philippe II, un état de la question* (Meletēmata 23, Athens, 1996), where a description of the coins of Philip can be found at pp. 21–25 for the silver and pp. 49–51 for the gold.

Despite the criticisms of M. J. Price,[4] I still consider it likely, as E. T. Newell had already proposed, that two (not three) mints, located at Pella and Amphipolis, shared Philip II's silver coinage.

2. At a date still difficult to determine, Philip II began striking gold coins: staters on the Attic standard (±8.60 grams) and fractions of the stater; in the first issues, there are quarter-, eighth- and twelfth-staters, and then half-, quarter- and eighth-staters.

The staters (pl. 1, 10-11) show the laureate head of Apollo on the obverse and a racing *biga* [a two-horse chariot] on the reverse, driven by a charioteer who holds the reins in his left hand and a goad in his right; the legend is *Philippou*, as on the silver coins. The smaller denominations show the head of Herakles on the obverse, except the twelfths of the early issues, which have a head of Apollo. The types on the reverse are more varied, with the half-staters struck towards the end of the reign bearing a lion's head, the quarters a club and a bow, the eighths a thunderbolt, a *kantharos* [a stemmed, two-handled goblet] or a trident.

I have proposed allocating the gold coins, like the silver, between two mints, Pella and Amphipolis. Different officials oversaw the coining of gold and silver at that time. The marks of the "mint magistrates" placed on the reverse of the gold coins have therefore no connection with those on the silver.

The date at which Philip instituted his gold coinage has been much discussed (the discussion is far from over), and I reviewed the different proposals in my book *Monnayage et finances de Philippe II* (1996). I personally tend to prefer the "low" or late chronology: Philip's gold currency only appeared after the fall of Olynthus in 348.

Plutarch (*Alexander* 4.5) reports that Philip depicted his victory in the chariot races at Olympia on his coins, and it is reasonable to interpret the *biga* on his gold staters as the illustration of such a victory. Likewise, the victorious jockey of his tetradrachms very probably celebrates the triumph of his racehorse at the Olympic Games (Plutarch, *Alex.* 3.5). This type appears from the start of the coinage, on the reverse of the half-drachms and on the majority of the drachms, paralleling the type of the mounted king on the reverse of the tetradrachms. In the subsequent group, it replaces the type of the mounted king on the tetradrachms, and appears as well on the didrachms (in this group, as we have seen, the drachms and half-drachms were taken out of circulation in favor of a new denomination).

Philip's two mints, Pella and Amphipolis, seem to have functioned normally during his reign, without discernible interruption; and the pace of

---

4. "The coinage of Philip II," *NC* 139 (1979), pp. 234-40, a review of my book; see also his *Alexander*, pp. 85-89. I have set forth Price's arguments and my own view in my *Monnayage et finanaces de Philippe II*.

coinage production throughout this period is interesting to observe.[5] With silver, the volume of issues increases in the second part of the reign; with gold, after a somewhat slow start, the number of obverse dies in use starts to grow at a certain point. What is troubling, and even makes our attempts at understanding somewhat futile, is that the dating of the different groups has not yet been firmly established. We do not know just where to place the break between the coins struck during Philip's lifetime and those belonging to Alexander's reign, at least if we admit that the coinage of Philip continued under his successor—a point to which I shall return in a moment.

The production of gold coins, a metal Macedonian kings had not previously minted, considerably augmented the means Philip had at his disposal to make payments in hard currency. Gold was probably more than ten times as valuable as silver when the first staters were struck. Diodorus (16.8.6–7) wrote that, by intensively exploiting the gold mines of the region around the city of Philippi, the king amassed a huge fortune that contributed mightily to securing his supremacy in Greece. Thanks to the gold coins he struck, Diodorus continues, he assembled a great mercenary force and induced many Greeks to betray their country.

Although Philip also struck bronze coins (and copiously, it seems), it does not follow that the Macedonian economy at this period was "monetized." A royal coinage had existed in Macedonia from the reign of Alexander I (c. 498–c. 452), and at least a part of the population knew how to use coined money. But ancestral practices endured, especially in the hinterland, as well as in the urban centers. Reciprocal gift-giving, payments in kind, exchanges of services were all still in use. What can be presumed is that the regularity and volume of Philip's issues probably resulted in expanding coinage's use throughout the country.

The Financial Organization of the Macedonian Kingdom

M. B. Hatzopoulos, in his work cited above on Macedonian institutions under the monarchy, has gathered together important evidence on the kingdom's financial organization. He has commented, in particular, on the words that Alexander addressed to his soldiers as they were on the verge of revolt,[6] according to the oration Arrian accords him at Opis on the Tigris

---

5. *Monnayage* . . . *Philippe II* (Athens, 1996), pp. 69–75.

6. Arrian is the only author to place this mutiny at Opis; the other ancient historians (Diodorus, Plutarch, Curtius, Justin) situate it at Susa. Arrian himself also mentions (7.6.2–5) army unrest at Susa, but it is at Opis that, according to him, the Macedonians' anger exploded.

in 324. The king, Arrian reports (7.9.9), cried out that, after all he had endured, the only things left him were the royal purple and the crown because he possessed nothing in his own right: all treasures he amassed belonged to the Macedonians.

The long speech Arrian records, of which the passage cited is only a brief excerpt, represents a beautiful rhetorical set-piece, as F. R. Wüst[7] has indisputably demonstrated and as H. Montgomery has confirmed.[8] Some details, nevertheless, indicate that the original source behind the text was not unaware of certain aspects of Macedonian affairs. Hatzopoulos thinks that when Alexander declares that he possesses nothing in his own right, he is alluding to an administrative reality: there were funds of which the king, whom the Macedonians placed on the throne, was only the manager. Hatzopoulos refers to a passage in Curtius (10.6.20–23) for corroboration. At Babylon, on the day following Alexander's death, during an assembly that brought together Alexander's "principal friends and leaders of the forces," Meleager spoke to show his opposition to Perdiccas, ending his speech by exhorting the soldiers to plunder the treasures because, he said, "the people, surely, are the heirs of these royal riches" (WEH). The question is whether these statements of Alexander at Opis and Meleager at Babylon concern only the riches accumulated from the conquest of Asia, and I will make no pronouncement on this point.

Seen, likewise, from Hatzopoulos's perspective, two other literary texts are quite interesting. Diodorus (16.71.2) relates that Philip forced the Thracians to tithe to the Macedonians out of their income. Arrian (1.27.4) reports that Alexander required the people of Aspendus to pay the Macedonians an annual tribute.

Hatzopoulos also mentioned some inscriptions and coins. In a treaty between Amyntas III (393–370/369) and the Chalcidians, some levies are

---

7. "Die Rede Alexanders der Grosse in Opis, Arrian, VII, 9–10," *Historia* 2 (1953), pp. 177–88. Wüst concludes: "The speech in its structure, stylistic devices and approach to the material is clearly rhetorical" [cited in the original German, WEH: "Die Rede ist in ihrer Anlage, in ihren Stilmitteln und in der Einstellung zum Stoff eindeutig rhetorisch"]. Arrian did not resist the urge to record a beautiful piece of rhetoric full of commonplaces; Diodorus and Plutarch are content to say that Alexander intervened vehemently. Curtius (10.2.15–29) has him deliver an actual speech, also well composed, but less detailed (no reference to the treasures not belonging to Alexander but to the Macedonians); despite these differences, it is clear that the same source inspired both authors.

8. "The Economic Revolution of Philip II, Myth or Reality?" *Symbolae Osloenses* 60 (1985), pp. 37–47, esp. pp. 38–39. Montgomery has investigated especially the bravura passage of the Opis oration where Alexander attributes to his father Philip II the transition, in Macedonia, from nomadic to settled life.

to be paid not to Amyntas but to the Macedonians.[9] At Delphi, financial accounts of the Amphictyony for 325/324 mention a contribution of 10,500 staters (equivalent to five talents on the Delphic standard) that the Macedonians, not Alexander, made.[10]

In the second century, under the last two kings, Philip V and Perseus, the Macedonians struck some small silver coins (tetrobols and diobols) in their own name (*Makedonōn*), as well as some bronze coins; in addition, an issue of tetradrachms bears the legend "of the Amphaxian Macedonians" (*Makedonōn Amphaxiōn*), Amphaxitis being the region between the Axios and Strymon rivers. Hatzopoulos concludes that the Macedonians had formed a constituent body able to assume some political and financial responsibilities.[11] A close connection has been asserted, indicated by a common monogram, between these coins of the Macedonians and the royal coinage. In contrast, the bronze currency issued during the same period by some cities of the kingdom (Pella, Thessalonica, and Amphipolis) does not show any such connection with the king's coinage. I. Touratsoglou[12] has correctly deduced, it seems to me, that the issues in the name of the Macedonians were under the same authority as those of the sovereign.

[How to explain the production of these coins in the second century in the name of the Macedonians? N. G. L. Hammond has rightly dismissed the idea that the Macedonians sought to take advantage of the kingdom's relative weakness and to express any discontent. On the contrary, Hammond says, they acted in concert with the king for socioeconomic reasons: the ever widening use of coined currency in local transactions required the issue of a larger number of bronze coins and small change in silver, the king sharing this task with the Macedonians (and the cities).[13] Such an explanation is possible, but difficult to prove. Hammond also speaks of the profit accruing to the issuing authority from striking coins, an essential aspect of coinage, I think. In this light, it is understandable that the cities of the Macedonian kingdom issued a coined currency when they could: the revenue collected in this way went directly into their treasury and helped

---

9. *Macedonian Institutions Under the Kings* II (Athens, 1996), no. 1, pp. 19–20. See also P. J. Rhodes and R. Osborne, *Greek Historical Inscriptions, 404-323 B. C.* (Oxford, 2003), no. 12, and J. Pouilloux, *Choix d'inscriptions grecques* (Paris, 1960), no. 25. The translation of Rhodes/Osborne for the relevant lines (13–16) follows: "There shall be export and transport of the other things on paying dues, both for the Chalcidians from Macedon and for the Macedonians from the Chalcidians."

10. J. Bousquet, *Corpus des inscriptions de Delphes* (CID), II, no. 100, col. II, ll. 10–11.

11. Hatzopoulos, op. cit., I, pp. 232–38.

12. *The Coin Circulation in Ancient Macedonia ca. 200 B. C.-268-286 A. D.* (Athens, 1993), p. 72.

13. N. G. L. Hammond, *History of Macedonia* III (Oxford, 1988), pp. 464–66.

defray their essential local expenses. The issue is more complicated for the Macedonians. From a fiscal point of view, why would the king and the Macedonians share coinage production if the resources thus obtained were earmarked for the public treasury? Philip V and Perseus admittedly gave new impetus to the existing regionalization of Macedonia that developed more fully at this time (and that the Romans maintained).[14] The king could entrust the oversight of regional affairs and the provision of necessary funding to the Macedonians in the different districts. A regional role for the Macedonians might explain a coinage legend like *Makedonōn Amphaxiōn*. *Botteatōn* is also found on some coins, and it is probably correct to understand *Makedonōn* and to interpret "[coinage of the Macedonians] from Bottiaea,"[15] Bottiaea being the district extending to the west of the Axios River. The issuance of these coins would have garnered supplementary revenue for the regional treasuries under the Macedonians' management.]

Texts and inscriptions, on the other hand, mention fines and payments *to the king*. Thus, in an act of emancipation coming from Beroea in western Macedonia, dating to the reign of Demetrius II (239–229), it is stipulated that anyone who would re-enslave families whose freedom he had purchased would have to pay "for each person 100 gold staters and to the king another hundred for each person" (Burstein trans.).[16] Similarly, Diodorus (31.8.3) and Livy (45.18.7; 45.29.4, 11), recounting the decisions taken by Rome after the defeat of Perseus at Pydna in 168, report the decree requiring the people of Macedonia to pay the Romans half of the taxes they paid to their king.

Is it necessary to conclude from these pieces of evidence that the Macedonian State had two treasuries, the Macedonians' and the king's? In any case, a single office probably collected these various taxes: the fisc. Conceivably, the fiscal administration had to distinguish, depending on the case and circumstances, between two recipients, the Macedonians and the king, the two together constituting the public treasury. To outsiders, the distinction (if it actually existed) was either not apparent or really must have appeared a distinction without a difference. The sovereign occupied such a place in

---

14. Hatzopoulos, op. cit., I, pp. 231–60, "The Districts." He specifically cites the work of Touratsoglou mentioned above.

15. *Amphaxiōn* (without *Makedonōn*) is also found on the denominations smaller than tetradrachms; conversely, small denominations can carry *Makedonōn* spelled out and the name of the Amphaxians as a monongram.

16. Hatzopoulos, op. cit., II, no. 93, ll. 20–21. [The English version is from the documents collection translated by S. M. Burstein, *The Hellenistic Age from the Battle of Ipsos to the Death of Kleopatra VII* (Cambridge, UK, 1985), no. 54—WEH.] This inscription has great historical interest because it shows that the emancipation was concluded in the twenty-seventh year of Demetrius's reign, from which we learn that Antigonus Gonatas, his father, had taken Demetrius as his co-ruler.

Macedonian affairs that everything seemed to derive from the king. Demosthenes well illustrated Philip II's unlimited power when, in 349, at the beginning of the *First Olynthiac* (section 4), he explained to the Athenians the menace this adversary represented: "he is the sole director of his own policy, open or secret, . . . he unites the functions of a general, a ruler and a treasurer." For Demosthenes, Philip had total control of the public treasury, whatever the internal distinctions of Macedonian accounting were. No doubt Alexander appeared in the same light, although, on some occasions, he judged it useful to remember the rights of the Macedonians.

Besides the public funds that he managed in the name of the State, the sovereign surely possessed a privy purse that, under Alexander as under Philip II, did not take long to grow substantially. A share of booty reverted to the king; the crown property, constantly enlarged by military victories, also brought him private revenues, and other resources probably augmented his personal fortune further. When, in the speech at Opis, Alexander asserted that nothing belonged to him, he certainly was absenting himself from reality. Undoubtedly it was difficult, under monarchs as absolute as Philip and Alexander, to mark the boundary between the public treasury and their own property, to the extent that they used to dip into the State's funds freely.

Macedonian Finances under Alexander from October 336 to April 334

Evidence of Ancient Authors

Theopompus, according to Athenaeus (166f–167c), portrayed Philip II as a reprehensible manager (*oikonomos*) who squandered his resources.[17] In his speech at Opis, Alexander did nothing to polish the image of his father's financial conduct: at the latter's passing, he says (Arrian 7.9.6), the treasuries contained only 60 talents and a few gold and silver cups, and Philip, in addition, owed 500 talents. Alexander adds that Macedonia, at the time of his own departure in 334, could not adequately support its own inhabitants (a strikingly modest evaluation of Philip II's much vaunted social policy).

Nonetheless, the accomplishments of Philip's reign have been widely admired, both in Antiquity and in our own day. Even Theopompus, while constantly castigating this prince for certain faults (earning Theopompus the censure of Polybius [8.9–11]), did emphasize his exceptional valor. In

---

17. See my article, "Philippe II de Macédoine jugé par Théopompe," *NAC* 30 (2001), pp. 87–99. P. Goukowsky suggests to me that the information given in the Opis speech on the state of Philip II's finances at the time of his death goes back perhaps to Theopompus.

fact, Philip II accelerated the urbanization of Macedonia and the conquered countries.[18] He developed commerce and earned substantial revenues from mineral deposits, particuarly applying himself, as we have seen, to the reorganization of the gold mines in the region of Philippi. He endowed his country with a powerful army. His coinage was ample and coherent.

If we heed the words of the Opis speech, however, Philip supposedly left Macedonia on the verge of financial collapse. Is that credible? One answer might be that the author of the oration, employing standard oratorical techniques, has dramatized the situation in order to throw into better relief the wealth that Alexander subsequently acquired. In any event, one can ask if the figures given by Arrian (and by Curtius), assuming they were correct, are as catastrophic as they first appear. To be sure, Philip would not have left an overflowing treasury. But flush with his successes and confident about the future, he would have kept his cash reserves as low as possible and would have had recourse to credit, so as to devote as much money as possible to the enterprises he was directing.

This optimistic view is not what the Opis oration intended. Darkening the record even more, Alexander comments that he was obliged to borrow 800 additional talents. Although the text does not say at what moment, between October 336 and April 334, the young king had recourse to this loan, one imagines that it happened at the time of his accession because the figures furnished by the tradition are no longer the same when the crossing of the Hellespont occurs.

Plutarch (*Alex.* 15.2) in fact cites three sources on this point. According to Aristobulus, he says, Alexander had no more than 70 talents for his expedition's budget (*ephodion*); according to Douris, he could guarantee the maintenance (*diatrophē*) of his troops for only thirty days; according to Onesicritus, he was still in debt for 200 talents.

Scholars have interpreted this text in various ways. A. R. Bellinger and M. J. Price, for example, thought that Alexander left behind a debt of 200 talents, and this appears most plausible to S. Kremydi-Sicilianou.[19] F. Rebuffat,[20] on the contrary, thinks that the king borrowed this sum for the beginning of his campaign and that he departed, therefore, with 270 talents. Must we accept that, in addition to this loan, Alexander had 70 talents in his

---

18. Philip II's activity in this area appears throughout the first part of Hatzopoulos's book, and the latter also forcefully stresses the accomplishments of the king at pp. 473–76.

19. A. R. Bellinger, *Essays on the Coinage of Alexander the Great* (New York, 1963), pp. 36–37 and note 15; M. J. Price, *Alexander* (1991), p. 25; S. Kremydi-Sicilianou, "The Financing of Alexander's Asian Campaign," *Nomismatika Chronika* 18 (1999), p. 61.

20. "Alexandre le Grand et les problèmes financiers au début de son règne," *RN* 25 (1983), pp. 43–52, esp. pp. 50–51.

treasury and provisions for thirty days as well (Price, Kremydi-Sicilianou), or must we believe instead that the evidence of Aristobulus and Douris agrees, the one expressing in talents what the other translates into number of days? Another passage of Plutarch (*Moralia* 327E, *On the Fortune or the Virtue of Alexander* 1.3) would support this second viewpoint: "the great and glorious war-chest [*ephodion*] that Fortune had ready for him was only 70 talents, as Aristobulus says, though Douris says it was provision for only thirty days."

As for the 70 talents Aristobulus mentions, maybe Alexander carried off the reserve funds of the Macedonian treasury with himself, leaving Macedonia and its normal revenues in Antipater's charge. If that were the case, and if one could also interpret Philip's 70 talents mentioned in the Opis speech as a reserve fund, the correspondence between the two sums would be interesting.

According to the Opis speech, Alexander, at the beginning of his reign, had a debt of 1,300 talents (the 800 talents he borrowed at his accession plus the 500 talents owed by Philip). When Onesicritus writes that the king had a debt of 200 talents in April 334, it is probably necessary to understand either that Alexander had reimbursed 1,100 of the 1,300 talents he owed, or that he had liquidated the initial debt but had been forced to take out a new loan of 200 talents shortly before his departure for Asia. In either case, it is astonishing that the king had so small a treasury and that he advanced to Asia Minor with such meager resources.

Alexander's Resources

Not that Alexander wanted at all for sources of income between October 336 and April 334. Regular receipts (whose amount we do not know) enriched the State treasury. Hatzopoulos[21] has recently studied these exhaustively, and I need only summarize his analysis. Exploitation of the crown property represented a first source of revenue. Port duties also brought in important sums. Mines contributed to the wealth of the central authority. Hatzopoulos has commented on the passage where Arrian (1.16.5)[22] notes the attention that Alexander paid to the parents and children of Macedonians killed at the battle of the Granicus: he exempted them from real estate taxes, personal contributions, and levies on acquired goods. The real estate taxes were those paid to the crown by each person who had received a plot of royal territory; personal contributions included not only

---

21. *Macedonian Institutions* (1996), pp. 431–42. H. Berve, *Das Alexanderreich* I (Munich, 1926), pp. 304–6, provides a general list of Alexander's income sources and expenses; it does not deal specifically with Macedonia, but with the empire.

22. See also the remarks of A. B. Bosworth, *A Historical Commentary on Arrian's History of Alexander* I (Oxford, 1980), pp. 126–27.

military service obligations but also services like participation in public works projects that the State required of its citizens; levies on acquired goods probably refer to taxes on capital gains derived from the buying and selling of merchandise. In addition to these normal receipts, fines payable to the State (as opposed to the local authority) provided another revenue stream.

Alexander also profited considerably from his military expedition in the Balkans in 335 and from the sack of Thebes. His campaign against the tribes surrounding Macedonia was meant to pacify this entire region; it was also a means for the new sovereign to test his army and strengthen his standing through victory. Last but not least, it was the chance to obtain a regular flow of booty for himself and perhaps, in certain cases, to annex new lands that would augment the size of the crown estate. Arrian, who is well-informed on this campaign, mentions the booty taken from the Thracians (1.2.1) and the Getai (1.4.5), and Alexander's unbroken successes during these few months surely provided him with other occasions to get his hands on local treasures. Later, he pillaged an unbelievable quantity of precious objects at Thebes, and the sale of war prisoners into slavery netted 440 talents (Diodorus 17.14.1 and 4).[23]

These different cash inflows, we may suppose, permitted Alexander to reduce his debts considerably. Yet, if the tradition has not excessively falsified reality, Alexander lacked any financial cushion whatsoever when he launched his Asian offensive. How can we explain such a situation?

The Expenses of the Macedonian King

I will not dwell on the expenses incumbent on any government: paying its servants (civil and military), construction and maintenance of the central authority's buildings and equipment, organization of great religious ceremonies, sundry financial outlays and disbursements. These inevitable expenses probably absorbed a good deal of the public revenues.

The latter, if one can believe Justin (11.1.10), were somewhat diminished when Alexander, to mark his accession and to win over hearts, "exempted the Macedonians from all duties except military duty" (*Macedonibus immunitatem cunctarum rerum praeter militiae vacationem dedit*; WEH).

---

23. According to Athenaeus (4, 148d), Cleitarchus valued the Theban booty at 440 talents. So the tradition has confused the value of the booty and the sum garnered from the sale of prisoners, who numbered more than 30,000 (Diodorus 17.14.1; Plutarch, *Alex.* 11.12, gives the same number but does not say that it applied only to prisoners of war). P. Ducrey, *Le traitement des prisonniers de guerre dans la Grèce antique* (Paris, 1968, revised second edition in 1999), p. 252 and note 3, thinks that a total of 440 talents for 30,000 individuals is reasonable. Pliny the Elder reports (34.14, 35.98) that Alexander offered the Apollo of Cyme in Aeolis in Asia Minor a candelabrum seized at Thebes and that a painting of the artist Aristeides was shipped off to Pella.

Such a measure, if it had lasted, would have harmed the state budget considerably because the Macedonians, as we have seen, were liable for all sorts of taxes. But we may assume that the exemption in question, supposing that it actually existed, was temporary or consisted in debt forgiveness. Otherwise, the exemption from all duties granted to the families of the fallen at the battle of the Granicus would not make any sense: it would have sufficed to exempt them from military service, the only obligation that would have remained for the Macedonians, if the measure Justin describes were still in force.

What is more certain is that, between 336 and 334, the public treasury had to cope with military expenditures that were probably exceptional.[24]

Philip II, a few months before his assassination in 336, sent an expeditionary force into Asia of about 10,000 men under the command of Parmenio and Attalus (Polyaenus 5.44.4). After achieving mixed results and despite reinforcements brought by Calas, the Macedonians were forced to fall back and take up a position around Abydus[25] where they remained until Alexander's arrival in April of 334. It may be that the Macedonian treasury largely saw to the support and pay of these troops, who had taken up a defensive position and who therefore could not obtain many of their necessities locally.[26]

In Macedonia itself, war expenditures were steep. The maintenance of a sizeable army on Macedonian soil was undoubtedly normal: Philip II had needed to keep troops combat-ready. Alexander's force before Thebes in 335 gives an idea of the manpower the king could normally assemble: more than 30,000 infantry and at least 3,000 cavalry, according to Diodorus (17.9.3). Philip II commanded a comparable army at the battle of Chaeronea in 338 (Diodorus 16.85.5).

The army that crossed the Hellespont at the start of spring in 334 was not much larger. Arrian (1.11.3) indicates that the number of infantry almost surpassed 30,000 and that the cavalry were more than 5,000.[27] We

---

24. The study of A. Andréadès, "Les finances de guerre d'Alexandre le Grand," *Annales d'hist. économ. et sociale* 1 (1929), pp. 321–34, contains useful analyses.

25. P. Debord, *L'Asie Mineure au IVe siècle* (Bordeaux, 1999), pp. 421–26, is the most recent study of this campaign.

26. A. B. Bosworth, "Alexander the Great and the Decline of Macedon," *JHS* 106 (1986), pp. 2–3, has conjectured, basing himself on the composition of Alexander's army upon its departure for Asia, that this expeditionary force comprised about 3,000 Macedonians.

27. The evidence of the ancient authors does not coincide. There is a list, for example, in Berve, op. cit., p. 177, of the differing figures that have come down to us; there are analogous lists in P. A. Brunt, "Alexander's Macedonian Cavalry," *JHS* 83 (1983), p. 46, and in P. Green, *Alexander of Macedon 356-323 B. C.* (Berkeley, 1991), p. 530, note 8. Scholars have been forced to impose some order on these data. In addition to the authors already

owe to Diodorus (17.17.3–4) some welcome details. The infantry, he writes, comprised 12,000 Macedonians, 7,000 allied Greeks, 5,000 mercenaries, and 8,000 Odrysians, Triballoi, Illyrians, and Agrianians, for a total of 32,000 men, which Diodorus rounds to 30,000. The cavalry consisted of 1,500 Macedonians, 1,800 Thessalians, 600 other Greeks, and 900 Thracians and Paeonians, or 5,100 cavalry (4,500, Diodorus says).

In itself, therefore, this army was not at all extraordinary, judging by the force led against Thebes. The preparations for the Asian campaign, however, probably went to unusual lengths. The setbacks that Philip II's expeditionary force endured raised awareness that the enemy was not to be underestimated. One can imagine that Alexander took particular care about his men's equipment and that he monitored the quality of their artillery, military engineering, commissariat, and medical care.

Alexander, moreover, left behind 12,000 infantry and 1,500 cavalry under Antipater in Macedonia (Diodorus 17.17.5). He had to allow for forces sufficient to defend the national territory and to keep an eye on the Balkans and Greece. These infantry and cavalrymen were probably almost all Macedonians because the Greek allies did not have any reason to second a part of their troops to Macedonia. As for the mercenary recruits, it is possible that Antipater retained some of them, but one presumes that most were meant to depart with Alexander.

Summing up, therefore, Macedonia made a noteworthy effort in putting on a war footing 24,000 Macedonian foot soldiers and 3,000 horse, a probably unprecedented figure.

Alexander was also preoccupied with readying a fleet for war. Philip II possessed a certain number of vessels, which he used especially in his operations of 340–339 against Perinthus and Byzantium. Alexander, notwithstanding his reliance on his land force, certainly did not neglect his navy. The ancient authors do not provide us with clear information on this subject. N. G. L. Hammond's interpretation,[28] based on information from Diodorus and Arrian, interests me. The allies contributed 160 triremes, and it was on these ships, joined by additional merchantmen, that Parmenio crossed the Hellespont from Sestus to Abydus with the cavalry and the bulk of the infantry (Arrian 1.11.6). Arrian mentions these 160 triremes again (1.18.4) a few months later, when Nicanor, Alexander's admiral, was anchored with 160 ves-

---

cited, see also A. B. Bosworth, *A Historical Commentary on Arrian* I (Oxford, 1980), pp. 98–99; P. Savinel, *Arrien, Histoire d'Alexandre* (Paris, 1984), pp. 12–13; N. G. L. Hammond, *History of Macedonia* III (Oxford, 1988), pp. 22–27. By assuming that they counted the forces already stationed in Asia, we can explain the elevated numbers of Callisthenes (40,000 foot) and Anaximenes (43,000). Polybius (12.19.1) cites Callisthenes; Plutarch (Moralia 327E, *On the Fortune* . . . 1.3; cf. *Alex.* 15.1) cites Anaximenes.

28. Op. cit., pp. 24–26; on the way Hammond explains Justin's information, who tells us that the fleet was composed of 182 ships, see *ibid.*, p. 25.

sels at the island of Lade, opposite Miletus, these 160 ships constituting, according to Arrian, the "Greek" fleet. Alexander, on the other hand, had separated himself from the rest of the army when crossing the Hellespont: he went to Elaeus (south of Sestus, at the tip of the Thracian Chersonesus, and from there he sailed to the Achaean harbor in the Troad (Arrian 1.11.6). He had taken a portion of the infantry with him, and he commanded a group of sixty "long boats," that is, warships (Diodorus 17.17.2). Hammond, speculating that these sixty vessels represented the Macedonian fleet, makes the point that Alexander did not combine his Macedonian vessels with those of the allies, but that he preferred to entrust the former with protecting lines of communication and the latter with offensive actions.

It is practically impossible to estimate the sums Alexander had to lay out in Macedonia to pay his troops.[29] Too many questions arise and remain unanswered. In chapter 4, I will address the problem of the wages for the army and fleet Alexander had at his disposal in Asia Minor, a period when the surmises one can make are maybe less haphazard, despite serious and persistent uncertainties. For now, I will be content to propose some ideas on the Macedonian situation up to the crossing of the Hellespont (April 334).

To begin with the Macedonians, we know that military service was among their fundamental obligations, constituting one of those duties that the Greeks called "liturgies."[30] Normally, therefore, when he had to defend the soil of his homeland, the Macedonian soldier received no pay and perhaps enlisted under arms with at least some of the regulation kit. If the Balkan and Theban campaigns were presented as critical to homeland security, were the Macedonians content to divide among themselves the booty that accrued to them? Did they also have claims tantamount to wages? And what were the financial conditions when the general mobilization took place at the end of 335 and the beginning of 334?

As for the allied Greek cities, they probably readied the troops and ships they placed under Alexander's command at their own expense. It is reasonable to think that the pay and maintenance of the allied contingents

---

29. The article of R. D. Milns, "Army Pay and the Military Budget of Alexander the Great," in *Zu Alexander der Grosse, Festschrift G. Wirth,* ed. W. Will (Amsterdam, 1987), pp. 233-56, highlights these uncertainties well. I will return to it in the next chapter.

30. This is the term Arrian employs (1.16.5) when he enumerates the exemptions granted the parents and children of the Macedonians killed at the battle of the Granicus (cf. the discussion above, p. 26). They are specifically dispensed from the "liturgies" incumbent on their person and therefore, notably, from military service, as commentators have thought: see M. B. Hatzopoulos, *Macedonian Institutions,* p. 437. The latter notes that Alexander, in his speech at Opis, uses similar terminology (Arrian 7.10.4): "'Indeed, when a man died, glory came to him by his death, splendor in his funeral, and brazen images have been erected for most of them at home, while his parents enjoy the honor of being freed from every public duty ["liturgy"] and tax.'"

were charged to the Conqueror's account after the passage to Asia. But the pay and sustenance of the mercenaries were presumably his responsibility right from the time of their recruitment.

A passage in Plutarch (*Alex.* 15.3–4) shows that the Macedonian treasury, even after receiving the riches of the Balkan campaign and the booty plundered from Thebes, was incapable of meeting the expenses the sovereign had to settle before his departure in 334. Alexander, Plutarch says, "would not set foot upon his ship until he had enquired into the circumstances of his companions and allotted to one a farm, to another a village, and to another the revenue from some hamlet or harbor. And when at last nearly all of the crown property had been expended or allotted, Perdiccas said to him, 'But what are you keeping for yourself, my lord?' 'My hopes,' Alexander replied" [Loeb modified].

This passage is particularly interesting. It is hardly probable that Alexander acted out of pure generosity, or prodigality, or out of a simple concern to win friends. There is a more plausible explanation. The sovereign's Companions (*hetairoi*) had assumed partial responsibility for the Asian campaign's preparation. They might have participated in at least two ways, by lending money to the king and by equipping and training some units of new Macedonian recruits at their own expense. At the time of his departure from Macedonia, Alexander wanted to settle his accounts with them. Plutarch indicates how he did so: he drew upon the crown estate and especially, we may surmise, upon those recently conquered territories that had not yet been parceled out among the Macedonians.[31]

To summarize: it is credible that Alexander did not have much money at his disposal when he left Macedonia in April of 334.

Alexander's Coinage in Macedonia from October 336 to April 334

I showed in chapter 1 that the coinage of Alexander, with the types of Athena head and Nike for gold, and Herakles head and seated Zeus for silver, were not created in all probability before 333/332. So we must ask what currency the sovereign did use between his accession and this date, and especially in Macedonia from October 336 to April 334.

He could not, in fact, do without coinage. It is true, as I have said above, that many transactions were conducted in other ways. There were exchanges in kind and services in lieu of payment. We have seen how the

---

31. I rely on Hatzopoulos's judicious commentary on the Plutarch passage, op. cit., p. 436. The sentence of Justin (11.5.5) relating the same episode is less instructive but no less striking: "All his ancestral domains in Macedonia and Europe he distributed among his friends, declaring that Asia was enough for him" [Yardley trans.].

king liquidated his obligations by giving a piece of land or by ceding this or that source of revenue. Nonetheless, using coined currency had become normal in various activities. We may assume that certain orders placed abroad for provisions and materials were paid in coin; so, too, the salaries of mercenaries or foreign experts (architects, engineers, artists). In Macedonia itself, certain salaries were probably paid in coined currency, as were, admittedly, a portion of levies, taxes, and fines. Individuals occasionally effected sales and purchases in this way. In 1991 Hatzopoulos[32] published bills of sale from Amphipolis, the city that became Macedonian in 357 under Philip II: houses and fields are valued in silver drachms and gold staters, and there can be little doubt that the seller actually received silver or gold coins from the buyer. Here is the text of one of these transactions, the second of the collection: "Lykophron bought a house for 280 drachms from Menander. It adjoins the property of Kason, Droubis, and Nikander. Sparges was the registrar. The guarantor was Aglainos. Witnesses were Polyboulos, Poianthos, Arkhippos. All duties as well as charges related to the house are the buyer's expense" (WEH, after Hatzopoulos's text). Note that 280 drachms, the value of the house Lykophron bought, amounted to a little less than one-twentieth of a talent, which was worth 6,000 drachms. I provide this as a point of reference because I frequently cite sums in talents in my analyses.

The "Eagle" Tetradrachms

If Alexander instituted his coinage with the Athena head type for gold and the Herakles head type for silver after his departure from Macedonia, he possibly, even probably, struck a group of tetradrachms that we call "eagle" tetradrachms between 336 and 334. This group, because it offers no easy interpretation, warrants detailed examination.

The "eagle" tetradrachms (pl. 1, 12–13), on the obverse, bear a head of Zeus facing right, set within a dotted border; on the reverse, they show an eagle, wings folded and head turned, standing to the right on a thunderbolt. The legend is *Alexandrou*, the initial letters being inscribed in the field to the left, the final letters to the right. A newly discovered coin shows no symbol; on others, two symbols are placed on each side of the eagle, either an "oriental" headdress and a club, or the same oriental headdress and a short olive branch with two leaves (the headdress is shown horizontally and is more easily recognizable if the coins are rotated 90 degrees to the right).[33]

---

32. *Actes de vente d'Amphipolis* (Meletēmata 14, Athens, 1991).

33. On this group of tetradrachms, see my *Monnayage et finances de Philippe II* (1996), pp. 91–94. O. Bopearachchi has described the newly discovered coin I have just mentioned in *La circulation et la production monétaires en Asie centrale et dans l'Inde du Nord-Ouest*, Indologica Taurinensia 25 (Turin, 1999–2000), pp. 24–25, no. 54. The coin is part of a private collection from Peshawar, with a provenance from the "hoard" of Mir Zakah II (Mir Zakah is a village in Afghanistan).

A dozen examples are known today; the eight I have been able to examine first hand share five obverse and eight reverse dies. Statistically, the relation between the number of coins studied (eight) and the number of obverse dies found (five) leads one to suppose that several other obverse dies were employed in the striking of these tetradrachms.

Their weights vary. They are, for nine coins: 14.44 or 14.45 grams; 14.42 or 14.45 grams; 14.37 grams; 14.34 grams; 14.20 grams; 14.04 grams; 13.36 grams; 13.24 grams; 13.16 grams.[34] Judging by the heaviest weights, these coins have generally been thought to continue the weight standard of Philip II's tetradrachms, the majority of which weighed ±14.45 grams.[35]

Another eagle coin served as a blank for a coin of Patraus, king of Paeonia (to the north of Macedonia) from c. 335 to c. 315. E. Pegan revealed this overstriking in an article of 1968[36] that summarized the long debate the eagle tetradrachms had elicited. Because one of these examples (number nine on my list in the accompanying footnote) had been found in Pakistan (the former Punjab), several commentators preferred an eastern origin for this coinage, and it will be noted that another specimen (number eight on my list) was recently discovered in Afghanistan. Several western findspots, however, have been identified, which tip the scale in favor of a western mint. One coin wound up in Paeonia (the one Patraus overstruck), another was brought to light in Elis (number six on my list), and three others were part of a Thessalian hoard.[37]

Most scholars today think that Alexander struck the eagle tetradrachms in Macedonia at the start of his reign, before the inauguration of the Conqueror's great silver coinage (with Herakles head and seated Zeus), and they support this view with several arguments. First, these tetradrachms, as I have emphasized above, have a weight similar to those of Philip II. Second, their types are Macedonian: the head of Zeus is the obverse type on Philip II's

---

34. The references for these coins are as follows: 1. Catal. Hirsch 35 (1909), 704 (14.44g) and Catal. Egger 40 (1912), 575 (14.45g); 2. London; Price, *Alexander* 142*a* (14.45g), and U. Wartenberg, *NC* 157 (1997), p. 183, no. 6 (14.42g); 3. Paris; 4. Catal. Freeman and Sear, summer/autumn, 1994, B36; 5. Athens (from Monnaies et Médailles, Basel, 13 [1954], 1097), pl. 1, 12; 6. Catal. Berk, Oct. 26, 1994, 124; 7. Alpha Bank (Athens), pl. 1, 13; 8. Private Collection, Peshawar (Bopearachchi's example); 9. London; Price, *Alexander*, 142*b*.

35. See my *Philippe II* (1977), pp. 343–50; the tetradrachms at issue are those struck during Philip's lifetime and immediately after his death.

36. "Die frühesten Tetradrachmen Alexanders des Grossen mit dem Adler," *Jahrb. Numism. und Geldgeschichte* 18 (1968), pp. 99–111. The coin Patraus overstruck is now kept in New York at the American Numismatic Society; cf. *SNG*, Macedonia I, 1023.

37. U. Wartenberg, "The Alexander-Eagle Hoard: Thessaly, 1992," *NC* 157 (1997), pp. 179–88, esp. p. 183 and p. 188, nos. 92–94. Number seven of my list comes from this hoard.

tetradrachms, and the eagle with folded wings, turning its head, appears on small silver coins of Amyntas III (393–370/69) and on bronze coins of Perdiccas III (who preceded Philip II, 364–60). Alexander himself, in Macedonia, used the type of the eagle with folded wings, turning its head and perched on a thunderbolt, for drachms (and their fractions) of Attic weight, as well as for bronze coinage. Third, the Zeus head on the eagle tetradrachms stylistically recalls that appearing on Philip II's tetradrachms, especially in the issue marked with a *kantharos* that I have attributed to the Pella mint (pl. 1, 14).[38] Fourth, it is possible that the specimen of Patraus overstruck on the eagle tetradrachm belongs to the beginning of this ruler's reign. Pegan has drawn attention to one peculiarity: the head of Apollo placed on the obverse of the Paeonian overstrike is notable for a very evident pellet placed on the god's neck. It happens that coins of Patraus's predecessor, Lykkeios (c. 359/58–335),[39] have a pellet just as protuberant on the cheek of the same god. Pegan thought that the issues showing this characteristic were close in time and belonged to the end of Lykkeios's reign and the beginning of Patraus's. If, therefore, the coin of the latter which used the eagle tetradrachm as a blank were issued shortly after 335, the eagle tetradrachm in question would have to be dated to the time of Alexander's accession. Fifth, the legend on the eagle tetradrachms reveals a peculiarity: the letter *xi* of *Alexandrou* is formed by three horizontal parallel bars dissected by a vertical stroke, whereas the letter is usually represented by the three horizontal strokes alone. Now, on the earliest Alexander tetradrachms with Herakles head struck in Macedonia (pl. 1, 6)[40] the *xi* is written in the same way as on the eagle tetradrachms. One is led to conclude that the two coinages are roughly contemporary.

To sum up, then, one might accept that the eagle tetradrachms were produced in Macedonia soon after Alexander's accession. In this case, would they have been struck at Pella, because the Zeus head resembles the one engraved at Pella for Philip II's tetradrachms? Pella, anyway, would be preferable to Amphipolis for the following reason: as I will show later, the first Alexander tetradrachms with Herakles head issued at Amphipolis display exactly the same symbols as the last group of tetradrachms Philip struck at this mint. There is no chronological gap between the two series during which the eagle tetradrachms could have been produced. At Pella,

---

38. See my *Philippe II* (1977), pl. 15, nos. 343–48.
39. This king's name has also been transcribed in the forms "Lykpeios" and "Lyppeios." Cf. H. Seyrig, *RN* 4 (1962), pp. 205–6 (= *Scripta Numismatica*, Paris,1986, pp. 5–6); N. G. L. Hammond, *A History of Macedonia* II (Oxford, 1979), p. 75 and note 2.
40. In particular, tetradrachms having a prow turned to the right as a symbol (pl. 1, 6) display this form of the *xi*. They are surely to be placed at the very beginning of the Macedonian coinage with Herakles head; cf. Troxell, *Alexander* (1997), pp. 87–88.

in contrast, the same continuity does not exist between the last Philips[41] and the first Alexanders: the eagle tetradrachms would fit well into this mint's output.

This solution, however, does not completely satisfy. If these tetradrachms succeeded the last issue of Pella Philips, the Zeus head ought to be of the same style as that on the last Philips. It is nothing of the sort. The head of Zeus on the eagle tetradrachms is, in fact, close, as we saw, to that on the Philips marked with a *kantharos* and struck a certain number of years earlier.[42] Moreover, this stylistic analogy, while undeniable, is more an overall similarity than a detailed resemblance. The idea that the eagle tetradrachms could have been struck at a mint other than Pella or Amphipolis is also not to be excluded categorically. M. J. Price[43] thought of the mint at Aigeai, Macedonia's old royal "capital," in itself an acceptable suggestion. Yet one has to observe that Price does not think that the eagle tetradrachms were issued as an occasional and unique coinage at Aigeai; he would readily attribute several other coinage issues under Philip II and Alexander to this city, a debatable opinion,[44] it seems to me.

Questions arise not only from the style but also from the symbols present on the eagle tetradrachms. Setting aside the newly discovered coin, which bears no distinctive symbol, the other coins are marked either with a club and oriental headdress or with an olive branch and the same headdress. The club symbol appears on coins of Philip II and Alexander.[45] In contrast, the olive branch does not appear on any other Macedonian issue of this period. As for the oriental headdress (previously thought to be a prow or a plow), certain writers have difficulty accepting that it could have served as a symbol in Macedonia. More recently still, P. Debord wrote[46]: "The presence

---

41. The appellation "Philips," like "Alexanders" (cf. the discussion above in chapter 1, p. 4), is a convenient shorthand for the coins struck by these kings during their lifetimes and posthumously by others. The same situation obtains with the coins produced by Lysimachus and after his death with his name and types: "Lysimachi."

42. I have provided a synopsis of issues of Philips at Pella and Amphipolis in *Monnayage et finances de Philippe II* (1996), pp. 22–23 (Pella), and pp. 24–25 (Amphipolis).

43. *Alexander* (1991), p. 103.

44. I have analyzed and criticized this hypothesis in "Les tétradrachms macédoniens d'Alexandre," in *Studies in Greek Numismatics in Memory of Martin Jessop Price*, R. Ashton and S. Hurter eds. (London, 1998), pp. 241–43 (= *Études d'histoire monétaire et financière du monde grec* II, Athens, 1999, pp. 523–25).

45. It appears as symbol on the tetradrachms of Philip that I have attributed to Pella towards the reign's end, not chronologically far removed from the eagle tetradrachms, if the latter are to be dated towards the beginning of Alexander's rule. See *Philippe II* (1977), pl. 16, pp. 376–82.

46. *L'Asie Mineure au IVe siècle* (Bordeaux,1999), p. 484.

of the oriental headdress (as secondary symbol) would rather bring Sardis to mind and, in any case, an Anatolian mint, in the early phase of Alexander's Asian invasion."

Actually, this symbol, in all likelihood, is not a mark chosen by the central authority but a personal signature; one can envisage that a mint magistrate employed it in Macedonia because he was of Persian origin, or because he had a Persian-sounding name, or because he had some other motivation impossible to surmise. Nevertheless, this oriental headdress remains curious and puzzling.

In the end, the chronology of the eagle tetradrachms leaves room for doubt. We have seen that some indications suggest placing them at the beginning of Alexander's reign. Yet these arguments are not decisive. Pegan's observation about the pellet on the cheek and neck of Apollo in the time of Lykkeios and Patraus is interesting, certainly, but the coinage of these two kings has not yet been studied enough to permit precise dating of the different issues. I note that, according to N. M. Waggoner,[47] the coinage of Patraus in question "may well come toward the end of Patraus's reign rather than the beginning," contradicting Pegan's opinion. King Patraus ruled Paeonia from c. 335 to c. 315. If the eagle tetradrachm used as a flan was overstruck after c. 320, it can no longer be said confidently that it was issued to coincide with the start of Alexander's reign.

We must also not forget that the weight standard Philip II adopted for his tetradrachms enjoyed renewed popularity in Macedonia when, after Alexander's death in 323, posthumous issues of Philips were struck at Amphipolis and Pella.[48] In fact, usage of tetradrachms with the name and types of Philip II never ceased on Macedonian soil (or in the neighboring regions) from the beginning of his rule down to the start of the third century BC. The production of eagle tetradrachms, on the Philips' weight standard, might conceivably have then occurred just as well shortly after 336 as towards the middle or the end of Alexander's reign, or even after his death.

I will add that the peculiar form of the *xi* in *Alexandrou* appears not only on the first tetradrachms of Alexander at Amphipolis but also on some of his gold distaters with *kantharos* symbol, which began to appear, according to Troxell,[49] in the second part of the reign. It is worth noting that the *xi* does not have that strange form on the distaters with thunderbolt and trident, even though they belong to the same group as the *kantharos* distaters. The shape of this letter was therefore left to the engraver's initiative, so that the particular form in question can be found at any time in any mint.

---

47. *SNG*, Amer. Num. Soc. 7, Macedonia I, no. 1023.
48. See my *Philippe II* (1977), pp. 120–26; H. A. Troxell, *Alexander* (1997), pp. 51–72.
49. *Ibid.*, pp. 112–14 and 128.

The Thessalian hoard recently published by Wartenberg[50] might have shed some light on the eagle tetradrachms' chronology, were its composition better known. Aware of gaps in her information, Wartenberg refused to offer a precise date for its burial. She leads one to understand, however, that the hoard was probably buried well before the end of Alexander's reign. The lot she reconstituted may have contained, besides the three eagle tetradrachms I have noted, two Alexanders with Herakles head, some tetradrachms of Philip II, a didrachm from Larissa, some silver staters from Sicyon and others from Opuntian Locris and Thebes, and maybe some Athenian tetradrachms. Concerning the eagle tetradrachms and one of the Alexanders, she writes: "The later report stated that the tetradrachm [the Alexander] was generally more worn than the Eagle-tetradrachms, but I would hesitate to draw any conclusions from this."

To conclude, the eagle tetradrachm coinage still lacks satisfactory explanation: its date, the mint where it was struck, the oriental headdress symbol all still pose problems. The data available today suggest that these coins were probably issued in Macedonia at the start of Alexander's reign, but nothing is really definite, and we must await the discovery of new evidence.

The output of this currency was not insignificant: five obverse dies have been identified and others will undoubtedly surface. It was not, however, a really voluminous coinage, and it will be noted that no gold staters accompanied the tetradrachms (at least in the present state of our evidence). If Alexander limited his monetary activity between 336 and 334 to issuing these silver eagle coins, the contrast would be striking between the production rate Philip imposed on the mint in the closing years of his reign and that to which Alexander slowed it. Yet the latter, from all appearances starting in October 336, probably needed as much coined silver as his father did. It is hard to believe that the eagle tetradrachms (once again supposing that they date from the years 336–334) would have sufficed. In these circumstances, what currency did Alexander use after his accession?

The Continued Striking of Coins of Philip II after Alexander's Accession

A first hypothesis would be that Alexander found a sizable quantity of coins in the treasury his father left him. On reflection, this hardly appears likely. Even if Philip had not been the insouciant spendthrift Theopompus describes, even if his treasury contained more than sixty talents, the efforts he had taken in Greece, the preparations for the expedition that he launched against the Persians shortly before his death, and the expenses he

---

50. *NC* 157 (1997), pp. 179–88.

incurred for the great autumn festivals of 336 and his daughter's marriage suggest that he probably did not have plentiful cash reserves at the time of his assassination. The sixty talents Alexander mentions in his Opis oration, whether they were sixty or more, might well have existed partly as currency and partly as still uncoined metal.

I can offer another perspective by observing that Alexander might have continued striking his father's coins (that is, silver tetradrachms of ±14.45 grams with the types of Zeus head and victorious young rider, and gold staters of ±8.60 grams featuring an Apollo head and a *biga*). I recalled above that, in my study of Philip II's coinage, I had allocated his issues to two mints, Pella and Amphipolis. In the series of tetradrachms I attributed to Amphipolis, Group II ends with coins whose symbols are notably a prow, a stern, or a Janus-head (pl. 2, 1–3).[51] These same symbols, it so happens, show up on the first group of Alexanders struck at the same mint (pl. 1, 6 and 2, 4–6). So the two groups are closely connected. Because the first Alexanders were not, in all likelihood, produced in Macedonia before 332 (at the earliest), one is tempted to infer that the Philips in question were struck up until that date, the same mint magistrates having moved without a break from one coinage to the other. One could argue, of course, that the moneyers who served Philip up to 336 resumed their activity under Alexander in 332, but this strikes me as less plausible. A chronologically unbroken continuation seems to me easier to accept.

The Evidence of the Gold Stater Hoards

The examination of four hoards containing gold staters of Philip II and Alexander may help to confirm the idea that Alexander continued issuing Philips. These are the hoards from Corinth, Samovodene in Bulgaria, a 1967 Balkans find, and one from Mende in Macedonia, and they were probably all buried in the same time period, between 323 and 320 (or a little later).[52] The Corinth hoard comes from an official excavation and its composition is known with certainty. One can only hope that what has reached us from the

---

51. These symbols sometimes stand alone, sometimes accompanied by a bee. Two other symbols appear in this group of Philips: an *omphalos* [the "navel" stone of Delphi: WEH] and a rudder with its tiller; a rudder without tiller also appears in the first group of Alexanders struck at Amphipolis. Cf. most recently Troxell, *Alexander* (1997), p. 21.

52. I studied the first three of them in detail in my *Philippe II* (1977), pp. 257–64, nos. 2, 3, and 5. The fourth, from Mende, was discovered in 1983, after my book had appeared, and was published by Troxell, *Alexander* (1997), pp. 134–36. She re-examined and, on certain points, made corrections of the first three, pp. 115–18 (cf. the table on p. 121). It is she who suggested a burial around 323 or later for the Corinth hoard that M. Thompson and I had dated to 327–325. For the Samovodene hoard, that contains two of my Group III Philips, the date depends on the chronology proposed for the first Philips of this third group; cf. below, at the conclusion of chapter 3, pp. 71–72.

three others gives a representative picture of their original contents. In these four deposits, almost all the Philip II staters belong to my Group II, the group that was being issued at the time of Philip's death. Only the Samovodene hoard contained several staters (two of them have been recovered) belonging to my Group III, which began after Alexander's death in June 323.

The four hoards lead to the same conclusion: Philip's staters are clearly more numerous than Alexander's and they are generally as well-preserved as the Alexanders accompanying them. Gold coins, indeed, ordinarily undergo less handling than silver coins, and they are treated with more care. Gold also tends to circulate less than silver. In addition, gold burials, more so than silver, may have been formed by successive additions of carefully chosen coins[53] so that older specimens are as good looking as more recent pieces. If the coins do not carry a date (and that is the case with our staters), it is therefore impossible to classify them chronologically with reference to one another.

Were the four hoards under discussion built up little by little over a great number of years, or, on the contrary, were their constituents removed from circulation over a relatively brief span of time? The staters in the four hoards, although in good condition, betray signs of wear (Alexanders and Philips both) and therefore experienced some handling before being buried. Moreover, the four hoards have comparable compositions. The coins were apparently acquired in the same way: their owners presumably received them as payment after rendering a service or at the conclusion of a commercial transaction. I personally am not inclined to deny these hoards all chronological interest.[54]

Returning to the number of Philips and Alexanders in our four hoards: the Corinth hoard had forty-one staters of Philip and ten Alexanders (eight of them Macedonian); the Samovodene lot included forty-nine Philips of Group II and sixteen Alexanders (eight Macedonian); the Balkans hoard had twenty-four Philips and five Alexanders (three Macedonian); and Mende contained sixty-two Philips and eighteen Alexanders (eleven being Macedonian). So the preponderance of Philips is clear. This fact, as well as their being as well preserved as the Alexanders, led me to conclude that the production of Philip staters extended into the reign of Alexander. This hypothesis accords well with the view, widely shared today, that the gold coinage with the name and types of Alexander began only some years after his accession, just like his silver coinage with Herakles head.

---

53. This is how Balzac's *père* Grandet constituted his daughter Eugénie's dowry. For thirteen years he used to contribute a gold piece (surely freshly minted) for her birthday, for New Year's Day, and for his own birthday celebration.

54. A more detailed discussion of this question will be found in my *Monnayage et finances de Philippe II* (Athens, 1996), pp. 55–56 and 61–62.

The Philips Struck under Alexander

The difficulty with the hypothesis I am defending is that the volume of gold and silver Philips struck at the start of Alexander's reign cannot be evaluated with any certainty. It is impossible, in fact, to establish the boundary line between the issues produced before and after 336. To give a clearer view of the situation, I will recall some numerical data, calculated on the basis of the corpus of silver and gold coins of Philip II that I published in 1977.[55]

[I classified these coins in two series (A and B); in each, only Group II concerns us, that which covers the final years of Philip II and the first years of Alexander.

Tetradrachms (head of Zeus/young jockey with palm):
 Series A (Pella?), Group II: around 160 obverse dies (cf. pl. 1, 7 and 14)
 Series B (Amphipolis?), Group II: around 220 obverse dies (cf. pl. 2, 1–3)
Gold Staters (head of Apollo/racing *biga*)
 Series A, Group II: around 160 obverse dies (cf. pl. 1, 10)
 Series B, Group II: around 90 obverse dies (cf. pl. 1, 11)]

We do not know just when in Philip's reign Group II began (the tetradrachms and staters of Group II conceivably starting at different dates). It seems that for the coinage of this period, only a general observation is possible: the activity of the mints was undoubtedly significant. The ratio of gold to silver was about 1 to 10 around 336. A gold stater of ±8.60 grams was therefore worth about six tetradrachms of ±14.45 grams. In sum, the 250 dies put in service for the gold staters and the 380 dies engraved for the tetradrachms, during a period lasting between ten and twenty years, yielded a considerable money supply whose purchasing power was not trivial.

In one particular case, we may have a more precise indication. Group II of Series B contains issues that seem, at least in part, to have been struck concurrently (there are die linkages tying them together) and that, stylistically, can be placed at the end of Group II. The principal symbols identifying these issues (which we have discussed above, p. 38; cf. pl. 2, 1–3) are a prow, a stern, and a Janus-head (all sometimes accompanied by a bee, sometimes not). We have seen how the first tetradrachms of Alexander with Herakles head issued in Macedonia also carry these three symbols (pl. 2, 4–6) and how, in all probability, they directly followed the Philips in question.

---

55. I gathered these data in *Monnayage et finances de Philippe II* (Athens, 1996), p. 70. The original number of obverse dies has been estimated with the help of G. F. Carter's simplified method, "A Simplified Method for Calculating the Original Number of Dies from Die-Link Statistics," *Amer. Num. Soc. Mus. Notes* 28 (1983), pp. 195–206.

Suppose that the Alexanders' production began at this mint in 332. Because the Philips carrying the symbols just described form a closely-knit group, it is tempting to conjecture that they were struck in a relatively brief span of time and that they can be dated to the years 336–332. They themselves total about 160 obverse dies, while the dies for all the tetradrachms with the name and types of Philip II classed in my Group II (series A and B together) number 380. If the Philips with prow, stern, and Janus-head come from the mint at Amphipolis, as I believe, one can state that this mint, at the start of Alexander's rule, accelerated its production of silver coins. And what is true for the silver coins of Amphipolis probably also holds for its gold coins, as well as for the silver and gold coins from the mint at Pella.

I am inclined to think, therefore, that my Group II of Philips, both silver and gold, that had already attained a certain volume under Philip II, achieved greater scale during the first four years of Alexander's reign, from October 336 to c. 332 (the latter year is conjectural and may have to be downdated slightly).

Alexander and the Coinage of Philip II

Gold and silver coins with the name and types of Philip II would, therefore, have constituted Alexander's principal currency between October 336 and April 334. His eagle coinage, if it really belongs to this period, appears relatively secondary. Alexander's practice seems nothing short of astonishing. It would be understandable if the new king did not produce any coinage for a certain period of time. Philip had waited perhaps four years before inaugurating his own silver coinage.[56] But that Alexander, no matter what date we prefer for his eagle tetradrachms, continued to strike his predecessor's currency on a grand scale—such conduct poses a problem that has provoked numerous attempts at explanation.

J. R. Ellis has been a notable proponent of political motives, which I have set forth in my *Philippe II*.[57] Following Philip's murder, Alexander, he argues, would have had to display considerable energy to secure his position. He needed the support of Philip II's powerful companions,[58] and he realized that he had to show Philip special fidelity. Continuing to coin

---

56. See my *Monnayage et finances de Philippe II* (Athens, 1996), p. 14 (date of Philip's accession) and pp. 44–46 (start of Philip's coinage).

57. J. R. Ellis, *Philip II and Macedonian Imperialism* (London, 1976), pp. 235–39; cf. my *Philippe II* (1977), p. 437.

58. Ellis has defended the view that Alexander's cousin, Amyntas, the son of Perdiccas III whom Philip had driven from the throne, hatched a vast conspiracy against Alexander: "Amyntas, Perdikkas, Philip II and Alexander the Great, A Study in Conspiracy," *JHS* 91 (1971), pp. 15–24. P. Goukowsky, in E. Will and P. Goukowsky, *Le monde grec et l'Orient II* (Paris, 1975), pp. 251–53, has shown that Alexander certainly had to deal with problems

Philips was one of the manifestations of such filial piety. This is an interesting but debatable hypothesis. It did not take Alexander long, it seems, to eliminate whatever difficulties confronted him at his accession. The Macedonians proclaimed him king immediately upon his father's death, and a few weeks later Greece recognized his power and promoted him to leadership of the League of Corinth. In 335 his military successes were dazzling. I am not convinced that, in this context, a monetary fidelity towards Philip would have been, politically, particularly useful.

Commercial reasons could also be advanced. E. T. Newell[59] in 1912 thought that the Balkan populations had developed a deep attachment to this sovereign's coinage from the time of Philip II's reign. That is how he explained the renewed coining of gold and silver Philips after Alexander's death in 323: this currency was so popular in 336 that Alexander's did not succeed in supplanting it and the Macedonian authorities were compelled to resume its production. M. J. Price,[60] agreeing with Newell, added that the standard of the silver Philips was quite at home in the Balkans. Newell and Price thought that Alexander had begun to issue his own coinage from the end of 336, ceasing to strike Philips as of this date. But the motivations they proposed for the resumption of the latter after 323 could also explain why Alexander continued to issue them for some time after his accession. He may have judged it commercially advantageous to maintain a currency that was so well accepted in regions where Macedonia had large interests.

That Philips had begun to circulate widely and were appreciated in the Balkans before 336 is quite probable, but that the inhabitants of these regions would have preferred this coinage to all others I find harder to believe. What mattered to them, I think, was receiving a certain weight of good quality silver in exchange for their products. If Alexander (whose prestige after his accession was as great as his father's in these territories) had undertaken to produce his tetradrachms with the head of Herakles and his staters with the head of Athena in 336, I have no doubt that they would have been accepted everywhere as readily as the coinage of Philip II. As for the return to striking Philips after 323, I refer to my study of 1993,[61] in which I presented a detailed criticism of the suggestions of Newell and Price and where, taking a different tack, I tried to show how the Macedonian treasury meant by this measure to procure a needed resource.

---

upon his accession but that he quickly resolved them. N. G. L. Hammond's narrative of the early months of Alexander's reign in *History of Macedonia* III (Oxford, 1988), pp. 3–17, also seems to imply that he, too, thinks that the new king mastered the situation very rapidly.

59. *Reattribution*, p. 22.

60. *Coins of the Macedonians* (London, 1974), p. 23.

61. "Les deux monnaies macédoniennes des années 323–294/90," *BCH* 117 (1993), pp. 491–500 (=*Études d'hist. monétaire et financière du monde grec* III, Athens, 1999, pp. 1173–1182).

Price, despite thinking that silver Philips had ceased production immediately after Alexander came to the throne, accepted that the output of gold Philips might have continued for some time under the new king. The most probable explanation for this, in his opinion, was that loan covenants with Philip required repayment in gold Philips. Alexander would therefore have been obliged to strike this currency until he had liquidated all his father's debts. This is an ingenious idea, but it still raises a question: if Alexander had decided, from the start of his reign, to issue gold staters with his own name and types, why would these staters (of the same weight and fineness as Philip's) not have been just as acceptable as those of his father, after the latter's death?

Alexander certainly made numerous payments in coin at the start of his reign. Nevertheless, he apparently did not create his own great gold and silver currency before the end of 333. The silver eagle tetradrachms are the only possible personal coinage attributable to him before that date, a coinage whose volume appears insufficient for the currency needs of the Macedonian treasury during this period. The idea that Alexander continued to issue his father's coins seems to me compelling; several pieces of evidence appear to point in this direction. Why the young sovereign acted this way is the question. Answers of a political, commercial, or accounting nature are not totally convincing. Because it is dangerous to foist on Alexander sentiments or intentions of our own imagining, the problem remains unresolved. What can be said, if the views I have expressed have a basis in fact, is that the young king, in the first years of his reign, did not seek to impose a coinage with his own name and types in Macedonia.

Chapter 3

Coinage in Macedonia under Antipater from April 334 to June 323

Before leaving Macedonia, Alexander put Antipater[1] in charge of Macedonian and Greek affairs (Arrian 1.11.3). Diodorus (17.118.1) specifically says that Antipater received the title "viceroy in Europe." He therefore had complete authority to act in the king's name in Macedonia, with the power to handle current problems that came before the head (*archōn*) of the Thessalians and the hegemon of the League of Corinth. Alexander left him with 12,000 infantrymen and 1,500 cavalry (Diodorus 17.17.5), probably Macedonians for the most part.

Antipater's role was crucial during the eleven years from April 334 to June 323. He succeeded in keeping "Europe" under Alexander's authority, and he managed to send substantial reinforcements to the Conqueror, whose demands were great. These different activities imposed heavy financial burdens on Antipater that I will now attempt to describe.

Antipater's Financial Burdens from 334 to 323

I will deal here with only those expenses that can be considered exceptional, that is, as not arising from the everyday management of a state treasury.

---

1. On Antipater, see the detailed entry in H. Berve, *Das Alexanderreich aus prosopographischer Grundlage* II (Munich, 1926), no. 94. In addition to his activity as soldier and statesman, Antipater was also interested in philosophy (he had close ties with Aristotle), and he made a name for himself as an historian (he wrote the narrative of the Illyrian war, in which he participated).

Antipater's Campaigns

In 334 and 333, Antipater had to protect the Greco-Macedonian coastline and the Aegean Sea against the Persians' naval offensive. Memnon, Darius III's admiral, had had some success, taking control, notably, of Chios and Lesbos (Arrian 2.1.1–2). He died in the spring of 333, but his strategy endured. Antipater ordered Proteas to assemble a fleet of Euboean and Peloponnesian vessels. When Proteas learned that the Persian Datames was stationed with ten ships off Siphnos, he sailed from Chalcis in Euboea with fifteen ships and succeeded in capturing eight of Datames's ten, while Datames escaped with the remaining two (Arrian 2.2.4–5). Just one episode in the naval war of 333, it was still of some importance because it seems that Proteas's intervention protected Greece and a certain number of the islands. Perhaps the cities that furnished his ships partly financed their arming and maintenance, by virtue of their membership in the League of Corinth. Yet it is reasonable to think that Antipater incurred a large share of the cost. According to Curtius (3.1.20), Alexander sent 500 talents to Amphoterus and Hegelochus with the objective of freeing Lesbos, Chios, and Cos, and he remitted 600 talents to Antipater and those guarding the Greek cities. Perhaps this subsidy permitted Antipater to finance Proteas without draining the Macedonian treasury. But, as the remark in Curtius shows, the 600 talents were to be shared among several recipients; how much Antipater received is unknown.

He had, next, to repress the revolt of Memnon,[2] *stratēgos* of Thrace, whom Alexander had named to this post, previously occupied by Alexander of Lyncestis. Diodorus tells us (17.62.5) that "Memnon, who had been designated governor [of Thrace], had a military force and was a man of spirit. He stirred up the tribesmen [and] revolted against Alexander." A little later (17.63.1) Diodorus informs us that Antipater, having learned of agitation in Greece (we are in 331), "ended the Thracian campaign on what terms he could and marched down into the Peloponnesus with his entire army." The conflict with Memnon ended, therefore, in compromise. Memnon kept his command and remained quiet. Some years later, he left Thrace to convey to Alexander (whom he rejoined in the Punjab during the spring of 326) 5,000 Thracian cavalry "and besides these, 7,000 foot-soldiers from Harpalus and sets of armor inlaid with gold and silver for 25,000 men" (Curtius 9.3.21, Loeb modified).

The Spartan king Agis III had fomented this upheaval in Greece. Antipater vanquished him in a deadly combat near Megalopolis, probably at the start of spring 330.[3] Antipater commanded an army of 40,000, and he

---

2. Berve, op. cit., no. 499.
3. Cf. N. G. L. Hammond, *A History of Macedonia* III (Oxford, 1988), pp. 76–78.

encountered some difficulty, it seems, in gathering this number of soldiers.[4] In addition to the contingents that his Greek allies provided him, he probably recruited a number of mercenaries.

During the following years, from 330 to 323, Antipater apparently did not undertake any important military operations. One may imagine him, however, intervening militarily after the catastrophe that struck the new governor in Thrace, Zopyrion, Memnon's successor. He was "overwhelmed with his whole army by tempests and gales which suddenly arose. On learning of this disaster Seuthes [a Thracian prince] . . . forced his subjects the Odrysae to revolt. . . . Thrace was almost lost" (Curtius 10.1.44–45). This event can be dated to 325. A little later, in 324, Harpalus's arrival in Athens aroused tensions that Antipater had to keep an eye on and resolve. According to Diodorus (17.108.4–8), Harpalus, Alexander's close friend, had seriously abused his power and chose to flee from Babylon upon learning, at the end of 325, of the king's return from his Indian campaign. Leaving turmoil behind him in Greece, Harpalus sailed for Crete, where he was assassinated. Alexander's decree recalling exiles home created further difficulties. This decree, proclaimed at Olympia in August 324 (Diodorus 18.109.1), provoked lively discontent that certainly kept Antipater busy. I will return to the events of 324 later in this chapter.

These various episodes must have occasioned large expenditures. The preparations for army campaigns, as well as troop pay and maintenance, were undoubtedly very costly. Earlier I said that the Macedonians, for whom military service was an obligation, probably did not collect any wages during expeditions that could be deemed vital to homeland defense. But the State must have provided for at least part of their kit and, in any case, their food. There is reason to think that the proportion of Macedonians in the army raised against Agis was rather small. Moreover, the mercenaries Antipater enlisted represented a considerable financial cost that Alexander did not underestimate. When he was staying at Susa (at the very end of 331), he entrusted 3,000 silver talents to Menes who was to transport them to the coast and send to Antipater as many talents out of this sum as he required for the war against the Lacedaemonians (Arrian 3.16.10).[5]

---

4. A. B. Bosworth, "Alexander the Great and the Decline of Macedon," *JHS* 106 (1986), pp. 1–12, cites Aeschines 3.165 on this point: "it took a long time for him to marshal the army" (WEH).

5. This passage of Arrian is not without importance for the chronology of the war with Agis. If Menes received this order in December 331, the battle at Megalopolis had not yet been joined; cf. A. B. Bosworth, *A Historical Commentary on Arrian's History of Alexander* I (Oxford, 1980), p. 320.

The Reinforcements Sent to Alexander

Alexander's requests for additional manpower were numerous and urgent. A. B. Bosworth,[6] who drew up a list of the reinforcements Antipater sent, remarks that we do not know for sure the total number dispatched. This was not a matter of prime importance for the ancient authors, and they certainly did not trouble themselves to make an exhaustive accounting. I summarize Bosworth's reckoning.

In spring 333, newly married soldiers, who had been authorized, at the end of 334, to return to Macedonia for the winter (Arrian 1.24.1), rejoined Alexander at Gordion in Phrygia, accompanied by 3,000 Macedonian infantry, 250 Thessalian cavalry and 150 Eleans (Arrian 1.29.4).

A little later, in Paphlagonia, Alexander took some troops with him who had just arrived from Macedonia (Curtius 3.1.24), perhaps a new contingent, unless Curtius has located in this province what Arrian situates in Gordion.[7] According to Polybius (13.19.2), citing Callisthenes of Olynthus, as he was marching deeper into Cilicia, at the end of summer 333, Alexander received 5,000 foot soldiers and 800 horse from Macedonia. At the time of the battle of Issus, he was expecting additional soldiers from Macedonia (Curtius 3.7.8).

So, in 333, at least 8,000 Macedonian infantry and a good number of cavalry reinforced Alexander's army. This sum is a minimum because the two passages in Curtius, to take them into account, contain no numbers. In April 334, the king had crossed the Hellespont leading 12,000 Macedonian foot soldiers: he may have received an equal number in 333.

During the siege of Tyre (January–July 332), Proteas, who had protected the Greek littoral and the Aegean on Antipater's orders, arrived on a fifty-oared ship (Arrian 2.20.2). As Berve notes,[8] perhaps Proteas was not coming to join the fleet marshaled before Tyre but to secure the communication link between Antipater and the king.

At the beginning of autumn in 332, after the capture of Gaza, Alexander sent Amyntas to Macedonia with ten ships and with instructions to draft young men fit for military service (Diodorus 17.49.1; cf. Curtius 4.6.30). Not without effort (for there were slackers), Amyntas recruited a corps of about 15,000 men, including 6,000 Macedonian infantry and 500 cavalry; the rest were mercenaries. This contingent met up with Alexander's army at the end of 331, either at Babylon (Curtius 5.1.40–42) or between

---

6. *JHS* 106 (1986), esp. pp. 5–9.

7. Bosworth's hypothesis; cf. also on this point the discussion of J. E. Atkinson, *A Commentary on Q. Curtius Rufus' Historiae Alexandri Magni, Books 3 and 4* (Amsterdam, 1980), pp. 97–99, and on Issus, p. 181.

8. Op. cit., II, p. 47.

Babylon and Susa (Diodorus 17.65.1). The king had probably received several other contingents in the meantime: for example, in Egypt at the start of 331, almost 400 Greek mercenaries sent by Antipater and 500 Thracian horsemen (Arrian 3.5.1).

Bosworth rightly remarks that after 331 there are no further mentions of Macedonian reinforcements. This is probably owing to the spotty character of our sources. But Bosworth suggests that Macedonia had been so tapped that it had no more men to supply,[9] and he argues that Alexander, willfully ignoring this reality, considered Antipater in bad faith, conceiving a resentment towards him that contributed to the deterioration of their relationship. In spring 327, when he was in Sogdiana, the Conqueror dispatched three of his officers to Macedonia to carry out a new levy of soldiers (Arrian 4.18.3), a mission of which we do not know the outcome.[10] In 324, Antipater received a last royal command: in order to replace the 10,000 Macedonian veterans demobilized at Opis and entrusted to Craterus, he was himself to lead to Alexander an equal number of militarily fit Macedonians (Arrian 7.12.4). The king's death rendered the order null and void.

The reinforcements Alexander received after 331, it seems, consisted essentially of mercenaries recruited in different regions of his empire. Antipater, for his part, delivered 3,000 Illyrians in 330 and 8,000 Greeks in 328 (Curtius 6.6.35; 7.10.2). A veritable army showed up for Alexander in the Punjab in India in 326: around 30,000 infantry and 6,000 cavalry (Diodorus 17.95.4), including the men under Memnon, the former governor-general of Thrace, who also brought armament for 25,000. Diodorus adds that 100 talents worth of medical supplies were delivered as well. Antipater, I do not doubt, contributed to this huge convoy of 326, prompted, perhaps, by the three officers Alexander had sent to Macedonia the year before.

One appreciates the financial burden on Antipater that the incessant obligation to ready new recruits for Alexander represented. Their equipment, training, and support entailed heavy expenses, whether they were Macedonians or mercenaries. To be sure, not all the Greek and Balkan mercenaries depended on the Macedonian treasury. The Thracian governor presumably financed the recruits enlisted in his province, while contributions from the

---

9. Diodorus (18.12.2), in his treatment of the Lamian War that broke out upon Alexander's death, writes that "Macedonia was short of citizen soldiers because of the number of those who had been sent to Asia as replacements for the army."

10. One of the three officers sent to Macedonia was Menidas. He rejoined Alexander at Babylon in the spring of 323, with the cavalry under his command (Arrian 7.23.1). P. Goukowsky, *Diodore de Sicile, Livre XVIII* (Paris, 1978), p. 124, wonders if Menidas had not brought these horsemen from Macedonia.

Greek cities of the League of Corinth could serve partly to defray similar expenses.

Nonetheless, Antipater needed a lot of money, both to meet his own military costs, to maintain order in Greece for eleven years (334 to 323), and to satisfy his monarch's demands. We have seen that the king sent him funds in 333 and 331. No other subsidies are mentioned in the course of the following years. According to Diodorus, however, a fleet of 110 triremes transported considerable sums to Macedonia from the royal treasuries on Alexander's order at the very end of his reign.[11]

In reflecting on Antipater's financial situation, one must not forget that the receipts of the Macedonian treasury probably never stopped falling; the successive departures of huge contingents of able-bodied men for Asia could only slow exploitation of the land and reduce tax receipts. Homeward-bound Macedonians during these years were rare, it seems: a group was repatriated from the banks of the Oxus in 329 (Arrian 3.29.5), but that appears to be an exception. Besides, Alexander had decided to exempt the families of those fallen in combat from all their taxes to the State. This measure, first taken after the battle of the Granicus, became the rule, if the words of the Opis oration are to be believed (Arrian 7.10.4). Episodes like the sieges of Tyre and Gaza cost the lives of many men, as Bosworth has remarked. The Macedonian families who received royal exemptions were numerous.

Returning to the expenses that Antipater had to assume, the volume of the coinage he struck in Macedonia between 334 and 323 (and until his death in 319) attests to the large sums he had to handle in coin. I will now undertake a review of the Macedonian coinages issued during this period.

Antipater and Coinage Production in Macedonia from April 334

Antipater and the Coinage of Philip II

We can accept that Alexander's departure for Asia did not interrupt the production of gold and silver Philips in Macedonia, at least until Alexander's own coinage began. The Macedonian mints probably did not issue the latter before 332 and perhaps even a little later. Antipater, therefore, would have struck Philips for a certain time. An examination mentioned earlier seems to show clearly that there was no halt in silver coinage after Alexander departed; the same symbols (prow, stern, Janus-head) appear

---

11. Goukowsky, op. cit., p. 124, comments on this information, suggesting that the fleet and funds in question could have been sent to Macedonia at the time of the Harpalus affair.

on the last tetradrachms of Philip II belonging to Group II of my Series B and on the first group of Macedonian Alexander tetradrachms (pl. 2, 1–6).[12] What we affirm of the silver also has to hold for the gold: output of gold Philips probably continued at least until the first Macedonian gold Alexanders went into circulation.

I thought it tenable that after 336 the production of Philips was perhaps greater than before. Did Antipater maintain the same production rate that Alexander seems to have set for these coins? It is obviously impossible to answer this question with certainty. What can be said is that Antipater, after 334, had to bear heavy costs and that once the coinage of Alexander was introduced in Macedonia, it was struck in quantity, especially the silver tetradrachms. Antipater presumably had a constant need for currency throughout his time in office.

Antipater and the Coinage of Alexander: The Macedonian "Great Series"

The Macedonian production of silver and gold coins with the name and types of Alexander still poses numerous problems concerning both the location of the mints and the chronology of the issues. Without getting overly involved in technical details, I will try to present a brief overview of the matter.

The striking of silver Alexanders was entrusted almost entirely to a single mint. Newell, in *Reattribution* (1912) and in his publication of the Demanhur hoard (1923), assembled and dated the different groups of the series issuing from this mint, what I will call the "great series" of Alexander's silver coins from Macedonia. Newell based his classification on the die linkages tying the issues together, and he added highly convincing stylistic arguments as well. He derived his chronology from the dating of the Demanhur hoard (318 or the beginning of 317). The results thus obtained continue to be widely used, as the work of Price and Troxell shows.

The "great series" from Macedonia that Newell elaborated begins, as I have said, with the issues of tetradrachms having the symbols prow, stern, and Janus-head. There are other denominations accompanying the tetradrachms: didrachms, drachms, triobols, diobols, and obols.[13] The mint magistrates' signatures do not appear only in the form of symbols; they can also be monograms or single letters.

---

12. Troxell, *Alexander* (1997), pp. 87–88, has emphasized that this group was surely the first struck in Macedonia; it is, in fact, on the tetradrachms with prow, stern, and Janus-head (associated with the tetradrachms with thunderbolt and rudder) that the influence of the Tarsus model, which the Macedonian engravers had to copy, most clearly appears.

13. Troxell, *Alexander* (1997), pp. 30–40, studies these denominations in detail.

The legend on the tetradrachms is *Alexandrou* at first; after a time, the coins (pl. 2, 7–8) carry *Basileōs Alexandrou*. This lengthier legend only appears for a few years, and subsequent issues revert to the simple *Alexandrou* (pl. 2, 9–10).

This "great series" lasted a long time. I myself believe that it continued without interruption until the beginning of the third century BC.[14] The issuing mint maintained a very sustained production tempo. In the reign of Cassander (316–c. 297), the issues bore a *lambda* and a torch (pl. 2, 10) as principal signs for several years, and they are particularly abundant.

The "great series," in my opinion, was struck at Amphipolis, where I have also attributed my Series B of silver Philips (ending in the tetradrachms with prow, stern, and Janus-head I have just mentioned). This Amphipolis location has provoked discussion that is far from over. I can only record my disagreement with Price, who, having broken the "great series" in two, prefers to attribute the first part to Pella, reserving the second to Amphipolis.[15]

In addition to the "great series," it may be necessary to attribute to Macedonia, before 323, a small group of Alexander tetradrachms, comprising four issues with symbols of a boxer (?), a jumping athlete (pl. 2, 11), an ear of wheat, and a goat's head. About ten obverse dies were employed, not an enormous amount. The tetradrachms, however, are accompanied by some gold distaters and staters, on which one finds the boxer (?) and athlete symbols, as well as a comic actor (?) (pl. 2, 12), and a thunderbolt coupled with a letter or a monogram.[16] Newell first thought in *Reattribution* (1912) that this series could have been struck in Macedonia or in Thrace; later, in *Demanhur* (1923), he opted for an attribution to Sicyon that S. P. Noe reiterated in 1950.[17] But Troxell[18] showed in 1971 that this classification was not justified, and she suggested Macedonia as the point of origin, which seems to have won acceptance.

No other Alexander tetradrachms appear to have been issued in Macedonia before 323. So the disproportion is striking between the "great series," for which several hundred obverse dies were engraved from 332 to

---

14. See my article, "Les tétradrachmes macédoniens d'Alexandre," *Studies in Greek Numismatics in Memory of M. J. Price*, R. Ashton and S. Hurter eds. (London, 1998), esp. pp. 237–38. I there express my disagreement with Price's opinion, *Alexander* (1991), pp. 86–87 and 130, who breaks off the "great series" around 317 and who creates a new series that would begin around 320, struck in another mint. Troxell, *Alexander* (1997), pp. 49–50, also disputes Price's proposed arrangement.

15. Cf. my article cited in the previous note, pp. 240–44.

16. I have borrowed from Price, *Alexander* (1991), nos. 188–89 and 185–86, the identifications of the boxer (?) and comic actor (?) symbols. The question marks are his, not mine.

17. *The Alexander Coinage of Sicyon Arranged from the Notes of E. T. Newell with Comments and Additions by S. P. Noe* (Amer. Num. Soc., Num. Studies 6, 1950).

18. "The Peloponnesian Alexanders," *Amer. Num. Soc. Mus. Notes* 17 (1971), pp. 42–44.

323, and the small group with boxer (?), athlete, wheat ear, and goat head just described.

Under Philip II, the production of silver coins was shared rather equally, it seems, between two mints, located, in my opinion, at Pella (my Series A) and Amphipolis (my Series B). Between 336 and c. 332, Amphipolis seems to have outpaced Pella: the abundant issues from the former, with prow, stern, and Janus-head, apparently did not have their equivalent at the other mint. When striking of silver Alexanders began, the disproportion between the two production centers became unmistakable: Amphipolis obtained near exclusivity in this coinage.

If the "great series" was issued, as I believe, at Amphipolis, can the boxer (?) coins and the others be attributed to Pella? N. J. Moore thought so.[19] Price wondered if one could not entertain an attribution to Aigeai, the old Macedonian "capital."[20] He did not think a Pella attribution possible because he allotted this mint the first part of the "great series."

I do not know if the future will bring desired clarification and whether, one day, it will be possible to describe the organization of Macedonian coinage under Alexander and Antipater with complete assurance. Right now, the attribution of the "great series" of silver tetradrachms to Amphipolis seems to me most probable. How, then, can we explain why this mint, in the striking of silver coins during this period, so overshadowed Pella, which continued to be the kingdom's most important administrative center? Newell, who always defended the Amphipolis attribution of the "great series," emphasized the city's maritime activity (it controlled the port at Eion) that gave it an essential role in the exploitation of the silver mines.[21] Amphipolis is, in fact, situated quite close to Mt. Pangaion, whose rich silver deposits are well known. The two points Newell stressed must certainly be borne in mind: the currency payments Alexander and Antipater had to make were presumably destined mostly for overseas, whether to states or individuals, and maybe it seemed more convenient to concentrate the production of silver coins at Amphipolis. When Alexander undertook his Thracian campaign in 335, he left from Amphipolis (Arrian 1.1.5), which suggests that the city was a place of prime importance for military preparations. Perhaps the Amphipolitan mint proved its effectiveness on this occasion and subsequently remained the kingdom's prime coinage center. It was also at Amphipolis that the fleet assembled in 334 prior to leaving for Asia. Although the *Itinerarium Alexandri* from the fourth century AD is the

---

19. In her Princeton doctoral dissertation (1984), *The Lifetime and Early Posthumous Coinage of Alexander the Great from Pella*, reprised in her "The Silver Coinage of Alexander from Pella," *Ancient Coins of the Graeco-Roman World* (Nickle Num. Papers, 1984), pp. 41–56.
20. *Alexander* (1991), nos. 185–200.
21. Newell, *Demanhur* (1923), p. 67.

sole source of this information, there is no reason to doubt it—the author bases himself on Arrian, and whatever new he adds to Arrian does not appear to be the fruit of his imagination.

To interpret better, however, the preference accorded this mint (supposing, at least, that the "great series" is Amphipolitan), we will need more information on the sort of relationship existing between the city and the central government. Hatzopoulos[22] has shown that Amphipolis became a Macedonian city shortly after Philip II conquered it in 357; the citizen body now included numerous Macedonians, and the royal calendar replaced the city's own. Yet the city retained a fair number of its own institutions, such as its citizen assembly, thus enjoying autonomy in its internal affairs. It is quite possible that establishing a mint of Philip II within its walls was not an imposition but the result of negotiation. The mint's growth under Alexander might indicate the excellent relations between the monarch and the Amphipolitans.

As for the gold coinage with the name and types of Alexander under Antipater, it is less well known than one might think. Troxell[23] has advanced our knowledge considerably, but many points await clarification.

The question is when the first Macedonian gold Alexanders were struck. Their creation in Cilicia and Phoenicia, accepting this region as their source, probably does not occur prior to July 332. Their production in Macedonia possibly came after that of the silver Alexanders. If so, the striking of gold Philips would perhaps have continued beyond 330, something the abundance of this currency in the hoards buried after 323 would not gainsay (cf. p. 38).

One of the difficulties that the classification of Alexander's gold Macedonian coinage presents is the widespread use there of the *kantharos*, trident, and thunderbolt as symbols, symbols that are present as well on the gold Philips of my Group II (both Series A and B). It appears that these signs were employed for a long time and were not restricted to just one mint.

Thanks to die classifications and stylistic analyses, Troxell was able to establish a coherent series for Alexander's gold staters. The first group of this series bears the symbols of *kantharos* and trident (pl. 3, 1–4), the second the symbols *kantharos*, trident, and thunderbolt (pl. 3, 5–8). Die linkages do not tie the two groups together, but strong stylistic resemblances do. Troxell made a remarkable discovery: the staters (pl. 3, 1–4) that, according to Newell, formed Alexander's first gold coinage from Tarsus belong without any doubt to the series in question here, and so are Macedonian.

---

22. *Macedonian Institutions* (1996), pp. 181–84.
23. *Alexander* (1997), pp. 99–128. Troxell devoted the second part of her book to Alexander's gold Macedonian coins.

This series apparently comprises most of the staters Antipater struck in Macedonia during Alexander's lifetime. The coins are divided among 26 obverse dies, perhaps 30, if one adds some specimens to the series that probably, but not certainly, belong to it.

We have seen that the gold Philips struck at the end of Philip II's reign and at the beginning of Alexander's were produced from around 250 obverse dies. It is clearly impossible to determine how many dies were put into service after 336. Still, one supposes that many of them date from the period of Alexander. Ending the coining of these Philips (belonging to my Group II) about 330 would lead us to conjecture that the striking of gold was subsequently less abundant.

Two considerations, however, might qualify this opinion. First, it is impossible to date precisely when the production of my Group II gold Philips ceased. This output may have continued much longer than is commonly believed. If so, the issuing of gold Alexanders would have begun only in the second part of the reign and the number of dies engraved before 323 would have to be understood within the context of a relatively brief time span.

Second, it is necessary to add some distaters (weighing ±17.20 grams) to Alexander's gold staters from Macedonia. Troxell has sketched out their number[24] and divided them into three groups. Group A comprises examples with a *kantharos*, trident or thunderbolt as symbol (pl. 3, 9), and she connects Group A with the series of staters she established. Group B belongs to another series described above (p. 52, pl. 2, 12) that also includes staters and tetradrachms stamped with a comic actor (?), boxer (?), athlete, etc. Group C once again introduces the symbols of *kantharos* (pl. 3, 10), trident, and thunderbolt. Basing herself on study of the hoards and stylistic observations, Troxell thinks that the distaters of Groups A and B have to be placed, at least in part, before June 323, whereas Group C should rather be placed after this date. She noted twenty-two obverse dies in Group A, eight in B (and five for the staters), and three in C. If Groups A and B were partly produced prior to June 323, Alexander's gold coinage struck during his lifetime in Macedonia becomes more coherent because a fair number of distater dies (not forgetting the five stater dies associated with the Group B distaters) would complement the twenty-six or thirty stater dies that Troxell highlighted.

Which mints struck these coins? At the end of the classifications proposed in my *Philippe II*, I placed a large series of gold Philips with *kantharos*, trident, or thunderbolt at Pella, a series that reappears after 323. I would therefore be inclined to attribute the Alexanders stamped with the same symbols to Pella as well. Antipater will have concentrated production of silver coins at Amphipolis, gold at Pella. An objection immediately arises,

---

24. *Alexander* (1997), pp. 112–14.

however: if the issues with comic actor (?), boxer (?), athlete, etc., belong to Pella, as Moore conjectured, it would be difficult to locate the gold series with *kantharos*, trident, or thunderbolt at this mint. For now, it is therefore impossible to assert anything confidently concerning the attribution of Alexander's Macedonian coinage issues.

Philip II had entrusted the production of gold and silver currencies to different mint magistrates who used different symbols.[25] So we lack a key criterion for our classifications, the presence of identical marks on the coins in the two metals. The organization Philip put in place endured: the majority of the gold and silver Alexanders struck before 323 in Macedonia carry no sign common to the two metals. An exception is the group with comic actor (?), boxer (?), etc., where connections do exist between the gold and silver. If this group really was issued before 323, the exception is noteworthy. After 323, a clear trend emerges suggesting the same officials oversaw both metals.

The Macedonians, in this period, seem to have designated as "big staters of Alexander" the coins weighing ±17.20 grams that I have called distaters. Among the sales records from Amphipolis that Hatzopoulos published,[26] numbers 10A and 10B provide quite interesting information. They were both inscribed on the same stele and probably concern the same piece of property. The latter is priced in one of the records "at 170 [gold staters] of Philip" and in the other "at 85 big staters [—]."[27] So these big staters (*statēres megaloi*) have twice the value of staters; in short, they are distaters of ±17.20 grams. In the lacuna following mention of the big staters, Hatzopoulos proposed the restoration "*khrusōn philippeiōn,*" in other words, eighty-five big staters "of gold Philips." Yet this king does not appear to have struck gold coins of ±17.20 grams in Macedonia. The distaters with his name and types that we can cite have to be regarded as posthumous imitations,[28] and a group of specimens described by N. Breitenstein was probably the work of modern counterfeiters.[29] I would personally suppose that the Amphipolis inscription's big staters are the distaters Troxell described in her Groups A, B and C. I would suggest restoring not "*khrusōn philippeiōn,*" but "*khrusōn alexandreiōn,*" eighty-five big staters "of gold Alexanders." Hatzopoulos has kindly informed me that he regards this as epigraphically possible: the stone is broken on the left and the exact letter length of the line cannot be determined.

---

25. Similarly, a third team of officials oversaw the striking of bronze coins.
26. *Actes de vente d'Amphipolis* (Meletēmata 14, Athens, 1991), esp. pp. 48–49 and 84–85.
27. "Gold staters" is a restoration; after "big staters" there is a gap in the text.
28. See, for example, H. Gaebler, *Münzen Nord-Griechenlands* III, 2, *Die antiken Münzen von Makedonia und Paionia* (Berlin, 1935), p. 162, 1, pl. XXX, 19; N. Breitenstein, "Studies in the Coinage of the Macedonian Kings," *Acta Archaeologica* 13 (1942), pp. 242–43, fig. 2–3.
29. Op. cit., pp. 243–45, fig. 4–13.

Hatzopoulos dated sale 10B from Amphipolis to Alexander's reign. According to Troxell, the distaters that she catalogued were not issued before c. 325, and some of them were struck after 323. If the "big staters" of sale 10B are actually the distaters in question, the sale would have occurred around the time of Alexander's death or even a certain number of years later because this currency did not disappear from circulation the very moment its production ceased.

It is known that later, from the second half of the third century, the term "Philip," (*statēr khrusous*) *philippeios* in Greek, (*nummus aureus*) *philippeus*, shortened to *philippus*, in Latin, served to denote gold staters in general (those of Philip, Alexander, the Hellenistic kings).[30] If Hatzopoulos's restoration *khrusōn philippeiōn* in the Amphipolis inscription is correct, and if the "big staters" are in fact distaters of Alexander, one would have an example from the end of the fourth century of the generic use of the word *philippeios*. I am reluctant to accept this usage as possible at this date, and that is why I prefer to restore *alexandreiōn* in the lacuna rather than *philippeiōn*.

Sale 11 from Amphipolis,[31] occurring later than the two preceding sales, describes a transaction that was also conducted in staters of Philip. Hatzopoulos has remarked that the odd shape of the *omega*, with uplifted arms, is found in the letters of Demetrius II to Harpalus of Beroea, letters written in the thirty-sixth regnal year of Antigonus Gonatas, that is, after 250. It is possible that the expression *statēres philippeioi* in this sale 11 from Amphipolis was applied not only to staters of Philip, but also to other gold staters. This would then be one of the earliest examples of the broad use of the qualifier *philippeios*.

Reflections on the Chronology of the Silver Coinage Issued by Antipater with Alexander's Name and Types Beginning c. 332

The volume of gold coinage Antipater struck in Macedonia is not easy to assess, as we have just seen. We know neither for how long nor at what pace he continued to produce Philips. Moreover, if the series of gold Alexanders that Troxell has established belongs, apparently, to Alexander's reign, it is possible (according to Troxell) that the distaters of Groups A and B placed into circulation before June 323 were still being struck after this date. All these uncertainties make our evaluations hazardous.

In contrast, the "great series" of Alexander's silver tetradrachms that Antipater produced from c. 332 is much better known and permits us to make a certain number of interesting assertions.

---

30. See my *Naissance*, pp. 199–200.
31. Hatzopoulos, op. cit., pp. 49–52.

As I said above, Newell, in his 1923 publication of the Demanhur hoard, established how to arrange this "great series," the relative chronology of its constituent issues and their classification into groups.[32] Newell did not go beyond the year 318 because the hoard was buried in that year or at the beginning of 317. As we know, he thought that Alexander inaugurated his own coinage upon his accession, and Newell established eleven groups (A through K) starting c. 336, with 318 being the year of Group K, represented in his inventory by a single coin.

Troxell (I refer to her *Alexander* of 1997) accepted Newell's relative chronology, with a reservation about Group K, which could be either prior to or contemporaneous with Group J. But she modified Newell's absolute chronology because she dated the debut of the silver Macedonian Alexanders to 332. She went a little beyond 318/17, naming L the group that followed immediately after Groups J–K. Finally, she undertook to classify all these tetradrachms by obverse dies.

Because I personally think that the first silver Alexanders were not struck before 332 and therefore agree with Troxell's overall results, I will be content to report these proposals in tabular form insofar as they concern both her absolute chronology of Groups A through L and her estimate of the number of obverse dies used in each group.[33] My table brings together data on pages 26 (number of dies) and 96 (dating) of Troxell's *Alexander*.

[Each group contains a different number of issues.

The title *Basileōs* is added to *Alexandrou* in Groups G, H, I, K, J (Troxell resolutely placed Group K before J in her lists): cf. pl. 2, 7–8.

Some silver coins (tetradrachms and other denominations) with the name and types of Philip were issued concurrently with Alexanders of Groups K, J, L, and perhaps I. Troxell also estimated the number of obverse dies used for Philip's tetradrachms. I remind the reader that these tetradrachms show a head of Zeus on the obverse and a nude young horseman holding a palm branch on the reverse.]

The table prompts several observations.

First, all the groups from A to J are represented in the Demanhur hoard. The production of Group J, for which Newell reckoned forty-four specimens, was, if not terminated, at least nearing its end by the time of the coins' burial (in 318 or early 317) because all this group's known issues are

---

32. Newell counted 4,826 tetradrachms in toto for the treasure (all Alexanders); the hoard probably contained more than 8,000 coins: cf. *IGCH* 1664. O. H. Zervos, "Additions to the Demanhur Hoard of Alexander Tetradrachms," *NC* 140 (1980), pp. 185–88, added 1,125 specimens to Newell's list; this supplement did not alter either the general character of the hoard or its dating.

33. In doing her estimate, Troxell used the simplified method of G. F. Carter, *Amer. Num. Soc. Mus. Notes* 28 (1983), pp. 195–206.

Table 3.1

Groups	Estimated Number of Obverse Dies	Troxell Dates	Observations
A	88		
B	49	A–D: 332–326	
C	18		
D	76		
	231 dies in total		
E	241	E–F: 325–323	
F	89		
	330 dies in total		
G	114		110 obv. dies for Philips of K, J [In Group K, almost all the issues are stamped with Λ, with or without another sign.] [Three symbols appear in Group J: ear of wheat, crescent, laurel branch (pl. 2, 8); another sign often present is the letter *pi*.]
H	109		
I	70	G, H, I, K, J: 322–317(?)	
K	10		
J	33		
	336 dies in total		
L	232	316–	47 obv. dies for Philips of L. [A monogram formed of the letters *pi* and a minute *omicron* within the *pi* appears on all the coins of Group L; this monogram is associated with ten different symbols, including a sheaf of wheat and a crescent (pl. 2, 9).]

found in the hoard. So we have a valuable chronological reference point for the dating of our "great series."

Second, on Troxell's chronology, the title *Basileōs* that characterizes Groups G through J would have first appeared only in 322, after Alexander's death, and would have stopped being inscribed in 317.

Newell had placed the first issue bearing *Basileōs* around 325. Troxell's redating is of interest not only for the chronology of Macedonian coins but also for that of several other imperial coinages showing the same title.

Third, the production of silver Alexanders was clearly more important at Amphipolis than at other imperial production centers. It is by far the best represented mint in the Demanhur treasure: Zervos counted 2,005 Amphipolitan tetradrachms; Babylon comes next, with 820.[34] Following

---

34. *NC* 140 (1980), pp. 185–88; Newell had tallied 1,582 Amphipolitan Alexanders and 630 from Babylon.

Troxell's chronology, the first four Amphipolitan Groups, A through D, total 230 obverse dies, in about seven years, which gives an annual average of 32 or 33 dies. Group E breaks all the records: 241 dies in a period of no more than two years, maybe much less. Later, Groups G and H, followed by L, are themselves relatively abundant.

One need not think, however, that the pace of monetary output changed noticeably in Macedonia as of c. 332. Of course, it is necessary to add the gold coinage, of which I spoke a little earlier, to the silver coins struck after this date. But already in the years preceding 332, the Macedonian gold and silver issues had been truly ample. I would rather be inclined to speak of a steady production tempo throughout this entire period. The grand endeavors of Philip II, Alexander's conquests, and the successor kings' struggles for power kept the currency needs of the Macedonian authorities at a high level.

Fourth, the 241 obverse dies used in Group E, associated with the 89 dies of Group F, have attracted the attention of scholars, who have sought to explain this abrupt takeoff in Amphipolitan silver production. Troxell[35] referred to M. Thompson's brilliant 1984 article[36] as follows: "This is the period to which Margaret Thompson has dated the opening of Alexander's Asiatic mints and the sudden large expansion of activity in others. The reason for this heightened activity in Asia Minor was the need to pay discharged troops, mercenaries, and others, who were sent home in large numbers starting in 325, and who would have been fully paid only upon arrival at home. The same situation would have obtained in the mainland, and the large Group E is reasonably explained as struck in expectation of and during the return of the earliest troops. The relatively large succeeding Groups F, G, and H would then reflect the same continuing need."

Thompson's arguments warrant closer examination.

M. Thompson on Coinage Production in Alexander's Mints and the Return of Demobilized Soldiers

Thompson thought she detected a net increase in the production of Alexanders throughout the empire in the last two years of the reign. In 325/24 and 324/23, mints that had not previously issued this coinage allegedly began to strike it. Thompson puts Miletus, Colophon, Abydus, Side, and Egyptian Alexandria in this latter category. Earlier output centers

---

35. *Alexander* (1997), p. 91.
36. "Paying the Mercenaries," in *Festschrift für Leo Mildenberg*, A. Houghton ed. (Wetteren, 1984), pp. 241–47.

stepped up their activity markedly, for example, the great Macedonian mint (Amphipolis) and Lampsacus. Production at Miletus was considerable right from its opening; at Amphipolis and Lampsacus, the momentum accelerated. Miletus and Lampsacus stand out for the prominence accorded gold coins (18 and 24 obverse dies respectively, Thompson writes).

In 325/24, she continues, Alexander made an important decision. He ordered his generals and satraps in Asia to demobilize their mercenaries (Diodorus 17.106.3). The Conqueror probably issued his edict at the end of 325 or the beginning of 324, upon his return from India by way of the Gedrosian Desert and Carmania. He had learned that some of his subordinates in command of troops were revolting against him (their misdeeds during his absence prompting them to fear the worst punishment). Alexander effected some demobilizations himself: at Susa or Opis he sent home about 10,000 Macedonian veterans (Arrian 7.12.1; Diodorus 18.12.1 puts their number over 10,000), and he may have released a part of his mercenaries as well. He charged Craterus with the Macedonians' repatriation and oversight of their safe conduct on the march (Arrian 7.12.3).

These men, Thompson adds, whether Macedonian or mercenary, had probably drawn only a small fraction of their salary during the preceding years, for they did not need much money while on the expedition. Their provisions were guaranteed, and it would have hardly been convenient for them, and even endangered their security, were they to be carrying and protecting sums that grew to be sizeable. Bonuses for bravery augmented, in fact, their regular pay, as did royal largesse. An accounting system enabled each man to receive his due at the end of the campaign.

It was not at Babylon, in Thompson's view, that all the soldiers were paid in 324/23. The monetary activity of the Babylonian mint, as we know it, was not sufficient to meet the currency needs at this time. It was only once they were back home, or at least close to their final destination, that the Macedonians and mercenaries would have collected the sums legally due them. This arrangement had ostensibly two advantages: it assured the safety of the men until their journey's end and it was an incentive for them to return home directly, rather than to wander about in marauding bands.

This would explain, according to Thompson, the sudden feverish activity that visibly took hold of the mints in Asia Minor and Macedonia. They would have had to strike considerable quantities of coins, for it was these regions that provided the majority of the soldiers whom Alexander and the satraps enlisted. These men were not only numerous (several tens of thousands, probably), but in the majority of cases the pay in arrears must have amounted to quite a sum, many of the combatants having served with Alexander for at least several years, some as many as ten.

Thompson's thesis has found favor. No one seems to have questioned it, including myself in earlier writings. The idea that soldiers on a long military campaign were only paid at its conclusion has been accepted and applied to other episodes.[37]

A Critique of the Thompson Thesis

Now, however, it seems to me that Thompson's case is not as solid as I once thought. In this chapter on Macedonia, I will examine from a specifically Macedonian perspective the arguments Thompson has set forth (with the intention of returning to the problem when I study coinage production in the other regions of the empire).

I will pose three questions: (1) Did Alexander's soldiers, especially the Macedonians, wait until their return home to receive the bulk of their pay? (2) If Troxell's chronology is correct, is not another explanation possible for the increase in coinage at Amphipolis in 324 and 323? (3) Is this chronology the only one possible, and could not this rise in coinage output suit another episode in Macedonian history just as well?

As for my first point, Thompson supposed that the men of the army had no practical need for money during Alexander's expedition because their maintenance was guaranteed. This is only a hypothesis. We do not know if the commissariat provided all of the soldiers' provisions. The men might have had to supplement their mess by buying food in the markets, the *agoras*, which traveled along with the army. Thus, in 401, during the expedition of Cyrus the Younger, the mercenaries who arrived in the region Xenophon calls Arabia (the country along the left bank of the Euphrates) were forced to buy wheat in the Lydian market at an exorbitant price because they needed provisions.[38] Many soldiers, moreover, had wives and children to feed: in 324, Alexander decided to keep the children born of Macedonian fathers and Asian women close by him (Arrian 7.12.2), and it is also probable that not all of the Macedonians went off on the expedition by themselves but that a certain number of Macedonian wives accompanied their husbands right from the start of the campaign. We also learn that many soldiers were deeply in debt, and that when, in 324, the king resolved to free them from this burden, he had to pay 20,000 talents according to Arrian (7.5.3) and Justin (12.11.3) and 9,870 talents according to Curtius (10.2.11) and Plutarch (*Alex.* 70.2). These debts, one presumes, were contracted when salaries had already been paid, and Alexander, moreover, expresses astonishment at this situation in the speech Arrian attributes

---

37. I suggested that the mercenaries Artaxerxes II hired for the reconquest of Egypt between c. 379 and c. 370 received only a portion of their pay in the theater of operations (the Persian quartermaster general was located at Ake in Palestine), and that they pocketed the rest of their salary in Cilicia, upon their return from the expedition. Cf. *Naissance*, pp. 224–25.

38. *Anabasis* 1.5.6; on this passage, cf. *Naissance*, pp. 147–48.

to him at Opis (7.10.3): "Furthermore, if you contracted debts, I did not make it my business to discover why, despite the enormous sums you gained by pay and plunder, whenever a besieged place was plundered, but I discharged them all." We can therefore assume, it seems to me, that the soldiers of Alexander's army had money at their disposal, some of them a great deal, sometimes even more than the total of their salary and the booty they got their hands on. I mentioned above the army of Cyrus the Younger. Xenophon (*Anabasis* 1.2.11) reports that Cyrus did not pay his troops on a regular basis and that he owed them more than three months back salary. The men, Xenophon writes, "went again and again to [Cyrus's] headquarters and demanded what was due them." It was not, apparently, common practice to leave the soldiers without pay for long.[39]

Arrian (7.12.1–2) mentions that Alexander paid their wages to some 10,000 Macedonians being mustered out at Opis in 324 (that is, what was still forthcoming to them), "not only for the time already served, but also for that of their journey home."[40] The king in a fit of generosity made each individual a gift of one talent (or 1,500 tetradrachms), a considerable sum for a soldier who typically earned less than 100 tetradrachms a year.

Thompson thought that there was no need to take Arrian literally and believe that the Macedonians in question pocketed their money at Opis itself: they received it, she felt, only in Macedonia. Yet Arrian's text appears quite clearly to say the opposite, and one may imagine that Alexander's concern that Craterus accompany these men on their homeward journey was owing in part to the large sums they carried. Ten thousand men would surely have been able to defend themselves on their own, but would they have remained a united body unless Craterus and his guard maintained discipline? Craterus, we know, had also received the order to replace Antipater, "to take charge of Macedonia, Thrace and Thessaly and the freedom of the Greeks" (Arrian 7.12.4). His mission with the veterans only served to slow his arrival at Pella, so that he had not yet reached it before Alexander's death. Alexander would have stressed the safety of the 10,000 Macedonians as the top priority. Without doubt, he wanted to be certain that they all returned home, but this does not exclude the possibility that he also desired to safeguard the money they were carrying.

If salaries were disbursed at Susa or Opis, one may ask how exactly did Alexander do so. Did he use unminted metal (gold or silver)? Did he include *objets d'art* (in his Opis oration, he refers to gold crowns awarded

---

39. See the remarks of G. T. Griffith, *The Mercenaries of the Hellenistic World* (London, 1935), pp. 265–66.

40. In this passage, Arrian leaves no doubt that the Macedonians, like the mercenaries, did receive a salary. I discuss this point at the start of chapter 4.

some soldiers for their bravery—Ar. 7.10.3)? Did he resort to payments in cash (in gold darics, for example, or in his own currency, if he had any ready money)?

To return to Thompson's thesis, observe how she describes what supposedly took place in Macedonia: "For men from Greek mainland and northern districts, Amphipolis would be the primary source of reimbursement." In her view, the Amphipolitan mint would, therefore, have struck enough coins to pay both Alexander's 10,000 discharged Macedonians and Greek and Balkan mercenaries.

[It is extremely difficult to estimate the amount of currency essential to such an operation. One would have to know, in fact, how many men, beyond the 10,000 Macedonians, were expecting to be paid and how much each was owed. Assuming that we are sufficiently informed on the number of dies used at Amphipolis in 324–323 for both gold and silver, we still do not know how many coins a single obverse die could produce on average.

I will try, nonetheless, to make an estimate, just for the 10,000 Macedonians.

Each of them had received a bonus of one talent, equal to 6,000 drachms or 1,500 tetradrachms. Multiplying by 10,000 gives a total of 15 million tetradrachms.

I will posit somewhat arbitrarily that these men were infantrymen and that they had served with Alexander for ten years: they are, indeed, depicted as veterans, and at least some of them (in what proportion, though?) had probably left Macedonia in 334. I will suppose just as arbitrarily that their salary in cash was a drachm per day, paid monthly.[41] Each man would therefore have collected 30 drachms a month, or 360 drachms, that is, 90 tetradrachms, a year. In ten years, he would have earned 900 tetradrachms,[42] and as there were 10,000 discharged home, we would have a total of 9 million tetradrachms, almost all in arrears because on Thompson's hypothesis the soldiers had spent practically nothing of their wages. This 9 million figure would probably understate the actual case because Alexander knew how to reward generously, and the bonuses he distributed over these ten years were numerous.

---

41. On the question of how much salary, cf. the discussion below, p. 74. As for the number of months pay was disbursed, texts from the Hellenistic period show that the winter months may not have been pay periods: cf. F. de Callataÿ, *L'histoire des guerres mithridatiques vue par les monnaies* (Louvain, 1997), pp. 399–400. Because Alexander's expedition continued over ten years without a break, I have supposed that salaries were paid in all twelve months of the year.

42. If this sum is not far off, Alexander would have awarded each man a bonus (1,500 tetradrachms) clearly superior to the wages earned in ten years of campaigning.

To be free and clear with the 10,000 discharged Macedonians in 324, Antipater, on Thompson's hypothesis and according to my calculations, would have had to produce currency worth 24 million tetradrachms, with partial settlement of this sum possible in gold (gold and silver at this time being in a ratio of 1:10).

Suppose that the Amphipolis mint devoted all its activity to this task. In 324 and 323, adopting Troxell's chronology, Amphipolis had 330 obverse dies in service for its tetradrachm issues (Groups E and F). Troxell, moreover, believes the issuance of distaters (her Groups A and B) started about this time, and it used 30 obverse dies (but how many of them were in service before June 323?). A gold distater weighed the same as a tetradrachm (±17.20 grams) and was worth ten times more; so a distater die could be thought of as producing the equivalent of 10 tetradrachm dies in value. The chronology for staters is more uncertain (their striking could have started several years before 324/23): they, too, total about 30 obverse dies, equal to 150 tetradrachm dies.

I come now to a particularly delicate point: how many coins can we reasonably estimate one die could strike?[43] I propose, with all due hesitation, to fix this number at 20,000.

---

43. T. V. Buttrey judges that any estimation of this sort is impossible, "Calculating Ancient Coin Production: Fact and Fantasies," *NC* 153 (1993), pp. 335–52; "Calculating Ancient Coin Production II: Why It Cannot Be Done," *NC* 154 (1994), pp. 341–52. F. de Callataÿ presents a measured response, "Calculating Ancient Coin Production: Seeking a Balance," *NC* 155 (1995), pp. 289–312. Cf. also *Annali* 44 (1997) for exchanges by Buttrey and Callataÿ, pp. 63–76, and Callataÿ's article, "Le volume des émissions monétaires dans l'Antiquité," pp. 53–62. Essential reading as well is Callataÿ's latest contribution to this problem, "Le taux de survie des émissions monétaires antiques," *RN* 155 (2000), pp. 87–109. Ph. Kinns, studying the short-lived coinage struck for a few months at Delphi in 336 to 335 by the Amphictyons, thought he had found some relatively precise indications about what occurred in this particular mint: "The Amphiktionic Coinage Reconsidered," *NC* 143 (1983), pp. 1–22. Earlier, E. J. P. Raven, "The Amphictionic Coinage of Delphi, 336–334 BC," *NC* 10 (1950), pp. 1–22, had dealt with this question. Kinns reexamined the numismatic and epigraphical data. Having estimated the number of obverse dies used originally for this coinage and having calculated with the help of inscriptions (knowledge of which had improved between 1950 and 1983) the approximate weight of the silver coined (between 125 and 175 talents, he thought), he was able to conclude that in this coinage, as far as the staters were concerned, each obverse die had struck on average between 23,333 and 47,250 coins. Kinns's arguments seemed solid and the numbers he obtained have since then been cited as trustworthy evidence. But P. Marchetti, "Autour de la frappe du nouvel amphictionnique," *RBN* 145 (1999), pp. 99–113, esp. p. 109, has questioned Kinns's results. He thinks that the weight of the silver coined by the Amphictyons did not exceed 105 talents and perhaps was only 61 talents and 30 minas. In this case, the average yield of an obverse die would fall somewhere between 23,333 and 14,350 coins. Marchetti has revised his article more precisely, "Révision des comptes à *apousiai*," *BCH* 123 (1999), pp. 405–22, where he maintains that the silver coined weighed "*at most*" (his italics) 105 talents and "quite probably" 61.

On this basis, the 330 tetradrachm dies would have produced 6.6 million coins, and around 15 (?) distater dies would have produced the equivalent of some 3 million tetradrachms. Adding the 30 stater dies would produce the equivalent of 3 million tetradrachms more, for a grand total of 12.6 million tetradrachms.

The result of these calculations, with every allowance for their serious uncertainties and the objections they will surely provoke, is that no argument based on Macedonian coinage production at this period rules out Thompson's theory. Such a rejection would have been possible if this production had been ridiculously low in comparison to the sums desired. This is apparently not the case.]

Instead, what really serves to shake Thompson's thesis, at least as it concerns Macedonia, is that the 10,000 veterans Alexander discharged do not appear back home either in 324 or 323. Craterus, their escort, arrived with them in Cilicia, where he stayed for some time, because he was still there in 322. He departed only at the end of spring or the beginning of summer that year, when Antipater, having difficulty with the Greeks in Thessaly, requested reinforcements from him (Diodorus 18.16.4; cf. Arrian, *Affairs after Alexander* 12). Craterus took 6,000 out of the 10,000 veterans under him, the other 4,000 remaining in Cilicia or its environs for the time being.[44] After enlisting some mercenaries along the route, he joined up with Antipater in Thessaly and helped him to win the victory at Crannon (September 322).

Craterus's presence in Cilcia in the early days of 322 is surprising. Recall that Alexander ordered him not only to repatriate the Macedonians but also to replace Antipater. He apparently gave these instructions right after the end of the soldiers' mutiny at Susa or Opis during the spring of 324. If Craterus started shortly thereafter, he would have arrived in Cilcia during the summer of that year. The province was about 950 miles from Babylon;[45] at an average speed of fifteen to twenty miles a day,[46] he would have reached Cilicia within two months. Is it an order from Alexander, anxious, perhaps, for better intelligence about Antipater, which might have kept Craterus in Cilicia? Or is it, rather, in Babylonia that Craterus awaited

---

44. See on this point N. G. L. Hammond, "Alexander's Veterans after His Death," *Greek, Roman and Byz. St.* 25 (1984), pp. 54–55 (=Hammond, *Collected Studies* III, Amsterdam, 1994, pp. 134–35). Also, P. Goukowsky, *Diodore de Sicile, Livre XVIII* (Paris, 1978), p. 129.

45. On the routes and (their length) connecting Babylonia to the western part of the Persian Empire, cf. P. Briant, *From Darius to Alexander: A History of the Persian Empire*, Eng. trans. from the original French by P. T. Daniels (Winona Lake, IN, 2002) pp. 357–61.

46. For rates of march and Alexander's army, cf. D. W. Engles, *Alexander the Great and the Logistics of the Macedonian Army* (Berkeley, 1978), pp. 153–56, for a nuanced discussion of this question.

the king's final decision, not departing until spring of 323? In any case, it is reasonable to think that he learned the news of the king's death in Cilicia and that he decided to stay put, pending further developments. As for the 10,000 Macedonians, one may well suppose that a long sojourn in Babylonia would not be displeasing because they would have been able to participate in the great pageants organized for the funeral of Hephaestion and to enjoy the other attractions of Babylon. On the other hand, one may wonder whether they would have patiently endured a new and lengthy stay in Cilicia if their pay and bonuses awaited them in Macedonia. We should not forget, either, that Craterus left 4,000 of them in Cilicia in 322 and that the other 6,000, taken to Thessaly and then brought back to Asia, may have wound up never seeing their native country again.

So the Amphipolis mint did not have to strike coinage in 324–323 to pay the Macedonian veterans. Would the Greek and Balkan mercenaries have presented themselves for payment? We have no evidence on this matter. Concerning the mercenaries' conduct in general, over the two years in question, a passage in Diodorus gives pause. The first reason he advances (17.111.1) to explain the uprising of the Greeks immediately after the death of Alexander is the following: "The king had ordered all his satraps to dissolve their armies of mercenaries, and as they obeyed his instructions, all Asia was overrun with soldiers released from service and supporting themselves by plunder. Presently they began assembling from all directions at Taenarum in Laconia . . ." Leosthenes, whom they had chosen as their leader, hired them out to Athens and the Greeks to fight against Macedonia. Diodorus's description of these vagabond bands arriving at Cape Taenarum does not square with what should have been occurring if these men had been obliged to return to their respective homelands (or at least near the latter) in order to collect their several years' worth of pay.

But, someone will object, could not the hoards buried in the Balkans a little after 323 provide evidence about the payments made to Thracian mercenaries around this time? I referred above, p. 38, to two hoards found in this region, one from Samovodene in Bulgaria and one called "Balkan," both containing gold Philips and Alexanders. Did mercenaries or merchants introduce these coins? Assuming that at least some of the coins probably wound up in the mercenaries' hands, when exactly were the two hoards buried? If they were deposited around 320 (a possibility), the staters they contained could have belonged to soldiers recruited for the Lamian War or the joint expedition of Antipater and Craterus in Asia (see below on these two events).

Turning to the second of the three questions I raised earlier, suppose that Troxell's proposed chronology for the different groups of coins from Amphipolis is correct. Are there not other possible reasons for the large size of Group E? Recall that in 324 Antipater received the order from Alexander to bring him "drafts of Macedonians in their prime to replace the men being sent home" (Arrian 7.12.4, Loeb modified). Antipater then had to undertake a new draft of around 10,000 men (the number of repatriated Macedonians), and he would have led them on their way, according to the king's instructions, if the latter's death had not intervened. This last levy for Alexander, of which Antipater was solely in charge, certainly entailed an increase in expenses and required striking a greater quantity of coins.

It is probable, moreover, that Antipater, during this same year, 324, had to intervene in Greece and distribute bribes to win support. As I noted above at the beginning of this chapter, the arrival of Harpalus in Athens stirred up some trouble, and the agitation was at its height when Alexander had his decree proclaimed at the Olympic Games, in August 324, requiring Greek cities to take back those whom they had exiled (Diodorus 17.109.1). Diodorus (18.8) presents this edict as the second reason for the Greek uprising. The proclamation Nicanor read at Olympia shows the role Antipater was to play: "'King Alexander to the exiles from the Greek cities. We have not been the cause of your exile, but, save for those of you who are under a curse, we shall be the cause of your return to your own native cities. We have written to Antipater about this to the end that if any cities are not willing to restore you, he may compel them.'" (Diodorus 18.8.4, Loeb modified).

My third observation bears on the uncertainty of the dates proposed for the different groups of tetradrachms from Amphipolis.

Thompson, adopting Newell's proposed chronology, placed Group G in 325/4, where the title *Basileōs* appears for the first time, while she assigned Group H to 324/3–323/2. These two groups, according to Troxell's estimates, used 114 and 109 obverse dies respectively, what might be considered a large output. Now, still employing Newell's dating, Group E, which would have lasted the two years 327/6 and 326/5, is by itself larger (241 obverse dies) than Groups G and H together (and these would have lasted three years). Yet no text speaks of soldiers returning to Macedonia or the neighboring regions during the years 327/6 and 326/5.[47] The previous discharge of Macedonians and Thessalians took place in 329 (its precise size not stated), at the end of spring or the beginning of summer, when Alexander was on the banks of the Oxus (Arrian 3.29.5). No other measure of this sort is mentioned prior to the beginning of 324.

---

47. Alexander went on to India in autumn of 327. Not only did he not authorize any discharges in 327/6 and 326/5, he called, rather, for strong reinforcements (cf. p. 49). When he was at Ecbatana three years earlier (spring 330), he dispatched the Thessalian cavalry and the other allies to the coast (Arrian 3.19.5). Arrian's precise words are that he released them "giving the agreed pay in full and adding as a personal gift 2,000 Talents." There is the clear impression that the soldiers received the money owed them at Ecbatana itself (and not upon their arrival home). Alexander kept with him only those who wanted to continue in his service as mercenaries: many stayed on (Arrian 3.19.6).

Troxell modified Newell's chronology: according to her calculations, Group E falls in 325/4 and 324/3. This change in dating, far from damaging Thompson's thesis, seems, on the contrary, to lend it some support, since the large demobilizations of Macedonians and mercenaries take place in 324 and Group E's production surpasses the other groups of the Macedonian mint. Indeed, Troxell thought her redating supported Thompson's hypothesis.

If this redating were reliable, Group E would presumably have begun only during the summer of 324, after Alexander's decision had become known in Macedonia and the authorities there could reasonably believe that it was time to anticipate the arrival of 10,000 veterans (who in fact, as we know, never came).

If one were to lower Troxell's proposed date for Group E by just a year, supposing that the latter's sudden increase in output began in the summer of 323, the military preparations Antipater was compelled to undertake would properly explain this surge in production. In fact, immediately after Alexander's death (June 10, 323), the Greeks under Athenian leadership openly revolted against Macedonian power. The war, called "Lamian,"[48] only concluded in September 322, with Antipater's victory at Crannon in Thessaly. Antipater left quickly for the campaign, probably at the end of the summer or the beginning of the fall of 323, taking with him 13,000 infantry and 600 horse (Diodorus 18.12.2). He charged his lieutenant Sirrhas[49] with recruiting more men in Macedonia, for his expeditionary force was far too small to stand up against the Greek army commanded by Leosthenes. Antipater took up a defensive position at Lamia and had to summon Craterus to his aid, who, as we have seen, arrived from Cilicia with 6,000 Macedonians and a contingent of mercenaries. He also summoned Leonnatus, satrap of Hellespontine Phrygia, who managed to gather 20,000 infantry and 1,500 horse (Diodorus 18.14.5). A. B. Bosworth[50] has supposed that Leonnatus's recruits were essentially mercenaries, with the Macedonians mustered by Sirrhas thrown in. Antipater had to maintain all these assembled reinforcements in addition to his own troops, for which he probably needed huge sums of silver (and gold) coins. He probably had to bribe various Greek politicians as well. Such a combination of needs would have prompted the Macedonian mint to order the engraving of a clearly larger than normal number of dies, as in the case of Group E. If we accept the evidence of Diodorus (18.12.2), according

---

48. A good survey of these events is found in Ed. Will, *Hist. Polit. du monde hellén.* I (2nd ed., Nancy, 1979), pp. 29–33, and Chr. Habicht, *Athens from Alexander to Antony*, English trans. by D. L. Schneider from the original German (Cambridge, MA, 1997), pp. 36–42. Inscriptions also call this war "the Hellenic War."

49. The manuscripts call this person "Sippas;" cf. Goukowsky, op. cit., p. 20, note 3.

50. *JHS* 106 (1986), p. 8.

to whom 110 triremes transported considerable amounts of money to Macedonia at the end of Alexander's reign, Antipater's finances would not have been deficient in 323, and he would have been able to step up coinage output at Amphipolis.

Antipater's huge financial needs did not cease with the battle of Crannon. At the end of 322 he wanted, with the aid of Craterus, to pacify the Aetolians (Leonnatus had died in combat). He never completed this operation because he and Craterus decided to leave for Asia and cross the Hellespont with their army, when they learned what Perdiccas and Eumenes were up to. Perdiccas thereupon left the scene, taking his troops to face Ptolemy, while Craterus in turn was slain in a battle with Eumenes. During summer of 321, Antipater arrived at Triparadeisos in Syria, where he was named regent of the empire and guardian (*epimelētēs*) of the two kings, Philip III and Alexander IV. At the end of 321, he transported them to Macedonia.[51]

By proposing to change the date of Group E, I merely wanted to show how a slight alteration in Troxell's chronology endangered the Thompson thesis as it related to Macedonia. Some will object that these dates have been calculated off a very solid chronological reference point, the Demanhur hoard, whose burial occurred in 318 or early 317. Consequently, it is appropriate to leave a sufficient period of time before this *terminus ante quem* for Groups G through J, to whose importance the number of dies in use attests: 114 for G, 109 for H, and 70 for I. We should not forget, either, that Groups K and J included tetradrachms (and staters) with the name and types of Philip II.[52]

I can only reply that the duration assigned each of these groups is arbitrary. Group E, for example, despite its 241 dies, was essentially struck in perhaps a few months, if the demand for coined silver was really urgent when the Lamian War broke out. Seleuceia on the Tigris provides a good example of a mint's ability to engrave an unusual number of dies in a very short time. Under Phraates IV, between March and May or September 27 BC, the Seleuceia mint used around 180 dies for its tetradrachms. Whether the time involved was three months or seven is uncertain; an average of some 60 dies would have been engraved per month in the former case, 26 in the latter.[53] Be that as it may, it is clear that the 241 dies of Group E and the 89 of Group F from Amphipolis could have been

---

51. The chronology of events in this period has been much discussed; P. Briant, *Antigone le Borgne* (Paris, 1973), pp. 216–21, provides a good overview.

52. For the tetradrachms, see the table above in this chapter, p. 59. Their issuance required engraving about 110 obverse dies.

53. See F. de Callataÿ, *Les tétradrachmes d'Orodès et de Phraate IV* (Studia Iranica, Cahier 14, Paris, 1994), pp. 37–42, esp. p. 40; the author's comparisons with other mints (p. 41) are instructive. It was during the time when Phraates IV opposed Tiridates *Philorhōmaios* that all these dies were engraved.

readied in a relatively short space of time,[54] between the summer of 323 and the start of autumn 322, so that Troxell's proposed dating of Groups G through J between October 322 and October 318 is still feasible.

I will add two further remarks.

First, Troxell concluded that the title *Basileōs* was inscribed on the Amphipolitan tetradrachms only after Alexander's death. On her dating, this title would have appeared in 322/1. She conjectured that *Basileōs Alexandrou* designated King Alexander IV (born in the autumn of 323).[55] The title *Basileōs*, applied to Alexander IV and Philip III (*Basileōs Philippou*, cf. pl. 8, 6), would have monetarily marked the period of the double monarchy. Troxell's argument seems convincing to me.[56] The inscription *Basileōs Philippou* disappeared upon the death of Philip III in the autumn of 317. Shortly afterwards, Cassander supplanted Alexander IV, who had just turned six, placing him and his mother Roxane under house arrest in the citadel of Amphipolis (Diodorus 19.52.4). All reference to the young king would have been suppressed, and the coin legend would become again *Alexandrou*. It is to be noted that in Macedonia, while the Alexanders with *Basileōs Alexandrou* are numerous, those bearing the name of Philip III are exceedingly rare. At present, only one issue is known,[57] belonging to a series Newell attributed to Pella because it does not fit in the great series from Amphipolis. This near absence of Philip III's name on Macedonian coins is curious, especially after Antipater took custody of the two kings at the end of 321.

The second of my two comments concerns Troxell's 320 or 319 dating for the Macedonian appearance, concurrently with the Alexanders, of the first posthumous tetradrachms with the name and types (and weight standard) of Philip II. This dating seems plausible to me. I have commented elsewhere[58] on the reemergence of these coins of Philip II (in gold and

---

54. In the chronological overview she presents in her *Alexander*, p. 95, Troxell puts Group F in 323/2.

55. A. B. Bosworth, "Perdiccas and the Kings," *Classical Quarterly* 43 (1993), pp. 420–427, thinks that Perdiccas would have waited until the end of summer or the start of autumn 322, to proclaim the one-year-old Alexander IV as king. If the legend *Basileōs Alexandrou* designates Alexander IV, the first coins bearing this inscription would have been issued at the earliest in 322/1, which accords with Troxell's proposed chronology.

56. Troxell, op. cit., pp. 96–98. She notes that Newell, in *Reattribution* (1912), held that Alexander never inscribed this title on his coins during his lifetime; Newell later changed his opinion.

57. Price, *Alexander*, p. 114, P1, pl. 116. See my article in *Studies in Greek Numismatics in Memory of M. J. Price*, R. Ashton and S. Hurter eds. (London, 1998), pp. 239–40 (= my *Études d'hist. Monétaire et financ. du monde grec* II, Athens, 1999, pp. 521–22), where I have called "No. 3" the series to which the issue in question belongs.

58. "Les deux monnaies macédoniennes des années 323–294/290," *BCH* 117 (1993), pp. 491–500 (= *Études d'hist. monétaire* III, Athens, 1999, pp. 1173–82).

silver, staters and tetradrachms together with their fractions). I have explained this phenomenon (whereby Macedonia, in effect, simultaneously struck two coinages, of different weights in silver, for at least two decades) from a fiscal perspective, denying the commercial or political reasons other authors have advanced; I alluded to this debate above, at the end of the preceding chapter. Because the reissuing of Philip II's tetradrachms probably commenced around 320–319, it is tempting to place the resumption of production for the gold Philips around the same date. Troxell did not rule out this possibility, but she prefers to separate the gold and silver and to place the appearance of these gold Philips a little before the silver tetradrachms.[59] I will not take a stand on this point. I am reluctant, however, to accept that the Macedonian administration treated the two metals separately.

Antipater had his hands full between April 334 and June 323, and again from 323 to 319. With responsibility for securing the *"pax Macedonica"* in the Balkans and Greece, and required to send his king reinforcements increasingly difficult to muster, he was led to strike coins as abundantly as Philip II had done in the second half of his reign and as Alexander did from 336 to 334. Would he, in addition, have had to anticipate the remuneration of the Macedonians and some of the mercenaries Alexander released from service in 324? Some have thought so, but I believe we ought to be more prudent, not taking for granted something that is only a debatable conjecture, however brilliant it may seem.

Circumstances led Antipater to strike the new coins of Alexander in large quantities. The silver had the beardless head of Herakles and seated Zeus as types, and the gold had Athena's head and Nike with a *stylis*. Thanks to its millions of produced and exported tetradrachms, Amphipolis, the empire's preeminent mint, contributed powerfully to this coinage's widespread popularity in the Mediterranean world.

---

59. On these posthumous series of Philip II struck after 323 in Macedonia, see my *Philippe II* (1977), pp. 56–59 (Pella, silver, Group III), pp. 120–26 (Amphipolis, silver, Groups III and IV), pp. 195–98 and 248–50 (Pella, gold, Group III), pp. 228–30 and 251–52, (Amphipolis, gold, Group III). Troxell expressed her views on the dating of the first of these gold Philips on pp. 117 and 122–23 of her *Alexander* (1997). It is clear that, if they were issued only after c. 320, the date of the burial of the Samovodene hoard (Troxell describes it at p. 117) should be lowered, and I would see no major objection to this.

Chapter 4

Alexander and Coinage in Western Asia Minor

After having crossed the Hellespont at the start of spring in 334, Alexander became the master of western Asia Minor within a matter of months; Lycia, Pamphylia, Pisidia, and Phrygia fell next. One year after his arrival in Asia, he cut the Gordion knot in King Midas's ancient Phrygian capital.

The Greek and Roman historians insisted on the paucity of Alexander's resources at the beginning of his campaign. Modern historians have reiterated this assessment. In order to judge objectively, we would need to know how much money Alexander had to expend during the spring of 334 to meet his troops' payroll. This point raises particularly delicate problems. We would also need to know the amount of financial resources his early victories provided. This latter point remains as imprecise as the first.

Is It Possible to Estimate the Monthly Cost of Alexander's Army during His Stay in Asia Minor?

R. D. Milns, in a previously cited article,[1] has listed the reasons that make such an investigation highly speculative. Without going into too many details (because I do not seek to add anything new to the question), I would like to examine the principal difficulties Milns has emphasized.

Alexander's army had three categories of combatants, he notes, and they need not have been remunerated or rewarded in the same way.

First, did the Macedonians (I pass over the different relations that could obtain between the king and the cavalry and between the king and

---

1. "Army Pay and the Military Budget of Alexander the Great," in *Zu Alexander der Grosse, Festschrift G. Wirth*, W. Will ed. (Amsterdam, 1987), pp. 233–56.

the infantry) customarily receive a wage? Milns shows that the first positive indication on this question appears only at the end of 326, when Alexander joins battle with the Mallians in India, and there is mention of a Macedonian who is called *dimoiritēs*, that is, someone who receives a double wage (Arrian 6.9.3; 6.10.1). This passage is a valuable piece of evidence, but we would like to know at what point the Macedonians started getting paid. Milns is inclined to think that they received a salary from the start of the expedition in 334, a view I share. The crossing into Asia could no longer be presented as a campaign whose objective was the defense of Macedonia. This was a war of conquest that very shortly would draw the army far from its departure point. The Macedonians became soldiers just like the others. One can speculate that they had received financial guarantees before setting forth on the adventure. Arrian (7.12.1), relating the events he places at Opis in 324, writes, as we have seen, that the king paid their wages (*misthophora*) to the 10,000 decommissioned Macedonians to cover the time that had elapsed and the time to be spent on their homeward journey.

Second, did Alexander or the cities pay and maintain the contingents sent by the member cities of the League of Corinth, contingents that could have comprised citizens and mercenaries? I myself will assume that they were the king's responsibility from the time they came under his command. Arrian (1.20.1) gives Alexander's discovery that he was short of cash as one of the reasons for the discharge of the allied fleet in summer 334 (cf. the discussion later in this chapter). This leads one to think that he himself underwrote fleet-related expenses.[2]

Third, did the mercenaries recruited in the Balkan territories conquered by Philip II and Alexander receive wages, despite their condition as subjects of the Macedonian king? Or did they receive only shares of booty? And what about the mercenaries not hailing from subject regions? Milns is certainly right to pose these questions. I would be inclined to think that all these men pocketed a fixed monthly salary, but in the absence of information doubts linger.

There is another difficulty, just as considerable: we do not know the amount of the salaries, nor do we know if each man was personally responsible for his food or if the army command provided a food allowance (*sitēresion*) in addition to the salary paid in currency (*misthos* or *misthophora*). An inscription from Athens (IG II², 329) created the impression that Alexander's *hypaspistai* (his elite infantry) received a drachm a day and that this sum probably did not include their food.[3] Milns has shown that this text, which is full of lacunae, could be interpreted in several ways and that the only evi-

---

2. Milns, op. cit., p. 238, doubts this interpretation, however.
3. See, for example, G. T. Griffith's interpretation of this text, *The Mercenaries of the Hellenistic World* (Cambridge, UK, 1935), pp. 297–98. M. Launey, *Recherches sur les armées hellénistiques* II (Paris, 1950), pp. 750–51, shares Griffith's opinion.

dence on which to make any inference is a passage in Arrian (7.23.3). This describes the new military units (*taxeis*) Alexander organized in 324, when he decided to include Persians in his army. Arrian says that each squad had a Macedonian *dekadarkhēs* at its head, someone who had previously commanded a group of ten men, the number being subsequently raised to sixteen. The *dekadarkhēs* had a Macedonian *dimoiritēs* (a double wage-earner) at his side and a Macedonian *dekastatēros* (who received a salary of ten staters). The squad comprised, in addition, twelve Persians and another *dekastatēros* who marched behind them. The *dekastatēros*, Arrian makes clear, was paid less well than the *dimoiritēs* but better than an enlisted man.[4]

It seems clear to me that the ten staters the *dekastatēros* received were ten silver tetradrachms, representing his regular monthly salary. The ancients often used to designate with "stater" the most important denomination of a currency series, whether gold or silver. Thus, in the system used on Aegina, the silver coin of ±12.20 grams was considered a stater, just like the silver coin of ±8.60 grams at Corinth. In Egypt, under the Ptolemies, the silver coin of ±14.30 grams, described in our catalogues as a tetradrachm, was called a stater, as we know from papyri. In Athens, this appellation would have suited the coin of ±17.20 grams, but the Athenians seem to have employed the term tetradrachm exclusively. Yet that did not prevent this denomination from receiving the name stater in the other states using the Athenian weight standard. As for gold coins, judging by weight standards similar to the Athenian, the ±8.60 gram coin was called a stater, and that is how scholars have taken to calling all the coins of this weight. Among the Persians, the term stater was applied to the daric of ±8.40 grams.

The *dekastatēros* of Alexander's army surely did not receive ten gold staters. Such a sum would have been excessive for a monthly salary; this soldier would have earned the equivalent of fifty tetradrachms a month (on the 1:10 ratio, gold to silver, one gold stater of ±8.60 grams was worth five tetradrachms of ±17.20 grams), that is, nearly two tetradrachms a day. Milns, however, has not ruled out this possibility, thinking that the mixed units Arrian mentions were elite corps created by Alexander and provided with salaries off the normal scale. I do not agree with Milns on this point. Ten gold staters, on the other hand, would represent too small an annual

---

4. Arrian, *Affairs after Alexander* 24.12–13 knows of another appellation, *hēmiolios*, a soldier who merited receiving one-and-one-half times the usual pay, owing to his bravery. This term also appears, perhaps, in the pseudo-Aristotelian *Oeconomica* 2, 34 a: Antimenes of Rhodes, to whom Alexander entrusted the finances of Babylon, might have been a *hēmiolios*, but this is an uncertain textual emendation (cf. below on Antimenes in chap. 7). Polybius, 5.42.1 and 5.79.5, mentions at the start of the reign of Antiochus III (223 BC) a superior officer, Theodotus, called *hēmiolios*: this fellow had distinguished himself as an enlisted man and had kept this prestigious title.

salary (only a little more than four tetradrachms a month and a half-drachm per day).

Rather, a *dekastatēros* probably received the equivalent of ten silver tetradrachms per month, these tetradrachms being considered as coins of Attic weight because Alexander had adopted this standard for his silver money at the end of 333, when he inaugurated his coinage with Herakles head and seated Zeus. Moreover, the Attic standard had been well known in the East for a long time. A sum of ten tetradrachms a month, that is, one drachm and two obols a day (eight obols in all), seems completely normal for a soldier with some extra responsibilities. Arrian informs us that an enlisted man earned less and the double-earner (the *dimoiritēs*) earned more. All one can conclude from this information is that the enlisted man received more than half the salary allowed the *dekastatēros* (meeting the condition that the latter's pay was less than that of the *dimoiritēs*), in other words, more than four obols.

Milns emphasizes that most often we do not know the precise extent of the army's manpower. I mean to arrive at a rough approximation of Alexander's expenses during his first months in Asia Minor. Here, for once, we are relatively well informed on the number of men under his command in April 334. The land forces, including the troops stationed in Asia Minor since the end of Philip II's reign, numbered around 45,000 men, infantry and cavalry together (cf. pp. 28–29). The naval forces, according to Hammond, consisted of 160 allied vessels and 60 Macedonian. A trireme usually had an average complement of 200 men. Although the strictly Macedonian fleet probably included other ships besides triremes, a calculation based upon the presence of 200 men per vessel gives, perhaps, an acceptable estimate. We arrive at a total of 44,000 sailors, a figure close to what we obtained for the land force.

I am now going to propose two hypotheses; they will appear bold but are meant only to provide an order of magnitude. I will suppose, first, that after crossing the Hellespont, all the soldiers and sailors received a salary paid by the king; and second, that this salary amounted to an average of a drachm a day, an estimate Milns uses, treating it as a "conservative average."[5]

Thus, in 334, the payroll for some 89,000 men in Alexander's army would have come to about 89,000 drachms a day, that is, about 15 talents (a talent comprising 6,000 drachms), for a monthly cost of 450 talents.

However one interprets the ancient authors' evidence on the state of Alexander's finances in April of 334, this sum of 450 talents far surpasses the means he had at his disposal, according to the historical tradition. But he knew that he would not have to pay the wages immediately;

---

5. Op. cit., p. 254.

we have seen that the Younger Cyrus kept his mercenaries waiting for at least three months. Alexander could therefore hope that if the fortune of battle went his way, he would acquire resources on the spot, which would provide him with the funds he needed. Like all conquerors, he had confidence in his own star.

From the Battle of the Granicus to the Capture of Sardis: How Alexander's Financial Situation Evolved (Spring 334)

The victory of the Granicus (end of May 334) provided Alexander the financial infusion he needed to continue his campaign. In the battle's aftermath, he named Calas satrap of the region (Hellespontine Phrygia) that the Persian Arsites had previously governed. The latter fled to Phrygia where he committed suicide because he was held responsible for the Great King's defeat (Arrian 1.16.3). It was he, in fact, who had persuaded the King to ignore Memnon's proposed strategy. Alexander had the population pay the same tribute taxes (*phoroi*) that they had paid Darius (Arrian 1.17.1). He sent Parmenio to take possession of Dascylium, the provincial satrap's seat, which Parmenio did without difficulty because the Persian garrison had fled (Arrian 1.17.2). Although Arrian does not give any other details and does not say whether Parmenio found any silver reserves, I do not imagine that the latter returned from Dascylium empty-handed.

For Sardis, the texts are more forthcoming. Sardis was the seat of the satrapy that included Lydia and Ionia at this time.[6] Spithridates, the territory's governor under Darius III (Arrian 1.12.8), had just been slain at the battle of the Granicus (Arrian 1.16.3). Mithrenes, the Persian commander of the garrison stationed on the city's acropolis, and its civic leaders surrendered the city without a fight. Mithrenes turned the citadel over to Alexander, as well as the cash (*ta khrēmata*) in his control (Arrian 1.17.3). Diodorus, in his narrative of this episode (17.21.7), speaks of the *acropoleis* (plural) of Sardis and the *treasures* (*thēsauroi*) stored therein. Sardis was the great royal city of the Persians in the western part of the empire. One presumes its treasury contained substantial sums.

Alexander placed Asander, son of Philotas, in charge of the satrapy; he named Pausanias, one of the Companions, commander of the citadel, the post Mithrenes held previously; and he charged Nicias with the allocation

---

6. On the history of this satrapy, see P. Briant, *From Cyrus to Alexander: A History of the Persian Empire*, English trans. from the original French by P. T. Daniels (Winona Lake, IN, 2002), pp. 700–707; P. Debord, *L'Asie Mineure au IVe siècle, 412-323 AC* (Bordeaux, 1999), pp. 116–57. On Alexander's arrival at Sardis, see Briant's "Alexandre à Sardes" in *Alexander the Great, Reality and Myth*, Jesper Carlsen ed. (Rome, 1993), pp. 14–17.

and collection of tribute taxes (*tōn phorōn*).[7] This division of labors prompted G. T. Griffith's interesting comment that Alexander wanted to diminish the satraps' power under the Persian regime as a way of lessening the risk of rebellion.[8] Satraps, according to Griffith, enjoyed absolute authority in their individual provinces, especially as far as the tax base was concerned and the income derived therefrom. So the following problem arises: does the fact that Arrian names three high officials left by Alexander in Sardis mean that each of them reported directly to the king? If so, would this system differ from the Persian?

Bosworth[9] rejected Griffith's suggestion, noting that Nicias was a nobody, a Greek, not a Macedonian, whose patronymic goes unmentioned. He would not have been able, according to Bosworth, to counterbalance Pausanias's authority. Alexander, therefore, did not intend to restrain the satrap's prerogatives; he would have left the previous arrangement unchanged.

I, too, believe that Alexander generally adopted the bureaucratic institutions of the Great King in Asia. The question is whether the satrap was all-powerful in his province. What exactly was the chain of command between Spithridates, satrap of Lydia and Ionia, and Mithrenes, commander of the citadel (*phrourarkhos* in Greek) and keeper of the treasure (*gazophylax*) stored there? When Alexander entered Babylon, he met, as at Sardis, "the guardian of the citadel and of the royal funds," a man named Bagophanes (Curtius 5.1.20). One supposes that the *phrourarkhos-gazophylax* (it is uncertain whether the two functions were always combined) and the collector of taxes were normally subordinate to the satrap. Yet one may well imagine, too, that they could receive a direct order from the Great King at any time and that they did not respond to an unusual request from the satrap save with the sovereign's assent.[10] The care Alexander took (judging by what we are told about Lydia, Egypt, and Babylonia) to divide the responsibility for the upper echelons of provincial administration among several, separately named people betrays, in my opinion, his imitation of the Persian model and the regard he had for its effectiveness.

---

7. A. B. Bosworth, *Historical Commentary on Arrian's History of Alexander* I (Oxford, 1980), pp. 129–30.

8. "Alexander the Great and an Experiment in Government," *Proc. Cambridge Hist. Soc.* 190 (1964), pp. 23–39.

9. Op. cit., p. 130; E. Badian, "The Administration of the Empire," *Greece and Rome* 12 (1965), p. 173, note 3, also considered Nicias "an insignificant person."

10. P. Briant, in his conclusion at a colloquium in Bordeaux on Persian gold and Greek history, *REA* 91 (1989), pp. 328–30, deduced from several examples that the Great King exercised strict control over the financial doings of his provincial representatives.

Note on the Revenues of the Great King and Alexander

While the ancient authors tell us that Alexander received tribute (did he maintain, as in Hellespontine Phrygia, the same rates as under Darius III?), they do not specify the amount. Herodotus (3.89–96) has provided valuable evidence on the sums Darius I (522–486) established for each of the tax regions of his empire. Although the latter's successors probably altered these amounts in accordance with changes in regional resources, the amounts in Herodotus nonetheless provide interesting points of reference. The difficulty is that each region encompasses several districts and the share of each district is not stated precisely. Thus, the Hellespontine Phrygians are grouped with the Thracians of Asia, the Paphlagonians, the Mariandynians, and the Cappadocian Syrians: all these together usually paid a tribute of 360 Babylonian talents, that is, 420 Attic talents (or Euboic, as Herodotus calls them). Second on Herodotus's list, the Lydians are grouped with the Mysians, the Lasonians, the Cabalians, and the Hytennians, and they together rendered the king 500 Babylonian talents (equal to 583 Euboic-Attic talents). The total tribute paid to Darius I on Herodotus's reckoning amounted to "14,560 Euboic talents," the last (and twentieth) region, the Indians, delivering 360 talents of gold dust, with one gram of gold, Herodotus says, worth 13 of silver.

These tribute amounts, some of which involved non-currency payments (grains, horses, eunuchs), when taken together quite probably enriched the royal treasury, whether they were sent to the central fisc at Susa or were partly kept in satrapal depositories. But they did not represent all the revenues the Great King derived from his provinces—far from it. The sovereign, in fact, also received very numerous gifts, he benefited from an entire series of regular or special taxes (on commercial traffic, on production, on the sale of slaves, etc.), he had direct or indirect control of many mines, he derived income from the crown property, and he obtained many services in kind. The satrapal coffers, moreover, had claims to different taxes and also to gifts. Concerning all these revenues, I refer to the research of P. Briant.[11] We do not have detailed knowledge of how the royal and satrapal bureaucracies managed them; whatever was not needed for the efficient running of the empire was saved as bullion (Herodotus 3.96).[12]

---

11. *From Cyrus to Alexander: A History of the Persian Empire*, Eng. trans. by P. T. Daniels (Winona Lake, IN, 2002), pp. 388–410. Cf. below, chapter 7, p. 229, where I provide Herodotus's evidence on Babylonia.

12. Briant has commented on the Herodotean passage in question, op. cit., p. 408. This is what Herodotus says: "The tribute is stored by the king in this fashion: he melts it down and pours it into earthen vessels; when the vessel is full he breaks the earthenware away,

According to Justin (13.1.9), Alexander was taking in 30,000 talents annually from his empire by the end of his reign. Berve,[13] and Beloch before him, wondered whether this figure was not exaggerated, observing that Antigonus in 315, according to Diodorus (19.56.3), received only 11,000 talents from his possessions when he was master of all Asia. M. Asperghis[14] has thought that Herodotus's numbers for the Great King and Diodorus's for Antigonus represented the sovereign's operating income (revenues minus the satraps' expenses) and that Justin's figure for Alexander corresponded to the empire's gross revenues, of which the king's net was only a fraction. I am not so sure. The 14,560 talents Herodotus accords Darius I might have increased over time (as E. Cavaignac, whom Asperghis cites, supposed); in addition, Alexander's realm included regions absent from Herodotus's list: Macedonia, European Thrace, Thessaly and, to a certain degree, Greece (the allied contributions). Moreover, Alexander never exempted "Persis," that is, the Persian heartland, from any tax assessment, as the Achaemenid monarchs had done (Herodotus 3.97). As for the 11,000 talents of Antigonus, it is worth noting that the latter had no possessions in Europe, that he had no power in Egypt, and that India had probably slipped out of his control. In short, I do not consider it improbable that Justin's 30,000 talents represented the total of the tribute taxes Alexander received in 323, and that he added in numerous other receipts as well.

Alexander's Financial Situation during Summer 334

After he captured Sardis, Alexander probably stopped worrying about his treasury. Around two and one-half months had elapsed since he crossed the Hellespont, and the soldiers, galvanized by success, knew they were certain to be paid. To important inflows like Sardis's, more modest contributions were surely added. Alexander, while still stationed at Sardis, sent Calas and Alexander, son of Aeropus, to take possession of the countryside (*khōra*)

---

and when he needs money [*khrēmatōn*], coins [*katakoptei*] as much as will serve his purpose." Briant [commenting on a French version similar to the Loeb's given here—WEH] objects to a too specific translation that uses words like "money" or "coins." He prefers something like "When the king needs silver, he chips off pieces of metal sufficient to meet his requirements." Undoubtedly the king used metal for numerous, non-monetary purposes; Briant's point may be well-taken, although the standard translation may still be preferable.

13. *Das Alexanderreich* I (Munich, 1926), p. 312 and note 1.

14. "Populaton—Production—Taxation—Coinage. A Model for the Seleucid Economy," in *Hellenistic Economies*, Z. Archibald et al. eds. (London–New York, 2001), pp. 69–102, esp. p. 78.

Memnon controlled (Arrian 1.17.8); this was undoubtedly another opportunity to enrich the royal treasury.[15]

The Conqueror's financial ease appears in the gifts he began to lavish. When he moved from Sardis to Ephesus, where he installed the democracy in power, he ordered (*ekeleuse*) the Ephesians to pay to the city's great goddess, Artemis, the tribute taxes (*phoroi*) that they had previously paid to the Barbarians (Arrian 1.17.10). He was still stationed there when the inhabitants of Magnesia and Tralles came to hand over (the verb is *endidonai*) their cities to him. He sent troops to take possession of the latter, and he dispatched another contingent of equal size to occupy the still unconquered cities of Aeolis and Ionia. Among other measures he ordered (*ekeleuse*) discontinuance everywhere of the tribute taxes (*phoroi*) that the Barbarians had received (Arrian 1.18.1–2). During the succeeding weeks, he made similar decisions benefiting other Greek cities, notably in Caria: these cities were declared *aphorologētoi*, exempt from tribute (Diodorus 17.24.1).

How to interpret these exemptions from tribute? Would Alexander deliberately deprive himself of a substantial and recurrent source of revenue? Ephesus, for example, which was the greatest port in western Asia Minor, undoubtedly paid relatively high taxes. By diverting this amount to Artemis's sanctuary, Alexander was giving up no small sum, at a time when he was not yet overly wealthy. One may suppose that in certain cases these exemptions represented a temporary gift that was not renewed. One or several other contributions, just as onerous in total, but differently perceived by the communities concerned, replaced the *phoros*, whose name evoked for the Greek cities of Asia the Great King's imposition. Here is what Edouard Will has written on this subject: "The suppression of the tribute (symbol of subjection) was compensated for by the requirement of the *syntaxis* (war "contribution"), a manipulation of language that the Athenians had already started when they founded their Second Confederacy."[16] A decree of Alexander relating to Priene that has elicited much commentary seems to

---

15. On the *khōra* of Memnon, see P. Debord, *L'Asie Mineure au IVe siècle, 412–323 AC* (Bordeaux, 1999), pp. 434–35.

16. In E. Will and P. Goukowsky, *Le monde grec et l'Orient: Le IVe siècle et l'époque hellénistique* (Paris, 1975), p. 459. A. Andréadès, *A History of Greek Public Finance*, Eng. trans. by C. N. Brown (Cambridge, MA, 1993), p. 80, tried to define the principal terms for taxation employed in Greek antiquity: *phoros* (tribute paid by subjects to their master); *syntaxis* (contribution paid for a common objective); *telos* (indirect tax); *eisphora* (extraordinary direct tax). These distinctions are probably accurate in themselves, but the vocabulary of the ancient authors does not always display the rigor we would like (cf. the remark of S. M. Sherwin-White cited below).

support Will.[17] It distinguishes between the tribute taxes (*phoroi*) exacted from the inhabitants of the royal domain belonging to Alexander and the *syntaxis* from which the city has been liberated thanks to the sovereign's kindness (the people here are probably to be seen as the Prienians from Naulochum who are now part of Priene proper and to whom the same privileges accorded other Prienians have been extended).[18] Delving into the meaning of *syntaxis*, Sherwin-White noted that this term, when taken in the sense of "contribution," "tax," often appears as the equivalent of *phoros*. She concluded: "The suspicion anyhow arises that few Prienians in the 280s, at the time of the inscription of the [edict of Alexander], took that clause to mean anything else than a grant of fiscal immunity, *ateleia*."[19] Priene would then have been one of the cities benefiting from a long-lasting exemption from taxation. I do not think, however, that this dispensation from *syntaxis* meant exemption from all that was owed the king. We have seen the quantity of taxes that the Great King and the satraps received over and above the tribute. Alexander quite probably maintained these taxes and perhaps structured them in such a way that he did not lose much in the end.

If one can accept that Alexander's treasury, after Sardis, no longer faced serious problems, one piece of evidence does seem to show that the sovereign still stayed attentive to the state of his finances, at least for a time. It is known that after capturing Miletus, Alexander decided to dismiss his fleet (Arrian 1.20.1). I observe that this dismissal probably did not affect the Macedonian fleet (consisting of 60 vessels, according to Hammond's conjecture noted in chapter 2), but only the allied 160-ship contingent. Diodorus (17.22.5) usefully specifies that Alexander kept only a few ships of the latter force "which he employed for the transport of his siege engines. Among these was the allied Athenian contingent of twenty ships" (Loeb modified). So about 120 or 130 vessels were returned to their cities of origin.

Arrian sets forth the reasons behind Alexander's decision in two passages. When Parmenio argued for a naval battle, Alexander offered three

---

17. P. J. Rhodes and R. Osborne, *Greek Historical Inscriptions* (Oxford, 2003), No. 86. In a fundamental study, S. N. Sherwin-White, "Ancient Archives: The Edict of Alexander to Priene, A Reappraisal," *JHS* 105 (1985), pp. 69–89, emphasized that this edict of Alexander belonged to a group of documents inscribed on one of the two *antas* of the entry of the *pronaos* and on the adjacent wall; the decree (which in fact is an excerpt of the original decree) was not inscribed during Alexander's lifetime but under Lysimachus and represents an archival document.

18. On this interpretation, see P. Debord, op. cit., p. 440.

19. See, also, the opinion of A. B. Bosworth, *Historical Commentary* I, pp. 280–81; "It is known that Alexander extracted contributions for his war effort. The *syntaxis* from which Alexander exempted Priene falls in the same category, a once-for-all contribution quite different from tribute."

arguments in rebuttal (1.19.7–8). First, the Persian fleet was far more numerous and better trained than the Greco-Macedonian fleet. Second, the Macedonian soldiers were better deployed elsewhere and not in an untrustworthy environment like the sea. Third, a naval defeat would deliver a decisive blow to the army's prestige and would provoke the Greeks to revolt. In the second passage (1.20.1), Arrian repeats the first two reasons and adds two more: Alexander was short of money, and "further he reflected that as he now controlled Asia with his land troops, he no longer needed a navy, and that by capturing the cities on the coast he would break up the Persian fleet, since they would have nowhere to make up their crews from, and no place in Asia where they could put in."

Diodorus (17.22.5), commenting more briefly on Alexander's decision, says that after the capture of Miletus, the naval force had nothing to do and was proving costly. He adds (17.23.1) that, according to some sources, the Conqueror was acting like a good general by depriving the Macedonians "of all hope of escape by flight" (they would not be able to use the Greek ships to leave Asia).

Bosworth has cast a critical eye on Arrian's reasons and has emphasized the weaknesses in the arguments the latter ascribes to Alexander.[20] He concluded that Alexander, if he really thought to vanquish the Persian navy on land, was committing a "colossal" mistake, on which the Great King was unable to capitalize. In fact, Alexander, confronting Memnon's naval offensive launched in the spring of 333, had to reactivate a naval force capable of containing the enemy attack. Curtius (3.1.20) writes that "the allies were ordered, as was provided by their treaty [in the League of Corinth] to furnish ships to guard the Hellespont." A little further on (4.5.14), he mentions a contingent of 160 ships placed under the command of Macedonian officers, the same number he had given for the allied triremes at the time of the crossing of the Hellespont in April 334.

Some scholars do not judge Alexander's strategy after the capture of Miletus as severely as Bosworth. L. A. Thomassen, for example, attributes to the Conqueror a long-term view that would justify the decision to dismiss the Greek fleet.[21] But what especially interests me in this episode is that Arrian, as one of his reasons, gives the scarcity of funds then troubling the king, something Diodorus seems to confirm when he emphasizes that naval expenses were running high. Bosworth does not think that Alexander could have experienced financial difficulties during the summer of 334. He observes that during the winter of 334/333, the king, while at Gordion in

---

20. Op. cit., pp. 141–43.
21. *The Aegean War of Alexander the Great, 333-331* (unpub. diss., Penn. State Univ., 1984), pp. 8–14.

Phrygia, sent 500 talents to two of his officers stationed in the Hellespont and 600 talents to Antipater and the others overseeing the Greek cities (Curtius 3.1.20: cf. above p. 46).

Reading the texts of Arrian and Diodorus without any preconceptions leaves the impression that Alexander himself, not the Greek cities, was paying the expenses of the Hellenic fleet. Milns (cf. the discussion at the start of this chapter) wondered, nonetheless, whether the issue here was not, rather, a monetary advance from the king, which the allies subsequently reimbursed. I am not inclined to accept this suggestion. The 160 Greek triremes employed about 32,000 men whose salary could come to roughly 160 talents per month. If we were to add in expenditures for food and ship maintenance, a total cost of 200 talents per month would not appear excessive.

By sending the great majority of these ships back home (about 120 out of 160, or three-fourths of the total), Alexander in effect would be saving around 150 talents per month. In the summer of 334, the king might not yet have had so rich a treasury at his disposal that he did not need to economize. The tax levies ordered in Hellespontine Phrygia and in Lydia-Ionia had not yet yielded their full measure, perhaps, and the treasures captured on the march might have been seriously depleted to settle debts and meet the army payroll in arrears. In short, while not bereft of funds, Alexander at this point in his career might still have had to consider his finances when thinking about what to do with the allied fleet. As P. Goukowsky has remarked to me, this fleet was useless outside the sailing season; the king was economizing by releasing it at this time, knowing that he could recall it when he thought it helpful.

Alexander's Monetary Practice in Asia Minor

Currency was surely required to meet Alexander's expenses in Asia Minor from the spring of 334 in a certain number of cases. To have enough of the necessary funds on hand, the king could have opened a mint in the region. Nothing, though, entitles us to suppose that he had any of his own coins struck in Asia at this time. Would it have concerned him that his current coinage was basically gold and silver pieces with the name and types of Philip II? Yet when he inaugurated his own great coinage with his own name and types after Issus (autumn 333), he seems to have let Asia Minor continue without any royal mint for several more years. Two questions require clarification. From what date can we detect the presence of one or more such mints in this region of the empire? If this date turns out relatively late, what can explain the Macedonian authority's delay?

Attribution of a Coinage with the Name and Types of Alexander to Western Asia Minor

When Newell published the Demanhur hoard in 1923, he isolated three series of coins that he proposed attributing to western Asia Minor. He suggested attributing the first series to Lampsacus, the second to Sardis, and the third to Miletus. He situated a fourth series at Phaselis or Side, in southwestern Asia Minor. Later, as his own personal collection grew, Newell was led to increase the number of functioning mints in this region. He proposed four more: Abydus, Teos, Colophon, and Magnesia on the Maeander.

Newell, in fact, had succeeded in establishing seven distinct series for western Asia Minor (I omit Phaselis or Side), based upon die linkages, stylistic similarities (an area where he was particularly gifted), sequences of symbols and monograms, technical peculiarities, and the different indicators discernible to the numismatist's practiced eye.

Identifying the production centers was a subtle task, and on this point several of Newell's surmises must be considered as only hypotheses. One of the series occasionally carries (not on the earliest issues, but only after a certain time) a forepart of Pegasus as a symbol (pl. 3, 11). Because the latter constituted the coinage type *par excellence* of Lampsacus in the preceding period (used notably on the gold staters struck there under the Persians, pl. 3, 12), Newell argued for attributing the series in question to this city. One may object that the symbols and monograms appearing on Alexander's coins of this period are generally the marks of those in charge of the issues (whom we call the "mint magistrates") and do not represent an official seal. For example, another group of coins also with the Pegasus forepart has been assigned to Abydus (pl. 3, 13). Moreover, in western Asia Minor, the Pegasus forepart was used as a coinage type in the fourth century not only at Lampsacus but also at Adramyttium in Mysia. This latter city was certainly less important and its coinage less brilliant, but one cannot say that the Pegasus forepart was a type peculiar to Lampsacus.

Another attribution, however, appears a little more certain. In one of Newell's established series, the second group, to whose coherence die linkages attest, continued at the beginning of the third century with issues bearing a monogram (pl. 3, 14) undoubtedly Miletus's, for, a little later on, it is accompanied by a lion twisting its head beneath a star, the well-known Milesian symbol (pl. 3, 15). In view of this, the assignment of the second group in question to the Milesian mint can be considered certain.

Margaret Thompson, starting from her teacher Newell's arrangement of his collection, pushed the organization of these coinages much further.

In 1955, collaborating with A. R. Bellinger,[22] she drew up a rich methodological and historical introduction and published for each of Newell's seven series a list of successive issues on which she made apposite comments. Then, in 1983, she produced the corpus of Alexanders from Sardis and Miletus down to the beginning of the third century, following, in 1991, with the corpus of Alexanders from Lampsacus and Abydus.[23]

Thompson retained Newell's proposed attributions without discussion: Lampsacus, Abydus, Sardis, Teos, Colophon, Magnesia on the Maeander, and Miletus.[24] Price in his *Alexander* took a much more critical stance and urgently entreated his readers not to place anything but limited confidence in these geographical identifications. Observing (as Thompson had too) that several series show an interruption of some years in the sequence of their issues, he wondered whether, at Miletus, for example, the first and second group actually belonged to the same series. No absolutely certain link exists between them; and while the second group, on which the symbol and monogram of Miletus appear, was certainly struck in that city, as we have seen, one might still envisage another mint for the first group. Price was also surprised that a center like Pergamum was excluded from Newell's list, and he highlighted how fragile the Colophon attribution was. He nevertheless preferred provisionally keeping the sites Newell and Thompson named, not wishing to replace one set of hypotheses with another, equally unverifiable. The absence of Ephesus is also surprising, the most active port of western Asia Minor. Troxell emphasized this point and asked, with great hesitation, if a group of gold coins assigned to Salamis on Cyprus might not have an Ephesian origin.[25]

---

22. M. Thompson and A. R. Bellinger, "Greek Coins in the Yale Collection, IV: A Hoard of Alexander Drachms," *Yale Classical Studies* 14 (1955), pp. 3–45.

23. *Alexander's Drachm Mints* I: *Sardes and Miletus* (Amer. Num. Soc., Num. Studies 16, New York,1983); *Alexander's Drachm Mints* II: *Lampsacus and Abydus* (Amer. Num. Soc., Num. Studies 19, New York, 1991).

24. In "The Alexandrine Mint of Mylasa," *NAC* 10 (1981), pp. 207–17, Thompson assigned to Mylasa another group of drachms (accompanied by some tetradrachms) that had been attributed for a long time to an "uncertain mint." Since this series did not begin until around 310 or even 300, I do not speak of it here. Cf. Price, *Alexander* (1991), pp. 313–14, and F. Delrieux, *RN* 155 (2000), pp. 35–46. The latter approves of assigning this group to Mylasa and suggests attributing it to Pleistarchus, who became master of Caria a little after 300 and remained in possession of this province until about 290.

25. "A New Look at Some Alexander Staters from 'Salamis'," in *Travaux de numismatique grecque offerts à G. Le Rider*, M. Amandry and S. Hurter eds. (London, 1999), pp. 359–67, esp. p. 367.

What we need to know is whether a gold and silver coinage with the name and types of Alexander existed in Asia Minor in the fourth century, from a date we have to determine. We can truly take as given that such a coinage belonged to this region of the empire. Its constituent series are distinct from Alexander's currency struck at the same period in Macedonia, Cilicia, Phoenicia, Cyprus, Egypt, and Babylon. More specific observations in addition to this general argument do not leave any doubt that these series belong to Asia Minor.

All writers have noted that Alexander's coinage in Asia Minor at the end of the fourth century is conspicuous for its prolific gold staters and abundant silver drachms, whereas the tetradrachms, so well represented among the other royal coinages, were produced somewhat sparingly. The vast quantity of Alexander's drachms from Asia Minor has particularly caught commentators' attention. F. de Callataÿ[26] has shown that although these drachms considerably outnumber the gold staters associated with them, their total purchasing power was clearly inferior (one stater being worth twenty drachms).

Curiously, the gold Alexanders, in Newell's and Thompson's seven designated centers, were paired after a certain date and for only a few years with issues of gold staters, varying in number by mint, with the name and types of Philip II (head of Apollo/*biga* [two-horse chariot]; *Philippou*; pl. 3, 21–22).[27] I will come back to this point later in the chapter.

I have mentioned the presence of a series of silver Alexanders originating from southwestern Asia Minor, according to Newell (pl. 3, 20), which he suggested assigning to Phaselis or Side. Price accepts that these coins were struck in Lycia-Pamphylia, but he takes no stand on the mint (which could just as well, he said, be Aspendus or Selge). Nonetheless, he assigns the series to Side, putting a question mark after the attribution.[28] This coinage differs from that of the mints of western Asia Minor: drachms are rare, there are a few staters, but tetradrachms predominate. So we are dealing with a series that can be geographically allied to western Asia Minor, but forming a distinct entity.

---

26. "Réflexions sur les ateliers d'Asie Mineure d'Alexandre le Grand," in *Trésors et circulation monétaire dans l'Anatolie antique*, M. Amandry and G. Le Rider eds.(Paris, 1994), pp. 19–35.
27. "Posthumous Philip II Staters of Asia Minor," in *Studia Paulo Naster Oblata*, S. Scheers ed. (Louvain, 1982), pp. 57–61.
28. M. Thompson, "The Cavalla Hoard," *Amer. Num. Soc. Mus. Notes* 26 (1981), pp. 44–48; Price, *Alexander* (1991), pp. 363–64. Thompson associates another series with the series Newell describes, marked by a pomegranate, the symbol of Side; it is not certain, as Price comments, that the two series come from the same mint.

Chronology of Alexanders Struck in Western Asia Minor in the Years Following the Macedonian Conquest

The Chronologies of Newell, Thompson, and Price

In his *Demanhur*, Newell apparently thought that the first Alexanders from Sardis could have been struck c. 333,[29] and this dating corresponds with his overall view of Alexander's coinage. Just as he placed the start of the great royal coinage a little after the king's accession in 336, so he was inclined to think that the Conqueror did not delay in opening one or more mints in the territories of which he became master. So we have to expect "high" datings in Newell's work for the different monetary series.

To tell the truth, Newell never paid much attention to the chronology of the Asia Minor Alexanders. In contrast, Thompson, thanks to her in-depth studies of this coinage, wound up dating the early issues of each series relatively precisely. Sardis, the region's administrative capital and site of a Persian mint, inaugurated the striking of Alexander's coinage in Asia Minor around 330. Magnesia on the Maeander would have immediately followed suit (c. 330/329), with Lampsacus next (329/328). The other mints waited a little bit longer: Abydus, Colophon, and Miletus would have started about 325/324, Teos around 324/323. Price suggested some adjustments to this scheme, on two items in particular: he would have Abydus begin earlier, about 328, and Magnesia later, about 325.

Thompson and Price agree on one point: these Asia Minor mints started their royal coinage during Alexander's reign, between c. 330 and 324/323. For the succeeding years, the chronology rests on harder data. On one hand, Philip III's name replaces Alexander's. We sometimes read *Philippou* instead of *Alexandrou* beside the seated Zeus on the tetradrachms and drachms and beside Nike on the staters. Philip III, proclaimed king during the summer of 323, was put to death at the start of autumn 317; the appearance of his name can only fall between these two dates. Furthermore, as I have said, these mints struck a group of gold staters with the name and types of Philip II starting after 323, providing us with a *terminus post quem* for the Alexanders bearing the same symbols and monograms.

A Chronologically Important Piece of Evidence: The Hoard of Alexander Drachms Discovered in the Near East in 1993

C. A. Hersh and Troxell[30] published this hoard of drachms with the name and types of Alexander that appeared in four lots on the American

---

29. Op. cit., p. 36.
30. "A 1993 Hoard of Alexander Drachms from the Near East," *AJN* 5-6 (1993–94), pp. 13–42.

market early in 1993. These four lots had such similar content that no one doubted they belonged to one and the same hoard. No reliable information could be given on the coins' findspot.

The 1,412 coins Hersh and Troxell examined were all drachms, almost all struck in the mints in question of western Asia Minor.[31] Nearly all the specimens were in excellent condition ("remarkably fine," the authors write). We find ourselves, then, in a special situation: the four lots examined probably represent the core of the hoard (no other lot of this sort appeared on the European and American markets at that time); the coins are sufficiently numerous so that we can make firm conclusions; and because the coins are very well preserved, we are probably dealing with a group of drachms withdrawn from circulation shortly after they were struck.

It is notable that not one of the 1,412 drachms studied bears the legend *Philippou* and that, at the same time, the issues constituting the hoard end just before this legend starts occasionally replacing the legend *Alexandrou*. Thus, for Sardis, Thompson's Group XIII is represented in the hoard; her group contained some drachms with the inscription *Alexandrou* and (for the first time at Sardis) some with *Philippou*. Hersh and Troxell, however, did not catalogue a single hoard specimen inscribed *Philippou*.

They dated the burial of the hoard to "very probably" 322, bearing in mind that the decision to substitute Philip III's name for Alexander's on some coins was taken a little after summer of 323. At the present time, it is the earliest known deposit of drachms with the types of Alexander. It antedates by some months, it seems, the 1964 hoard from Asia Minor that also does not contain specimens with the legend *Philippou* but does include some coins from Lampsacus and Abydus of a possibly slightly later date than those of our deposit. Next in our body of evidence comes the hoard of Sinan Pascha, buried, according to Thompson, in 317, towards the time when Olympias had Philip III executed.[32]

---

31. The authors counted 1,370 coins deriving from these mints. Thirteen other specimens could not be classified because their marks were off flan or obscured by deposits (from oxidation); presumably most of them were also struck in Asia Minor.

32. Hersh and Troxell present a comparative table of the three hoards' contents, op. cit., pp. 18–19. Thompson described the 1964 Asia Minor hoard and Sinan Pascha in *Alexander's Drachm Mints I: Sardes and Miletus* (New York, 1983), pp. 81–89. The Asia Minor hoard contains a dated Alexander drachm, issued at Tyre (Ake) in year 22. Thompson writes that this year 22 corresponds to 324 BC (by which I understand the Macedonian year running from October 325 to September 324). That would mean that year 1 of Tyre corresponds to 346/345, but I myself am of the opinion that this year 1 falls in 347/346 and that year 22 is equivalent therefore to 326/325; cf. below in chapter 5, pp. 127ff.

Just suppose for the moment that the 1993 Near Eastern hoard analyzed by Hersh and Troxell was hidden in 322. One salient fact catches our attention: the hoard does not include a single drachm from Colophon or Teos. Of course, the production from Teos is relatively modest and the fact that it does not appear in this deposit could, strictly speaking, be owing to chance. The Colophon mint, however, was quite active. The absence of any specimen from Colophon in such a vast hoard (1,412 coins) seems to indicate that the mint had not yet begun striking Alexanders at the time of the burial or had been striking them too short a time for the coins to attain wide circulation. So Hersh and Troxell rightly conclude that the early Alexanders from Colophon, and probably those from Teos as well, date to around 322 at the earliest. It will be noted that the 1964 Asia Minor hoard, rich with 88 drachms, contained one from Colophon. We have seen that the burial of this hoard perhaps occurred only a few months after that of our 1993 deposit. So it is at the time when these two groups were assembled and buried that the Colophon mint would have begun its output of Alexanders.

Of the five other mints in Asia Minor (Lampsacus, Abydus, Sardis, Magnesia on the Maeander, and Miletus) present in the 1993 Near East hoard, Hersh paid special attention to the one at Magnesia. He demonstrated, based upon a study of the die linkages, that the early issues of this mint (cf. pl. 3, 16) were more concurrent than consecutive and were to be dated shortly before Alexander's death, not around 330/329, as Thompson had accepted (Hersh dated the hoard to 322). Hersh's adjustment accords with Price's suggestion that Alexander's coinage from Magnesia started about 325.

Similarly, if we accept 322 as the date of the hoard's burial, Miletus would have begun its output of Alexander's around 325. Of the 755 Milesian drachms from the deposit, 733 belong to Thompson's Group I (cf. pl. 3, 17), 2 to Group II, 20 to Group III. All are very well preserved, like the other coins of the hoard, as I have already said.

The drachms from Abydus, numbering 160, are split between Thompson's Groups I and II (cf. pl. 3, 13). The hoard's evidence therefore favors her "low" dating (with the first coins of Alexander from Abydus coming around 325/324) rather than Price's "high" chronology (who proposed 328 instead of 325/324).

That leaves Sardis and Lampsacus.

Alexander's coinage from Sardis begins with six issues of gold staters with his name and types. The fourth issue also includes some drachms (one obverse die), the sixth some tetradrachms (one obverse die) and some drachms (one obverse die also). The existence of these six gold issues (18 obverse dies) led Thompson to think that the Sardis mint had struck Alexanders from c. 330. But she herself showed that common obverse dies linked the six issues: "Clearly," she wrote, "some at least of the symbols must have been employed concurrently. In all probability, the issues with griffin's head, tripod and bucranium—and possibly with serpent as well—were in simultaneous production" (the coins with griffin head [pl. 3, 18], tripod, bucranium, and serpent represent issues III–VI). One is justified in thinking that we are dealing here with a concentrated production over a relatively short time span. The mint continued to operate in this way, since some issues of drachms, a little later, were struck concurrently, as Troxell has demonstrated (Groups IX–X, XI–XIII, XII–XIII). To sum up, one could, it seems, have the Alexanders from Sardis begin around the same date (c. 325/324) as those from Magnesia, Miletus, and Abydus. All the issues of Sardis drachms Thompson noted, down to her Group XIII, are represented in the 1993 Near East hoard, and all the specimens are in very good condition.

As for Lampsacus, 253 of the hoard's 268 drachms belong to Thompson's Group V, and it was this group that was being produced when the deposit was assembled. This is a large group, marked with differing monograms and an image of Artemis with torches (usually described as Demeter: cf. pl. 3, 19). Some variants, absent from our deposit, appear in the 1964 hoard from Asia Minor (see above). Thompson's first four groups are very small in comparison.[33] In this case too, one is inclined to think that the Alexander coinage of this mint commenced not around 329/328 but later.

To conclude, based on the data the Near East hoard provides, and accepting that the latter was buried about 322, one may adopt a chronology on which the mints of western Asia Minor would not have started striking coins with the name and types of Alexander before the last years of his reign. Hersh and Troxell were not opposed to this idea: "With Abydus, Magnesia and Miletus all now seemingly commencing operations only ca. 325, is it necessary to assume that Lampsacus and Sardes started as early as 330?"[34] I myself, when commenting on the hoard,[35] took the same position, proposing that none of these coinages be dated before 325.

One hoard of silver drachms prompted the "low" chronology I have just presented. We need independent confirmation. Is this dating compatible

---

33. Group I in Thompson's collection, *Lampsacus and Abydus* (New York, 1991), p. 11, is composed of some tetradrachms and a single drachm: no drachm of this issue is present in the 1993 Near East hoard. The contents of Groups II–IV are also quite few in number, providing the 15 drachms of this deposit that are additional to the 253 specimens of Group V.

34. Op. cit., p. 38.

35. "Alexander in Asia Minor," in *Coins of Macedonia and Rome, Essays in Honor of Charles Hersh*, A. Burnett, U. Wartenberg, and R. Witschonke eds.(London, 1998), pp. 49-57 (= *Etudes d'histoire monétaire et financière du monde grec* II, Athens, 1999, pp. 529–37).

with the evidence of gold stater hoards whose burial can be dated to the time of Alexander's death? Some Alexander staters from Lampsacus, Abydus, Sardis, and Miletus belonging to these mints' early issues were part of the hoard of Saida (Sidon); two Milesian staters were present in the Mende hoard, and we further note that some coins attributed to Salamis on Cyprus, but struck, perhaps, in Asia Minor (Ephesus? cf. p. 86), are part of hoards from Corinth, Samovodene, and the Balkans. I have already indicated (p. 38) that the last four hoards mentioned were probably buried after Alexander's death, in 323–320 or even a little later. As for the Saida hoard, if we may judge by the lists at our disposal (the problem is knowing if we can be entirely confident), it, too, seems to have been buried closer to 320 than 323 (cf. p. 139). In these circumstances, the "low" chronology I favor could be accepted, because these staters, whether struck just before or after Alexander's death, had time to wind up in Phoenicia, Greece, Macedonia, and the Balkans before c. 320.

Alexander Coinages from Western Asia Minor and Thompson's Theory on the Paying of Demobilized Mercenaries

The new dating just suggested is not, at first sight, inimical to Thompson's thesis, whose principal points I set forth in the preceding chapter. In her view, in fact, the need to pay demobilized mercenaries on Alexander's orders at the start of 324 would explain the opening of Alexander mints in 325/324 and the rise in output at that time from other, already existing mints. Payments were to be made as close as possible to the soldiers' respective homelands, and that is why she says the mints of western Asia Minor were especially busy, because many of these men came from that region or from the islands of the Aegean and from central and southern Greece. Since the released mercenaries, according to Thompson, numbered in the tens of thousands and had, in some cases, to receive salaries in arrears, output at the mints was particularly heavy during the two years 325/324 and 324/323.

I had the occasion (in chapter 3) to express some doubts about the validity of this interpretation as it concerned Macedonia and the mint at Amphipolis. So I am led to ask whether it may not be appropriate to assume the same critical stance about Asia Minor as well.

Accept for the moment that the hoard Hersh and Troxell published was buried, as they thought, around 322. The absence in this deposit of any coinage attributed to Colophon and Teos supports the assumption, as we have noted, that these mints did not strike any Alexanders before the king's death on June 10, 323. Moreover, in examining the issues from Lampsacus, we can affirm that the activity of this mint became truly prolific only after Thompson's Group V. That group seems to have been in full production at the time of the hoard's burial because different secondary markings appear in the 1964 Asia Minor hoard, of only slightly later date. So we cannot take as certain that Group V from Lampsacus started before June 323. As for the mint located in southern Asia Minor, at Side (?), it, too, does not appear to have issued Alexanders from 325/324, the date Thompson and Price suggested. Its output of tetradrachms begins, in fact, with coins bearing the legend *Basileōs Alexandrou* (cf. pl. 3, 20), and serious reasons exist for thinking that the title *Basileōs* would have appeared on coins only after Alexander's death (cf. p. 71).

Thus three mints (Colophon, Teos, Side) that, according to Thompson, would have played a monetary role (during 325/24 and 324/23) in paying the demobilized mercenaries probably did not begin issuing Alexanders until after June 323. A fourth mint, Lampsacus, seems to have attained real scale in its production only shortly before the hoard's burial, that is, in the months following Alexander's death. These observations are bound to weaken Thompson's case.

The four other mints (Abydus, Sardis, Magnesia on the Maeander, and Miletus), as soon as they undertook issuing Alexanders, achieved a volume of coinage that was hardly negligible, striking staters, tetradrachms, and drachms (Abydus, Sardis), or only staters and drachms (Magnesia, Miletus). If one were to accept Hersh and Troxell's date of c. 322 for the hoard's burial and date the beginning of these coinages to 325/324, one might accept Thompson's explanation as plausible.

Yet I still must point out that the date Hersh and Troxell proposed for their hoard rests on the idea that the name of Philip III was inscribed on some Alexanders from 323/322. In fact, we do not really know this for sure. Bosworth suggested that Perdiccas, who still possessed some power at this time, succeeded in determining Alexander's succession at the end of summer or the beginning of autumn 322, proclaiming the one-year old child Alexander (IV) king and thereby instituting a double monarchy (Philip III had been so designated from the summer of 323).[36] Supposedly the legend *Philippou* appeared on the Alexanders in the latter part of 322, parallel to the legend *Alexandrou* referring to Alexander IV (with the title *Basileōs* often, but not always, accompanying *Alexandrou* or *Philippou*). This is how the double monarchy would have manifested itself monetarily. Alexander's name, which evoked the Conqueror, was by far the more frequent. After Alexander IV died in 310, the legend *Alexandrou* on the posthumous Alexanders reverted unambiguously to its earlier significance: it was the great Alexander's name people now understood on the coins.

---

36. "Perdiccas and the Kings," *Classical Quarterly* 43 (1993), pp. 420–27. See above, p. 71, note 55.

If Bosworth is right, and my hypothesis sound, one would be led to date the burial of Hersh and Troxell's hoard a little later than they thought. The time gap would not be large but invites some questions. For example, only the first two issues from Abydus represent that series in the hoard: the series could only have begun, therefore, at the end of 323 and could not have been directly involved in paying the decommissioned mercenaries in 324. I do not think we can go any further at this time, and I am ready to accept that this series or some other started before Alexander's death. Some of the released mercenaries were in the service of the satraps of Asia Minor, and it would not be surprising if they received coins struck in that locale upon their demobilization.

Nonetheless, if we take the chronological slippage of my theory as a possibility, we would still have to connect most of this earliest Alexander currency of Asia Minor to the events following Alexander's death on June 10, 323. Briefly to recall the facts, already set forth at the conclusion of the preceding chapter: Craterus in Asia Minor and Leonnatus in Hellespontine Phrygia recruited mercenaries in response to the appeal of Antipater who was fighting the "Lamian" War in Greece. After defeating the Greeks at Crannon (September 322) and waging war for some weeks in Aetolia, Antipater and Craterus left for Asia Minor, where Perdiccas and Eumenes on their side had gathered some forces. During the following years, the struggles among the successors knew only brief interludes of calm and threw numerous territories of the empire into confusion. Presumably, in the majority of cases (I do not say all), the coins of Alexander issued at this time in Asia Minor and elsewhere were primarily directed towards the preparations for these campaigns and troop payments. The extent and duration of these conflicts would explain the amount of coinage produced.

After June 323 the generals of Alexander quite naturally struck coinage with the name and types of the dead king. None among them had the power to issue coins of his own, while the two kings, Alexander IV and Philip III, were mere figureheads. The name of Philip III appeared on some coins, but the coinage types remained those of the great Conqueror. Even after Antigonus, whom his rivals immediately imitated, took the title king in 306, the production of Alexanders did not break off (it only ceased in Egypt, where Ptolemy had stood aloof from 315–310). So many coins with the name and types of Alexander were put into circulation that this currency assumed a decisively dominant place in international trade. When the new kings inaugurated their own coinages and stopped striking Alexanders (or at least produced them only periodically), a certain number of cities took up the practice, finding commercial and financial advantage in the issuance of these coins, as I have tried to show elsewhere.[37]

---

37. Cf. *Annuaire du Collège de France 1996–1997*, p. 821 (= *Études d'histoire monétaire et financière* III, Athens, 1999, p. 1099); also, "Sur un aspect du comportement monétaire des

Remarks on the Alexander Drachms of Asia Minor Issued at the End of the Fourth Century and the Beginning of the Third

What is unique in the late-fourth-century Alexander series from Asia Minor is, as we have seen, the striking abundance of drachm issues in comparison to the other coinages from the rest of the empire. At Amphipolis, Side, Tarsus, Tyre and Sidon, and Babylon there exist an imposing number of tetradrachms and, depending on the mint, more or less large numbers of gold staters; drachms are not absent, but they occupy only a small place in these mints' production. By contrast, in Asia Minor, if one thinks in terms of coinage inventory, the proportion is reversed. Take Sardis as an example. Thompson, in her corpus of the coinage, which covers roughly the last quarter of the fourth century, noted 242 obverse dies for the drachms, against 59 for the staters and 48 for the tetradrachms.[38] Now, a stater was worth twenty drachms and a tetradrachm was worth four drachms. The purchasing power of drachms issued from 242 dies was therefore far inferior to that of staters issued from 59 dies and only a little higher than that of tetradrachms issued from 48 dies. In terms of money supply, the staters from Sardis represented nearly three-fourths of the total value of metal coined then at that mint. F. de Callataÿ has rightly highlighted this point.[39] His accurate and compelling observation notwithstanding, the extraordinary profusion of Alexander drachms struck at this period in Asia Minor continues to surprise.

Scholars have entertained two explanations. First, Alexander may have ordered the Asia Minor mints to issue drachms for the entire empire. O. Mørkholm did not reject this interpretation.[40] Thompson, although she favored the idea that Alexander had a monetary policy that aimed to provide his realm with a uniform currency, did not think that he sought to organize production tightly.[41] The mints, she said, seem to have acted with complete independence in accordance with local needs, as I certainly believe.

---

villes libres d'Asie Mineure occidentale au IIe siècle avant J.-C.," in *Les cités d'Asie Mineure occidentale au IIe siècle avant J.-C.*, A. Bresson and R. Descat eds.(Bordeaux, 2001), pp. 37–63, esp. pp. 52–53 (= *Études*, pp. 1330–31).

38. *Alexander's Drachm Mints* I (1983), p. 40 ("Synopsis of the Coinage," where it is necessary to take account of note c).

39. "Réflexions sur les ateliers d'Asie Mineure," in *Trésors et circulation monétaire en Anatolie antique* (Paris, 1984), p. 20. Callataÿ has made the same calculations, arriving at comparable results, for Miletus, Lampsacus, and Abydus, the three other mints included in Thompson's corpus. A drachm was worth a quarter of a tetradrachm and a twentieth of a stater.

40. *Early Hellenistic Coinage* (Cambridge, UK, 1991), p. 50.

41. *Yale Classical Studies* 14 (1955), p. 7.

Moreover, if the chronological framework I set forth above corresponds with what actually happened, the massive issuance of Alexander drachms in Asia Minor would have occurred after the Conqueror's death, at a time when the empire had already begun to split apart and when a central authority, practically speaking, no longer existed.

Or could the abundance of these drachms in Asia Minor be owing to well-established regional custom? It has been observed that in the fifth and fourth centuries, the Persians struck gold darics (whose weight was quite close to Alexander's staters) at Sardis, the satrapal residence of Lydia and Ionia, and perhaps at Dascylium, where the satrap of Hellespontine Phrygia resided,[42] and that they also struck silver sigloi whose weight was barely heavier than drachms'. The preference for staters and drachms after 330 would follow from the habit of using darics and sigloi. Price in mentioning this explanation did so cautiously because, he said, several years separate the first staters-drachms from the last darics-sigloi "and it is not possible . . . to postulate direct continuity."[43] One could answer Price that the Persian coinage did not disappear from circulation immediately, if it ceased production in 334. Thompson, who herself considered the connection between the pairings stater-drachm and daric-siglos probable, recalled, as well, that if one were to find large-denomination coins (tetradrachms) in the coinage of the cities of Asia Minor under the Persians, one would also encounter quantities of smaller denominations, notably drachms, on Rhodian or Persian weight standards. In fact, one only has to page through the second volume of Babelon's *Traité* or a corpus such as that of B. Deppert-Lippitz on Miletus to be convinced of the importance of small denominations in fourth-century Asia Minor.[44] "Monetization," the use of coined money, had grown in urban centers: note how bronze coins complemented coins in precious metals for use in small, everyday transactions. Officials in charge of the western Asia Minor mints, when they began to strike Alexanders, would not, therefore, have changed any of the region's monetary customs by issuing a fair number of staters (replacing darics), a moderate quantity of tetradrachms, and an imposing volume of drachms.

Drachms, in general, most often had a limited circulation. In addition to be being less convenient than staters and tetradrachms for large payments and therefore less well-suited for big commercial transactions, they could be subject to the manipulations of the issuing authority, which had a ten-

---

42. See my *Naissance*, pp. 133–39.

43. *Alexander* (1991), p. 208.

44. E. Babelon, *Traité des monnaies grecques et romaines* II, 2 (Paris, 1910); B. Deppert-Lippitz, *Die Münzprägung Milets* (Typos V, Aarau-Frankfurt-Salzburg, 1984).

dency to give them (as to other small denominations) a weight below the norm[45] and, one may imagine, to debase the metal ever so slightly. So the nominal value of these coins could be perceptibly higher than their intrinsic value. Accordingly, there was every advantage in using them within the territory of the issuing government (where they were accepted at their nominal value), and this served to limit their diffusion considerably.

The Alexander drachms of late-fourth-century Asia Minor did not experience this fate. They circulated not only in Asia Minor but also in the most varied regions of the Greek world during the Hellenistic Age.[46] They also had remarkable longevity. A hoard found in the excavations of Gordion, Phrygia's ancient capital, was buried at the end of the third century or the beginning of the second. Of the fifty drachms it contained, forty-six were Alexander coins from Asia Minor.[47] A deposit of twenty Alexander drachms of this provenance, unearthed at Susa, was buried even later, probably after the middle of the second century.[48] By this time the coins were well worn, but they still circulated. They had been so prolifically produced between c. 325–323 and the early third century, that, despite hoardings and the disappearances due to various causes, they were still being used in transactions a century and a half later. For a long time, the Seleucid kings struck very few drachms with their names and types: in their kingdom, the Alexander drachms in question formed the core of this denomination's coins.[49]

These coins could, on occasion, have possibly served for large payments. Thus, to cite an example, the people of Colophon opened a subscription for the reconstruction of their ramparts around 310. One of the

---

45. See, for example, the remarks of O. Picard, "Les monnaies des comptes de Delphes à *apousia*," *Comptes et inventaires dans les cités grecques* (Neuchâtel-Geneva, 1988), pp. 91–101, and "Monnaie *holoschérès*, monnaie de poids réduit, *apousia* en Eubée, à Délos et ailleurs," *Kharaktēr* (Mélanges M. Oikonomidou, Athens, 1996), pp. 243–50.

46. One may refer to recent studies like those of F. de Callataÿ, in *Trésors et circulation monétaire en Anatolie antique* (Paris, 1994), esp. pp. 33–34, and of I. Touratsoglou, "The Price of Power: Drachms in the Name of Alexander in Greece," *Eulimene* 1 (Rethymno, 2000), pp. 91–118 (the tables on pp. 109–18 are quite telling).

47. D. H. Cox, "Gordion Hoards," *Amer. Num. Soc. Museum Notes* 12 (1960), pp. 27–33. On the burial date, see F. de Callataÿ's comment, *RBN* 129 (1983), pp. 41–42; also my "Sur le frai de certaines monnaies," in *Mélanges de la Bibl. de la Sorbonne offerts à André Tuilier* 8 (Paris, 1988), p. 78 (= *Études* I, Athens, 1999, p. 249).

48. G. Le Rider, *Suse sous les Séleucides et les Parthes* (Mém. Mission Archéol. en Iran, 38 [Paris, 1965]), pp. 243–44; *Mélanges de la Bibl. de la Sorbonne* 8 (1988), pp. 77–79 (=*Études* I, pp. 248–50).

49. See G. Le Rider, "Les alexandres d'argent en Asie Mineure et dans l'Orient séleucide au IIIe siècle avant J.-C," *Journal des Savants*, 1986, esp. pp. 26–27, and *Annuaire de Collège de France*, 1996–1997, pp. 817–18 (= *Études* III, Athens, 1999, pp. 1206–7, and 1095–96).

donors, Eudemos, son of Pyrrhos, a Macedonian, offered 10,000 Alexander drachms.[50] Payment was made, conceivably, in the form of 10,000 one-drachm coins. But, in fact, it could have been consummated in staters, tetradrachms, and drachms. If so, the accountants of Colophon would not have judged it necessary to go into the details; according to normal Greek practice, the value of the whole sum was expressed in drachms.

For these drachms to have acquired such popularity, it was essential, first of all, that they had a true weight upon leaving the mint and that their metallic composition was above suspicion. Hersh and Troxell found it impossible to weigh the 1,412 specimens of the hoard they published, a real pity because we are deprived of a precious piece of metrological evidence. Happily, Thompson did furnish the weights of a significant number of specimens from the Asia Minor hoard, buried immediately after Hersh and Troxell's. These weights are high, around 4.30 grams. One ventures to say that the officials in charge of production saw to it that the coins were exactly fourths of a tetradrachm. As for their metallic standard, I have no doubt that it was excellent, but one would still like to have some metallic analyses done.

These drachms benefited, besides, from the prestige that the name and types of Alexander conferred on them. They also profited from the fact that Alexander tetradrachms had acquired the status of an international coinage, and they themselves did not fail to obtain this eminence in turn. Their omnipresence in the Hellenistic world for more than a century is proof positive. They circulated everywhere and enjoyed an advantageous exchange rate. It is possible that some cities of Asia Minor striking the drachms in question continued to issue local ("epichoric") drachms simultaneously, practicing the system of double coinage established in Macedonia after the death of Alexander and whose mechanics I have tried to describe.[51] The Alexanders would have been the preferred coinage for foreign transactions, while the local coinage of lighter weight would have taken precedence in transactions effected domestically. Coins issued elsewhere, if they were not Alexanders, would have been subject to exchange, and the exchange process, as we know, was a substantial source of income.[52]

---

50. B. D. Merritt, "Inscriptions of Colophon," *Amer. Journal of Philol.* 56 (1935), pp. 358–72; cf. L. Migeotte, *Les souscriptions publiques dans les cités grecques* (Geneva-Quebec, 1992), no. 69, and J. Melville Jones, *Testimonia numaria* (London, 1993), p. 326, no. 384.

51. "Les deux monnaies macédoniennes des années 323–294/290," *BCH* 117 (1993), pp. 491–500 (= *Études* III, Athens, 1999, pp. 1173–82).

52. On this topic, see the reflections of M.-C. Marcellesi, "Commerce, monnaies locales et monnaies communes dans les Etats hellénistiques," *REG* 113 (2000), esp. pp. 334–43.

Why Would the First Alexanders from Asia Minor Have Been Struck at a Relatively Late Date?

The foregoing analyses generally concluded that Alexander probably waited quite some time before striking his coinage in western Asia Minor. Apparently, no royal mint opened there before 325/324, and it is even possible that the number of these mints was originally rather smaller than Newell, Thompson, and Price believed.

This is somewhat surprising. We can understand why Alexander did not proclaim himself monetarily in 334. But when he created his currency after his victories at Issus and Tyre, he could have ordered this coinage to be produced in Asia Minor. During the spring of 331, when he had left Egypt and was stationed at Tyre, he put Coeranus of Beroea in charge of the gathering (*ksullogē*) of tribute taxes (*phoroi*) in Phoenicia, while he ordered Philoxenus to collect (*eklegein*) them in Asia Minor west of the Taurus Mountains.[53] It seems that no coinage measures accompanied this financial reorganization. Former chronologies, placing the first Alexanders' appearance at Sardis around 330, are unlikely to be correct, as we have seen. Yet one would have thought that in the rich and highly monetized provinces of western Asia Minor Alexander's royal coinage would have been issued without delay. This currency would have replaced the Persian royal coinage and demonstrated Alexander's authority. It would, moreover, have assured much greater financial independence to the regional satraps who, in addition to meeting their current expenses, had to recruit mercenaries for Alexander[54] and sometimes to conduct military operations, as Calas, satrap of Hellespontine Phrygia, did in Paphlagonia (Curtius 4.5.13). A comparison

---

53. See Bosworth, *Historical Commentary* I, pp. 279–82, who criticizes Badian's thesis that the original function of Philoxenus was collecting the war contributions (*syntaxeis*) owed by the Greek cities of Asia Minor. P. Goukowsky, *Le monde grec et l'Orient* II (Paris, 1975), p. 318, thinks that Alexander created financial districts (encompassing several satrapies) and that their overseers made their payments to the army treasury at first, and subsequently to the central treasury in Babylon under Harpalus.

54. Curtius 6.6.35 reports that Alexander received 26,000 infantry and 300 horsemen from Lydia in 330; Curtius also indicates (7.10.12) that in 328 Asander arrived from Lydia at Alexander's camp with 4,000 infantry and 500 cavalry; this Asander, son of Philotas, had been named satrap of Lydia-Ionia in 334 (Arrian 1.17.7). In early 333, he helped the satrap of Caria, Ptolemy, to conquer the Persian Orontobates (Arrian 2.5.7); he left Lycia in 328 to rejoin Alexander, and it is probable that the mercenaries he led were recruited not only in Lycia but in the other provinces of western Asia Minor. The two Curtius passages show that this part of the empire had been tapped as much as the other provinces; one may speculate that other mercenary contingents, not mentioned by the ancient authors, were enlisted there and sent to Alexander.

comes to mind with Antipater in Macedonia, who had the same sorts of expenses but who himself struck the coins he needed.

It is fitting, therefore, to wonder whether Alexander may not have had some special reason to refrain from striking his currency in western Asia Minor until 324. We need, first of all, to examine the relations between the Macedonian king and the Greek cities of this region.

Alexander and the Greek Cities of Asia Minor According to Four Historians

Modern historians are very divided on this issue. I will cite only four authors. W. W. Tarn in 1927 argued forcefully that Alexander had restored "their original freedom" to the cities of Asia Minor and that he dealt with them "as free allies."[55] One could argue, according to this view, that the Conqueror found it impossible to replace the striking of local coins, a sign of freedom, with that of a royal mint, a sign of subjection.

E. Bickerman, a few years later, in 1934, argued just the opposite.[56] After the battle of the Granicus, the Greek cities of Asia Minor did not become Alexander's allies and consequently did not obtain the status of free and independent cities. On the contrary, Alexander, applying the Greek rules of war, considered himself their master, making no distinction between the Greek and barbarian cities, and rewarding those who rallied to him while punishing those who resisted. According to Bickerman, the cities merely went from domination by the Persians to domination by Alexander, whose authority was sometimes more severe than his predecessors'. Basing himself on the classifications of the numismatists of his time, Bickerman wrote that Alexander reserved the striking of gold and silver in Asia Minor to himself, thereby depriving the cities of a right they used to enjoy under the Persians and which was one of the manifestations of their local self-rule. Tarn, in 1950, undertook to demolish Bickerman's thesis point by point, a case of one passage in an ancient historian being interpreted by two authors in a diametrically different way.[57]

Cl. Préaux, in a frequently overlooked study, scrupulously examined the texts of Diodorus and Arrian that Bickerman and Tarn discussed.[58] She

---

55. Tarn's chapter in the *Cambridge Ancient History* VI (1927 edition), p. 371.

56. "Alexandre le Grand et les villes d'Asie," *REG* 47 (1934), pp. 346–74. Bickermann, pp. 347–48, reviewed opinions previous to his, beginning with J. Droysen, whose book, translated from German into French under the direction of A. Bouché-Leclerq, appeared in Paris in 1883 (*Histoire de l'Hellénisme*, pp. 233–36). Bickerman even cites a proposal of L. Flathe from 1832.

57. *Alexander the Great*, Volume II: *Sources and Studies* (Cambridge, UK, 1950), Appendix 7, "Alexander and the Greek Cities of Asia Minor," pp. 199ff.

58. "Les villes hellénistiques principalement en Orient, leurs institutions administratives et judiciaires," in *Recueil de la Société Jean Bodin* VI: *La ville*, first part (Brussels, 1954), pp. 75–88.

reacted against the overly dogmatic character of their arguments and concluded that Alexander did not apply Greek rules of war in all cases (as Bickerman insisted) but often used a cautious pragmatism. Still, he acted as master; the autonomy of the cities, Préaux wrote, "did not rule out subject status, even if it was called freedom."

I will also mention the important article of E. Badian, published in 1966, where this eminent historian essentially reasserts Bickerman's position.[59] He differs, however, from both Bickerman and Tarn on one still debated point. Based on the appearance of the word *syntaxis* in the Priene inscription mentioned earlier in this chapter (pp. 81-82), and noting that the members of the League of Corinth paid the king a *syntaxis*, he thought that the Greek cities of Asia Minor were included in the League. Bosworth and S. M. Sherwin-White[60] have criticized this opinion.

Alexander, Successor of the Great King

I myself would like to emphasize the similarities evident in Asia Minor between Alexander's political conduct and the Great King's.

In 386, Artaxerxes II claimed the cities of Asia as his own, as well as the islands of Clazomenae and Cyprus. This solemn assertion, as Xenophon reports it (*Hell.* 5.1.31), did not change the ancestral policy of the Persians regarding their vassals in any way. The cities in question enjoyed considerable autonomy in internal affairs, as the handsome silver tetradrachms that the Ephesians copiously issued during the fourth century strikingly illustrate. On the obverse these show the ethnic (abbreviated) of the city's inhabitants, while on the reverse they carry the name of an Ephesian mint magistrate; the types of bee and stag's head along with a date palm refer to the goddess of Ephesus, Artemis. These coins attest to the Ephesians' local self-rule. Cyzicus, with its impressive series of electrum staters, Lampsacus, with its gold staters, and the silver currency issues of many other cities provide similar testimony.[61]

The subject status of these cities, however, was a fact. The obligation incumbent on them not to pursue a foreign policy contrary to the interests of the Great King made their position clear. So did their having to pay the sovereign annual tribute (the *phoros* of the Greek texts) and having probably

---

59. "Alexander the Great and the Greeks of Asia," in *Ancient Society and Institutions, Studies Presented to V. Ehrenberg*, E. Badian ed. (Oxford, 1966), pp. 37–69.

60. Bosworth, *Historical Commentary* I, pp. 280–81; Sherwin-White, *JHS* 105 (1985), esp. pp. 84–86. Many historians before Badian held the view that the Asia Minor cities were members of the League of Corinth, and P. Green takes it up anew on pp. 187–88 of the 1991 edition of his *Alexander of Macedon 356–323 BC*.

61. See my *Naissance*, pp. 174–77.

to set aside for him a percentage of their receipts from numerous other taxes. Finally, they had to submit to the satrap's authority and the occasional presence of a garrison. We should add that the Great King was inclined to support the oligarchic faction in a city and to establish tyrannies from time to time, following the principle Thucydides sets forth in a speech attributed to the Thebans (3.62.3–4).[62]

After his victory at the Granicus (May 334), Alexander made no changes to the administrative structures the Persians had put in place. We have seen how Calas, in charge of the satrapy of Hellespontine Phrygia, received the order to collect the same tribute taxes (*phoroi*) that existed under the Great King. Likewise, at Sardis, Alexander was content to replace Persian personnel with men from his own staff: he did not alter the existing system itself (cf. p. 78).

On the other hand, his attitude towards the Greek cities seems at first glance to have been quite different from the Persian king's. The ancient authors celebrate the liberation of the Greeks,[63] democracies replacing oligarchies, the gaining of autonomy, and freedom from tribute. What are we to make of this?

I note, first of all, that the Conqueror's decisions were unilateral and depended on his goodwill. It was he who gave the order (the verb used is *keleuein*) to end the oligarchies and abolish the tribute. These decisions were not the result of a mutual agreement and were immediately revocable in case of any disobedience, as the example of Aspendus shows (Arrian 1.26.2, 3, 5; 1.27.1–4). Bickerman rightly insisted on this point.

As for the liberation of the Greeks of Asia, R. Seager and C. Tuplin have shown that, between 400 and 386, this notion had become a slogan used to justify the self-interested interventions of Sparta and Athens in the region. It is noteworthy, they observe, that the Greeks of Asia never asked to be liberated.[64] By the same token, in the time of Philip II and Alexander, the cities of Asia do not appear to have been in a hurry to throw off Persian sovereignty.[65] The welcome Alexander received in Asia Minor at the start of

---

62. Tacitus, *Annals* 6.42.2, makes the same observation about the king of the Parthians, Artabanus II, and the city of Seleucia on the Tigris.

63. Diodorus 17.24.1, recounting Alexander's passage through Caria, reports that Alexander had undertaken the war against the Persians to liberate the Greeks.

64. "The Freedom of the Greeks of Asia: On the Origin of a Concept and the Creation of a Slogan," *JHS* 100 (1980), pp. 141–54.

65. One notes that, according to Diodorus (16.89.2), Philip II, looking to become *hēgemōn* of all Greece after Chaeronea, let it be known that he wanted to undertake the war against the Persians in the name of the Greeks and to punish the Persians for having profaned temples. No mention is made of liberating the cities of Asia Minor. Likewise, Isocrates, *Philip* 120–23, urges Philip II on to the war that would permit him to conquer Asia Minor (up to

his campaign was rather muted.[66] His victory at the Granicus and his rapid advance rallied the hesitant, but he still had to fight more battles, notably at Miletus.

Change of regime was the hallmark of the liberation Alexander proclaimed. Not that Alexander preferred democracies to oligarchies (the opposite would seem more natural), but the new regimes, which owed him everything, were sure to be especially loyal.

I will not rehearse the problem of tribute exemptions, discussed earlier. In fiscal matters, other obligations incumbent upon administered territories often compensated for measures apparently in their financial favor. I can scarcely believe that Alexander would totally and definitively deprive himself of revenues whose lack would have seriously compromised the proper functioning of the provinces concerned and the cash flow of his own treasury.

As for the cities' local autonomy, Alexander could not have done much better than the Great King, who on this issue, we know, showed himself to be quite liberal. Arrian (1.18.2) writes that Alexander gave the order to restore (*apodounai*) to the cities their own laws. But the Persians had never suppressed these laws. Would Arrian, whether deliberately or not, have altered the historical reality? It is also understandable that some cities like Magnesia and Tralles submitted (capitulated, Bickerman says) to the Conqueror and that, having them at his mercy, he gave them back the autonomy in internal affairs they used to have under the previous regime.

The Great King not only permitted the Greek cities of Asia Minor to strike their own currency; he also apparently refrained from producing his own royal coinage (darics and sigloi with the type of the archer king) in any of them. His satraps and army marshals sometimes used the mint of an autonomous city, but their coins were different from the Great King's and their issues were probably subject to special conditions.[67] Presumably Alexander, who was so careful to proclaim the autonomy of the Greek cities, could not show himself to be less generous than the Persians had been in coinage matters. When he created his own personal coinage in 333/332 in Cilicia and Phoenicia, Alexander also had it struck in Macedonia without delay. If, as it seems, he waited several years before opening

---

a line running from Cilicia to Sinope), to found cities there where migrant poor could live, and so create a buffer protecting Greece; if Philip did not achieve all this, at least he would wind up easily liberating the cities of Asia. In this large Isocratean program, liberation of the Greeks comes last.

66. See Badian's remarks, *Ancient Society and Institutions*, pp. 40 and 43–44; P. Briant, *From Cyrus to Alexander: A History of the Persian Empire*, Eng. trans. by P. T. Daniels (Winona Lake, IN, 2002), pp. 855–57.

67. See my *Naissance*, pp. 231–32.

other royal mints in western Asia Minor, that can be partly explained, I think, by the pledges he made in 334/333 to the region's cities.

Two objections to this viewpoint will arise. First, the Great King, in Asia Minor, had produced darics and sigloi at Sardis, a royal city and satrapal residence, and perhaps at Dascylium as well, where the satrap of Hellespontine Phyrgia had his palace. Could not Alexander have issued his coinage from 332 in these two mints, if he had wanted to? Second, is a city's issuing of royal currency incompatible with autonomy?

As for the first point, concerning Dascylium, the city is not heard of after Parmenio took possession of if it in the wake of the battle of the Granicus.[68] Did Calas, the new satrap, install himself there or did he prefer to reside elsewhere? We are better informed about Sardis. The city remained the satrapal seat of Lydia and Ionia, and received favorable treatment from the Conqueror. In return for the welcoming attitude of the Persian Mithrenes and the leading men of Sardis, Alexander allowed the inhabitants of Sardis and Lydia to be free and to use their ancestral laws (Arrian 1.17.2). Badian observed that the Persians had certainly not abolished the "ancestral laws" of the Lydians and that the liberty Alexander accorded them meant that he did not enslave the population.[69] Badian is probably right about the first point, but it is hard to go along with him on the second. Briant's analysis[70] has convincingly shown that the people of Sardis enjoyed internal autonomy under the Persians, perhaps more restricted than that of a city like Ephesus, but nonetheless real.[71] It is quite possible, contrary to what Badian thought, that Alexander added to the liberties of Sardis, according its people the same privileges as the Ephesians, as Briant has cautiously speculated. If that is right, one could accept that, monetarily speaking, Alexander recognized no big difference between Sardis and the Greek cities of Asia Minor. Sardis, nevertheless, was and remained a satrapal city, reporting

---

68. Tomris Bakir, "Archäologische Beobachtungen über die Residenz in Daskyleion," *Dans les pas des Dix-Mille*, P. Briant ed., *Pallas* 43 (Toulouse, 1995), pp. 269–85, remains rather unclear on the history of this city after 334.

69. Op. cit., pp. 44–45.

70. "Alexandre à Sardes," in *Alexander the Great, Reality and Myth*, J. Carlsen ed. (Rome, 1993), pp. 18–23.

71. Bosworth, *Historical Commentary* I, p. 129, writes concerning the passage in Herodotus, 1.155–57: "There is a tradition in Herodotus that after Cyrus' conquest Lydian institutions were entirely remoulded in order to transform the people into pliant subjects." Herodotus says that after the revolt of Pactyes, Cyrus regretted having given the city to the Lydians, that is, having left Sardis with its own internal autonomy. Croesus deterred him from resorting to overly severe retaliatory measures and counseled him to direct the Lydians to non-military activities. It is possible to interpret this text differently from Bosworth. The Lydians would preserve their freedoms on condition that they lived peacefully and loyally recognized Cyrus's sovereignty.

directly to the royal administration and more receptive than the Greek cities to that administration's demands. It is very possible that Sardis was the site where the first Alexander coinage of western Asia Minor was struck.

As for the second objection, it is conceivable that a community enjoying internal autonomy did not necessarily suffer a diminution of its liberties if it struck royal coins for the sovereign's account. Far from being an imposition, this activity could have resulted from a negotiation and belonged to the category of services rendered. The city would have received tax refunds in return and benefited, moreover, from an increase in coinage transactions in its territory, if at least some of the royal currency it struck were spent there. Finally, the city would not have lost the possibility of continuing its own coinage. In these circumstances, why was not such an arrangement made in Asia Minor from 332 but only some years later (if, at least, the chronology I have adopted is correct)? One might speculate that in 332 it was perhaps still premature, for reasons of general policy, to put an organization of this type in place. Around 325/324 (?), perhaps the satraps of Hellespontine Phrygia, Lydia-Ionia, and Caria proceeded gradually, beginning by striking Alexander's currency in the cities where they resided, before turning to other cities.

All this will remain problematic for as long as we cannot determine with sufficient precision in what mint and at what date each of the coinage series presented above was issued in Asia Minor.

The Currency Used in Asia Minor from 334 to the End of Alexander's Reign

Did Alexander Leave with a Supply of Macedonian Coins?

When Alexander left Macedonia at the start of spring 334, did he take a reserve of coins with him? At that time, the Macedonian coinage consisted of gold and silver coins with the name and types of Philip II and perhaps a certain number of "eagle" tetradrachms in Alexander's name.

Consider, first, the silver coins. No tetradrachm of Philip, no eagle tetradrachm of Alexander appears in the hoards of this period from Asia Minor. Nor has a single, isolated specimen, to my knowledge, been found in this region. The few coins that have been found farther to the east do not provide any significant evidence. A tetradrachm of Philip II belonged to the important hoard unearthed near Babylon in 1973, another to the hoard from Oxus.[72] An eagle tetradrachm was noted in the enormous deposit of

---

72. For the Babylonia, or rather Iraq, hoard, see Price, "Circulation at Babylon in 323 BC," in *Mnemata, Papers in Memory of N. M. Waggoner*, W. E. Metcalf ed. (Amer. Num. Soc.,

Mir Zakah II in Afghanistan, and another has a provenance from the bazaar in Rawalpindi, Pakistan (the former Punjab).[73] If Alexander had sacks of Philip II tetradrachms and eagle tetradrachms in his army treasury, they have left no trace in Asia Minor.

But perhaps he came supplied with gold Philips; they were more convenient than silver coins because of their clearly superior purchasing power and smaller bulk. Hoards found in the East containing gold Philips are rare. A single one was buried at a date not far removed from Alexander's passage through Asia Minor, the Saida (Sidon) hoard buried in the years 323–320.[74] Of the thousands of gold coins it contained, more than 302 (according to lists drawn up at the time of its discovery) were staters of Philip II, only 6 of which can be precisely classified. They belong to my Group II and were still in production in Macedonia when Alexander crossed the Hellespont. One could accept that the Conqueror carried at least some of the hoard's 302 Philips to Asia Minor and used them there, and that they were subsequently employed to pay more distant recipients. It is also possible, however, that the Philips of the Saida hoard wound up in Phoenicia by another route and that they never spent time in Asia Minor.[75]

To sum up, nothing clearly indicates that Alexander carried quantities of silver and gold Philips into Asia Minor.

New York, 1991), p. 72, no. 299. I have commented on the tetradrachm of Philip II it contains in *Monnayage et finances de Philippe II* (Meletēmata 23, Athens, 1998), p. 19, no. 8. For the Oxus hoard, see A. R. Bellinger, "Coins from the Treasure of the Oxus," *Amer. Num. Soc. Notes* 10 (1962), p. 57; no description was given of this coin. As for the hoard itself, its highly varied and chronologically disparate content is startling.

73. See chapter 2, p. 32. O. Bopearachchi has described the Mir Zakah I and II deposits in *La circulation et la production monétaires dans l'Asie centrale et l'Inde du Nord-Ouest*, Indologica Taurinensia 25 (Turin, 1999–2000), pp. 60–64.

74. I mentioned this hoard earlier in this chapter, p. 92, and I will come back again in the next chapter to the problem that dating its burial poses. The six identifiable gold staters of Philip II have been catalogued in my *Philippe II* (1977), p. 262.

75. Four other hoards found in the East contain gold Philips. The first poses a problem: discovered at Prinkipo, the most important of the Princes' Islands, to the southeast of Istanbul in the Sea of Marmara (the Propontis), it comprised 27 gold Philips, some electrum staters of Cyzicus, and some gold staters from Lampsacus and Pantikapaion (*IGCH* 1239). I have indicated that the Philips perhaps had another provenance (*Philippe II*, p. 255); in any case, the 27 coins belong to my Group I, struck during Philip II's lifetime, and could have been buried before Alexander's crossing to Asia. The three other hoards are later. That from Larnaka (Cyprus), was buried c. 300, that from Maeander c. 280–75, and that from Gordion at the end of the third century; see *Philippe II*, pp. 277–78, 282, and 283. In these three hoards, several Philips belong to my Group III, issued after 323.

Remarks on the Gold Staters of Philip II Struck in Asia Minor after 323

Earlier in this chapter, I mentioned the gold staters with the name and types of Philip II issued concurrently with issues by Alexander in western Asia Minor after 323 (gold Philips and gold Alexanders of the same weight, ±8.60 grams).[76] We can take as certain that the earliest of these gold Philips are later than 323 because the coins of Alexander with which their monograms and symbols associate them were not produced prior to that time. This was already evident in Thompson's lists, and today it seems that the beginning of Alexander's coinage in Asia Minor has been slightly downdated with even more assurance.

These gold Philips from western Asia Minor, struck in several mints (cf. pl. 3, 21, "Lampsacus," and pl. 3, 22, "Magnesia on the Maeander") are a little surprising. It is hard to believe that the hypothetical specimens Alexander brought in 334 or that came from Macedonia between 334 and 323 created such a stir that the masters of Asia Minor after 323 decided to have this coinage struck. How, then, are we to explain its production, a production, to be precise, that lasted only a few years[77] but did not lack volume?[78]

Thompson proposed a political interpretation. Having emphasized how precarious the succession after Alexander was in 323, she suggested that the striking of a coinage with the name and types of Philip II was a means of strengthening the position of Philip III. The Macedonian authority thereby supposedly recalled that Philip III was the son of the great Philip and that he occupied the throne legitimately. Upon his death in the autumn of 317, this coinage ceased because any propaganda effort was now beside the point.

I have shown that this hypothesis is not entirely satisfactory.[79] Macedonia is the other region where gold (and silver) Philips were struck after 323; if these issues were made in the interest of Philip III, their end should have coincided with the latter's disappearance from the scene (as Thompson

---

76. Thompson has described them in detail, "Posthumous Philip II Staters of Asia Minor," *Studia Paulo Naster Oblata*, S. Scheers ed. (Louvain, 1982), pp. 57–61.

77. The Maeander hoard (*IGCH* 1294; Price, *NC* 9 [1969], pp. 9–10), buried c. 280–75, contains some later gold Philips, struck in other mints; but, as Thompson observes, these (very rare) coins can be regarded as city issues, i.e., non-royal, and they raise other problems than those concerning us here.

78. Thompson noted twenty-eight obverse dies at Lampsacus, twenty-one at Abydus, fourteen at Teos, nineteen at Colophon-Magnesia (she observed die transfers between these two centers), one at Sardis, and one at Miletus.

79. "Les deux monnaies macédoniennes des années 323–294/290," *BCH* 117 (1993), esp. pp. 497 and 499–500 (= *Études* III, pp. 1179 and 1181–82).

wrote apropos of Asia Minor). Yet, the striking of gold Philips may have lasted until about 315 in Macedonia, while silver Philips continued on until the start of the third century. So I cannot agree with a view that sees this coinage as an instrument of propaganda. I prefer a financial and commercial explanation.

Western Asia Minor, and especially Hellespontine Phrygia, maintained close relations with Macedonia, Thrace, and the Black Sea region, where the gold coinage *par excellence* at this time was Philip II's. When, after 323, Antipater thought it useful (for fiscal reasons, in my view)[80] to renew the striking that he had probably suspended a few years earlier (cf. p. 71), he prolonged this coinage's dominance. It is understandable that the satraps of Asia Minor produced quantities of gold Philips for their transactions with the regions of northern Greece, where they had not only to buy products but also to recruit mercenaries. The currency was all the more appealing to them because it probably enjoyed an advantageous rate in these territories.

The findspots of the oldest hoards containing gold Philips from Asia Minor show, in effect, that these coins were originally intended for the territories I have mentioned. Some specimens are present in the Mende deposit, in Macedonia, buried c. 320; in the finds from Iasna Poliana, in Bulgaria (on the Black Sea), from Lergoutsch in Moldavia (north of the Danube delta), buried c. 315; and in that from "Northern Greece," hidden around 310–305. After 300, the findspots are more scattered, but this does not mean that the coins did not have northern Greece and the Balkans as their prime destination.[81]

We have seen that the issuing of gold Philips from Asia Minor did not begin before 323. One might suppose that it started immediately after Antipater reinstated the striking of this coinage in Macedonia and gave it an advantage in local transactions. Antipater's decision might have occurred only c. 320, if one accepted that striking the gold Philips recommenced at the same time as the silver (cf. p. 72). Such a dating for the first Philips of Asia Minor would not be incompatible, it seems, either with the overall chronology of Alexander's coinages with which their mint marks associate them, or with the evidence from the hoards (the Mende hoard, containing a Philip from Miletus, not having been buried, perhaps, before 320). As for the last of

---

80. *Ibid.*, pp. 497–99 (= *Études*, pp. 1179–81). I supposed that the gold (and silver) Philips acquired a certain added value at this time in Macedonia.

81. For the Mende hoard, cf. Troxell, *Alexander* (1997), pp. 134–36, esp. p. 135, no. 61. For the other hoards, cf. my *Philippe II* (1977), pp. 264 ff.; also, Thompson, *Alexander's Drachm Mints* I and II, noting especially the precision she brings, I, pp. 76–77, to the subject of the find *IGCH* 801.

these staters, I would place them about the time when the gold coinage of Philip II ceased being produced in Macedonia, perhaps around 315.

What Coins Were Used in Asia Minor Between 334 and 323?

I have tried to show that Alexander's crossing in 334 did not significantly modify the coinage situation of western Asia Minor. So we may suppose that the currencies used in this region before the Macedonian conquest remained in circulation and that some of them continued to be struck in local mints.

Thus, we can assume that the use of Persian darics and sigloi, which were chiefly produced at Sardis, did not suddenly cease upon Alexander's arrival. We shall see (in chapter 7) that he probably used this coinage in the East; when Harpalus, to whom the king entrusted chief responsibility for financial affairs, chose to flee at the end of 325, he arrived in Athens and disbursed 1,000 darics to Demosthenes, according to the *Lives of the Ten Orators* (846 A). If this is correct, one would conclude that Persian gold coinage continued to play an important role in the Greek world at this time. Darics are also mentioned in some inscriptions from Delphi between 336 and 324/323.[82] The currency of the Great King, therefore, did not disappear overnight, and western Asia Minor, which was used to this coinage, probably continued to employ it for some years, because Alexander does not seem to have made any attempt to withdraw it.

In addition to darics and sigloi, local coinages, which their cities probably did not cease producing, functioned under Alexander as they had under the Persians. The chronology of civic issues remains a bit uncertain. For a long time there was a tendency to think that Alexander's arrival in 334 prompted termination of the cities' coinages. I have explained why this is a debatable viewpoint and why we have to accept that certain coinage series begun prior to 334 did not experience any interruption (at least not immediately) after the Macedonian occupation and, therefore, continued to supply the region with coined metal. It would not be very convincing to cite cities like Byzantium, Chalcedon, or Kios, which remained off Alexander's route. But, nearer to the theater of operations, events do not seem to have affected the mint of Cyzicus, for example.[83] One may assume that it was similar with other cities that came into direct contact with the Conqueror.

---

82. See my *Naissance*, p. 198.

83. G. Le Rider, *Deux trésors de la Propontide* (Bibl. archéol. et hist. de l'Institut d'Istanbul, Paris, 1963), pp. 42–50 (Byzantium and Chalcedon) and pp. 54–55 (Cyzicus).

We have seen how, after the monetary decisions Alexander had taken in Cilicia and Phoenicia, the mint at Amphipolis in Macedonia started to produce important quantities of silver Alexanders and also some amounts in gold. These coins, meant in large part to pay non-Macedonians, spread over the Aegean, and surely some of them quickly wound up in Asia Minor, entering into local circulation and making known the sovereign's new currency. Some Alexanders from Cilicia and Phoenicia probably mingled in this region with Alexanders from Amphipolis.

In concluding this chapter, I will say that examination of the coinage series struck with the name and types of Alexander in Asia Minor at the end of the fourth century and the evidence of a great, recently published hoard of Alexander drachms have led me to think that these issues did not begin c. 330, as previously supposed, but rather c. 325/324 and that at first, perhaps, they were limited to a select number of mints. I think we can explain Alexander's restraint in this matter. In 334, he did not yet have any truly personal coinage. Moreover, the example of the Great King, who had not struck darics or sigloi outside his satrapal cities and who had left to the Greek cities wide latitude in coinage affairs, deterred Alexander from assuming a less conciliatory stance right away. The task for scholars in coming decades will be to determine, with the help of new information, when and where the Alexanders of Asia Minor made their first appearance. It will then be easier to understand for what reasons and in what conditions this currency began. What we can suggest for now is that Alexander, who presented himself as the liberator of the Greek cities, and his immediate successors, who loudly proclaimed these cities' freedom, had an interest in seeing to it that the production of royal coinage by a civic mint did not appear as a diminution of local autonomy or as an additional financial burden. On the contrary, one might envisage a monetary cooperation that would have brought the cities some advantages without hindering their own coinage, if they had one and wanted to continue it.

Chapter 5

Alexander and Coinage in Cilicia, Phoenicia, Syria, and Cyprus

Toward the middle of 333, Alexander arrived at the Cilician Gates, which he daringly traversed without mishap (Arrian 2.4.3-4). He descended toward Tarsus so rapidly that the Persian Arsames could not complete the scorched-earth tactic he had undertaken (Curtius 3.4.3; 3.4.15).[1] Alexander entered Tarsus, where he fell ill either from exhaustion, according to Aristobulus, or from bathing in the frigid waters of the Cydnus River, according to others (Arrian 2.4.7). Once recovered, he went on to conquer all of Cilicia, and then rejoined Parmenio, who had occupied the Assyrian (or Syrian) Gates, situated at the Beylan Pass, which leads from Iskenderun into the plain of Antioch. Upon learning that Darius had crossed the mountain a little farther north via the Amanic Gates and was encamped near Issus, Alexander doubled back and at Issus engaged in his second great battle against the Persian forces (autumn 333). His victory made him master of Syria (where he named Menon satrap, the son of Cerdimmas: Arrian 2.13.7). It also gave him *entrée* into Phoenicia, where he received the surrender of Straton, son of Gerostratos, the king of Aradus; the surrenders of the kingdoms of Byblos and Sidon followed. Tyre, whose king, Azemilkos, was absent, refused to open its gates, and it required a six-month siege (January to July 332) to

---

1. Curtius severely criticizes Arsames's conduct, who, he says, would have done better to defend the Cilician Gates and the mountain passes controlling descent to the plain more vigorously. Curtius says that Arsames was in charge of Cilicia (*Ciliciae praeerat*): had he been named satrap of the province as Mazaeus's replacement, or was he only acting for the latter when Mazaeus was summoned to Darius's presence? On this issue, see my *Naissance*, pp. 220–21.

overcome the city's resistance (Arrian 2.15–24). A little farther to the south, Gaza also put up a bitter fight (Arrian 2.25.4; 26–27). It was only at the beginning of autumn 332 that Alexander could make his way to Egypt.

Financial and Monetary Questions

These new territories brought the Macedonian king substantial financial resources. Curtius (3.4.14) specifically describes Tarsus as a wealthy city, *opulentum oppidum*, and one imagines the Macedonians got their hands on a treasury of considerable importance. According to Herodotus (3.90), Cilicia all by itself constituted an entire region among the tax regions of Darius I. The established tribute amounted to 500 Babylonian talents (or 583 Euboic-Attic talents), supplemented by 360 white steeds (delivered one a day, Herodotus says): Cilicia was renowned for its excellent horses. With reference to these, Herodotus provides an interesting detail: of the 500 talents, 140 were earmarked for the cavalry stationed in the province, with the remaining 360 going to the Great King. The following region (the fifth on the Herodotean list) stretched from the city of Posideion all the way to Egypt; it included Phoenicia, Syria (called Palestine), and Cyprus, but excluded Arab territory. This region paid a tribute of 360 Babylonian talents (420 on the Euboic-Attic system).

As I suggested earlier, these tribute amounts had probably risen since Darius I's time (522–486). The King also collected numerous other taxes of every sort. He benefited additionally from the services of the remarkable Phoenician and Cypriote navies, while the intense commercial activity of the region's cities, especially Tyre and Sidon, surely offered the opportunity for highly remunerative tax revenues.

We may presume that the treasuries of Cilicia and Phoenicia, of which Alexander had become master, were quite full and that he received valuable gifts. His victory at Issus, moreover, brought him rich booty (Arrian 2.11.10 gives the figure of 3,000 talents) and opened the road to Damascus where Darius III, after the battle, had deposited the largest part of his money and the belongings from which he never parted, even while on campaign (Arrian 2.11.10). Alexander dispatched Parmenio to take possession of the Damascus treasure. Curtius's narrative of this episode (3.13) reads like a novel. The Persian governor's betrayal of Darius, his feigned flight, the panic he provokes among the ranks, the plain strewn with riches, the weight of the booty, the traitor's final punishment, Curtius recounts it all in highly colorful terms. Here is his description of the plunder (3.13.16): "The sum of coined money was 2,600 talents, the weight of wrought silver amounted to 500 pounds. Besides these, 30,000 men were captured, with 7,000 pack-animals carrying burdens on their backs" (Loeb modified).

Sometime after the Macedonians' arrival in Tarsus (summer 333), a monetary event of great consequence occurred: Alexander created his own silver currency with the types of Herakles head and seated Zeus holding an eagle. The gold currency with the types of Athena head and Nike holding a *stylis* appeared a little later. For the tetradrachms, it is owing to the dates inscribed on the Alexanders from Sidon that we know for a certainty that this coinage existed in 333/332.

The Sidon Mint Began Striking Alexander Tetradrachms in 333/332 (October 333 to September 332)

The chronological evidence of the Sidon mint is so critical that I think it is worthwhile to set forth the details of the Sidonian issues of this period.[2] I will then examine the mints of Tarsus and Tyre.

Alexander entered Sidon towards the end of autumn 333. The population received him cordially. King Straton, whose loyalty appeared to waver, was stripped of power and replaced by Abdalonymus. Curtius (4.1.15–26) provides a moralizing account of this episode, all to the credit of the new sovereign.

An Alexander coinage was produced at Sidon, following on the issues of civic types begun under the Persians a century before.[3] Identifying the Alexanders from this mint has not been difficult, because initially the first letter, and subsequently the first two letters of the city's name appear legibly on the coins. In the supply of Alexanders of this period, marks in local or Greek script indicate the coins' provenance so that numismatists can distinguish, to their general satisfaction, those issues struck in this region, in Phoenicia, on Cyprus, and, in one case, in Syria. The use of Phoenician and Cypriote (at Amathus) shows that the Macedonian administration sometimes entrusted the operations of the mints to non-Greek officials and allowed the latter a certain latitude. The use of these Phoenician or Cypriote signs, however, was generally short in duration. It lasted longest at Tyre.

The Alexanders from Sidon can be divided into five groups.

[Group One: the coins (we only know tetradrachms at this point) carry the Phoenician letter *sade*, Sidon's initial, "S," and are dated in Phoenician as year 1 (*aleph*; pl. 4, 2) and year 2 (*beth*).

Group Two: the coins (gold staters, tetradrachms, and small change in silver) are almost all marked with the letter Σ or the two letters ΣI, Sidon's

---

2. E. T. Newell studied them in *The Dated Alexander Coinage of Sidon and Ake* (New Haven, 1916), hereafter cited as *Sidon and Ake*. See now M. J. Price, *Alexander* (1991), pp. 435–44.

3. On these issues, see, for example, the short but instructive account of C. M. Kraay, *Archaic and Classical Greek Coins* (London, 1976), pp. 288–89.

Greek initials; they are not dated, but their style and die linkages confirm that they come between Groups One and Three (pl. 4, 3–4).

Group Three: the coins regularly bear ΣI; they are dated in Phoenician from year 7 to year 10 (from *zayn* to *yod*; cf. pl. 3, 5–7: numbers five and six carry the letter *teth*, the ninth letter of the alphabet; number seven carries the letter *yod*, tenth in the alphabet).

Group Four: the dates are now written in Greek; they go from *kappa* (year 10 in Greek numeration, cf. pl. 4, 8) to *omega* (year 24); it seems at first glance as if the switch from the Phoenician to the Greek alphabet occurred during year 10, and that is how Newell unhesitatingly read the situation in *Sidon and Ake*, as did Price in his *Alexander*. But in *Demanhur* (1923)[4] Newell proposed another interpretation: we have no Sidonian coin marked with a *lambda* (year 11), a surprising gap because the mint seems faithfully to have maintained the annual rhythm of its issues. Newell wondered whether a Phoenician engraver had not made a mistake: having received the order, in year 11, to inscribe the date in Greek, he traced the Greek letter K, the equivalent in Phoenician of *kaph*; now, *kaph* is the eleventh letter of the Phoenician alphabet, and it is this letter the coins would have carried if the date had continued to be written in local script. Newell's idea seems attractive to me, and we ought not to reject it out of hand, in my opinion.

Group Five: the coins are dated from year 1 to year 4 (A-Δ); die linkage and style make the group's place in the series certain (pl. 4, 10).]

The succession of alphabetic letters inscribed on the reverse of these Alexanders has always been interpreted as a year-by-year enumeration of issues. I do not believe this is debatable, since logic requires it, and stylistic observations and the study of coin hoards corroborate it as well. The Alexanders are dated at Tyre, too, and the correspondence in the hoards between the dates from Sidon and Tyre is significant. The Phoenician practice of indicating the year on coins goes back to the Persian period.

As for the dates of the Sidon Alexanders, two questions arise: What is the year of the first issue (marked by the letter *aleph*)? How are we to interpret this succession of letters?

The first question has elicited different answers.[5] As we shall see, however, only one is tenable, that which places year 1 in 333/332, between October 333 and September 332 on the Macedonian calendar. For even

---

4. Pp. 131–33.
5. In the *Annuaire de l'École pratique des Hautes Études 1968/1969* (Paris, 1969), pp. 182–86, I have set forth in detail the different working hypotheses. To wit: R. Dussaud, *RN* 12 (1908), pp. 445–54, thought that year 13 of Sidon, during which Philip III's name replaces Alexander's, was the year of Alexander's death and Philip's accession, i.e., 324/323; the

though we are dealing with Phoenicia, coins with the name and types of Alexander, constituting official instruments of the Macedonian administration, were surely dated according to the Macedonian calendar as it was used by the royal chancellery for all acts bearing the sovereign's seal.

[Scholars who study Sidonian chronology have noted that on some coins of the year 13 and on all those known from years 14, 15 (pl. 4, 9), and 16, Philip III's name replaced Alexander's. Philip III, declared king during the summer of 323, was assassinated at the start of autumn 317; his name, which had regularly appeared from year 13 to year 16, no longer figures on the coins from year 17. This suggests that year 16 was his last regnal year, i.e., 318/317; indeed, he probably died more toward the beginning of 317/316 than at the end of 318/317, but it is rather unlikely that Alexanders were struck in his name during the first weeks of autumn 317 at a time when he was a dead issue politically.

If, then, year 16 corresponded to 318/317, year 1 would fall in 333/332.

A piece of numismatic evidence, on which I. L. Merker has commented astutely, confirms this dating.[6] On one occasion, Ptolemy, satrap of Egypt, had some tetradrachms struck at Sidon with his name and types (horned head of Alexander covered with an elephant skin/eagle standing on a thunderbolt).[7] The two letters ΣI, placed on the reverse to the left of the eagle, confirm the issue's attribution to Sidon. What is particularly interesting about these coins is that they carry a date, indicated by the letter X, the twenty-second of the alphabet. So this date corresponds to year 22 in the Sidonian dating system, probably the date applied to the Sidonian Alexanders;[8] with year 1 corresponding to 333/332, year 22 falls in

---

coins would be dated according to an era of Alexander whose year 1 would coincide with his coming to the throne, i.e., 336/335 (E. J. Bickerman, *Chronology of the Ancient World*, London, 1968, p. 74, seems to approve of Dussaud, but his presentation is unclear); G. Kleiner, on the other hand, situated year 16, the last during which Philip's name was inscribed on the coins, in 317/316, right at the start of autumn 317, before this ruler's execution, which gave 333/332 as year 1 (*Alexanders Reichsmünzen*, Berlin, 1949, pp. 24–29, esp. p. 25); finally, J. Rouvier, "L'ère d'Alexandre le Grand en Phénicie," *REG* 12 (1899), pp. 362–81 (cf. *RN* 7 [1903], pp. 239–51), and Newell situated year 16 in 318/317 and wound up for year 1 with a date of 333/332, the year of Alexander's arrival in Sidon and the installation of Abdalonymus.

6. "Notes on Abdalonymus and the Dated Alexander Coinage of Sidon and Ake," *Amer. Num. Soc. Mus. Notes* 11 (1964), pp. 13–20, esp. pp. 13–14.

7. Merker knew of two specimens of this issue, produced from the same obverse die but from different reverse dies.

8. Merker noted two Alexander tetradrachms from Sidon, marked with the same letter, *chi* (one obverse die, two reverse): cf. Price, *Alexander* (1991), nos. 3511–12; Newell knew of only one.

312/311. Now it was precisely during the spring of 312 when Ptolemy made himself master of Sidon, after defeating Antigonus's son, Demetrius, at Gaza (Diodorus 19.86.1).[9] He prudently left the city some months later, when he learned that Antigonus had joined forces with Demetrius and was preparing to march against him (Diodorus 19.93.5–7; Pausanias 1.6.5; Plutarch, *Demetrius* 5–6). His stay in Phoenicia, nevertheless, was probably long enough to provide him the opportunity to produce an issue of Sidonian tetradrachms at the beginning of the year 312/311 (October 312 to September 311).]

We can therefore confidently accept that the first Alexander tetradrachms from Sidon, marked with year 1, were struck in 333/332. And so we possess an extremely valuable chronological reference point for the study of Alexander's coinage.

As for the second question raised above, how are we to interpret the numbering of the Sidonian Alexanders? Newell[10] suggested either that the battle of Issus (autumn 333) inaugurated an era of Alexander or that the new king Abdalonymus marked his regnal years in this way; Merker recalled these two possibilities without proposing any other. At Tyre, the dates correspond to the local ruler's regnal years in all probability, and that is why one might entertain the same interpretation for Sidon. Both theories come up against a difficulty: after the last and twenty-fourth letter of the alphabet, Ω, the enumeration begins all over again with the first letter, Α. Would using the era of Alexander have lasted only twenty-four years at Sidon and a new era (which?) been initiated? Or, indeed, would the reign of Abdalonymus have lasted just twenty-four years and would the numbers 1 through 4 that appear on the last Sidonian Alexanders designate the regnal years of his successor? I prefer to think instead, with Bickerman,[11] that these numbers 1–24 and 1–4 are simply annual marks coinciding with the opening of the mint and meant to distinguish the issues year by year.

After this brief overview of the mint at Sidon, we can accept that the name of Philip III was inscribed on this city's Alexanders only from 321/320 (year 13) and that it was regularly maintained until his death. Of course one cannot extrapolate from Sidonian practice to the other mints of the empire. But what makes this information important is that we have no other evidence by which to date the appearance of the legend *Philippou* on the coins of this period with certainty. The only other mint whose issues are

---

9. Ptolemy had already occupied Phoenicia between 320 and 315; Demetrius Poliorcetes controlled Sidon and Tyre until 287, when Ptolemy took long-lasting possession of Phoenicia, with the exception of Aradus and its mainland territory.

10. *Sidon and Ake*, p. 23.

11. *Chronology of the Ancient World*, p. 74; in alphabetic numbering, where the numbers 1 to 24 are indicated by the letters from Α to Ω, there are frequent examples where the number 25 is written ΑΑ, 26 is written ΒΒ, etc.

similarly dated, Tyre, never replaced *Alexandrou* with *Philippou*. In the previous chapter, I mentioned Bosworth's theory, which argued that Perdiccas did not definitively arrange the succession to Alexander until the end of summer or the beginning of autumn 322. I suggested, in this vein, that one might accept that the legends *Basileōs Alexandrou* and *Basileōs Philippou* (eventually shortened to *Alexandrou* and *Philippou*) were not employed before 322/321. The evidence from Sidon, isolated as it is, does not authorize us to conjecture that this practice first occurred only in 321/320.

I note, finally, that it was in 325/324 (year 9, pl. 4, 6) that the Sidon mint changed the position of Zeus's legs on the tetradrachms: the right leg, which previously was parallel to the left, is now drawn back. The other dated mint, Tyre, adopted this new posture in 322/321 (year 26 of Tyre), and the great Macedonian mint, Amphipolis, took it up around 315. It appears, with rare exceptions, on all the Alexanders from the end of the fourth century and during the third and second centuries. The Sidonians seem to have invented this "new style."

Alexander at Tarsus

The Tarsus Coinage of the Persian Satrap Mazaeus

During the Persian period, the inhabitants of Tarsus and Cilicia were among those peoples who, while under the power of the Great King, preserved local autonomy. Several authorities shared the province, including local dynasts and cities along the coast whose governing class and many of whose citizens were Greek in origin. The Great King's principal spokesman in the fifth century was the master of Tarsus, Syennesis, whose name modern authors use both as a proper name and as an official title, as in the phrase "the syennesis of Tarsus." This ruler seems to have lost his importance in the fourth century: the ancient authors no longer mention him. Yet we cannot establish that the Great King eliminated him.[12]

Artaxerxes III (359/358–338) had designated the Persian Mazaeus as governor of Cilicia, or, in any case, had confirmed him in office, if one prefers to place Mazaeus's nomination a little earlier, around 360. Diodorus (16.42.1) gives him the title *arkhōn*. Some time later, this high official also received responsibility for the Transeuphrates region, that is, Syria and Phoenicia. A group of his coins bears an inscription saying that he was "overseer of the Transeuphrates region and Cilicia." I indicated above (in the first footnote of this chapter) that some have wondered whether he still held this position in Cilicia at the time Alexander took control of Tarsus.

---

12. For Cilicia in the Persian period, I refer to the citations I gave in *Naissance*, pp. 207–37 (the chapter entitled "Le Grand Roi et le monnayage des dignitaires de l'Empire").

[The army marshals in Cilicia in the fourth century, successively Tiribazos, Pharnabazos, and Tarkumuwa, struck silver staters at the Tarsus mint on the Persian weight standard (10–11 grams) bearing their names (written in Aramaic) and types of their own choosing. It seems that these three individuals had an essentially military function, which would lead one to think that the local ruler of Tarsus, the syennesis, still preserved some political role. Mazaeus himself, as satrap, combined military and civilian responsibilities. The coinage he issued deserves our close attention because the figures of Baal of Tarsus (*Baaltars*) placed on the reverse of his coins are directly related to the images of Zeus engraved under Alexander. I will recall, before broaching this subject, that these Persian high officials produced coinage only with the Great King's assent; and I have suggested that the latter, for political reasons, avoided striking his gold darics and silver sigloi with the archer king as type anywhere else but in his royal mints (at Sardis and perhaps Dascylium). The coinage of his grandees, when produced, for example, at Tarsus, probably did not look like a royal coinage, either in its types, which evoked local features, or in its weight, which was double that of the royal siglos.[13]]

Mazaeus issued five groups of silver staters of Persian weight. Three of them have been attributed, without much discussion, to the Tarsus mint, while the classification of the other two has invited various hypotheses. I provide a brief description.[14]

[Group 1: Baaltars seated left, head in profile, holding a scepter in his left hand and an ear of wheat and a grape cluster in his right; the name of Baaltars, in Aramaic, is written to the right in the field; *on the reverse*, a lion attacking a deer; above, the name of Mazaeus in Aramaic; the scene is shown within an incuse square (with or without a dotted border) or in a linear circle (pl. 1, 3–4).

Group 2: Baaltars, head facing; he holds a scepter in his left hand; an eagle perches on his right, which also holds a wheat ear and a grape cluster; his name is written in Aramaic; *on the reverse*, lion attacking a bull; above, the name Mazaeus in Aramaic.

Group 3: Baaltars, seated left, head in profile, holding a scepter in his right hand, the left arm wrapped in a fold of his cloak; to the left, an ear of wheat and a grape cluster; to the right, the god's name in Aramaic; *on the reverse*, lion attacking a bull above two rows of fortified walls; Aramaic legend in half-circle: "Mazday (Mazaeus) overseer of the Transeuphrates and Cilicia" (pl. 6, 4).

Group 4: Baaltars as in Group 3; there is neither wheat ear nor grape cluster to the left; same inscription; *on the reverse*, lion advancing left; name

---

13. *Ibid.*, pp. 231–32.
14. For a more detailed description, *ibid.*, pp. 211–12.

of Mazaeus in Aramaic; the lion advances on uneven terrain, sometimes undulating, or on a dotted line; on some other coins, a star is placed above him, with a large lunar crescent below.

Group 5: Baaltars seated right, on a chair with back, wearing a headdress evoking the double crown of Upper and Lower Egypt;[15] in his left hand he holds a scepter ending in a lotus flower, in his right hand a lotus flower; his name, in Aramaic, is inscribed to the left; *on the reverse*, lion crouching to the left; above, a bow; there is no legend.

Newell ascribed Groups 4 and 5 to Myriandrus (which he imagined became the future Alexandria ad Issum, modern Iskenderun, which was in fact located some distance away). J. D. Bing preferred an Issus attribution. C. M. Harrison thought that the lion appearing on Mazaeus's Babylonian tetradrachms under Alexander followed directly upon the lion placed on the reverse of Group 4. In her opinion, this group was the last Mazaeus struck under Darius III, and the issuing mint should be located wherever it was that Mazaeus spent the time between 333 (Alexander's capture of Cilicia) and 331 (capture of Babylon). According to L. Mildenberg and E. Levante, Groups 4 and 5 are from Tarsus, just like Groups 1 through 3.[16]]

Alexander's Tetradrachms from Tarsus

The attribution of a group of Alexander tetradrachms to Tarsus rests principally on the fact that the Zeus of these tetradrachms and the chair on which he sits closely resemble the Baaltars and chair of Baaltars appearing on the obverse of certain Persian staters produced by Mazaeus at the Tarsus mint. The similarity between the Zeus illustrated in pl. 1, 1 (cf. pl. 4, 11–12) and the Baaltars of Mazaeus's Group One (pl. 1, 3–4) is striking. Every writer has emphasized this stylistic relationship, which is evident not only in the overall presentation of the two divinities (the left profile, the parallel legs, the scepter held in the left hand, etc.) but also in a great number of details (beaded and flowering scepter, footstool, chair decorations, etc.). As Price wrote, "the same engravers clearly turned from cutting dies for the Persians to producing those

---

15. This double crown is called *pschent* in Egyptian, *basileion* and *basileia* in Greek: cf. H. Seyrig, "Deux notes d'épigraphie relatives aux cultes alexandrins," *Annuaire de l'Institut de philol. et d'hist. orientales et slaves* 13 (1953), Mélanges Isidore Lévy, pp. 608–9 (= his *Scripta Varia*, Paris, 1985, pp. 728–29). On the coins we are describing, this headpiece is roughly sketched rather than accurately drawn; it is more a question of an imitation or evocation.

16. E. T. Newell, *Myriandros-Alexandria kat'Isson* (New York, 1920 = *AJN* 53 (1919), pp. 16–29; J. D. Bing, "Reattribution of the 'Myriandros' Alexanders: The Case for Issus," *AJN* 1 (1989), pp. 1–24; C. M. Harrison, *Coins of the Persian Satraps* (dissertation, Univ. of Pennsylvania, 1982), pp. 361–66; L. Mildenberg, "Notes on the coin issues of Mazday," *Israel Num. Jour.* 11 (1990–91), pp. 9–23 (= *Vestigia Leonis*, 1998, pp. 43–53); E. Levante, *SNG Switzerland* I, Levant-Cilicia (1986), no. 181 (note).

of the imperial Macedonian coinage. Details of the throne, drapery, and figure can be closely compared in the two series."[17] Price concluded that there was no serious break in the output of the Tarsus mint: the Alexander tetradrachms took over very quickly where the silver Persian staters left off.

Tarsus was quite probably the first eastern mint to strike Alexander's tetradrachms. To be sure, the Zeus of the Alexanders from Sidon is also quite close to the Baaltars of Mazaeus, and one could imagine a Sidonian artisan, charged with engraving a Zeus for Alexander, copying the Baaltars of our Group One; in this case, Tarsus's production of Alexanders would have started only after Sidon's. If I entertain this possibility, it is because of the suggestion that Alexander inaugurated his coinage in the wake of the battle of Issus, when he would have been halfway between Tarsus and Sidon. I personally am also inclined to think that Alexander's coinage debuted after Issus. But even so, it seems plausible to me that the Conqueror ordered the Tarsus mint, rather than a neighboring one, to strike his first tetradrachms. It was at Tarsus that he had coins with the type of Baaltars, in whom he instinctively recognized Zeus, right before his eyes; when he decided to transform Baaltars into Zeus on the reverse of his tetradrachms, it is plausible that he ordered an engraver from Tarsus to set the image. Moreover, he had been holding Tarsus for two or three months when he joined battle at Issus; Tarsus is where he had named those who were to be responsible for local and provincial administration; and it was in this city that he could strike his very own coinage with complete confidence, at a time when he was proceeding to the conquest of Phoenicia where he had still to establish the signs of his power.

Tarsus would therefore possess a glorious and prestigious claim: its mint would have been the first in the entire empire to produce the great silver coinage of Alexander that was to have such a brilliant and lasting posterity. For, we may recall, several details in the presentation of the Zeus type led us to conclude that the first Alexanders struck in Macedonia were engraved according to a model from Tarsus. I set forth in chapter 1 the arguments favoring this thesis, and they, to my mind, outweigh those to the contrary.

Is it possible to determine why Alexander decided, around the end of 333, to strike his own silver coinage?

When and Why Alexander Decided to Issue His Own Silver Coinage with the Types of Herakles Head and Seated Zeus

The close ties between the first Alexanders from Tarsus and certain of the Mazaeus staters led Price, as I have said, to think that the same engravers

---

17. *Alexander* (1991), p. 369.

remained at work and that the two series succeeded one another without much of an interruption. Because Alexander entered the city after the start of summer 333, one might suppose that it was during that time, while he was staying in Cilicia, that he inaugurated his silver coinage with Herakles head.

The situation was favorable. A royal dynast had reigned at Tarsus in fealty to the Great King, and the Tarsus mint had produced coins for the former. In the fourth century, Persian high officials had struck plentiful series of silver staters there. Alexander's coinage, consequently, would fit in very naturally with this sequence of issues.

Moreover, the Macedonian king found himself in a position quite different from that in western Asia Minor. Here, the slogan of freeing the Greek cities no longer applied. His expedition had openly become a war of conquest. He had seized territories where the Greek element was not in the majority. In Cilicia, the population of a city like Tarsus was probably of local origin for the most part, with the native born outnumbering the Persians and Greeks resident there. Alexander could act as he pleased and fully exercise his prerogatives by right of conquest.

Finally, one might argue that his discovery of the Baaltars type gave him the idea for creating a personal coinage emblazoned with a seated Zeus.

All these arguments have to be considered. Yet, up until this time (summer 333), Alexander displayed no discernible need to innovate in monetary matters. He was content to employ the kinds of coins he found along his route for operations requiring the use of currency. Why all of a sudden at Tarsus would he have decided to inaugurate a coinage with his name and types? There was nothing special about his entry into this city: Parmenio was sent with light-armed troops to extinguish the fire Arsames had set (Curtius 3.4.15). Alexander arrived a little later, apparently without any particular fanfare.

I would thus be tempted to connect the creation of Alexander's silver coinage to a more decisive event: did not Alexander make this decision following the great victory at Issus, won during the autumn of 333? Zervos thought as much, without commenting on the idea.[18] Of course, our desiring to have the start of a coinage or a monetary reform coincide with a single event, whether political or military, is dangerous. C. M. Kraay[19] has warned against it, citing object lessons that counsel the greatest caution. It is certain that a government's adoption of a new currency or modification of an

---

18. *NC* 142 (1982), p. 177; cf. above, chapter 1, p. 13.

19. *Greek Coins and History* (London, 1969). Kraay has assembled numerous instances where scholars have committed serious errors by associating a given monetary event with a precise historical occurrence. He writes, p. 2: "But if the coins are placed in a wrong context, they may constitute formidable obstacles to the true understanding of major episodes of ancient history."

existing system frequently derive from fiscal and economic imperatives that can manifest themselves just as easily in settled as in more dramatic times.

The case of Alexander is admittedly a little different. He spent the thirteen years of his reign waging war, and his brilliant successes followed upon one another uninterruptedly. Whatever the date suggested for the commencement of his coinage, it would have to come in the wake of one of his exploits. All the Conqueror's successes did not, however, have the same repercussions. Some of them enjoyed only local importance. Others, in contrast, opened up new, perhaps unexpected vistas for the hero, and prompted him to undertake actions equal to the occasion.

The victory at Issus was resounding, even if Darius continued the struggle and serious obstacles (Tyre, Gaza) soon loomed on the Macedonian king's route. The historical tradition has transmitted the text of letters that the two protagonists exchanged,[20] where the vanquished proposes increasingly favorable terms to the victor and Alexander responds to Darius scathingly. Although this evidence needs to be viewed quite critically (Briant's skepticism seems to me the right approach), the proposals Arrian (2.14.8–9) attributes to Alexander probably show rather accurately what the Conqueror and Macedonian propaganda wanted to convey at this time. Here is what Alexander supposedly wrote to Darius: "You must then regard me as Lord of all Asia and come to me. . . . And in future when you send to me, make your addresses to the king of Asia, and do not correspond as an equal, but tell me, as lord of all your possessions, what you need."

After Issus, therefore, Alexander portrayed himself as the new master of all Asia, as the ever-triumphant ruler over the immense empire that once belonged to the Great King. The victory legitimated this claim. If Alexander was bound to create a coinage with his name and types, now was the acceptable time, it seems to me. In these territories where every local dynast struck his own coins, the issuing of his own currency provided the Conqueror with an additional way to broadcast his sovereignty effectively. His name and types would eclipse those of the satrap Mazaeus, as well as those of the Phoenician and Cypriote princes; his coinage would become the royal coinage of the entire region.

Such might be the confluence of events and motivation that determined Alexander, toward the end of 333, to create his own tetradrachms

---

20. Bosworth, *A Historical Commentary* I (Oxford, 1980), pp. 227–29, has commented on the problem of the letters Darius and Alexander exchanged after Issus. P. Briant, *From Cyrus to Alexander: A History of the Persian Empire*, Eng. trans. by P. T. Daniels (Winona Lake, IN, 2002), pp. 832–40, has studied them convincingly in depth. He does not deny the reality of diplomatic overtures between the two sovereigns after Issus, but he thinks that the texts Diodorus, Plutarch, Curtius, and Arrian transmit are the result of Macedonian falsification, and his argument is compelling.

with Herakles head and seated Zeus. I will not pretend, however, that this convergence is the only one possible. It looks highly probable to me, but one might well imagine, as I have said, that it was in Tarsus, before Issus, that Alexander made this decision. In any case, the existence of Alexander tetradrachms is attested in 333/332: whatever circumstance may have provoked their birth, it occurred before the end of September 322.

Comments on the Types of Alexander's Tetradrachms

The types Alexander placed on his silver tetradrachms have a very pronounced Macedonian and Greek character. Even so, they do not lack ties with eastern cults, and they were probably selected in part for this very reason.

Herakles and Zeus were unquestionably the two great Macedonian divinities. Herakles was considered the ancestor of the Temenid dynasty to which Alexander belonged. The mythical founder of this dynasty, who came from Argos, was indeed Temenos, Herakles's direct descendant, and the ties of the Temenids with this divinity are frequently mentioned. Isocrates, especially, in the passage where he asks Philip II to take Herakles as a model (*Philip* 105–110), points out to the king that this god was the author (*arkhēgos*) and ancestor (*progonos*) of his race (*genos*). Macedonian sovereigns often chose Herakles as a coinage type. Philip II put Herakles's beardless head on the obverse of his silver didrachms and drachms, as well as on the obverse of his gold half-, quarter- and eighth-staters. We saw above (p. 11) Alexander's piety to this god.

Zeus was the lord of Olympus whose southern slopes had sheltered the first Macedonians. He was, moreover, the father of the hero Macedon. Numerous pieces of evidence attest to the veneration surrounding him in Macedonia.[21] I will recall here that king Archelaus I (413–400/399) established the Olympia at Dion in Pieria in his and the Muses' honor, and that Demosthenes (*On the Embassy* 192) depicts Philip celebrating this festival after the capture of Olynthus. On Macedonian coins, the eagle of Zeus is seen under Archelaus I, Amyntas III, and Perdiccas II. Philip II put the god's head on the obverse of his tetradrachms, and it also appears on the obverse of Alexander's "eagle" tetradrachms, which carry on the reverse the god's eagle and thunderbolt (cf. above, p. 32).

If Macedonia particularly honored Herakles and Zeus, the rest of the Greek world was fervent in their cult, and they also suited perfectly the eastern countries Alexander had conquered or was going to conquer. In

---

21. W. Baege, *De Macedonum Sacris* (Diss. Halle, 1913), pp. 1–19, gives a list of various texts and documents.

Tarsus, the indigenous god Sandan (or Sandon, Sandes, Sandas), whose animal was the lion, was assimilated to Herakles;[22] the latter is also shown in his Greek aspect on the silver staters from the first half of the fourth century with the legend *Tersikon*: his head in three-quarter profile, with lionskin headdress, appears on one issue; another shows him struggling with the lion;[23] and obols of Persian weight, probably struck during the time of Mazaeus, likewise bear Herakles's facing head.[24] The Greeks also considered the great god of Tyre, Melkart, to be an avatar of Herakles.[25] When relating Alexander's arrival before Tyre, Arrian (2.16.1) says as follows: "At Tyre there is the most ancient temple of Heracles of which there is any human recollection, not the Argive Heracles, son of Alcmene, for a Heracles was honored at Tyre many generations before Cadmus sailed from Phoenicia..." Arrian (2.16.2) adds: "The Egyptians too worship another Heracles, different from the Heracles of Tyre and the Heracles of Greece." Earlier, in the fifth century BC, Herodotus (2.44) was already writing: "I took ship to Tyre in Phoenicia, where I heard that there was a very holy temple of Heracles... and in converse with the priests [learned] that the temple of the god was founded when Tyre first became a city, and that was 2,300 years since." Herodotus adds that he saw another sanctuary at Tyre dedicated to Herakles under the name of Herakles of Thasos, and that he found on Thasos a sanctuary of Herakles the Phoenicians had established.[26]

As for the type of Zeus Alexander chose, it could not help but evoke their Baals for the people of the Near East, their god who ruled heaven and earth. Just as the Macedonians could recognize their Zeus in the Baal of Tarsus, so the inhabitants of these regions could find some connection in the two images, as they beheld the Alexander Zeus in a pose identical to that of Baaltars holding a scepter and an eagle, as Baaltars sometimes did.

---

22. L. Robert, *Documents d'Asie Mineure* (Paris, 1987), pp. 54–55 (= *BCH* 101 [1977], pp. 96–97); P. Chuvin, "Apollon au trident et les dieux de Tarse," *Journal des Savants* (1981), pp. 319–25.

23. C. M. Kraay, *Archaic and Classical Greek Coins* (London, 1976), pl. 60, 1038 and 1041.

24. G. Le Rider, "Un trésor d'oboles de poids persique," *Trésors et circulation monétaire en Anatolie* (Paris, 1994), pp. 13–14 (= *Études d'histoire monétaire et financière* II, Athens, 1999, pp. 743–44).

25. On the Melkart of Tyre and Herakles, see H. Seyrig, "Héraclès-Nergal," *Syria* 24 (1945), pp. 69–74 (= *Ant. Syriennes* 4 [1953], pp. 8–13); E. Will, "Intégration des divinités orientales dans la civilisation gréco-romaine," *Mythologie gréco-romaine, Mythologies périphériques* (Paris, 1981), pp. 158–59 (= *De l'Euphrate au Rhin*, Beirut, 1995, pp. 108–9).

26. On this passage of Herodotus, see H. Seyrig, "Quatre cultes de Thasos," *BCH* 51 (1927), pp. 185–98, and "Note additionnelle," *ibid.*, pp. 369–79 (= *Scripta Varia*, Paris, 1985, pp. 534–47 and 585–89); J. Pouilloux, *Recherches sur l'histoire et les cultes de Thasos* (Paris, 1954), pp. 20–21 and 352–57.

The silver currency Alexander inaugurated in 333 would show images, therefore, that, while featuring the divinities' Greco-Macedonian aspect, did not appear totally foreign to eastern natives.

Alexander and Tyre

The siege of Tyre was long and difficult. It lasted more than six months, from January to July 332, and caused Alexander moments of despair. The ancient authors emphasized his technical prowess in constructing a causeway between the shoreline and the island of Tyre, the latter protected by mighty ramparts (Arrian 2.18.2–3). The battles were deadly. The Macedonians suffered around 400 fatalities (Arrian 2.24.4). The Tyrians lost 8,000 men, of whom 2,000 perished after the cessation of hostilities (they were crucified: Curtius 4.4.16-17);[27] women and children remaining on the island were sold into slavery (Diodorus 17.46.4), while according to Arrian (2.24.5), the victor sold 30,000 prisoners, Tyrian and foreign.

But a part of the population was saved. A good number of women and children had been sent to Carthage, a Tyrian colony (Diodorus 17.41.2; Curtius 4.3.20; Justin 11.10.14). The Sidonians who entered the city with Alexander (they were an auxiliary corps of the Macedonian army) saved 15,000 Tyrians at the last moment (Curtius 4.4.15–16). Moreover, the king spared those of the enemy who had taken refuge in the sanctuary of Herakles. These included the most important Tyrian magistrates, the king Azemilkos, and some Carthaginian envoys who had come to the mother country to honor Herakles, following an ancient custom (Arrian 2.24.5). By resettling new inhabitants, Alexander saw to it that the city was not too depopulated (Justin 18.3.19).

We should not underestimate the damage the city endured, but neither should we exaggerate it. Curtius does speak of "ruin" (*excidium*), but he employs this word in a sentence of lyrical flight: "Having therefore suffered many disasters and having risen again from their ruin, now at last wholly restored by long-continued peace, they are at rest under the protection of Roman clemency" (4.4.21). The other ancient authors, Arrian and Diodorus, are quite discreet about the ravages of the siege. One might even infer from Diodorus (17.46.6) that the city never ceased being habitable: during the siege, a resident of Tyre heard Apollo say in a vision that he was going to leave the city, so the Tyrians bound the god's statue to its pedestal

---

27. Arrian 2.24.4 gives the figure of 8,000 dead. Diodorus 17.46.3–4 says that the surviving Tyrian combatants numbered more than 7,000 and they were all massacred "except a few"; he then adds Alexander ordered crucified all those who were of military age, and these numbered not less than 2,000.

with chains of gold (Diodorus 17.41.7–8). Alexander, after his victory, had the chains removed[28] and then performed magnificent sacrifices in honor of Herakles (Diodorus 17.46.5), a ceremony that may have taken place inside the city on the altar of Melkart's sanctuary. So not everything would have been destroyed.

Some months later, in the spring of 331 on his way back from Egypt, the king spent several days at Tyre. According to Arrian's account (3.6.1–2), he sacrificed once more to Herakles, organized athletic and artistic competitions, received a delegation from Athens, and took major administrative actions.[29] If Tyre had been an utter ruin in July 332, Alexander would have chosen another stopping point in April 331. Surely the Conqueror was too prudent to allow the total destruction of such a strategically and commercially important city, whose outstanding services he could draw upon.[30]

Tyre, Not Ake, must be the Location of an Alexander Mint

It was accepted opinion until 1976 that a handsome series of silver and gold Alexanders was struck in a Phoenician mint located at Ake (Akko, Acre). Then A. Lemaire published an article questioning this opinion and proposing Tyre as the site where the series under discussion was issued.[31] Lemaire's arguments convinced me immediately and completely.

The series, which Newell had closely studied (*Sidon and Ake*), begins with three issues of tetradrachms, with a thunderbolt as a mark, or an M sometimes associated with what is variously described as a pellet or globule (pl. 4, 13), or the letters $\Sigma\Omega$.[32]

---

28. "The king . . . gave orders that the god should be called 'Apollo Philalexander'."
29. He put Coeranus in charge of the tributes from Phoenicia and Philoxenus of those from Asia Minor (cf. above, p. 99); he made Harpalus overseer of the treasure he carried with him; perhaps at Tyre, or while en route between Tyre and Thapsacus, he named the new satraps of Lydia and Syria (Arrian 3.6.4–8).
30. See the apposite reflections of H. Seyrig, "Sur une prétendue ère tyrienne," *Syria* 34 (1957), p. 97 (= *Ant. Syr.* 5 [1958], p. 159).
31. "Le monnayage de Tyr et celui dit d'Akko dans la deuxième moitié du IVe siècle avant J.-C.," *RN* 18 (1976), pp. 11–24; see also the same author's "Populations et territoires de la Palestine à l'époque perse," *Transeuphratène* 3 (1990), pp. 59–63; "Le royaume de Tyr dans la seconde moitié du IVe siècle avant J.-C.," *Atti del II Congresso intern. di studi fenici e punici* I (Rome, 1991), pp. 131–49, esp. pp. 133–36 and 146–48; "Histoire et administration de la Palestine à l'époque perse," in E.-M. Laperrousaz, *La Palestine à l'époque perse* (Paris, 1994), pp. 37–39.
32. See Newell, *Sidon and Ake*, p. 39ff., and M. J. Price, *Alexander* (1991), pp. 408–14. A marked stylistic similarity connects the three issues just mentioned; in addition, obverse die linkages connect the second and third issues with subsequent coins bearing the letter *ayn*.

The following group bears the Phoenician letter *ayn* (pl. 4, 14 and 5, 1). Another group follows, where a *kaph* is added to the letter *ayn*: that is, an inverted, reverse "k" and o (pl. 5, 2; the *kaph* after a while has a simplified form); these two letters appear subsequently on all the issues. A date written in Phoenician soon accompanies them, beginning with year 20 and progressing to year 39 (cf. pl. 5, 3–4: year 26 and year 28). Next, year 39 is followed by year 8 and the series concludes with year 11 (pl. 5, 6). Other than the *ayn/kaph* inscription and date, no other mark is inscribed in the field of the reverse except for an *aleph* that appears on several coins of the years 26–29 and the Greek letters TY that appear on bronze coins of large and small diameter. Some of the large bronzes are dated year 26 while others are not dated (pl. 5, 5); the small bronzes are not dated either and also do not carry the letters *ayn* and *kaph*.[33]

The interpretation of the two letters *ayn* and *kaph* as the initials of Ake goes far back. In his *Numismatique d'Alexandre le Grand*, published in 1855, L. Müller (p. 303) noted that J. Pellerin, in the eighteenth century, had proposed this explanation, which Müller favored. Newell, with his customary talent, lent considerable strength to this opinion. In his view, Alexander began striking coins at Ake during the siege of Tyre; Ake, he wrote, was a strategic position that the Macedonians had securely occupied since the start of 332 and that was still quite useful after the capture of Tyre when they attacked Gaza. The dates (year 20 to year 39), Newell continued, are those of a local dynast whom Alexander maintained in power. In hoards like Demanhur containing dated coins from Sidon and "Ake," one notes most often a difference of fourteen years between the two datings.[34] Take, for example, the Demanhur hoard: its latest Sidonian tetradrachm is from year 15, that from Sidon from year 29; because it is certain that year 1 of Sidon is to be placed in 333/332, year 1 of "Ake" falls in 347/346.[35] Newell concluded that the ruling dynast of Ake, when Alexander arrived, had been in power since this date and that he apparently kept his throne until the

---

33. Cf. J. and A. G. Elayi, *RN* 153 (1998), pp. 107ff.

34. In the Akçakale hoard which I have published with N. Olcay, *RN* 30 (1988), pp. 42–54 (= *Études d'hist. monétaire et financière du monde grec* II, Athens, 1999, pp. 761–79), the difference is fifteen years.

35. Price, *Alexander* (1991), pp. 406–7, puts year 1 of Ake in 346/345; he thinks, in fact, that the beginning of the year at Ake did not necessarily coincide with the beginning of the year as observed by the Sidonians when they started to strike Alexanders. For Price, this dating has the advantage that in 346/345 the Persians reestablished their power over Phoenicia, after the revolt of Tennes, king of Sidon, had compromised it. They would then have installed a new prince at Ake, completely loyal to them. Putting aside any discussion of the mint's location (which, I am convinced, is Tyre and not Ake), I think that the Macedonians, for their official documents (and Alexander's coins are official documents), imposed the use of the Macedonian calendar on the conquered territories.

year 39 (= 309/308). The following dates (year 8 to year 11, cf. pl. 5, 6) are more difficult to explain, and I will come back to them.

For a long time, scholars of Phoenicia have accepted without discussion the existence of an Alexander mint at Ake and the presence of a king in 332 who allegedly came to power under the Persians and obtained the goodwill of the Macedonian conqueror. The history of Ake was thereby considerably enriched.[36]

Without doubt Ake had genuine strategic importance. Between 380 and 370, Pharnabazos, leader of the Persian army, used it as a base of operations when Artaxerxes II entrusted him with the reconquest of Egypt (Diodorus 15.41.3; Strabo 16.2.25). Still, one might observe that not a single text attests to Ake as the capital of a royal territory, and no coinage from the Persian period can be attributed to Ake. On the contrary, it seems that this site belonged to the kingdom of Tyre. Lemaire, who shares this opinion, notes that a graffito, uncovered at Abydos in Egypt and dating from before Alexander, mentions a man from Ake who is described as Tyrian.[37]

On the other hand, is it not startling that a great city like Tyre, which had coined so prolifically under the Persians, saw its coinage activity cease in the time of Alexander until the end of the fourth century? Attribution of an Alexander currency comes only after 305–300.[38] Would the Tyre mint have remained dormant for nearly thirty years, when the other cities of Phoenicia, large and small, were continually or occasionally issuing Alexanders? This monetary demotion of Tyre seems strange, especially considering how rapidly the city overcame the shock of its defeat in 332.

So Lemaire's proposal to attribute to Tyre all the Alexander coinage Newell had attributed to Ake was greeted with great interest. His arguments are solid and, in my view, decisive.

Lemaire's novel idea[39] was that the letters *ayn/kaph* do not designate a place but a person. It frequently occurred in Phoenicia under Persian domination that the name of the local dynast was inscribed on the currency he issued, and it happened rather often that his regnal years were also indicated. If, then, the two letters in question refer to a king's name, they can represent either the first two letters of this name (abbreviation by shortening) or the name's first and last letters (abbreviation by contraction); the latter is numismatically well-attested in Phoenicia, in both the

---

36. M. Dothan has excavated the site of Akko; cf., e.g., "Akko: Interim Excavation Report, First Season, 1973/1974," *Bull. American Schools of Oriental Research* 224 (1976), pp. 1–48. Dothan died before being able to synthesize his work on Akko.

37. *Transeuphratène* 3 (1990), p. 60.

38. E. T. Newell, *Tyrus rediviva* (New York, 1923); M. J. Price, *Alexander* (1991), pp. 444–47; C. A. Hersh, "Tyrus rediviva reconsidered," *AJN* 10 (1998), pp. 41–59.

39. *RN* 18 (1976), pp. 11–24.

Persian and Greco-Roman periods, as well as in other regions like Syria and Asia Minor.[40]

It so happens that we know of a king whose contracted name would be written *ayn/kaph*: it is '*zmlk*, in Greek Azemilkos, the sovereign who ruled the Tyrians when Alexander arrived before the city. When Tyre fell, Azemilkos sought refuge in the temple of Melkart-Herakles, and the Conqueror spared him (Arrian 2.24.5). Lemaire suggests that he retained his throne.[41] This is a plausible supposition, in my opinion, because Alexander could be generous: when the kings of Cyprus came to offer homage, he forgave their earlier attitude, judging that they had supported the Persians more out of duress than free choice (Arrian 2.20.3). Azemilkos could have argued in his own defense that he was absent from Tyre at the time when the Tyrian delegation's response provoked Alexander to undertake the city's siege. According to Arrian (2.15.7), the Tyrian ruler was then at sea with the Persian admiral Autophradates. Azemilkos must have had real negotiating skills if his reign truly lasted thirty-nine years, for, after the death of Alexander, the Macedonian successors fought over Tyre and Sidon bitterly, not making it easy for a local ruler to retain his crown.

I note that, on Lemaire's hypothesis, the Greek letters TY on the bronze coins of the year 26 and on other undated bronzes (pl. 5, 5) can be seen as the beginning of Ty(riōn), "of the Tyrians." One might object, as Price did, that we are dealing here with a mint magistrate's signature: on the silver coins of the years 26–29, the Phoenician letter *aleph* that I mentioned above may designate an official of the mint. This objection is not to be dismissed, but the resolution of TY into Ty(riōn) is tempting.

We have seen that after the year 39, the last year of Azemilkos, dates going from year 8 to year 11 follow, always accompanied by the letters *ayn/kaph*. Lemaire interprets these dates as the regnal years of a sovereign who would have originally been associated in rule as coregent and who assumed sole power only after the eighth year of his mandate; this new king could also have been called Azemilkos[42] or had another name beginning

---

40. See the examples H. Seyrig collected, *Notes on Syrian Coins* (Num. Notes and Mon. 119, New York, 1950), pp. 23–28. Lemaire, *RN* 18 (1976), p. 17, found an example of this type of abbreviation on an issue from Byblos in the Persian period. Seyrig established the same practice on the coins of Aradus from the second and first centuries BC, noting some similar cases at Tyre (first century BC), Cilicia, Smyrna, in an inscription from Hauran, and at Gabala in the time of the emperor Commodus.

41. Diodorus 17.46.6 and 47.1–6 is mistaken in locating at Tyre an episode that occurred at Sidon; it is, in fact, at Sidon, not Tyre, that Hephaestion named Abdalonymus king with Alexander's authorization and approval; cf. P. Goukowsky, *Diodore de Sicile, Livre XVII* (Paris, 1976), p. 200.

42. He would have been the son or grandson of his predecessor; Lemaire, op. cit., p.21, remarks that there are several examples in Phoenicia of grandsons having the names of their grandfathers.

with *ayn* and ending with *kaph*, as in the case of the dynast from Byblos, Adrimilk (Adramelek). This conjecture seems as plausible to me as Newell's, who calculated the years 8 to 11 from a Phoenician period of Antigonus the One-Eyed, a period attested only by this single piece of numismatic evidence.

Price, in 1979, recognized the merits of Lemaire's proposal, but he did not agree.[43] In 1991, in his great inventory of Alexander's coins, he attributed the entire series to Ake, without the slightest question.[44] This is very regrettable in my view because his book will remain the standard in the field for a long time. People will continue to cite Ake, without challenge, as a great Persian and Alexander mint[45] with the historical consequences that this entails (thus Antigonus's Phoenician period still has a long life ahead of it). I myself think it highly improbable that Ake struck coins under the Persians or under Alexander and his immediate successors. It is at Tyre, "a city worthy of note in the memory of later times both for its ancient origin and its frequent changes of fortune" (Curtius 4.4.19), where it is appropriate, I am persuaded, to attribute the coinage series marked with the letters *ayn/kaph* (or simply *ayn* at the start).

Beginning and End of Alexanders from Tyre

The first Tyrian Alexanders bearing a date (always in Phoenician) are of the year 20 of Azemilkos. We have observed that there was probably a fourteen-year difference between the Tyrian and Sidonian datings; if that is true, Tyre's year 20 then corresponds to Sidon's year 6 and falls accordingly in 328/327 (putting year 1, we have seen, in 347/346).

Several undated issues precede the coins of the year 20, bearing in succession the following marks: thunderbolt, M, $\Sigma\Omega$ the Phoenician letter *ayn*, and the two letters *ayn/kaph*.

Tyre fell in July 332. Theoretically, the mint could have commenced producing Alexanders from the end of the Macedonian year 333/332 that concluded in September 332. Yet even if one accepts that the city resumed activity quickly, it might be preferable to put the opening of Alexander's mint only in 332/331. Alexander's sojourn at Tyre in the spring of 331 was, perhaps, the occasion for this opening because the Conqueror's passage actually did entail large expenses that had to be settled at least partly in

---

43. "On Attributing Alexanders, Some Cautionary Tales," in *Essays in Honor of Margaret Thompson*, Otto Mørkholm et al. eds. (Wetteren, 1979), pp. 241–46.

44. *Alexander* (1991), pp. 405–7.

45. In the collection *Coin Hoards* 8 (1994), Ake is cited unquestioningly as one of the mints of Alexander: cf., for example, nos. 185, 189, 201. Similarly, Troxell, *Alexander* (1997), p. 80, nos. 29 and 31, speaks of the Ake mint without raising the slightest doubt.

coined currency. Festivals were organized; an Athenian delegation was welcomed, undoubtedly with pomp and circumstance; Amphoterus left with a fleet for the Peloponnesus, and the Phoenicians and Cypriotes were ordered to fit out 100 additional ships to join up with him. Some Phoenician soldiers were probably incorporated into Alexander's army, for Arrian (*Indica* 18.1) reports that the king, as he was selecting crews in 326, on the banks of the Hyphasis (a tributary of the Indus), "picked out all the Phoenicians, Cypriotes, and Egyptians who had followed the expedition up-country." Among these men, some had probably been recruited in 331.

The Macedonian king's financial requirements in spring 331 might therefore have prompted him to start coining Alexanders at Tyre. In Newell's classification, the mint struck only silver tetradrachms at first. I will examine later a suggestion of Price[46] in which a puzzling group of gold coins that Newell put at the beginning of Sidon's coinage would revert, perhaps, to Tyre (Ake for Price); I myself will propose attributing it to Tarsus.

Year 39, Azemilkos's last (assuming, as I believe, he really is the person concerned), falls in 309/308. The eighth year of his successor could also correspond to 309/308: the same obverse die has been linked to some reverse dies of year 39 and of year 8, in which case year 11 (pl. 5, 6) would correspond to 306/305. This year 11 marks the end of the Alexander coinage at Tyre bearing the name of the local king and the latter's regnal years in Phoenician.

One will recall that the Alexander coinage of Sidon also ceased in 306/305. This is not, perhaps, a simple coincidence, but it is difficult to explain. At this time, Phoenicia was under the control of Antigonus, who had become its master after driving out Ptolemy at the end of 312 or the start of 311. Should one see in the monetary events at Tyre and Sidon an intervention by Antigonus? In 306, in the wake of his son Demetrius's dazzling victory over Ptolemy at Salamis, Antigonus took the title of king and conferred it on Demetrius. He was now at the height of his power. But why would he have interrupted the coinage of the two cities in question? If he did it deliberately, the reason for his decision remains unclear.

After this interruption, Sidon never resumed issuing an Alexander coinage. Tyre, in contrast, struck gold and silver Alexanders again soon after. So it seems Newell rightly attributed to this latter city a group of coins characterized on the reverse by the presence of two Greek monograms in circles (pl. 5, 7)[47] with one of the monograms sometimes replaced by a club (in a circle, or not). Some tetradrachms with Alexander types continue the

---

46. *Alexander* (1991), p. 436.

47. Cf. above, p. 128 and note 38; Hersh has assembled a considerably enhanced corpus of this coinage.

series, but in the name of Demetrius. The latter, after the disaster of Ipsus in 301, held on to a part of Phoenicia, notably Tyre and Sidon. Newell dated this new Tyrian coinage between c. 306/305 (therefore following hard upon the issues marked with Phoenician letters) and c. 287, the date at which Ptolemy won back Tyre and Sidon from Demetrius. Price noted that the coinage in question was a limited issue, needing little time to produce, and beginning perhaps later than Newell thought. That was also Hersh's opinion, who suggests it started after the battle of Ipsus.

[Before leaving the problems of Tyrian chronology, I would like to mention a group of silver coins whose production was in progress when Alexander arrived in Phoenicia. These are coins of Tyre having a bearded archer god (Melkart?) upon a winged hippocamp as an obverse type and an owl with a scepter and flail as a reverse type. A date in Phoenician (from year 1 to 17) is inscribed near the owl (pl. 5, 8: year 15); from year 1 to 4, a letter may or may not precede the date, either a *beth* (year 1), *mem* (in years 1, 2, and 3), or *ayn* (years 3 and 4), and an *ayn* always precedes the date from year 5 on.[48]

Lemaire, in 1976, recalled the hypotheses[49] surrounding this group of coins and I refer to his treatment. A misunderstanding about the coins' weight has misled the discussion. Didrachms of Attic weight have been recognized, an identification acceptable to Lemaire, but to me impossible. The coins are too heavy to have been struck on this standard. If they were Attic standard, they would not weigh more than 8.60–8.65 grams. To be sure, several of them do not weigh this much, whether as a consequence of wear and tear or the mint's own negligence. But it is evident from glancing at the catalogue lists[50] that the "legal" weight was clearly higher than 8.60–8.65 grams. Several specimens weigh between 8.70 and 8.95 grams, which does not at all accord with the Attic standard. It is right to reject this identification and to speak of a Tyrian standard, of a Tyrian shekel.[51]

---

48. H. Seyrig gives a table of these signs in "Sur une prétendue ère tyrienne," *Syria* 34 (1957), p. 95 (= *Antiquités syriennes* 5 (1958), p. 157). A letter does not precede the date on some coins from the years 2, 3, and 4.

49. *RN* 18 (1976), pp. 11–14.

50. See, e.g., E. Babelon, *Traité des monnaies grecques et romaines* II, 2 (Paris, 1910), p. 626; G. F. Hill, *BMC Phoenicia* (London, 1910), pp. 231–32; J. and A. G. Elayi give a long list of weights in *Trésors de monnaies phéniciennes et circulation monétaire* (Paris, 1993), in their inventories of the Tell Abu Hawam hoard, pp. 173–81, and the Gaza region hoard, p. 186. They put "Attic standard" in quotation marks, thus demonstrating their own doubt about this identification.

51. Tyre had previously used the standard called "Phoenician," and had struck coins of c. 14 grams and c. 3.5 grams; Sidon conformed to the same standard, but struck coins of c. 28 grams and c. 7 grams. On the relation between the two coinages, see C. M. Kraay, *Archaic and Classical Greek Coins* (London, 1976), p. 288 (Kraay thinks that the 7 gram coin is the core of this system, and it is to this coin he gives the name "shekel").

Finds in a grotto of Wadi-Daliyeh (fourteen kilometers to the north of Jericho, about twelve west of the Jordan) provide, it seems, a reference point for dating these coins. The grotto served as a refuge for some Samaritans who had burned the Macedonian governor of Syria alive, Andromachus; Alexander exterminated them in 331 (Curtius 4.8.9–11). Aramaic papyri found in the grotto are not later than 331, and the coins found with them are probably not to be dated later than this. They include some Tyrian shekels of the series we are interested in, with the latest from year 15. Unfortunately the information provided on the objects in the find is incomplete and confused. J. and A. G. Elayi, in attempting to rectify this, wonder if the coins mentioned all came from the grotto and if some of them might not have been gathered from other spots on the site.[52]

Suppose, however, that the shekels of year 15 were not issued after 331. Because the latest date known for the coins of this weight is year 17, we can conclude that this coinage was struck, for the most part, before Alexander's arrival. The majority of specimens, we have seen, bear the letter *ayn*. Since this letter likewise appears on a group of Alexanders where it has been interpreted as the initial of Azemilkos, it has been suggested that the series with Tyrian types also carried the initial of the same Azemilkos and that these coins and the Alexanders were dated by this sovereign's regnal years, where year 1 corresponds to 347/346, if our interpretation of the Alexanders is correct.[53] The final two issues of Tyrian shekels, from years 16 and 17, would therefore fall in 332/331 and 331/330, at a period when Alexander was master of the city and had already, I think, inaugurated his own personal coinage.

Lemaire, in 1976, was only able to mention a single shekel of year 16 and one from year 17. He hesitated to accept them. J. Rouvier had described the one from year 16, but because its location was unknown, it was impossible to verify this scholar's reading. As for that of year 17, well known from its location in the British Museum, it is a plated coin whose official character is therefore uncertain.[54] The Elayis, nevertheless, seem to

---

52. See A. Lemaire, op. cit., pp. 12–13; J. and A. G. Elayi, *Trésors de monnaies phéniciennes* (Paris, 1993), pp. 216–18, inventoried nine coins: an Athenian tetradrachm, a stater of Mazaeus, a small, pseudo-Athenian coin, a small coin of Sidon and five specimens from Tyre belonging to our series.

53. It is surprising, on this theory, that Azemilkos did not initial the shekels of years 1 and 2, waiting until year 5 to sign his coins; but to tell the truth, a similar phenomenon is observable at the beginning of Alexander's Tyrian coinage: the first issues carry Greek signatures with a partly contemporary group marked with an *ayn*. It is only afterwards that the signature *ayn/kaph* appears along with Azemilkos's regnal years.

54. J. Rouvier, "Numismatique des villes de la Phénicie," *Journal intern. d'archéol. numis.* 6 (1903), p. 276, no. 1818 (cf. Lemaire, op. cit., p. 22); G. F. Hill, *BMC Phoenicia* (1910), p. 232, no. 42; two other specimens of the British Museum (*ibid.*, nos. 33 and 38 bis), dated as year 3 and year 13, are likewise plated.

have observed other shekels bearing these dates, because they write that "some specimens"[55] confirm issues for the years 16 and 17.

Some small fractions, weighing less than a gram, with winged hippocamp and owl armed with flail and scepter as types, have been associated with the shekels in question. They are dated, but an initial does not precede the date. Kindler published a hoard discovered at Akko in 1962 and made known other specimens from the same site. He read dates going to year 26. If we are dealing here with Azemilkos's coinage, he struck smaller denominations of the shekel with Phoenician types until 322/321. But the Elayis, in their new study of the hoard,[56] have expressed certain misgivings about these readings. To judge, we await their planned corpus of Tyrian coinage of the Persian era.]

The First Gold Coins of Alexander; Importance of the Capture of Tyre; Role of the Tarsus Mint; General Remarks on the Types

I have set forth the arguments supporting the belief that the first tetradrachms of Alexander with the types of Herakles head and seated Zeus first appeared either in summer 333 or, more likely, during the autumn, some weeks after the battle of Issus. When should we place the start of the gold coins with Athena head and Nike holding a stylis? It is hardly probable that Alexander inaugurated his gold coinage before having his silver coinage in place. Despite the gold Philips and the darics of the Great King, silver remained the coinage metal of choice in the Greek world, the one best adapted to the majority of transactions. Gold, whose intrinsic value was considerably higher, suited, to be sure, major payments, but it was less practical for more ordinary exchanges. Although we cannot be completely certain that the creation of Alexander's tetradrachms preceded that of his gold staters, this is a reasonable assumption. I hasten to add that the time gap separating these two events was probably not very long. Gold darics glorified the Persian sovereign: Herodotus (4.166) reports that Darius I (522–486) instituted this coinage as a memorial (*mnēmosunon*) of his reign.[57] When, after Issus, Alexander was declared lord of Asia and of Darius III, he could not delay issuing his own gold currency.

Nike holding the *stylis* on the reverse of Alexander's staters evokes more than a one-off maritime victory: like Zeus holding the scepter, she proclaims absolute sovereignty. Now, according to Arrian (2.17), Alexander

---

55. A. Kindler, *Eretz-Israel* 8 (1967), pp. 318–24 (cf. Lemaire, op. cit., p. 14 and note 1); J. and A. G. Elayi, op. cit., p. 218, in their commentary on the Wadi Daliyeh hoard.

56. Elayi, op. cit., "Trésor d'Akko 1962," pp. 163–68.

57. See my *Naissance*, pp. 167–68.

delivered an oration to his army explaining his decision to vanquish Tyre. Whether this oration is authentic or not, its content is realistic. Alexander expresses his ambition to secure control of the seas. The capture of Tyre, he says, would bring possession of all of Phoenicia, and therefore of the largest and most powerful fleet; with the Cypriote fleet rallying to his cause in turn, the sea would incontestably belong to the Macedonians. Arrian merely proclaims what actually happened. Once the siege of Tyre had begun, the king of Aradus (Gerostratos) and the king of Byblos (Enylos) deserted the Persian admiral Autophradates and brought their fleet over to Alexander; the kings of Cyprus followed their example (Arrian 2.20.1, 3). Tyre's fall securely established the Conqueror's maritime rule, and he could justly adorn his gold coins with Victory wielding a naval emblem. I would place the first circulation of Alexander's earliest staters after July 332.

Can we determine which mint inaugurated this coinage? In order to make the train of thought easier to follow, I will start by setting forth Newell's conclusions. Indeed, his classifications have long been standard.

He attributed three groups of staters between the years 333 and 327 to Tarsus[58]: the first and second display the same symbols, a *kantharos* or a trident, while the third has an amphora or trident.

The coinage that can confidently be assigned to Sidon begins (cf. p. 113, and pl. 4, 1–2) with silver tetradrachms dated from year 1 (333/332) and year 2 (332/331). The first Sidonian gold staters appear in the following group, which has no date (pl. 4, 3) but which clearly covers the period years 3 to 6 (331/330–328/327); all, or nearly all, these coins have a palm decorated with a fillet as a symbol, and on a fair number of them the letters Σ or ΣI, the initial letters of the city's name,[59] are inscribed.

At Tyre, the Phoenician letter *ayn* marks the earliest known issue of staters (pl. 5, 1), and it also appears on a group of tetradrachms. Three closely related issues of tetradrachms precede these coins.[60] Because the Tyrian mint probably opened only in 332/331, it is perhaps in the following year that the gold coinage began.

One relatively important group of gold coins presented Newell with a problem of attribution and chronology. It comprises eight gold issues, two of them including not only staters but also distaters. A symbol distinguishes each issue: a wreath (pl. 1, 2 and 5, 9), caduceus (pl. 5, 10), club, thunderbolt, star (pl. 5, 11), grain of wheat, ivy leaf, *kantharos*. The examples with wreath are spread over six obverse dies, those with the caduceus over two; in each

---

58. "Tarsos under Alexander," *AJN* 52 (1918), pp. 90–94.
59. Newell, *Sidon and Ake*, pp. 10–11; Price, *Alexander* (1991), p. 439.
60. Cf. the discussion above, p. 126 and note 32.

of the other issues, a single obverse die is known, and two dies of double staters must be added (issues with club and star).

These coins present three stylistic peculiarities. First, on the earliest wreath coins (pl. 1, 2 and 5, 9), the helmet of Athena is decorated with a serpent (sometimes with a star in the serpent's coils); on the other wreath coins and on seven other issues, the helmet is decorated with a griffin or a lion-griffin (cf. pl. 5, 10–11). Second, from the caduceus issue on, two small Nikes are sometimes placed on the transverse bar of the stylis (pl. 5, 10–11). Third, the legend *Alexandrou* is inscribed left of Nike, not right.[61]

Newell thought that all these staters formed a coherent entity while Price, more accurately it seems to me, noted that no die linkage had been found among the issues and that the striking of this coinage, therefore, probably lasted some time.

In *Sidon and Ake*, Newell proposed an attribution to Sidon between the end of 333 and October 331, in other words, 333/332 and 332/331. He thought that it was the gold captured from the Persians at Issus and Damascus that was coined. Sidon, he maintained, had become rather experienced in coinage production during the previous period, and Alexander, with the siege of Tyre on his hands, had the Sidonian mint operating at capacity. Newell emphasized the resemblance between the head of Athena on our staters and that on the first staters confidently attributed to Sidon. One will also note that on these same Sidonian staters, the legend *Alexandrou* is similarly inscribed left of Nike.[62] The fact that our issues are not dated from the years 1 and 2 of Sidon, as the contemporaneous issues of tetradrachms are, is not a serious objection. It happens that gold and silver are not always handled in exactly the same way; moreover, from year 3 to year 6 (a period when neither silver nor gold Sidonian coins carry a date), the staters are marked with a palm decorated with a fillet, a symbol not appearing on the tetradrachms.

Newell, however, was not completely satisfied with the Sidonian attribution. According to Hill,[63] Newell had raised in conversation the idea that our group of gold coins was produced in Damascus after the victory of Gaugamela (October 1, 331), at the same time as the tetradrachms where the letters ΔA appear.

Price rejected this suggestion, arguing that Damascus had not struck coinage under the Persians and that nothing indicates that an Alexander mint opened in this city immediately (note that Newell dated this opening only after Gaugamela). Unsatisfied himself, Price wondered if our gold

---

61. Newell, op. cit., pp. 7–8 and 21–26; Price, op. cit., pp. 436 and 438.
62. Newell, op. cit., pl. I, 15–18 and II, 2.
63. "Alexander the Great and the Persian Lion-Gryphon," *JHS* 43 (1923), p. 159, note 8.

coins were not from Tyre (Ake in his mind); he established a connection between the thunderbolt functioning as a symbol on one of our issues and that on all the earliest Tyrian tetradrachms. I will only comment that such a symbol is far too common to use as a criterion for a convincing classification. Finally, in his *Alexander*, Price kept the Sidonian attribution.

A recent reassessment by Troxell (confirming an intuition of F. de Callataÿ)[64] leads me to propose another possibility. Troxell, I said, has shown that the two earliest groups of staters assigned by Newell to Tarsus (with the symbols of trident and *kantharos*) were in fact Macedonian. Leaving the third group aside (with amphora and trident as symbols), she concluded that the first gold coins that could confidently be assigned to Tarsus were those bearing the plow as symbol (pl. 5, 12), whose first appearance is commonly dated to 327.

Tarsus was an important mint under Alexander. In the great Demanhur hoard, buried in 318 or early 317, Tarsus ranks third in the number of its tetradrachms, behind Amphipolis and Babylon. It would be surprising if the Tarsus mint did not strike gold coins before 327, when Sidon and Tyre had already been producing them for some years. Its strategic position, which the Persians greatly appreciated,[65] between western Asia Minor and the Near and Middle East, gave it a leading role in the movement of troop reinforcements, provisions, and matériel. It is not too much to think, perhaps, that Cilicia was a center for military training and equipping in the years after 333, as it was under the Persians, and that warships were built in the province's dockyards. The output of gold coins would not, therefore, have been superfluous from 332/331: we may well suppose that the Macedonian authorities at Tarsus had to shoulder heavy costs, a part of which had to be settled in currency. That is why I propose assigning to the Tarsus mint the eight gold issues under discussion: they would fall between c. 332/331 and c. 327.

Two stylistic observations support this attribution to Tarsus. First, the griffin or lion-griffin appearing on Athena's helmet in these issues is also present on the issue with plow and the other issues from Tarsus (pl. 5, 12–13). Second, in examining the stater with plow (pl. 5, 12) illustrated by Price in his plate X (no. 3009), I believe I can distinguish two small Nikes decorating the transverse bar of the stylis. This peculiarity, a characteristic, one will recall, of several specimens from our eight issues, likewise appears

---

64. *Alexander* (1997) pp. 101–11, esp. pp. 108–9. F. de Callataÿ had floated the idea in an unpublished note from 1983, a copy of which is to be found at the American Numismatic Society.

65. On Cilicia's role under the Persians, see P. Briant, *From Cyrus to Alexander: A History of the Persian Empire*, Eng. trans. by P. T. Daniels (Winona Lake, IN, 2002), pp. 498–500, and my *Naissance*, pp. 207–37, esp. p. 222.

on later staters from the Tarsus mint (pl. 5, 13), but it does not figure on coins from either Sidon or Tyre.[66]

The objection will doubtless arise that, on the plow staters, the hairstyle of Athena is a little different from the style on our staters. To explain this discrepancy, I suggest that the mint recruited another engraver at this time, perhaps after a more or less lengthy interruption in the striking of the gold coins. All mints experience stylistic evolutions of this sort.

Since Sidon and Tyre, to all appearances, did not produce staters prior to 331/330, it is probably our group of eight issues that inaugurated Alexander's gold coinage. If my attribution to Tarsus is correct, this mint would have a double claim to fame, not only for having put into circulation Alexander's first tetradrachms but also his first gold staters as well.

Just as the head of Herakles and the Zeus engraved on the tetradrachms from Tarsus served as models for the other mints, so the different production centers copied the head of Athena and the Nike with stylis on the staters. The stylistic similarities evident among the types from Tarsus, Sidon, and Tyre should not surprise us, therefore. Close ties united these three mints at the start of Alexander's coinage. Newell noted that Sidon and Tyre had utilized an identical obverse die for an issue of tetradrachms. He thought that the engraver of this die was transferred from Sidon to Tyre and spent some time in the Tyrian mint; this man then came to Tarsus, where his handiwork is visible.[67] This is probably not an isolated example. Not only iconographic models, in all likelihood, passed from mint to mint: the artisans did too.

In examining the types the Macedonian king chose for his gold coins, Zervos[68] concluded that, in contrast to those on the silver coins, they referred rather more to Alexander himself in his invincibility. Upon his arrival in Asia, at Ilion, he received from Athena (Ilias) the assurance of her support (Diodorus 17.17.7), and for this reason he put her countenance on the obverse of his staters; as for the type on the reverse, I have shown that it proclaimed Alexander's conquest of the seas. I will add, however, that Athena was venerated in Macedonia, and notably at Pella, where she was honored under the name of Athena Alkidemos.[69] Her presence on the gold

---

66. Price, *Alexander* (1991), pp. 376–77, nos. 3040, 3041, 3043; these coins have *Basileōs Alexandrou* as the legend. As for the griffin and lion-griffin on Athena's helmet, it is to be noted that this ornament also appears at Sidon and Tyre (only on the early issues at the former and almost without exception at the latter).

67. Newell, *Sidon and Ake*, p. 53, and *Tarsos under Alexander*, p. 81; cf. Price, *Alexander* (1991), pp. 407 and 370.

68. *NC* 142 (1982), p. 173.

69. A. B. Brett, "Athena Alkidemos of Pella," *Amer. Num. Soc. Museum Notes* 4 (1950), pp. 55–72. The epithet "Alkidemos" appears in a passage of Livy (42.51.2), where Perseus at

coins could not fail to speak directly to the Macedonians. The cult of this divinity was widespread throughout the Greek world, and the image of the helmeted goddess was known in the East, where the tetradrachms of Athens had circulated in abundance. One will note, nevertheless, that on Alexander's staters, the goddess does not wear an Attic but a Corinthian helmet, like the Athena on the coins of Corinth.

Other Coinages of Alexander in Phoenicia, Syria, and Cyprus

Tarsus, Sidon, and Tyre were not the only mints in the region to produce coins of Alexander during his lifetime. Some Syrian and Cypriote mints also participated in this activity, and they present us with two problems. First, several mint attributions, taken as settled ever since Newell's publication of the Demanhur hoard in 1923, are not certain. Second, the precise chronology of the issues is hard to establish: where to divide those issues struck prior to June 10, 323, from those coming after? Fortunately, we do possess some helpful indications. The appearance, at certain mints, of the name of Philip III, gives a valuable reference point; the title *Basileōs* was probably written only after Alexander's death, perhaps only in 322/321 (cf. p. 117). Lastly, for the gold coins, the hoards of Corinth, Samovodene, the Balkans, and Saida provide interesting chronological signposts, while the great hoard from Demanhur, buried in 318 or early 317, provides a particularly welcome *terminus ante quem* for the tetradrachms.

[I would like to add a few words on the burial date of the Saida (Sidon) hoard.[70] This huge deposit, consisting of 7,000 to 9,000 gold coins, was discovered in three tranches, in 1829, 1852, and 1863. Only forty or so specimens[71] have been identified so far in public collections; enlightened

---

Pella "sacrificio . . . Minervae, quam vocant Alkidem, confacto" [having sacrificed to Minerva, whom they call Alkides—WEH]. These last words have been emended to "quam vocant Alkidemon, facto" [having sacrificed to Minerva, "whom they call 'Defender of the Folk'"—Loeb]. A terracotta statuette from the second century BC, discovered in the excavations of Pella, represents an Athena with bull's horns, and it has been suggested that this object could be a copy of the cult statue of Athena Alkidemos. There is a good reproduction in R. Ginouvès, ed., *La Macédoine de Philippe II à la conquête romaine* (Paris, 1993), p. 110, no. 97, where L. Kahil has written the text of the pages dealing with the iconography of the gods and myths.

70. See *IGCH* 1204, where there is an up-to-date bibliography as of 1973, when the inventory of these Greek coin hoards was published. Nothing more is known of the deposit discovered in 1829; the deposits of 1852 and 1863 were enclosed in lead vases, the ensemble found in a garden in the suburbs of Saida.

71. U. Westermark, "Notes on the Saida Hoard," Nordisk Num. Årsskrift 1979–80, pp. 22–35, has accurately catalogued these coins.

amateurs fortunately drew up partial lists in the nineteenth century. According to these lists, the latest staters from Sidon were from year 10 (324/323), the latest from Tyre from year 24; the fourteen year difference between the Sidonian and Tyrian dates corresponds to what is most often attested elsewhere and so one presumes that the hoard was buried either during 324/323 or in the early months of 323/322. The fact that the find was made at Sidon itself reinforces this surmise, permitting one to think that local coins were much in evidence there.

Yet Westermark preferred to speak of the years 323–320 for the burial, and Thompson has written: "If one takes account of only the Alexander material, the record is consistent with a burial after Alexander's death, but perhaps closer to 320 than to 324."[72] In any case, the incomplete nature of our information on the hoard's contents demands prudence. Some later coins from Sidon and Tyre belonged, perhaps, to the original deposit. Moreover, some specimens not belonging to the hoard may have been included in the reports made at the time. In short, the Saida hoard cannot be dated with any great precision.]

Aradus is another Phoenician mint that was relatively active in addition to Sidon and Tyre under Alexander. Alexander accepted the surrender of the Aradians and their territory on the adjacent mainland, and Straton, the son of king Gerostratos, placed a golden crown on Alexander's head (Arrian 2.13.7–8). Gerostratos himself at the time was with the Persian admiral Autophradates, but he switched to Alexander's side shortly afterward, when the latter was besieging Tyre (Arrian 2.20.1). F. Duyrat has established a corpus of Aradian coins from the time of the Macedonian conquest.[73] The mint put marks on its Alexander coinage, allowing easy attribution of this group of issues: first, the letter A, then Phoenician letters indicating Aradus, then a monogram where the initial letters of Aradus are immediately recognizable (pl. 5, 14).[74]

An issue of tetradrachms produced at another mint carries the two Phoenician letters *ayn* and *yod*. Newell interpreted them as the initial letters

---

72. *Alexander's Drachm Mints I: Sardes and Miletus* (New York, 1983), p. 72.

73. *Aradus hellénistique, étude historique et monétaire*, doctoral thesis, University of Paris, now published at Beirut, 2005, by the Institut français du Proche-Orient, Bibliothèque archéol. et histor., Volume 173.

74. Price, *Alexander* (1991), pp. 414–19. On the first issue of tetradrachms, one reads, besides the letter A, the letter Γ, that Newell, probably correctly, considered the initial of a mint magistrate; one could also think of the initial of king Gerostratos, but the subsequent issues carry other letters (Δ, B, M, etc.). The Phoenician letters are the same as on the coins the Aradians struck before Alexander; for their interpretation, see Price, p. 414.

of king Ainel (Enylos in Greek), dynast of *Byblos*, who, along with Gerostratos, came over to Alexander.[75] This attribution has not been questioned. But another attribution Newell made to Byblos is debatable: a group of Alexander staters and tetradrachms shows a monogram, in which Newell discerned the name of king Adramelek (pl. 6, 1), Enylos's successor. Price stressed the tenuousness of this classification.[76] Not only is the deciphering of the monogram rash, but the presence of a king Adramelek[77] in Byblos after Enylos remains highly conjectural.

Neither Beirut nor Marathus seem to have produced Alexanders during the Conqueror's reign. It is possible, however, that Carne, a coastal city belonging to the kingdom of Aradus, struck some tetradrachms before June 323.[78]

In Syria, an Alexander coinage of tetradrachms quite probably began at the Damascus mint before Alexander's death.[79] Since Damascus did not strike coins under the Persians, the Macedonian governor of this province must have innovated. The presence of the letters ΔA on all these tetradrachms confirms the attribution to the Damascus mint (pl. 6, 2). All the known issues are represented in the Demanhur hoard buried in 318 or early 317. The mint's activity was thus limited in time and could have been concentrated over a few years.

Newell[80] located another Syrian center for producing Alexanders at Myriandrus, without any compelling reason, as Price has emphasized.[81] Alexandria ad Issum, some distance away, was thought to have replaced Myriandrus in Hellenistic times. Newell's intuition might have been right: a mint could have been opened at *Alexandria ad Issum* shortly after Alexander

---

75. *Demanhur* (1923), pp. 124–25.

76. Op. cit., p. 430.

77. A king Adramelek did reign at Byblos; he is known from coins on which his name and title as king of Byblos are written in Phoenician. These coins are to be dated before Alexander's time; cf. now J. and A. G. Elayi, *Trésors de monnaies phéniciennes* (Paris, 1993), pp. 85 and 107–14.

78. Price, op. cit., pp. 429, 432–33.

79. *Ibid.*, pp. 398–401. We have seen, a few pages above (p. 136), that Newell thought of attributing a group of gold staters to Damascus, but this does not seem tenable.

80. "Myriandros-Alexandria kat'Isson," *AJN* 53 (1919, 2), pp. 32–42. This Alexander coinage would continue a coinage of Mazaeus in the same mint, cf. above, page 119 (Groups Four and Five of Mazaeus). I have mentioned the other proposed locales.

81. Price, op. cit., pp. 401–4.

founded this city, if indeed he was the founder.[82] Stylistically, the coins (mostly tetradrachms) are to be associated with those from Tarsus and Phoenicia. This Syrian mint, whichever it was, seems to have been shut down around the time of the Demanhur hoard's burial (318–17).

As for Cyprus, I will begin with the Alexander mint of *Salamis*, to which Newell assigned a large production of gold staters during Alexander's lifetime (cf. pl. 6, 3), along with two issues of tetradrachms with bow as symbol. Price went along this attribution,[83] but recently Troxell has doubted the staters are from Cypriote Salamis.[84] Her personal hunch, she writes, led her to assign them, rather, to western Asia Minor. I have remarked above that Troxell was rightly surprised that the powerful city of Ephesus has not been included on the list of Asia Minor mints that struck coinage for Alexander and his immediate successors. She wondered, considering it a mere conjecture, whether "Ephesus" could not take the place of "Salamis" for this series of gold staters and their fractions. Several of these staters were present in the Saida hoard.

As for the tetradrachms marked with a bow (either by itself or with the letter B), their attribution to Salamis is possible. Newell in turn assigns a series of tetradrachms and staters to this mint after June 323; their principal symbol for many years is a rudder.

Some staters and tetradrachms carry a monogram that we may unhesitatingly identify as that of *Citium*. All the tetradrachms (and drachms) of Citium[85] have *Basileōs Alexandrou* as a legend and are therefore probably later than 323; the staters do not mention the royal title and would therefore have been struck before the tetradrachms, during Alexander's lifetime (yet it does happen that some gold coins without the title are contemporary with tetradrachms bearing the *Basileōs* legend).[86] Some of the Citium staters were

---

82. H. Seyrig, *Syria* 47 (1970), p. 309, note 1, has posed the problem clearly. He is inclined to accept Alexander as the founder because an ancient text indicates as much; P. M. Fraser, *Cities of Alexander the Great* (Oxford, 1996), pp. 20–23, does not agree, judging it more probable that the city was founded after the Conqueror's death. See also M. Sartre, *D'Alexandre à Zénobie* (Paris, 2001), p. 116. Getzel Cohen now provides a complete overview of the issue in *The Hellenistic Settlements in Syria, the Red Sea Basin, and North Africa* (Berkeley, 2006).

83. Newell, "Some Cypriote Alexanders," *NC* 15 (1915), pp. 306–8; Price, op. cit., pp. 390–92. Price did, however, cast doubt on the attribution of some of the staters to Salamis.

84. "A New Look at Some Alexander Staters from 'Salamis'," in *Travaux de num. grecque offerts à G. Le Rider*, M. Amandry and S. Hurter eds. (London, 1999), pp. 359–67.

85. Newell, *NC* 15 (1915), pp. 301–6; Price, *Alexander* (1991), pp. 384–86.

86. This could be the case in Macedonia, where no gold coins bear the title *Basileōs*, when some at least are probably contemporary with tetradrachms bearing this title. But it is not certain that the tetradrachms and the gold coins in question come from the same Macedonian mint. In another series, of eastern origin, sometimes attributed to Aradus but prob-

part of the Saida hoard. If the latter was buried in 323 or 322, there would be an argument for the gold coinage of Citium commencing prior to Alexander's death. But, as I said, the date of the hoard is probably later.

Troxell reattributed a group of Alexanders with prow symbol to Soli.[87] The list she established includes a stater and a half-stater with the legend *Alexandrou*; the other staters, products of four dies, carry the title *Basileōs*, while all the tetradrachms bear the simple legend *Alexandrou*, with certain among them having Zeus's right leg moved backwards. Troxell would date the entirety of this coinage between 325/323 and 319/318, but she is cautious about this chronology.

It does not seem possible to assign an Alexander coinage earlier than June 323 to any other Cypriote mint (Amathus, Paphos).

Some Comments on the Volume of Alexander Issues from Cilicia, Phoenicia, Syria, and Cyprus up to c. 318

The great hoard of Demanhur (containing, it will be recalled, a Sidonian specimen from year 15, issued therefore between the beginning of October 319 and the end of September 318) was in all probability hidden in 318 or perhaps early in 317. This hoard, remarkable for the impressive number of its Alexander tetradrachms (nearly 6,000 coins have been inventoried), provides an almost complete prospectus of the mints that, prior to the end of 318, had issued Alexander's coins. By an interesting coincidence, some of the mints belonging to the region we are studying, Tarsus, Myriandrus/Alexandria ad Issum, Damascus, and Citium, do not seem to have continued the production of this currency for long after 320. In any case, none of their issues currently known is later than 318, because the latest among them are represented in the Demanhur hoard. The date of 318, therefore, seems to represent a good reference point for our investigation.

A precise assessment of the volume of the different coinages from Cilicia, Phoenicia, Syria, and Cyprus will not be possible until we possess a corpus of all the mints that will provide us with the number of dies used in each issue. The data collected by Newell concerning Tarsus, Sidon, Tyre, and Myriandrus/Alexandria ad Issum are extremely valuable in this regard, but

---

ably produced elsewhere, *Basileōs* appears only on the tetradrachms, most in the name of Philip III: cf. Price, op. cit., pp. 422–24; P138–158, 3336–38. Likewise, at Salamis on Cyprus, in a group of coins with the rudder symbol where many (but not all) the tetradrachms have the title *Basileōs* in their legend, no stater bears it: cf. Price, op. cit., p. 393.

87. "Alexanders from Soli on Cyprus," in *Studies in Greek Numismatics in Memory of M. J. Price*, R. Ashton and S. Harter eds. (London, 1998), pp. 339–44.

they are now old and need updating.[88] Troxell has assembled a classification by dies of the coins with prow symbol that she has reassigned, as we saw, from Amathus to Soli on Cyprus. But this is a relatively limited group and, besides, Troxell's study dealt only with the coins and the documentation at the American Numismatic Society. They surely make a solid contribution to the knowledge of this coinage, but more is needed. The only exhaustive corpus we possess at present is Duyrat's for Aradus, already mentioned.

Concerning the other mints of the region, in the absence of a corpus, we may arrive at an approximation of their output by consulting the Demanhur hoard that I outline below. Even so, it must be said that one cannot be entirely confident about this inventory's figures, which sometimes seem to contradict other evidence.

F. de Callataÿ, in his quantitative survey of 1997,[89] sought the original number of dies by applying statistical formulas to the number of coins and dies inventoried. He did this for Tarsus and Myriandrus/Alexandria ad Issum using lists Newell had compiled. Duyrat has done the same thing for Aradus. I have not undertaken such calculations, believing that, overall, the data at my disposal were not sufficiently precise.

[In the following conspectus, I will first provide an overview of the output of the six mints for which die surveys exist (Tarsus, Sidon, Tyre, Aradus, Myriandrus/Alexandria ad Issum, Soli); I will then present the numerical data from the Demanhur hoard.

The issues of Sidon and Tyre, because they are dated, pose no chronological problem. For the other mints, I accept that the title *Basileōs* did not appear before 322/321.

Tarsus (according to Newell). Following the suggestion advanced above (page 137), I assign to Tarsus the gold issues Newell collected at the beginning of his catalogue of Sidonian coinage (*Sidon and Ake*, pp. 7–8, series I, Group A; Price, *Alexander*, 1991, p. 438).

From c. 333/332 to 323/322 (without the title *Basileōs*):

a) From 333/332 to c. 327:
   Gold Staters: 13 obverse dies + 2 distater dies
   Tetradrachms: 27 obverse dies

b) From c. 327 to c. 323/322:
   Staters: 1 die

---

88. Newell, *Demanhur* (1923), p. 151, provided a more complete status report of the number of dies put to use in these four mints up to 318.

89. *Recueil quantitatif des émissions monétaires hellénistiques* (Wetteren, 1997), no. 267 (pp. 247–48, Myriandrus/Alexandria ad Issum) and nos. 268–69 (pp. 248–50, Tarsus); in this work, the author has given each time the estimates obtained by F. Carter's formula and that of W. W. Esty.

Tetradrachms: 14 dies (there are also some drachms and half-drachms)

From 322/321 to 319/318 (legend: *Basileōs Alexandrou*):
Staters: 6 dies
Tetradrachms: 26 dies (two of which were already in use at the end of the preceding group)

Newell raised the total number of tetradrachm dies, here 65, to 69 in *Demanhur*, p. 151.

Sidon (according to Newell and Price).[90] No Sidonian issue apparently occurred in year 11 (323/322) unless Newell was right in suggesting that the coins marked with the Greek letter K do not date from year 10, but year 11.

From 333/332 (year 1) to 324/323 (year 10, indicated by the Phoenician letter *yod*:
Staters: 9 dies (one and the same die was used from year 7 to the start of year 10; two new dies were engraved in year 10)
Tetradrachms: 13 dies

Coins marked with the letter K: year 10 (324/323) or year 11 (323/322):
Staters: 4 dies (one of them already having been used for the *yod* staters)
Tetradrachms: 1 die

From 322/321 (year 12) to 319/318 (year 15):
Staters: 7 dies
Tetradrachms: 7 dies

The total of 21 dies for the tetradrachms became 24 in *Demanhur*, p. 151; I trust Price's figures (*Alexander* [1991], p. 437) and keep 21 as the number.

Some smaller denomination coins in silver and bronze coins were struck at Sidon between 333/332 and 318/317.

Tyre (according to Newell and Price).
Up to 324/323 (year 24 of Tyre):
Staters: 8 dies (of which one in 325/24, one in 324/23)
Tetradrachms: 17 dies (of which one in 325/24, one in 324/23)

From 323/322 (year 25 of Tyre) to 319/318 (year 29 of Tyre):
Staters: 9 dies
Tetradrachms: 9 dies

In *Demanhur*, p. 151, the total number of tetradrachm dies is not 26 but 25.

---

90. Price, *Alexander* (1991), p. 438, has slightly revised Newell's data for Sidon and Tyre.

The Tyre mint issued some silver fractions during this period; one bronze issue is known for the year 322/321.

Aradus (according to Duyrat).
>Up to c. 323/322 (without the title *Basileōs*):
>>Staters: 2 dies
>>Tetradrachms: 14 dies

>From c. 322/321 to c. 319/318 (legend: *Basileōs Alexandrou*):
>>Staters: 10 dies + 1 distater die
>>Tetradrachms: 182 dies

Issues with the legend *Philippou* on the staters and *Basileōs Philippou* on almost all the tetradrachms (Price, *Alexander* [1991], nos. P138–P158); some coins with the legend *Alexandrou* or *Basileōs Alexandrou* are a part of this group:
>Staters: 13 dies
>Tetradrachms: 68 dies

The attribution to the Aradus mint of this group in the name of Philip III, which does not carry the monogram of Aradus, has been discussed and debated; no tetradrachm of this group is present in the Demanhur hoard, which leads one to think that these coins were struck at the very end of Philip III's reign, that is, a little before autumn of 317.

Myriandrus/Alexandria ad Issum (according to Newell).
>Up to c. 323/322 (without the title *Basileōs*):
>>No gold issue is known
>>Tetradrachms: 10 dies

>From c. 322/321 to c. 319/318 (with *Basileōs*):
>>Staters: 1 die
>>Tetradrachms: 15 dies

I have followed Newell's classification. Price introduced into the group with *Basileōs* some tetradrachms where this title does not appear. The last Alexander coins of the mint are in the name of Philip III and so are not later than 318/317.

Newell did not revise the number of tetradrachm dies in *Demanhur*.

Soli on Cyprus (according to Troxell).
>Between 332 and 319/318:
>>Gold: 1 die + 1 half-stater die (without *Basileōs*)
>>   4 dies (with *Basileōs*)
>>Silver: 13 dies (without *Basileōs*)

For the other mints of the region, sufficiently precise lists of the number of dies employed do not exist. As I said above, the Demanhur hoard furnishes possibilities for comparison among the various mints. Newell catalogued 4,826 tetradrachms from this deposit. Zervos was able to add 1,125 specimens,[91] giving a grand total of 5,951 coins. I have followed this last survey of data in the table presented below of the region's production centers we are investigating. I also note the numbers attained by the Macedonian mint at Amphipolis and the mint at Babylon (data in italics). All the coins are tetradrachms. For Tarsus, Sidon, Tyre, Aradus, Myriandrus/Alexandria ad Issum, and Soli, I record the number of obverse dies counted between 333/332 and c. 319/318, the hoard having been buried in 318 or early 317.

Amphipolis	*2,005*
Babylon	*820*
Tarsus	549 (69 dies)
Damascus	428
Aradus	371 (196 dies)[92]
Tyre	256 (26 dies)
Myriandrus/Alexandria ad Issum	207 (25 dies)
Citium	142
Sidon	133 (21 dies)
Salamis on Cyprus	132
Byblos	80
Soli	40[93] (13 dies)
Paphos	24

The mints of Beirut, Carne, Amathus, and Marion are represented by only a very small number of specimens.]

The Damascus mint seems to have been one of the region's most active, as far as silver is concerned, so it is regrettable that no corpus has been undertaken for it. The case of Aradus is surprising: its output, judging by the number of coins present in the hoard, would seem markedly inferior to Tarsus's, yet judging by the number of dies in use, the Aradus mint quite outdistances the latter.[94]

---

91. "Additions to the Demanhur Hoard of Alexander Tetradrachms," *NC* 140 (1980), pp. 185–88.

92. This figure represents the total number of dies used in the first two groups from Aradus described above; the third group, in the name of Philip III, is perhaps not from Aradus and, in any case, is completely absent from the Demanhur hoard.

93. In *Demanhur*, Newell attributed to Amathus one tetradrachm with eagle symbol (which he identified as a dove) and 31 prow tetradrachms; these last were in fact struck at Soli, as Troxell has shown. Zervos, following Newell's classification, raised the number of tetradrachms at Amathus from 32 to 41; I propose accepting that Zervos did not find any other eagle specimen and that 40 coins bear the prow symbol.

94. An exhaustive corpus of Tarsus, Sidon, Tyre, Myriandrus/Alexandria ad Issum, and Soli would certainly reveal numerous other dies, but the gap would probably remain considerable between the new numbers and what Duyrat has given for Aradus.

The sum total of tetradrachms struck in this geographical area comes to 2,371, surpassing the number from Amphipolis (2,005). Yet the Macedonian mint, based upon the number of dies engraved at this period (and supposing that the number of coins per obverse die was, on average, roughly equivalent from one mint to the next), ought by itself to have attained an output far larger than that of all the mints of Cilicia, Phoenicia, Syria, and Cyprus.

In her recent study of Macedonian coinage under Alexander and his immediate successors, Troxell sought the number of obverse dies used at Amphipolis for the tetradrachms struck between c. 332 and c. 318.[95] She came up with 740 dies.[96] This figure apparently surpasses the number of dies in service during the same period by the group of regional mints under discussion. So we have to wonder why the specimens from Amphipolis are not more plentiful in the Demanhur hoard. The same question also arises when observing the Babylon mint's place in the hoard, represented there by 820 specimens.[97] At Babylon, the total number of obverse dies made for tetradrachms up to 318 BC rises to 172, according to Newell.[98] If the hoard gives a fair picture of the relative production of the Macedonian and Babylonian mints, the tetradrachms from Amphipolis ought to be not two and one-half times, but four times more numerous than those from Babylon. This observation seems to show that the deposit buried at Demanhur in Egypt consisted of coins coming mostly from Babylon and the coastlands of the eastern Mediterranean. A portion of the output from Amphipolis was undoubtedly directed towards payments in Macedonia itself and its neighboring regions. One would like to have a hoard from the Balkans or Greece, comparable in date and size, to Demanhur. This is not the case, one infers, consulting the list Price provided.[99]

What conclusion can we draw about the coinage activity of the mints belonging to the region of Cilicia, Phoenicia, Syria, and Cyprus? Each of the production centers struck moderate amounts of silver; there was just one exception, Aradus between 322/321 and c. 319/318, when the Aradians engraved nearly 200 tetradrachm dies, coming close, in this four-year period, to the record achieved at Amphipolis. Conversely, Tarsus, Sidon, Tyre, Myriandrus/Alexandria ad Issum, Soli, and Aradus prior to c. 322/321 (to cite only

---

95. *Alexander* (1997); cf. above, pp. 58–59. She gives the total on p. 26.
96. So as not to skew comparisons, I mention here the total of dies inventoried, not the total Troxell estimated using Carter's simplified formula (whereas in chapter 3 above, I used the estimated number of dies).
97. I will come back again to the Babylon mint in chapter 7.
98. *Demanhur* (1923), p. 151.
99. *Alexander* (1991), pp. 50–52.

those mints of which we know approximately the number of tetradrachm dies) employed *on average* from 1 to 5 dies annually, not an enormous figure.

Gold coin production, however, supplemented silver, permitting the issuing authorities to have at their disposal a relatively significant purchasing power overall. We do not know if the relative value of the two metals, which was theoretically 1 to 13.33 under the Persians,[100] remained the same under Alexander or if it went to 1 to 10, as in Greece. Taking the latter rate, a stater was worth 5 tetradrachms, a distater 10 tetradrachms. Accepting my attribution of a relatively large group of gold coins to Tarsus, the mint, between 333/332 and c. 327, would have circulated staters produced from 13 dies and distaters from 2 dies; in silver terms, this gold coinage's value would equal that of tetradrachms struck from 85 dies (supposing a stater die struck as many coins as a tetradrachm die). Tarsus would therefore have put into circulation no small money supply between 333/332 and c. 327.

Tyre and Sidon, as well, resorted to striking gold coins to obtain the funds they deemed essential for payments. Damascus was content with producing tetradrachms, but Aradus (especially from 322/321), Citium, and Soli also used gold coinage (recall that the series usually attributed to Salamis comes, perhaps, from another center, situated in Asia Minor), so that, finally, the amount of currency produced between 333/332 and 319/318 in the area of Cilicia, Phoenicia, Syria, and Cyprus was a sum to be reckoned with. If it remains inferior to that from Macedonia (where gold was coined too, with handsome issues of distaters), it still represents, taken as a whole, a noteworthy contribution to the coinage needs of the empire.

Macedonia's primacy in this domain is understandable. I set forth above (chapter 3) the range of expenses that Alexander and political circumstances imposed on Antipater. Macedonia was, besides, the sole center producing the royal coinage at this time in a very vast region (Greece, Thrace, the Aegean). It is not surprising, therefore, that Antipater found that he needed to issue a particularly abundant coinage and that the Amphipolis mint was the most active of the entire empire.

The Coinages of Cilicia, Phoenicia, Syria, and Cyprus in the Last Two Years of Alexander's Reign (325/324 and 324/323)

I have already shown, apropos of Macedonia and western Asia Minor, how I tried to test Thompson's hypothesis[101] according to which the

---

100. On the ratio 1:13.33, an Alexander stater would have been worth a little more than 6.5 tetradrachms; on this ratio, cf. my *Naissance*, pp. 157–64.

101. "Paying the Mercenaries," in *Festschrift für Leo Mildenberg*, A. Houghton et al. eds. (Wetteren, 1984), pp. 241–47.

decommissioning of mercenaries Alexander imposed on all satraps in 324 provoked a sudden increase in the royal coinage throughout the empire, whether through an already existing mint raising its output or through the opening of additional mints at this time. The intended objective, according to Thompson, was to pay out the salary of these men in locales closer to their respective homes.

In her article, Thompson did not bring up the region we are studying, for the good reason that no such monetary phenomenon has been observed there. Yet one presumes that the governors of this region, like other satraps, had mercenaries in their service and that they obeyed the order immediately upon its receipt.[102] So I do not think it otiose to examine the coinage issues struck at this period in Cilicia, Phoenicia, Syria, and Cyprus.

Starting with Tarsus, and accepting my attribution there of the group of eight gold issues that I dealt with at length above,[103] one may say that Tarsus's production in the two metals was relatively robust during the years after Alexander's passage in 333, and that it fell off in the second part of the reign (the known staters with plow symbol are the issue of a single obverse die), only to pick up with renewed vigor following the king's death. There is no evidence at Tarsus that permits us to assert that the decommissioning of mercenaries in 324 occasioned an increase in coinage.

At Sidon, October 325 to September 324, a single stater die was in service, and this die, already employed in 327/326 and 326/325, remained in use until 324/323;[104] for silver, only a single tetradrachm die is known in 325/324. Suppose we accept Newell's suggestion concerning the production of the next two years, 324/323 and 323/322. In 324/323, there was a first stater die, ending its service begun three years earlier; a second die functioned only in 324/323; a third die was also used in 323/322, with two new dies engraved in 323/322. As for tetradrachms, a single die was made for them in 324/323. Now suppose we reject Newell's suggestion and date the coins marked with the letter K to 324/323, not 323/322. Five stater dies (the first in its fourth year of use) and two tetradrachm dies would have been in service in 324/323. If this is correct, one would like to know the

---

102. Alexander had Phoenician and Cypriote mercenaries in his army (Arrian, *Indica* 18.1), but the order he gave to the satraps did not apply to himself; perhaps he sent back those soldiers who were no longer fit for service, as he did at Susa or at Opis with the Macedonian veterans.

103. Pp. 135–138.

104. The use of one and the same die over four years is worth noting; on this question, see O. Mørkholm, "The Life of Obverse Dies in the Hellenistic Period," in *Studies in Numismatic Method Presented to Philip Grierson*, C. N. L. Brooke et al eds. (Cambridge, UK, 1983), pp. 11–18.

amounts of coinage struck both before June 10, 323, and in the months following Alexander's death. The Sidonians might have been caught up, after the king's passing, in events that relaunched their mint's activity.

At Tyre, the mint's production tempo remained quite steady in 325/324 and 324/323 (one stater and one tetradrachm die each year). It accelerated slightly in 323/322 and 322/321.

The contrast with the Aradus mint is striking: up to c. 323/322, 2 stater dies and 14 tetradrachm dies were in use; from c. 322/321 to c. 310/318, Duyrat has counted 10 stater dies, 1 distater die, and 182 tetradrachm dies.

There is not much to say concerning the other regional centers. Myriandrus/Alexandria ad Issum seems to have augmented its output a little following Alexander's death. At Soli on Cyprus, the chronology of the tetradrachms is not clear to me. For the other mints, Damascus, Citium, Salamis, and Byblos, the absence of a corpus makes any determination impossible.

Despite this, it seems that the evidence of the coinages from Tarsus, Tyre, and Aradus (Sidon's being annoyingly ambiguous) can be extrapolated to the entire region without too much risk. No coinage activity worth noticing appears at these three mints in 325/324 or 324/323; it was either in the early part of Alexander's reign (at Tarsus, in my view) or after his death (at Tarsus, Tyre, and especially Aradus) that the issues were most abundant. So in the present state of our knowledge, Cilicia, Phoenicia, Syria, and Cyprus do not provide any support for Thompson's thesis. I repeat what I observed above, that she did not mention this area in her article.

Arrian (7.19.5) provides an interesting piece of information. In spring 323, some weeks before his death, Alexander sent Miccalus of Clazomenae with 500 talents to Phoenicia and Syria in order to "hire recruits or purchase men accustomed to seafaring. For Alexander was planning to colonize the coast along the Persian Gulf and the islands there." If Miccalus changed these 500 talents into coined gold and silver, the production of the mints drafted for this purpose would naturally have increased for the duration of his mission. But presumably the king's death on June 10, 323, prevented Miccalus from carrying out the task. What became of the 500 talents entrusted to him?

Various events significantly affected our region in the period following June 10, 323. Craterus was in Cilicia with the 10,000 Macedonian veterans Alexander had placed in his charge; he left in 322 with 6,000 of them to help Antipater in Thessaly (cf. above, p. 66). At the settlement in summer 323, Eumenes obtained Cappadocia and Paphlagonia, which he had to begin pacifying. He received help from Perdiccas in 322–321, whose presence in Cilicia is known, for Antipater decided to confront him there (Diodorus 18.29.7). But Perdiccas, preferring to attack Ptolemy first, headed towards Egypt, passing through Syria, staying at Damascus (Arrian, *Affairs after Alexander* 28), and finally arriving at the Nile. There, conspirators in his own entourage assassinated him. Antipater, traversing Cilicia, arrived at Triparadeisos in northern Syria where the adversaries of Eumenes and the dead Perdiccas reunited. At the same time, Attalus, who commanded the fleet of his stepbrother Perdiccas, left the Egyptian coast for Tyre, which its governor Archelaus surrendered, also transferring to Attalus a sum of 800 talents that Perdiccas had left behind (Diodorus 18.37.3–4).

Antigonus, at Triparadeisos, was commissioned to defeat Eumenes, on whom he immediately declared war. Antipater died in 319. A little later the same year, Ptolemy invaded Syria, which Laomedon, the satrap, was unable to defend, and Ptolemy won over the cities of Phoenicia, where he stationed garrisons (Diodorus 18.43.1–2). Eumenes overturned Ptolemy's power in these regions in 318, recruiting mercenaries with the offer of high wages and enlisting men similarly in Cilicia and on Cyprus (Diodorus 18.61.4–5). Ptolemy reacted by directing his fleet towards Zephyrion in Cilicia (Diodorus 18.62.1), but Eumenes would probably have succeeded in conquering Phoenicia had not Antigonus confronted him with an army of elite troops. As Antigonus approached Cilicia, Eumenes chose to leave for the eastern provinces of the empire, the "upper satrapies."

After 322, the region encompassing Cilicia, Phoenicia, Syria, and Cyprus was, therefore, the theater of events that quite probably increased currency needs. The presence of troops, the preparation for military expeditions, the recruiting of mercenaries all led successive officials to strike supplementary issues of Alexanders at the existing mints. Aradus, between 322 and 318, was the region's most active monetary center by far, judging by the corpus we have at our disposal. Perhaps the various adversaries on the scene sought out the Aradians in particular for their noteworthy and favorable geographical position: their island is situated halfway between Tarsus and Tyre and, via their adjacent mainland territory, they had easy lines of communication with northern (Aleppo) and southern (Damascus) Syria.

Alexanders and Local Coinages

Did the opening of a royal mint in a city producing its own currency necessarily entail the latter's interruption? The answer remains uncertain because the chronology of the coinages concerned is not sufficiently determined. The cases of Tarsus and Cilicia also hold special interest: the monetary series, of both royal and local types, are sufficiently well dated and therefore permit observations where hypothesis is less than usually rampant.

We have seen that Alexander at Tarsus began to issue silver tetradrachms of Attic weight, with his name and types, probably a little after his victory at Issus, that is, during the autumn of 333. This coinage seems to have continued without interruption until around 320–318 and to have been accompanied by gold staters, likewise of Attic weight, with the Conqueror's name and types. The early tetradrachms are marked on the reverse with what is variously called a pellet or globule, an A, or a B (pl. 1, 1 and 4, 11–12).[105] The subsequent tetradrachms have a plow for principal symbol (see the stater illustrated on pl. 5, 12); various signs appear in the field, among which, once again, is the letter B.

Contemporaneous with these royal issues of Attic weight, the Tarsus mint produced two series of silver staters of Persian weight (between 10 and 11 grams).

[The first series (pl. 6, 5) displays *on the obverse* Baaltars seated to the left, legs parallel, holding in his right hand a flowering scepter; a part of his mantle is wrapped around his left arm; his name is inscribed behind him in Aramaic; in front of him, a wheat ear; under his seat, one reads T, M, I, or Σ. *On the reverse*, above two rows of fortified wall, a lion is shown attacking a bull; left of the lion, a club is placed obliquely; the letter B occasionally appears in the field.[106] Associated with these staters are small coins of ±.60 grams (sixteenths) with a head of Athena, right, wearing an Attic helmet, on the obverse, and a Boeotian shield and the letters B or BA on the reverse.

The second series *on the obverse* carries an image resembling Baaltars, but the right leg is drawn back and his name is not inscribed in the field; in place of the name, on one coin, *Balakrou* appears in Greek (pl. 6, 6)[107] and, on other coins, the letter B (pl. 6, 7); a symbol can be placed near the B, and it also occurs that only a symbol appears in this part of the field or even that no mark (whether letter or symbol) appears there; in front of the Baaltars, wheat ear and grape cluster; beneath the seat, T, M, I, or Σ. *On the reverse*, there is a head of Athena almost full-face, wearing an Attic helmet topped with three plumes; various marks are sometimes present in the field. There also exist sixteenths of a stater: Athena head facing/Boeotian shield decorated with thunderbolt, star in the field.]

The silver staters of the first series, in their obverse and reverse types, continue the staters from Tarsus of the Persian satrap Mazaeus that I have described above, Group 3 (p. 118, cf. pl. 6, 4). On the obverse, Baaltars has

---

105. The pellet, which is sometimes the only discernible mark, can also accompany the letter A or B; there are sometimes even four small pellets above the A.

106. Newell, *Tarsos under Alexander*, p. 85, notes that in this case there is usually no letter beneath the seat on the obverse.

107. This unique coin bearing the name of Balacrus was found in the collection H. von Aulock, cf. *SNG von Aulock* 5963. The American Numismatic Society subsequently acquired it. Cf. H. von Aulock, "Die Prägung des Balakros in Kilikien," *Jahrb. für Num. und Geldgesch.*14 (1964), pp. 79–82.

exactly the same posture, with a part of his mantle around his left arm; he holds the same scepter and his name is inscribed in the same way in Aramaic; it is evident, however, that the god on our coins is without a footstool and that the symbol is just a wheat stalk. On the reverse, the type is also the same, but the legend in Aramaic, giving the name of Mazaeus and his titles, has been omitted. These few differences lead one to think that our staters are later than Mazaeus's; the presence of the letter B as a mint magistrate's mark confirms that we are no longer in the Persian period.

The second series admits of no doubt: the name Balacrus is written in its entirety on one of the staters, that of Baaltars in Aramaic has disappeared, and the god no longer has parallel legs. As for the motif on the reverse (Athena head), it does not belong among the types of Mazaeus either.

Balacrus, who acts here as moneyer, has been identified, correctly, it seems, as the satrap and general Balacrus, son of Nicanor,[108] whom Alexander placed in charge of Cilicia immediately after the battle of Issus (Arrian 2.12.2, Diodorus 18.22.1). Before the end of Alexander's reign, he was slain in nearby Pisidia by the inhabitants of Isaura and Laranda, whose cities Perdiccas destroyed shortly after, in late 322 or early 321 (Diodorus 18.22.2–8 relates the Isaurians' heroic conduct). Bosworth asked whether the death of Balacrus did not occur around 331.[109] If it is right to think of the Balacrus on the coinage as identical with the satrap of Cilicia, it is appropriate to extend this individual's life a little longer because dating the two series of Persian staters before 331 does not look feasible. It is therefore preferable to date Balacrus's death "shortly before Alexander's" (Berve—"*kurz vor Alexanders Tode*"), around 324 (Goukowsky).

The stater where the name Balacrus appears was struck from the same reverse die as a stater whose obverse carries simply the letter B. The inference that this letter B is Balacrus's initial finds support from the fact that a sixteenth-stater belonging to the first series carries the letters BA. Must we go further and also see Balacrus's initial in the letter B on the tetradrachms of Attic weight with the name and types of Alexander? Price thought so.[110] I can come to no conclusion on this point because we are too poorly

---

108. Cf. the entry in H. Berve, *Das Alexanderreich* II (Munich, 1926), no. 200; cf. also P. Goukowsky, *Diodore de Sicile, Livre XVIII* (Paris, 1978), p. 134. After the capture of Tyre, Socrates received a command in Cilicia (Curtius 4.5.9), not the satrapy, given to Balacrus, but probably a military post.

109. *Historical Commentary* I (Oxford, 1980), p. 219 (taking up the hypothesis he had earlier suggested in *Classical Quarterly* 24 [1974], p. 58). Socrates's Cilician command after the taking of Tyre (Curtius 4.5.9) was probably a military post, if one accepts that Balacrus exercised his office as satrap up to c. 324, as is probable.

110. *Alexander* (1991), p. 370.

informed about the organization of the mints, whose quality control system could, moreover, vary from one mint to the next. If Price was right, we would have to note that Balacrus the satrap apparently shared responsibility for Alexander issues with two other individuals, the one who signed himself with a pellet and the one who signed with the letter A. For the staters and the denominations of Persian weight, there is nothing surprising, it seems to me, in the satrap's having to guarantee nonroyal coins of local character, whose circulation, with rare exceptions, was limited to the province he governed. Balacrus would have only been following the example of his predecessor Mazaeus, who always inscribed his name in its entirety on the staters he struck. Von Aulock suggested that the legend *Balakrou* indicated that Balacrus was attempting to increase his personal prestige and that he reverted to the single letter B on Alexander's orders. We could also speculate that the satrap, launching a new series with a different reverse type, thought it a good idea to vouch publicly for the first issue by putting his entire name on it.

As for the letters T, M, I, Σ placed beneath Baaltar's throne, it has been well demonstrated that they are the initials of Tarsus, Mallus, Issus, and Soli (in Cilicia). Because reverse die linkages connect the coins bearing these letters, numismatists have deduced that the coinage was centralized at Tarsus and that the letters relate to the financial contribution each of the cities made to the issues. At the beginning of the fourth century, a comparable system seems to have functioned under the Persian grandee Tiribazos:[111] on staters of the same types, there appear either the letter T or the first letters (in Greek) of Soli or Mallus, or the legend *Issikon*, and these inscriptions probably also indicate the currency runs each city financed. Was the coinage of Tiribazos all produced at Tarsus or did each city strike its own share? A corpus would show whether there were die linkages among the coins.

Thus, under Alexander, the Tarsus mint produced two sorts of coins: a royal coinage bearing the king's name, and a local coinage anonymous except for the issue in the name of the satrap Balacrus. The two coinages differed from one another in types and weight. The Persian staters did not constitute merely small change that would have been restricted to minor transactions. Weighing around 11 grams, they were suitable for varied commercial activities, and they continued in the province to play the role they had under the Persians.

How to explain the simultaneous issue of these two coinages? One possibility is that they did not have the same purpose. The royal currency was meant to circulate throughout the empire and was automatically accepted everywhere. The staters of the Baaltars type, on the contrary, though favored in transactions within Cilicia, lost all attraction outside the

---

111. See my *Naissance*, pp. 209 and 215.

provincial borders. But why did the Macedonian authority permit the striking of such a coinage? It would seem natural to extend the use of the royal currency to all transactions.

Newell offered one explanation.[112] The peoples of the East, he said, were particularly devoted to their customs, and Alexander, in all his conquests, showed himself respectful of local traditions. The Cilicians were attached to their staters with the Baaltars type, and the king, according to Newell, granted permission to the four great commercial centers of the province, Tarsus, Mallus, Issus, and Soli, to issue, at their expense, the coinage that they would have been very reluctant to forgo.

I will not comment on Newell's explanation, which introduces a psychological element difficult to assess. I have tried instead to find a practical reason of a fiscal nature for the maintenance of the Cilician coinage. Each city had its own expenses to finance; it could generate a revenue stream by issuing regional currency that would benefit from an added value in local transactions because foreign coins would have to be exchanged. The royal coinage certainly enjoyed a special status, but the circulating currency of this period still included many different coins struck elsewhere than Cilicia, the majority of them probably dating from the years prior to Alexander's arrival.

The four Cilician cities struck silver staters and some sixteenth-staters. In contrast, bronze coins produced at the Tarsus mint from c. 333[113] bear the name and types of Alexander. Currency in this metal was not a novelty in the region, but until then it had not been struck in quantity, it seems. The Macedonian administration needed bronze coins for its payments, which probably led to a greater "monetization" of retail commerce.

In Phoenicia, Syria, and Cyprus, no local coinage under Alexander exists comparable to the Cilician staters of Persian weight. Scholars have sometimes held that cities and dynasts struck coins of small denomination concurrently with the Alexander currency. Newell, for example, wrote: "Thus for Cyprus, while large quantities of Alexander staters, tetradrachms, drachms, and bronze pieces were all coined in the island mints, still, at the same time, small denominations of Rhodian weight and bearing local types were allowed to be issued. In Aradus and Byblos small denominations with local types were struck along with the regular Alexander issues."[114] As for Phoenicia, Newell's opinion clashes with that of J. and A. G. Elayi, according to whom "the issuing of Phoenician coins of civic types totally ceased after Alexander's conquest."[115]

---

112. *Tarsos under Alexander*, pp. 87–89.

113. Price, *Alexander* (1991), pp. 373, 375, 378.

114. *Tarsos under Alexander*, p. 88; Newell, we must note, does not provide any precise chronology, and his theory concerns both Alexander's reign and the years following the latter's death.

115. *Trésors de monnaies phéniciennes et circulation monétaire* (Paris, 1993), p. 333.

The publication of the corpus that these two scholars are preparing for Phoenician coinages is awaited with interest. In fact, only a gathering of the evidence will allow us to establish accurate chronologies. At Tyre, as we have seen, the question of Azemilkos's personal coinage urgently needs resolution. One would also like to know the monetary condition of Cyprus during this period more precisely.

If the absence, during Alexander's lifetime, of any issue of local currency in Phoenicia, Syria, and Cyprus were to be confirmed, we could still not conclude that the Conqueror had forbidden this kind of coinage. His conduct towards Cilicia, his tolerance towards the regional dynasts, lead one to think he would not have been averse to the striking of a coinage other than his own (on the condition, I suppose, that this coinage responded strictly to local needs). But rather than engage in speculation, it is better to await the proper resolution of chronological questions.

In any case, the coin hoards from the end of the fourth century found in this region seem to show that the currency produced in the area prior to Alexander's arrival continued in use after 333. The 1973 *Inventory of Greek Coin Hoards* (*IGCH*), the publication *Coin Hoards*,[116] and, for Phoenicia, the survey of the Elayis (*Trésors de monnaies phéniciennes*)[117] provide several examples of deposits in which local coins are mingled with coins of Alexander. Also note the presence in certain of these hoards of coins with Athenian types[118] (Athenian "owls" began to be imitated in the Levant, more or less accurately, from the end of the fifth century). By contrast, darics and sigloi of the Great King are conspicuous for their rarity.

Studying the lists drawn up by Price in his *Alexander* (1991), one has the impression that staters and tetradrachms formed the core of the royal coinage under Alexander and that silver fractions and bronze coins were struck sparingly.[119] The Macedonian authorities would have produced currency primarily to make large payments. This view probably needs some adjustment. On the one hand, Price's collection is not a corpus and does not indicate the number of dies used for the different denominations; on

---

116. This publication, with the objective to list, periodically, newly discovered hoards, first appeared in London in 1975; vol. 8 dates from 1994. Since then, a list of new hoards is appended each year to the *Numismatic Chronicle*.

117. In Cilicia: *Coin Hoards* 8 (1994), no. 210 (hoard buried c. 310); on Cyprus: *ibid.*, no. 198; in Phoenicia and Syria: *IGCH* 1517 (Elayi, no. XXII), 1506 (Elayi, no. XXIII), 1510 (Elayi, no. XXVI), 1509 (Elayi, no. XXXIV), 1507 (Elayi, no. XLVII). Cf. also Elayi, nos. XLVI and LVIII.

118. In a hoard found in Cilicia: *IGCH* 1421, and also in the Abu Shusheh hoard in Judaea: *IGCH* 1507 (Elayi, no. XLVII).

119. Thus, at Damascus, where a handsome series of Alexander tetradrachms was struck, no smaller silver denomination or bronze coin has been identified so far (Price, op. cit., pp. 398–401).

the other hand, bronze coins and small change in silver have not survived to the same extent as tetradrachms and staters. Their lesser value provided no incentive to save them, reducing their chances of survival for us; moreover, they wore out more rapidly than the large denominations[120] and disappeared from circulation more quickly. Finally, few amateur collectors, at least until recently, have shown interest in these small silver and bronze coins, so that the latter are often poorly represented in public and private collections.

The issuance of small denominations was all the more natural in those regions where the inhabitants of some localities were accustomed under the Persians to deal with coins of small value. The Aradians were the leaders in this, putting into circulation really tiny silver coins. The Al Mina hoard[121] contained fifty-one specimens: the ascertained weight lies between .04 and .11 grams. The deposit also included four coins from Sidon, three of them weighing between .58 and .76 grams; the fourth is described as one-thirty-second of a siglos (in other words, one-half of the three other coins).

The Elayis' survey includes several other deposits consisting of silver coins weighing less than a gram, with provenances from Byblos, Sidon, and Tyre. Some of these hoards were buried in Alexander's time, so one infers that the small change of the Persian period had not fallen out of use and that it complemented the small denominations issued by the Macedonian administration. It is clear that the Phoenicians had introduced the use of coined silver and bronze currency[122] in retail transactions well before 333.

---

120. H. de Nanteuil, "Le frai des monnaies d'or et d'argent," *Courrier numismatique* 16 (1928), pp. 3–29, wrote that coins in comparable circulation suffered almost the same yearly wear and tear (that is, the loss of weight from usage), no matter the coin's size: an obol of ± .72 grams lost as much weight as a tetradrachm of ±17.20 grams. Consequently, the life of an obol was much shorter than a tetradrachm's . F. Delamare, *Le frai et ses lois* (Paris, 1994) does not dispute this assertion, but he admits that there can be exceptions; cf. my thoughts, "Sur le frai de certaines monnaies anciennes et contemporaines," *Mélanges de la Bibl. de la Sorbonne offerts à André Tuilier* 8 (1988), pp. 70–83 (= *Études d'hist. monétaire et financière* I, Athens, 1999, pp. 241–54); also, my *Naissance*, pp. 68–69.

121. E. S. G. Robinson, *NC* 17 (1937), pp. 184–85, first published this hoard (discovered at a level dated by the excavator, C. L. Wooley, to 430-375); J. and A. G. Elayi, op. cit., pp. 62–67, have succeeded in locating 28 of the 55 coins and in completing their inventory thanks to notes Robinson left. Handling such tiny coins must have posed problems for the Aradians.

122. For the hoards containing Phoenician coins and buried in Alexander's time, cf. Elayi, op. cit., hoard of Qasr Naba, no. XXIII (*IGCH* 1506): sixteenths of a siglos (± .70 grams) from Byblos, Sidon, and Tyre found with an Alexander tetradrachm struck at Babylon and an obol probably issued at Sidon (there was also a Sidonian thirty-second of a siglos). The village of Qasr Naba is located between Zahleh and Baalbeck. Also, hoard from the Akko region, no. XXXIV (*IGCH* 1509) with sixteenths and thirty-seconds of a Tyrian siglos mixed in with Alexander bronzes from Tyre; hoard from the region around Gaza, no.

Of course, probably only a part of the population was involved in its use: the demands of urban life in large centers like Tyre and Sidon explain the beginning of this "monetization," which was so noticeable at Aradus as early as the beginning of fourth century, at least if the Al Mina hoard cited above was actually buried before 375.

In my view, the victories at Issus and Tyre were critically important for Alexander's coinage. It was following Issus (autumn of 333) that Alexander deemed it essential to issue his own currency as a way to proclaim his sovereignty in a region where Persian satraps and local dynasts had produced their own coins up till then. He began, apparently, by striking silver tetradrachms (the metal most commonly coined in Greece and the East), and he chose as reverse type a representation of Zeus inspired by one of the images of Baal with which Mazaeus had adorned his silver staters at Tarsus. Alexander briefly deferred the creation of his gold coinage, a means of payment useful in large, wholesale transactions but also an effective weapon against the prestige that the Great King gained from his darics. Alexander inaugurated this coinage when the capture of Tyre (July 332) gave him mastery of the sea, and this explains the presence of a stylis, a symbol of maritime power, in Nike's hand. The new coinage types were communicated to Antipater, who launched Macedonian production of the Alexander currency. It will be noted, however, on my proposed chronology, that no royal mint was opened in western Asia Minor at this time. Moreover, Alexander does not seem to have insisted on total control in coinage matters. The king of Tyre, for example, was able to inscribe his own name and regnal years in Phoenician on the reverse of the Alexanders he issued. The Cilicians continued to strike silver staters of Persian weight and Baaltars type. The coins produced by satraps and dynasts from the Persian era did not disappear from circulation. This conduct of Alexander, in a region where he could have imposed exclusive usage of his coinage without any difficulty, reveals, I believe, the Conqueror's monetary pragmatism, as my final two chapters will only confirm.

XLVI, with small coins of Aradus and Sidonian sixteenths of a siglos found with "Philisto-Arabian" coins and Babylonian Alexanders; Abu Shusheh hoard, no. XLVII (*IGCH* 1507): small and bronze coins from Sidon associated with some Alexanders, imitation Athenian coins, and "Philisto-Arabian" coins. For bronze issues prior to 333, cf., for example, by the same authors, "La dernière série tyrienne en bronze aux types civiques," *NAC* 27 (1998), pp. 129–39.

Chapter 6

Alexander and Coinage in Egypt

Tyre fell in July 332. After seeing to the city's condition and regrouping his forces, Alexander departed for Egypt. A redoubtable obstacle stood in his way, the fortress of Gaza, which the governor,[1] loyal to Darius, had decided to defend. It took the Macedonian army a two-month siege to prevail (Diodorus 17.48.7), and Alexander was wounded in the shoulder. All the men of Gaza died fighting. The Conqueror, Arrian says (2.27.7), enslaved the women and children, repopulated the city by bringing in inhabitants from the surrounding region (as he had done with the population of Tyre), and turned Gaza into a base of operations. Plutarch (*Alexander* 25.6) mentions the booty captured at the fortress. Alexander sent most of it to his nearest and dearest (his mother Olympias, his sister Cleopatra, and his friends); to his teacher Leonidas he made a gift of 500 talents of incense and 100 talents of myrrh in memory of some advice Leonidas had given him several years earlier.[2]

According to Plutarch (*Alex.* 26.1–2), it was after the siege of Gaza that Darius's splendid coffer[3] came into Alexander's possession, the "casket" in which Alexander decided to place his copy of the *Iliad* that Aristotle had given him[4] and that the king never ceased to read and annotate (Plutarch, *Alex.* 8.2).

---

1. He was named Betis according to Curtius (4.6.7), Batis according to Arrian (2.25.4).

2. As Alexander, during a sacrifice, was picking up two handfuls of incense, Leonidas recommended that he be less prodigal until such time as he became master of the land of spices.

3. P. Green, *Alexander of Macedon* (Berkeley, CA, 1991 edition), p. 245, thinks that this object belonged to the enormous booty Parmenio captured at Damascus and on the surrounding plain, where the traitorous Persian governor had feigned flight (Curtius 3.13; cf. Arrian 2.15.1).

4. Cf. chapter 1, p. 11.

Alexander in Egypt (November 332 to April 331)

If we suppose that the king left Tyre at the end of August and that Gaza detained him for two months, his arrival at the Egyptian border occurred in November 332 (he covered the distance from Gaza to Pelusium, roughly 125 miles, in six days of marching, while his fleet followed him by sea; Arrian 3.1.1). The Persian satrap of Egypt at the time was Mazaces, who had replaced Sabaces when the latter fell at the battle of Issus. During 332 Mazaces had had to fight the Macedonian Amyntas, son of Antiochus, who was in the service of the Great King. After Issus, Amyntas took his troops to Tripolis in Phoenicia, and then to Cyprus; from there he sailed to Egypt where he achieved some successes before the satrap annihilated him (Diodorus 17.48.2–5; Curtius 4.1.27–33; Arrian 2.13.2–3).

Impressed with Alexander's victories, and given his own diminished forces, Mazaces decided to welcome the Conqueror warmly. He surrendered Egypt and, at Memphis, delivered to Alexander more than 800 talents and all the royal goods and chattel (Curtius 4.7.4). Egypt had such an abundance of gold[5] that at least part of the Memphis treasure probably consisted of bullion. As for the value of what the victor obtained, presumably it was calculated in units of silver talents, as was customary.

Diodorus, who arrived in Egypt during the 180th Olympiad (60/59–57/56 BC), informs us (1.31.7–8) that it had the highest population density in the world, that it contained more than 30,000 cities and large villages under Ptolemy I, and that, according to his sources, its inhabitants had numbered around 7 million in the past and not less than 3 million in his own time.[6] So the conquest of such a province enriched Alexander considerably.

In the Egyptian capital, the Macedonian king sacrificed "to the gods, especially Apis, and held athletic and musical games; the most famous per-

---

5. See the recent work of Alfredo and Angelo Castiglione, *Das Goldland der Pharaonen* (Mainz, 1998), the German translation of a book originally published in Italian in 1995. The text, written in collaboration with J. Vercoutter and with contributions from several authors, has superb illustrations. The mines were located in the south, between the Nile and the Red Sea; the gold from Koptos and Kousch was celebrated. The Castiglioni have explored the region of Wadi Allaqi (right bank of the Nile, at the entry points to Nubia) and they think they have discovered the location of the ancient Berenike Pankhrysos ["the all-golden"—WEH] (the name is found in Pliny the Elder, *Natural History*, 6.170).

6. Almost all the manuscripts of Diodorus give this figure of 3 million: is it an error in the tradition? Several scholars have thought so, believing that the true reading of Diodorus's text showed that the number of inhabitants was 7 million in the past and that in the first century BC the number was not inferior. A passage in Josephus (*Jewish War* 2.385) seems to incline this way: the author writes that the Egyptian population, excluding Alexandria, reached 7.5 million. Prevailing opinion today, however, accepts the 3 million figure, which better suits, I may say, the papyrological evidence from the Roman period.

formers in both athletics and music came to him there from Greece" (Arrian 3.1.4). Contrary to what many modern authors have written, it is not certain that Alexander had himself solemnly crowned as Pharaoh at Memphis. S. M. Burstein[7] has reacted vigorously against this opinion, showing that it rests on the sole evidence of Pseudo-Callisthenes,[8] while no other ancient historian mentions such a crowning. Although Alexander was recognized as master of Egypt and consequently as Pharaoh, nothing indicates that he performed specific and essential Egyptian rituals. Arrian devotes considerable space to the Greek contests that Alexander organized and to his conduct as commander-in-chief; one may imagine that the sacrifices he undertook were meant as much for the Greek gods as for local divinities. It is to be noted that Arrian subsequently (3.5.2) says that Alexander, passing by Memphis again, paid homage to Zeus the king, and he emphasizes that the Conqueror once more celebrated athletic and artistic competitions.

Two events stand out during Alexander's stay in Egypt: his visit to the oracle of Ammon in the Siwah oasis,[9] and his choice of a site for the new city he decided to found under the name of Alexandria.[10] The ancient authors do not agree on their sequence. Arrian (3.2.1) and Plutarch (*Alex*. 26.6) put the city's foundation before the journey to Siwah, Curtius (4.8.1) and Justin (11.11.13) after. According to Ps.-Callisthenes (1.32.6–7), Alexandria was founded in the month Tybi, more precisely, on the twenty-fifth of Tybi, a date corresponding to April 7 in the Ptolemaic calendar. A certain number of commentators have taken this evidence seriously, all the more so since the city's horoscope likewise puts its birthday in April (but a few days later, on the sixteenth).[11] Since Arrian (3.6.1) tells us that Alexander returned to Phoenicia at

---

7. "Pharaoh Alexander: A Scholarly Myth," *Ancient Society* 22 (1991), pp. 139–45. Burstein cites in particular the narrative of P. Green, op. cit., p. 269: "So, on 14 November 332, the young Macedonian was solemnly instated as Pharaoh. They placed the double crown on his head and the crook and flail in his hands. He became simultaneously god and king, incarnation and son of Ra and Osiris; he was Horus the Golden One, the mighty prince, beloved of Amon, king of Upper and Lower Egypt."

8. *Le Roman d'Alexandre* I, 34 (translated with commentary by G. Bounoure and B. Serret, Paris, 1992): "The Egyptians enthroned him as king of Egypt, placing him on the throne of Hephaestus" (that is, Ptah).

9. On the Siwah oasis, see the report of J. Leclant, "*Per Africae sitientia*. Témoignages des sources classiques sur les pistes menant à l'oasis d'Ammon," *Bull. Inst. fr. d'archéol. orient.* 49 (1950), pp. 193–253.

10. On the site and plan of Alexandria, see A. Bernand, *Alexandrie la Grande* (Paris, 1998), pp. 31–73.

11. For an overview of the question, with earlier bibliography, see P. M. Fraser, *Ptolemaic Alexandria* (Oxford, 1972), I, p. 4, and II, pp. 3–4 (note 9); P. Goukowsky, *Diodore de Sicile, Livre XVII* (Paris, 1976), p. 207. Note that in the Julian calendar, Tybi 25 falls on January 20: a version of this account in the *Alexander Romance*, written in Roman times, speaks of the city's foundation in January.

the beginning of spring in 331, the city's foundation would have been his last act in Egypt and has to be dated after his journey to the Ammon oasis.

Ammon was not a new divinity for Alexander. Cyrenaeans (of Dorian origin from Thera) had spread his cult in Greece. As Leclant and Clerc have written,[12] the Cyrenaeans had adapted Ammon to Greek taste, raising him to the level of the Hellenic Zeus and creating a new iconographic type. Through their commercial relations with Sparta and Thebes, they propagated Ammon's cult and image in Greece. The god had a temple and oracle at Aphytis in Chalcidice, on the peninsula of Pallene (his only oracle apart from Siwah). Leclant and Clerc have demonstrated the devotion accorded him at the Macedonian court, a devotion that increased when Philip II became master of the Chalcidice in 348: "Such are the antecedents," writes Leclant, "of Alexander's famous pilgrimage to the oasis sanctuary in 331."

Alexander also named new officials to oversee Egypt. Arrian's comments (3.5.7) are worth citing: "It is said that he divided the government of Egypt among many officers, as he was strongly impressed by the character and defensibility of the country and did not think it safe to entrust the command of all Egypt to one man." Arrian goes on to observe that the Romans learned from Alexander to treat the country with special care, so that they sent knights, not senators, to be governors there. Diodorus (1.30–31) also emphasized Egypt's natural defenses that served to protect it well against external assaults.

In other provinces, power had been distributed according to the Persian practice among a satrap, a citadel commandant (or *phrourarkhos*), and a tax collector. In Egypt, Alexander was particularly careful to define responsibilities. Arrian (3.5.2–6) informs us of the royal appointments affecting the armed forces left behind on the banks of the Nile. In the same passage, he reports that the Conqueror named two *nomarchs* for Egypt, Doloaspis and Petisis, and that he divided all the provincial territory between them.[13]

---

12. *Lex. Icon. Myth. Class.*, I, s.v. Ammon, pp. 666–67.

13. One of these men probably received the government of Upper Egypt, the other of Lower Egypt. J. Yoyotte, "Le nom égyptien du 'ministre de l'Economie' de Saïs à Méroé," *Comptes rendus Acad. Inscr. et Belles-Lettres*, 1985, p. 82, writes that Doloaspis was "a Persian official judging by his name, and Petisis of Egyptian stock." H. S. Smith read the name Pediese in a fragmentary inscription on an *ostrakon* in demotic: "A Memphite Miscellany," in *Pyramid Studies and Other Essays Presented to I. E. S. Edwards*, J. Bains et al. eds. (Egypt Exploration Society, Occasional Publications 7, 1988), pp. 184–86. After Pediese the title of satrap appears in the inscription and Smith suggests, among other possibilities, the reading "Pediese the satrap." S. M. Burstein has identified this individual as the Petisis of Arrian (cf. H. S. Smith, in *Life in a Multicultural Society: Egypt from Cambyses to Constantine and Beyond*, J. H. Johnson ed., Chicago, 1992, p. 296). The title of satrap would correspond to "nomarch" in the Arrian passage, but the problem is that Petisis, according to Arrian, did not accept the office Alexander offered him.

Arrian adds, "Petisis, however, declined the power, and Doloaspis took it all.... The government of the neighboring country of Libya was given to Apollonius son of Charinus; and that of Arabia around Heroönpolis to Cleomenes from Naucratis."

This was not Cleomenes's only government post. Arrian (3.5.4) reports that, while Cleomenes was required to let the nomarchs[14] administer their districts ("nomes") as usual, he was to make sure that they remitted to himself the *phoroi* (taxes) they collected. Cleomenes, moreover, had received from Alexander the mission to build Alexandria (Ps.-Aristotle, *Oeconomica* 2.33 c; Justin 13.4.11). It is clear that Cleomenes needed a great deal of money in order to accomplish this major undertaking successfully, and that explains why Alexander diverted the revenues of Egypt to him. But in acting so, the king was not being entirely faithful to the principle of separation of powers that he had resolved strictly to observe in this country. Cleomenes, as governor of an Egyptian region, directed civil and military services; as chief treasurer, he had considerable financial power at his disposal. Finally, the mission to build Alexandria conferred on him a position of the first importance and entitled him to subordinate everything to the realization of this great endeavor. I will have more to say about Cleomenes in the course of this chapter.

Alexander left Egypt in spring 331. Did he issue any coinage before his departure? M. J. Price developed the theory that he struck a bronze coinage at Memphis between November 332 and April 331 which consisted of small coins (10–11 millimeters in diameter) with his portrait on the obverse. Before taking up this issue, we had better outline as succinctly as possible the evidence we have on monetary activity in Egypt prior to the Macedonian conquest.

Egyptian Coinage before 332: C. M. Kraay's Treatment

That excellent scholar of archaic and classical coins, C. M. Kraay, set forth the state of the evidence, as of 1976, on coinage produced in Egypt prior to 332.[15] He wrote that, despite its relations with Greece and its

---

14. Are we dealing with two, "grand" nomarchs designated by Alexander, or with ordinary nomarchs who headed the numerous districts (called "nomes") into which the country was divided? Yoyotte, op. cit., p. 82, favors the former explanation. P. Briant, *From Cyrus to Alexander: A History of the Persian Empire*, Eng. trans. by P. T. Daniels (Winona Lake, IN, 2002), p. 413, thinks that Arrian's text uses the term nomarch in two different senses: the nomarchs in charge of collecting taxes and remitting the sum to Cleomenes would have been district leaders. This is also the view of Bosworth, *Historical Commentary* I (Oxford, 1980), p. 277, who observes that Egypt was divided into forty-two nomes.

15. *Archaic and Classical Greek Coins* (London, 1976), pp. 294–95.

familiarity with the currencies of the Aegean, Egypt had struck very few coins under its native dynasties and the Persian kings. (Remember that the Persian Cambyses conquered Egypt in 525 to 522. The Persians lost it in 404, but Artaxerexes III regained it in 343 to 342.) Kraay demonstrated that hoards discovered there from the first part of the fifth century included coins from different parts of the Greek world.[16] These coins were occasionally cut into pieces and found with unminted metal and objects, and so were regarded, in short, as nothing more than silver ingots. Kraay established that in the second half of the fifth century and in the fourth century up to Alexander's time, Athenian tetradrachms occupied a dominant, if not exclusive, position in Egyptian hoards. That is why, he continued, the rare coinages occasionally struck on Egyptian soil were almost all imitations of Athenian coinage. He cited, first, the gold stater with Athena head and owl as types but on which we read, not the initials of Athens (AΘE), but "Taos" (written in *Greek*: cf. pl. 6, 8),[17] the name of the pharaoh most commonly spelled Takhos, who ruled from 361–359. Kraay next mentioned the pseudo-Athenian tetradrachms where the legend *in demotic* "Artaxerxes Pharaoh" (pl. 6, 9) replaces the Athenian initials. At the time Kraay wrote, in 1976, two specimens of this series were known, struck from two obverse and two reverse dies.[18] Finally, Kraay recalled the successive pseudo-Athenian coins in the names (in *Aramaic*) of Sabaces (pl. 6, 10) and Mazaces (pl. 6, 11), the last two Persian satraps of Egypt.

---

16. The Asyut deposit, buried c. 475 B. C., provides a handsome example of a hoard of this sort; cf. M. J. Price and N. M. Waggoner, *Archaic Greek Silver Coinage, the Asyut Hoard* (London, 1975): the two authors inventoried 873 silver coins of most diverse provenances.

17. Cf. Kraay, op. cit., pp. 76 and 295, pl. 12, no. 217; on the reverse a papyrus reed replaces the Athenian olive branch. The weight of the sole stater known is nearer a daric's than an Athenian stater's. Takhos declared himself independent of Artaxerxes II in 361 and was proclaimed pharaoh; the expedition he launched against the Great King in 359 failed, and Takhos, having been betrayed by his nephew Nektanebo, found refuge with Artaxerxes.

18. O. Mørkholm and A. F. Shore studied these two coins in, respectively, "A coin of Artaxerxes III" and "The Demotic Inscription on a Coin of Artaxerxes," *NC* 14 (1974), pp. 1–8. G. K. Jenkins, *NC* 15 (1955), p. 144, no. 20, published one of the specimens, that in the British Museum, but interpreted the legend incorrectly. The second specimen, acquired by the Coin Cabinet of Copenhagen, belonged to the hoard from Babylon published in 1973 (cf. Price, in *Mnemata, Papers in Memory of N. M. Waggoner*, W. E. Metcalf ed., New York, 1991, p. 71, no. 135). We can assume that Artaxerxes initiated the coinage after 343/2; he died in 338. It now seems certain that his successor Arses (338–336) took the crown name Artaxerxes (IV): E. Badian so concluded after studying the trilingual inscription found at the Letoön of Xanthos, "A Document of Artaxerxes IV?" *Greece and the Eastern Mediterranean in Ancient History and Prehistory, Studies Presented to F. Schachermeyer*, K. Kinzl ed. (Berlin, 1977), pp. 40–50. Thus, some of the tetradrachms in the name of Artaxerxes could have been struck by Artaxerxes IV.

Kraay emphasized that only one group of gold coins, without legend, issued perhaps by Nektanebo II (359–343), Takhos's successor, escaped the influence of Athenian types: a galloping horse appears on the obverse, two hieroglyphs that together signify "pure gold" on the reverse (pl. 6, 12).[19]

Kraay's study therefore portrayed Egypt in the fifth century and the first decades of the fourth as a country little inclined to issue coinage and, when it did so, being content, with perhaps one exception, to reproduce the types on Athenian currency. This leaves the strong impression that most Egyptians had not adopted the use of coinage; the idea that some pseudo-Athenian coins of Takhos, Artaxerxes, Sabaces, and Mazaces were meant for paying mercenaries or foreign creditors, not for internal commerce, reinforces this impression. The only real sign of an incipient "monetization" was the small bronze coins produced by Sabaces and Mazaces just before the Macedonian conquest.

Egyptian Coinage before Alexander: The Proposals of T. V. Buttrey

According to T. V. Buttrey, coins struck in Egypt before 332 were not limited to the few issues Kraay identified: they were more numerous than anyone ever suspected.

Buttrey based himself on an analysis of a hoard of 347 tetradrachms with Athenian types most likely found in the Fayum. He published his conclusions in 1979[20] without, regrettably, an accompanying publication of the hoard: only a few coins were illustrated. One must therefore rely on the author's assertions, an author, I hasten to add, of unquestioned competence.

According to Buttrey, the hoard contained only a very few coins struck at Athens itself; nearly all were of Egyptian origin, dating from the fourth century, although the eye of Athena was shown facing on all but one specimen. The two specimens known at the time, with the types of Athens and the name of Pharaoh Artaxerxes, mentioned above, provided a chronological reference point. Those two tetradrachms, very probably to be dated after 343/2, also show the eye of Athena facing, while the Athena head shares the style evident on a fair number of the Athena heads in the Fayum hoard. Buttrey, observing the stylistic variety and differing degrees of wear on the hoard's coins, thought that their striking extended over a period of

---

19. On the history of the first coin of this group found in Egypt, see A. O. Bolshakov, "The Earliest Known Gold Pharaonic Coin," *Rev. d'Egyptol.* 44 (1992), pp. 3–9.

20. "Pharaonic Imitations of Athenian Tetradrachms," in *Actes du 9e Congrès international de numismatique 1979*, 1 (Louvain la Neuve—Luxembourg, 1982), pp. 137–40; Buttrey summarized his observations at the 1979 Congress in "More on the Athenian Law Coinage of 375/374 BC," *NAC* 10 (1981), pp. 76–78.

time, and he added the important observation that some other large hoards found in Egypt have the same composition and characteristics as the Fayum hoard and so would date from the same decades. In total, some hundreds of dies would have been engraved for the striking of these fourth-century pseudo-Athenian tetradrachms.

Buttrey's analysis, if correct, would have two major consequences. First, we would have to correct the view that huge quantities of Athenian tetradrachms penetrated into Egypt in the second half of the fifth century: a large part of these coins would, in fact, be of Egyptian origin and date from the fourth century. The quality of their style, the precision of their weight, their technique of striking and Athena's facing eye let them be taken for authentic fifth-century Athenian currency, when we are dealing, according to Buttrey, with Egyptian issues of the following century. Second, we would have to accept that, between the two Persian dominations (404 and 343/2, 28th–30th Dynasties), the pharaohs, far from appearing almost dormant in monetary activity, would have produced a relatively abundant coinage, probably struck at Memphis and well-suited for paying mercenaries, who valued Athenian currency. Takhos's gold stater with the types of Athens would fit into this series, which the tetradrachms in the name of Artaxerxes and the satraps Sabaces and Mazaces follow.

Buttrey's argument is seductive. His conclusions, however, are so important for the monetary history of Egypt that one hesitates to adopt them before knowing the evidence better. I note that C. Flament has recently published a critical examination of Buttrey's proposals[21] in which he, too, cautions prudence but without assuming an entirely negative attitude.

The Syrian Hoard: Additional Data

In 1993, Price provided an inventory of 164 silver coins he had seen on the numismatic market.[22] Their provenance, in all probability, was a hoard brought to light in northern Syria, east of Aleppo, not far from the Euphrates. Most of them (142) were tetradrachms with Athenian types, and 18 undoubtedly belonged to Egypt: 10 were in the name of Pharaoh Artaxerxes (in demotic), 8 in the name of the satrap Sabaces (in Aramaic). The

---

21. "A propos des styles d'imitations athéniennes définis par T. V. Buttrey," *RBN* 147 (2001), pp. 39–50; Flament's article contains some interesting technical discussions. Carmen Arnold-Biucchi has undertaken the detailed study of the hoard, which is preserved in the Kelsey Museum in Ann Arbor.

22. "More from Memphis and the Syria 1989 Hoard," in *Essays in Honour of Robert Carson and Kenneth Jenkins*, M. J. Price et al. eds. (London, 1993), pp. 31–35.

other specimens were struck at Sinope, Cyzicus, Ephesus, Tarsus (Datames and Mazaeus), at Membog-Hierapolis (Abdhadad and Abyati), and at Tyre; 1 specimen was struck by a Persian high official (the king of Persia as archer/ a mounted Persian holding a lance). The hoard might have been buried around 333.

If it was truly discovered in northern Syria, the fact that it contains five coins issued at Membog-Hierapolis indicates, perhaps, that the find occurred in this great sanctuary's environs, situated to the west of the Euphrates, not far from the river, between Zeugma and Thapsacus. The currency struck in this area[23] and bearing the names of Abdhadad, Abyati, Mazdai (Mazaeus), and Alexander (the legends are in Aramaic) does not seem to have circulated widely, and consequently the presence in the hoard of the five specimens in question assumes some significance.

The ten Egyptian tetradrachms with demotic inscription (cf. pl. 6, 9) provide a few surprises. First, the coins are divided among numerous obverse dies that are to be added to the two we knew already. Therefore, this coinage was clearly more abundant than supposed, and all the more so because the number of dies is not much less than the number of surviving coins, which means statistically that future discoveries of specimens from this group will reveal still more dies. Second, among the specimens Price described, several have the Athena eye not facing but in profile; so they are harbingers of the issues of Sabaces and Mazaces, where the eye is also in profile. The presence on one of them of the symbol (a stylized thunderbolt?) characteristic of Sabaces's coins reinforces the connection between the coins with demotic legend and the satrap's tetradrachms. Finally, on some specimens, the demotic is written in a way that scholars find odd, and Aramaic letters are placed in the field.

H. Nicolet-Pierre, we note, has catalogued the pseudo-Athenian tetradrachms of Sabaces and Mazaces, observing eleven obverse dies for the former, only one for the latter. She paid particular attention to the legends and Aramaic letters and provided a useful commentary on the name of Sabaces, whose Iranian origin now seems assured. She also pub-

---

23. H. Seyrig, "Le monnayage de Hiérapolis de Syrie à l'époque d'Alexandre," *RN* 13 (1971), pp. 11–21 (= *Scripta numismatica*, Paris, 1986, pp. 171–81); L. Mildenberg, "A Note on the Coinage of Hierapolis-Bambyce," in *Travaux de numis. grecque offerts à G. Le Rider*, M. Amandry and S. Hurter eds. (London, 1999), pp. 277–84. Coinage in the name of Mazdai has recently been discovered: P. Bordreuil, *Civilisation du Proche-Orient*, série I, *Archéologie* 3 (1996), pp. 27–30, and *Comptes rendus Acad. Inscr. et Belles-Lettres*, 1998, pp. 219–27 (cf. G. Le Rider, *ibid.*, pp. 228–29, and A. Lemaire, *Mécanismes et innovations monétaires dans l'Anatolie achéménide*, Istanbul-Paris, 2000, pp. 136–38). One issue bears the Greek letters ΣΕ, very probably the abbreviation for "Seleukou" (cf. Seyrig, op. cit., p. 21, no. 14).

lished the small bronze coins in the name of these two satraps (pl. 6, 13: Sabaces; pl. 6, 14: Mazaces).[24] Of the eight tetradrachms of Sabaces contained in the northern Syrian hoard Price inventoried, only one (no. 161), it appears, was struck from an obverse die not recorded by Nicolet-Pierre.

Concerning the demotic legend distinguishing the tetradrachms in the name of Artaxerxes, Buttrey, taking up a suggestion of Mørkholm and Shore, thought that these coins with Athenian types and Egyptian language were not meant only for mercenaries and foreign traders, but also for the local population. C. M. Harrison has questioned this viewpoint,[25] observing that the use of demotic only permits us to say that the mint magistrate responsible for the legend was an Egyptian. It would be stretching things too far, she says, to conclude from this single fact that the coins were produced, at least in part, with Egyptians in mind; she adds that, following Buttrey's reasoning, we would have to conclude that a few years later the tetradrachms of Sabaces and Mazaces with Aramaic legend were struck for an Aramaic-speaking population.

Harrison's point is well taken. What one can say, I believe, is that Aramaic was the language used by Persian officials who struck coins in fourth-century Cilicia, and it is not startling to see Sabaces and Mazaces using it. Mørkholm, Shore, and Buttrey were surprised, I suppose, to find demotic where they expected Aramaic. Their interpretation certainly goes too far, but one does wonder why the Persian authorities allowed the Egyptian engraver to use his own language. Perhaps it was simply for a practical reason (there was no artisan in the mint who knew Aramaic) or for some other cause. The question, anyway, is worth asking.

The pseudo-Athenian tetradrachms that constituted nearly all of the Egyptian issues of the fourth century were certainly not suitable for everyday usage. At least that segment of the Egyptian population involved in commercial operations of a certain scale had begun to acquaint themselves with coined currency, and the last two satraps' issue of bronze coins is telling: there was a palpable need for coinage amidst the small transactions of daily life in that great urban center, Memphis.

---

24. "Les monnaies des deux derniers satrapes d'Egypte avant la conquête d'Alexandre," in *Essays in Honor of Margaret Thompson*, O. Mørkholm and N. M. Waggoner eds. (Wetteren, 1979), pp. 221–30. All ancient authors do not transcribe the name of Sabaces in this form; Newell thought this high official was an Egyptian, but Nicolet-Pierre agrees with the opinion of M. Sznycer, whom she consulted: Sabaces's name is Iranian. As for Mazaces, he was, like Mazaeus, of Persian origin.

25. *Coins of the Persian Satraps*, doctoral dissertation, Univ. of Pennsylvania, 1982, pp. 381–82.

Did Alexander Strike Bronze Coins in Egypt between November 332 and April 331 with His Portrait on the Obverse? Price's Theory

In 1981, publishing 217 coins discovered at Saqqara, the necropolis of Memphis, in the precinct for sacred animals, Price[26] described three small bronze coins, of 10–11 millimeters in diameter, found with two others of the same metal, one from Sidon, the other of indeterminate origin, but probably struck outside Egypt.

A young head appears on the obverse of the three bronzes, and its headdress poses an identification problem. In a descriptive note, Price presented it as an "oriental leather cap," while in his commentary he notes that it is shaped like a Phrygian cap; he finally interprets it as a helmet (I will come back to this). On the reverse of the three bronzes, there is a forepart of Pegasus, along with the letter A and a wreath (not having photos of the Saqqara specimens, I give, in pl. 6, 15–16, the reproduction of two coins, from an older find, at the British Museum, illustrated by Price in his *Alexander*, pl. 149).

Price recalled that Babelon[27] had attributed this coinage to a Persian satrap of western Asia Minor (who would have used the mint at Lampsacus, as indicated by the forepart of Pegasus, the city's emblem). Price neglected to note (an omission he shortly corrected)[28] that Troxell in 1977, publishing a coin of the American Numismatic Society (pl. 6, 17), had suggested assigning it to Mithradates I Callinicus, king of Commagene at the start of the first century BC.[29]

Price stressed that, in addition to the three specimens found together at Saqqara, another came to light on the same site (in zone five of the excavations), and that a fifth specimen, kept in the British Museum, had been

---

26. "Coins," in G. T. Martin, *The Sacred Animal Necropolis at North Saqqâra, The Southern Dependencies of the Main Temple Complex* (Excavation Memoir, No. 50, London, 1981), pp.157–65. The three bronzes in question are described on pp. 162–63 (nos. 173–75); the two bronzes with which they were found are nos. 182–83 (p. 165).

27. *Perses Achéménides* (Paris, 1893), p. 56, no. 379: the satrap would be Orontes; *Traité des monnaies grecques et romaines* II, 2 (Paris, 1910), pp. 121–22, no. 66: "Satrap unknown (Autophradates?)". J. Babelon, publishing this coin in his catalogue (no. 2900) of the Luynes collection, in 1930, did not take a position on the identity.

28. He cited this study in the article that he wrote during the following months and about which I will presently speak, "A Portrait of Alexander the Great from Egypt," *Norsk Numismatic Forening (NNF-NYTT)* 1 (1981), pp. 32–37.

29. "Greek Accessions: Asia Minor to India," *Am. Num. Soc. Museum Notes* 22 (1977), pp. 21–23. This specimen is heavier than the others, weighing 1.79 grams; neither the letter A nor the wreath is discernible on the reverse (as F. de Callataÿ has confirmed to me, after kindly examining the coin in New York at my request).

acquired in 1864 in a group containing more than 1,000 Egyptian coins. He concluded from these provenances that the coinage in question had to be Egyptian; the Greek letter A and the typically Greek symbol of the wreath would indicate that the coins were issued after the arrival of the Macedonians in the Nile delta.

Price, at first, clearly had questions about the youth's headdress on the coins' obverse. In the article he published some months later (cf. the footnote below), he no longer hesitated about interpreting it as a helmet, "normally known as the Phrygian or Thracian helmet." He associated this helmet with the one Alexander wears on the obverse of the famous so-called Porus decadrachm (pl. 8, 8)[30] on which the helmet is provided with a crest and two large side plumes, while on the bronzes the helmet is devoid of ornament. Yet we are dealing, he says, with the same head covering.

Price's conclusion is striking: the youthful head depicted on the coins from Saqqara can only be that of Alexander himself, making it the earliest known portrait of the Conqueror engraved during his lifetime, probably earlier than that of the "Porus" decadrachm. Price, in fact, was inclined to think that the Saqqara bronzes were struck during the Macedonian king's stay in Egypt, at the end of 332 or the beginning of 331. They were a natural continuation of the small bronzes in the names of Sabaces and Mazaces at the Memphis mint (pl. 6, 13–14),[31] the letter A on the reverse being the first of Alexander's name, who would have wanted to proclaim in this way that he had become master of the satrapy.

A similar juvenile head, with comparable headdress, appears as a symbol on the coins with the name and types of Alexander produced at Sardis (pl. 6, 19) and Abydus (pl. 6, 20), and also at the end of the fourth century on the silver didrachms of Leucas (one of Corinth's colonies) with Athena head and Pegasus types. Is it not correct, Price writes, to see in these symbols the head of Alexander? If so, its appearance at Leucas would establish a link with the Pegasus forepart on the bronzes of Saqqara. Pegasus was the emblem of Corinth, the type *par excellence* of its coins (and its colonies' coins). By placing a forepart of Pegasus on the reverse of his own bronzes, Alexander meant to emphasize that he was the general of the Greek cities of the League of Corinth.

Returning to the issue of the headdress, Price insists on the idea that the helmet is not the combat helmet with crest and plumes but the simple

---

30. See below, chapter 7, p. 248; this helmet with curved top is a Thracian helmet, of which examples have been found in excavations; cf. P. Bernard, "Le monnayage d'Eudamos," in *Orientalia Josephi Tucci memoriae dicata*, G. Gnoli and L. Lanciotti eds. (Rome, ISMEO, 1985), p. 68. I will come back to this study of Bernard in chapter 7.

31. These bronzes are illustrated in Nicolet-Pierre, op. cit., pl. 26, A–C.

helmet, familiar to his soldiers, that the Conqueror normally wore. Price observed that another way of depicting Alexander also appears in Egypt, at Naucratis, where the king is pictured bareheaded, hair streaming behind (cf. the design reproduced at pl. 6, 18). Indeed, he unhesitatingly recognizes Alexander's head on the bronze coins (15 millimeters in diameter) in the name of this city; on one side, they have a female head and the Greek letters NAY, the start of the ethnic *Naukratitōn*, while the head in question appears on the other side, with the Greek letters that start Alexander's name, AΛE.[32] According to Price, this issue was struck at Naucratis during the sovereign's reign, with Alexander's hair treated as it was on the later mosaic from the House of the Faun at Pompeii.[33]

To conclude, Price has stressed the "dramatic" importance of these small bronze coins struck, he thinks, in Egypt. Alexander, following the example of the last two satraps, his predecessors, displayed his portrait on coins, the first Greek to do so. His Memphis issue sought to reconcile his role as elected general of the League of Corinth with his position as conqueror of the Persians in the East. The Memphis coins would therefore provide contemporary evidence for one of the turning points of world history, and at the same time challenge the idea that Alexander had authorized only Lysippus and Pyrgoteles to sculpt his image.

P. Debord's Elaboration of Price's Interpretation

When writing his *Alexander* of 1991,[34] Price showed no hesitation about his thesis's validity, and his confidence cannot fail to impress his readers. So F. Smith, whose book probably came out in 2001,[35] has no reservations on the question, titling his first chapter "The Portrait of Alexander on Egyptian Coins."

P. Debord, who also favors Price's proposal, examined from this perspective some numismatic evidence that Price did not mention.[36] A certain

---

32. I have discussed these coins in "Cléomène de Naucratis," *BCH* 21 (1997), pp. 92–93.

33. This, the "Alexander Mosaic," is now preserved in the Naples National Museum; it illustrates the battle of Issus, with Alexander leading the Macedonians against Darius and Persian soldiers.

34. Cf. p. 496.

35. *L'immagine di Alessandro il Grande sulle monete del regno (336-323 AC)*, Materiali Studi Ricerche 19, Milan, Edizioni ennere. Although the book carries no date, it appeared at the end of 2000 or the beginning of 2001. [Le Rider cites the chapter title in the original Italian, "Il ritratto di Alessandro sulle monete dell'Egitto"—WEH].

36. *L'Asie Mineure au IVe siècle (412–323 Av J.-C.)*, Appendice 5, *Alexandre et les monnayages "perses"* (Bordeaux, 1999), pp. 479–92; the coins cited by the author are illustrated on pp. 490–91, pl. XI–XII.

number of coinages from Asia Minor do, indeed, show beardless juvenile heads wearing a headdress that encloses the cranium and ends in a havelock and ear flaps; the pointed top of the headdress either projects forwards above the head or is so bent that it is nearly or completely horizontal. Examples are known on bronze coins from Teuthrania in Mysia (pl. 6, 21), Cebren in the Troad, and Kios in Bithynia; on electrum coins from Mytilene, Phocaea, and Cyzicus; and on silver coins from Amastris in Paphlagonia. Numismatists have generally preferred to be cautious in their descriptions, speaking of a "juvenile head wearing an eastern headdress"; some have been more specific and opted for "beardless satrap," sometimes seeking even to identify the satrap; still others have seen divine countenances in these images, Attis, Mithras, or Men.

Debord himself recognizes the head of Alexander on these various coins, and, according to him, all these issues were therefore struck after 334 (a dating made possible by the uncertainty of current chronologies). Debord furthermore remarks that the earliest *certain* examples of a coinage representation of Attis or Mithras are clearly later. Because the idea of a "beardless satrap" is fuzzy, Debord thinks identifying the heads as Alexander's resolves the difficulties.

Alexander's image also appears, he thinks, as a symbol on an issue of Rhodian tetradrachms, as well as on gold and silver coins with the name and types of Alexander from the Sardis mint (an opinion Price shared). At Rhodes, as at Sardis, one does see, in fact, a small head in the field on the reverse wearing a headdress comparable to that we have described.[37]

Debord concludes that it is interesting how the cities where these coins were issued began by presenting Alexander "neither as Macedonian king, nor even as a new Herakles, but as satrap, and then as Persian king. Two possible explanations ensue: either Alexander personally chose to wear such dress at this time, the height of his career, or the cities saw in him the successor of the Persian satrap who governed them until then."

---

37. Debord likewise thinks that the horseman on the coinage issues of Membog-Hierapolis in Syria, wearing a conical cap, is Alexander (these coins are in the name of Alexander, written in Aramaic: cf. H. Seyrig, *RN* 13 [1971], p. 20, nos. 8–9, pl. II; L. Mildenberg, in *Travaux offerts à G. Le Rider*, M. Amandry and S. Hurter eds., London, 1999, p. 284, nos. 30–31). Similarly, according to Debord, the archer riding in a chariot discernible on a tetradrachm of the hoard found near Babylon in 1973 (Price, in *Mnemata, Papers in Memory of N. M. Waggoner*, W. E. Metcalf ed., New York, 1991, p. 70, pl. 15, 26–27) is Alexander, but it is actually an Indian archer, as Bernard has emphasized, op. cit., p. 75; see also P. Goukowsky, *Essai sur les origines du mythe d'Alexandre* II (Nancy, 1981), p. 3.

Comments on the Interpretations of Price and Debord

To sum up Price's position, the small bronze coins with juvenile head found at Saqqara were struck in Memphis in 332/331. On the obverse, they portray Alexander wearing a helmet, chronologically his earliest known portrait, while on the reverse the letter A stands for the beginning of Alexander's name and the forepart of Pegasus recalls the League of Corinth.

Can we accept such an interpretation unconditionally? I remark, first, on the very probability of the conduct attributed to Alexander. He arrived in Egypt as victorious king, crowned with glory. He had triumphed over Darius and was hailed as ruler of Asia. If he had decided to strike coinage at Memphis and to have his monetary portrait engraved for the first time, would he have been satisfied with issuing tiny bronze coins and reducing his name to its first letter? Is this the sort of help he would have chosen to promote himself to the cities of the League of Corinth? Although anything is possible, I find it difficult to follow Price on these different points.

I will rapidly review his arguments.

[As to the Memphis attribution, Price based it on two assumptions. First, coins with juvenile head were struck in Egypt (and here he seems to be on firm ground because five specimens have been discovered in that country). Second, the coins in question date from a period during which the Memphis mint was authorized to function, that is, a period prior to the opening of the Alexandria mint. For Price, this was not a problem because he placed the output of these coins at the time of Alexander's arrival in Egypt, in 332/331.

I will not discuss this dating, save to underline its hypothetical character.

I will comment, however, on the attribution to Egypt. Five specimens with juvenile head do, indeed, have an Egyptian provenance, four unearthed at Saqqara (three in the sacred animals' necropolis, the fourth in a different precinct) and the fifth from a commercial lot with no further details. I would like to draw attention to the specific conditions in which the three coins from the sacred animals' necropolis were dug up. They were found together, in company with two other small bronzes, one from Sidon, the other also non-Egyptian (Price's opinion), but too badly preserved to be definitely identified. This association suggests we not exclude the possibility that the three small bronzes with juvenile head had a foreign origin, like the two others. The coins from the necropolis of sacred animals published by Price are certainly nearly all Egyptian, being essentially Ptolemaic bronzes issued at Alexandria. One will note, however, in Price's inventory (in addition to the two coins accompanying the three small coins with juvenile head) a small bronze from Cnidos, another from Rhodes, a third of a Persian satrap, and a fourth from a dynast of Cappadocia(?). Small-denomination coins from Asia Minor and Phoenicia were therefore present in this necropolis, and when we ask ourselves about the attribution of the coins with juvenile head, we have to take this fact into consideration. Curiously, the unidentified specimen associated with the three small bronze coins carries a Pegasus type on the reverse while the bronze coins have a forepart of Pegasus: probably mere coincidence.

Concerning the headdress of the obverse, Price was right not to see in this an official Persian head covering. The tapered point at the top, which is more or less curved, suggests, as he said, a "Phrygian cap" or Thracian helmet. Alexander's helmet on the "Porus" decadrachm has a similar shape, but it is decorated with a crest and large plumes. The Conqueror at Memphis would have shown tremendous restraint in opting for a helmet devoid of ornament. On the specimen Troxell published,[38] the top of the headdress is almost vertical: perhaps the engraver was clumsy, but in any case we are not dealing here with the erect tiara, the *kidaris*, that only the Great King had the right to wear. I would like to go into more detail on this issue.

D. Schlumberger has studied the Persian royal headdress well.[39] He pointed out, referring to the official sculpture of the Achaemenids, that the Great King wore either a rather narrow, crenellated crown that permitted the top of the head to be visible (Darius I at Behistun, for example),[40] or a relatively tall, cylindrical tiara, denticulated or not (if the latter, it can be described as "pillbox"), as illustrated by the reliefs from Persepolis.[41] The Great King's gold darics and silver sigloi, themselves official documents, show the sovereign with a denticulated, cylindrical headpiece whose height is halfway between the Behistun diadem and the Persepolis tiara, the coin's small dimension possibly preventing the engravers from making the royal headdress larger. The famous "Persian vase," the work of the "Darius Painter," dating from c. 330, shows the Great King wearing a headdress with bent point; a beardless bodyguard with the same head covering stands nearby. As Villanueva-Puig has written, the Persian atmosphere of the scene

---

38. *Amer. Num. Soc. Museum Notes* 22 (1977), p. 22, no. 10, pl. 4. I indicated above (p. 171, note 29) that neither the wreath symbol nor the letter A is discernible on the reverse. Debord, op. cit., p. 480, note 14, seems to doubt that this coin and those of Saqqara belong to the very same group; the rendering of the head looks different to him on Troxell's specimen, whose heavier weight he also emphasizes. Nonetheless, the similarity of types is such that it is difficult to distinguish this coin from the others.

39. "La coiffure du Grand Roi," *Syria* 48 (1971), pp. 375–83.

40. A lovely reproduction of this can be found in R. Ghirshman, *Perse* (Paris, 1963), p. 236.

41. *Ibid.*, p. 186, no. 233; p. 198, no. 246; p. 205, no. 255. ["Pillbox," i.e., the ladies' hat style so called, translates the French *mortier*, the round, somewhat cylindrical hat of medium height worn by certain judges in France—WEH.]

depicted on the vase indicates "a certain knowledge of Achaemenid art, but springs even more from 'persianizing.'"[42] The headpiece attributed to Darius III and his servant is not authentic, being shown "*à la grecque*."

As for the satraps of the Great King, their headgear forms no projection above the head; when it has a point (not always the case), this is completely, or almost completely, flattened forwards.[43]

The last two satraps of Darius in Egypt, Sabaces and Mazaces, as Price observed, struck some small bronze coins that, on the obverse, probably display their portrait and, on the reverse, carry their name and a type chosen at their behest (pl. 6, 13–14). Alexander merely followed their example, according to Price. This is plausible, at first glance. Yet it is worth noting that Sabaces and Mazaces inscribed their name in full on these small bronzes, whereas Alexander was allegedly content with the letter A. The two satraps, besides, issued silver tetradrachms in their name with Athenian types (pl. 6, 10–11), something Alexander did not do, for he never produced any gold or silver coinage during his stay in Egypt, as far as we know. The idea that the Conqueror's sole monetary act there consisted in his continuing the small bronze coins of Sabaces and Mazaces strikes me, I repeat, as hard to accept.

Price saw a definite political intention in the choice of the forepart of Pegasus that adorns the reverse of the Saqqara coins. One may well ask if he has not accorded too much importance to a type that certainly evokes the Corinthian Pegasus but which also appears in the same form in western Asia Minor at Lampsacus (pl. 3, 12) and Adramyttium. It is of this geographical area, whose artists in general seem to have shown a predilection for the foreparts of animals, that one instinctively thinks when seeking to classify the Saqqara small bronze coins. It is not impossible that they were struck in Egypt, but this is not the country that springs to mind when first looking at them.

Finally, Price sought support in the bronzes of Naucratis (pl. 6, 18), which do seem to bear a head of Alexander. I will only say that we are dealing with a municipal issue of indeterminate date that could have occurred equally well during Alexander's reign as after his death.]

In short, Price's interpretation arouses misgivings. He was overconfident, it seems to me, when in *Alexander* he considered the question settled.

Turning now to Debord, his idea that several cities of Asia Minor represented Alexander as a Persian satrap on their coins appears rash. The Macedonian king, in 334, had not yet stopped proclaiming that he had come to liberate Asia Minor from the Great King's domination. Debord observes that, even so, Alexander did not alter the Achaemenid bureaucracy

---

42. "Le vase des Perses," *REA* 91 (1989), pp. 277–98, esp. p. 280, fig. 2.
43. See H. A. Cahn, "Le monnayage des satrapes: iconographie et identification," *REA* 91 (1989), p. 102.

much and that the newly appointed governors followed the practices of their predecessors. But Alexander was in no sense a satrap. He was the supreme sovereign, and if the cities, for whatever reason, had wanted to show him as Great King, they would have put the royal tiara on his head.

Similarly, I am surprised that a symbol appearing on the coins of Alexander from Sardis and Abydus (pl. 6, 19–20)[44] could have been identified as a head of Alexander in the guise of a Persian satrap. One symbol, in one mint, was only one mark among many others and, as far as we can tell, was chosen not by the city, but by the mint magistrates responsible for the issue.

I will make one objection to Debord of a strictly iconographic nature. On the coins he has illustrated in plates XI and XII of his work, the coverings worn by the different, beardless heads fall into two groups, it seems to me: those whose point is completely collapsed, as on nos. 6–8 and 17 of his plate XI and on nos. 1, 12, and 13 of XII, and those whose point rises above the head and bends forward, as on nos. 1–5 (the Saqqara coins Price commented on), 9–12 and 14 of his plate XI and on nos. 5–7 of XII. Only the headdresses of the first group can be associated with those of satraps; those of the second group, in contrast, belong to the category of "Phrygian caps" or Thracian helmets.

An effective riposte to Debord would require a convincing identification for these diverse heads. I can only express a personal impression. I see in these representations images of gods, mythological heroes or legendary creatures rather than likenesses of historical characters.

[Among the legendary creatures, I include the Amazons, reputed founders of several cities in western Asia Minor. They were chosen as types on Hellenistic and Roman coins, where they no longer sport the "Phrygian cap," previously their customary headdress. One might easily imagine that in the fourth century such a symbol (or even, conceivably, such a principal type) representing a beardless head decked out in this covering was the image of an Amazon.

P. Goukowsky, whom I consulted on this problem, wondered if we ought not to include Perseus among the various possibilities. This Argive Greek hero was, curiously, ancestor of both the Macedonian Temenids and the Persian Achaemenids. He counted Herakles among his descendants, who was himself an ancestor of Temenos, the mythical founder of the Macedonian dynasty. Some bold genealogies, moreover, playing on

---

44. The exact reference for these issues is as follows: for Sardis, M. Thompson, *Alexander's Drachm Mints* I (New York, 1983), p. 9, nos. 44–49 (staters, tetradrachms, and drachms); p. 15, nos. 96–104 (staters and drachms); for Abydus, Thompson, *Alexander's Drachm Mints* II (New York, 1991), p. 60, nos. 354–60 (drachms). See also Price, *Alexander* (1991), nos. 1565 and L19; and A. Davesne and G. Le Rider, *Le trésor de Meydancikkale* (Paris, 1989), nos. 891–92.

Perseus's name, located the kingdom of his wife Andromeda in Chaldaea or in Persia; one of their sons was called Perses who had, in turn, a son called Achaimenes, after the homeland of his grandfather, Achaia. This Achaimenes was allegedly the ancestor of the Achaemenids. Greek cities in Asia Minor, in the third quarter of the fourth century, could have chosen Perseus as a coinage type: this legendary figure established a bond between the two civilizations, Persia and Greece. Xerxes recalled this bond during the Persian Wars, when he sent a herald to the Argives, requesting their neutrality in memory of their common origin (Herodotus 7.150). Goukowsky pointed out to me that Perseus sometimes wears a "Phrygian cap."[45] I may add that the king of Macedon, Philip V (221–179), when he had himself depicted as a new Perseus on a series of tetradrachms, chose for headdress a winged helmet with forward-leaning point ending in a griffin's head.[46] Note that, according to Arrian (3.3.1–2), Alexander wanted to consult the oracle at Ammon partly to imitate Perseus and Herakles, who had consulted the oracle and to whose lineage he belonged. Plutarch (*Moralia* 332 A/ *On the Fortune of Alexander* 1.10) has his hero say that he is seeking to copy Herakles, that he is emulating Perseus, and that he is following in the steps of Dionysus.]

In the end, I am not persuaded that Alexander, during his journey in the Nile delta between November 332 and April 331, had his portrait engraved on small bronze coins issued at Memphis, as Price supposed. I do not believe that he had any coinage struck at all in Egypt during these five or six months. After his departure at the start of spring in 331, what happened, monetarily speaking, in Egypt? What did Cleomenes of Naucratis, who governed Egypt from 331 to 323, do in money matters?

Cleomenes of Naucratis, Master of Egypt from April 331 until the Aftermath of Alexander's Death

Alexander, as I have said, gave Cleomenes significant powers and resources, and he entrusted him, besides, with a mission of the first importance. Yet Cleomenes was not a member of Alexander's inner circle; he was not one of the "Companions." Coming from Naucratis (*ek Naukratios*, Arrian 3.5.4), he was probably unknown to the Macedonian king before the latter's arrival in Egypt. If the sovereign singled him out at this point, it

---

45. Cf. K. Schauenburg, *Perseus in der Kunst des Altertums* (Bonn, 1960), p. 118 and pl. 32, 1; 35, 1–2; 42. For another example, cf. *Lex. Icon. Mythol. Class.*, s.v. Perseus, no. 36 (a fourth-century silver ring in the Museum of Taranto).

46. M. J. Price, *Coins of the Macedonians* (London, 1974), pl. XIII, 74.

is probably because he had acquired a brilliant reputation in his own country. Naucratis, his native city, was noted for its lively commercial activity. It was situated on the Canopic branch of the Nile, the westernmost of the delta, and after the founding of Alexandria it was located quite close to the new capital. According to Herodotus (2. 178–79), the pharaoh Amasis (570–526) decided to grant Greek cities a place (the only one in Egypt) where they could build their temples and carry on trade with the Egyptians. Herodotus records that the cities of Chios, Teos, Phocaea, Clazomenae, Rhodes, Cnidos, Halicarnassus, and Mytilene founded a large sanctuary, the Hellenion, at Naucratis. Archeological discoveries, indeed, attest to Aegean merchants conducting business at Naucratis before Amasis's reign. But we can trust, on the basis of Herodotus's text, that this pharaoh meant to legalize the status of the settlement (Herodotus calls it a *polis*) and that he made decisions favoring the Greeks.[47]

One can imagine Cleomenes getting his political and financial education in this prosperous city where, prior to the Macedonian conquest, Greek merchants concentrated and organized their activity. He presumably became a famous authority, his expertise recognized well beyond his city's limits. In any case, Alexander heard him spoken of favorably and was sufficiently taken with his talents to trust him. When the king left Egypt in April 331, Cleomenes was promoted to the top position.

The ancients made no mistake about this. Two authors very close in time to these events, the orator who delivered *Against Dionysodoros* and the author of the second book of the *Oeconomica*, included among the works of Aristotle, described Cleomenes's power in unequivocal terms. *Against Dionysodoros*, found among the orations of Demosthenes, was delivered, perhaps, just after the death of Cleomenes, who probably survived until the late 323 or early 322. At section 56, we read "When Cleomenes was ruling (*Kleomenous . . . arksantos*) in Egypt" (WEH), meaning that he was governor there. The second book of the *Oeconomica* probably dates from the end of the fourth century. At section 33 a, it tells us that Cleomenes held the office of satrap in Egypt (*satrapeuōn*). The verbs *arkhein* and *satrapeuein* often seem in cases of this sort to denote the same function,[48] although we cannot generalize.

---

47. On Naucratis, see M. M. Austin, *Greece and Egypt in the Archaic Age* (Proceed. Cambridge Philol. Soc., Suppl. 2, 1970), pp. 22–33; J. Boardman, *The Greeks Overseas* (London, 1973), pp. 108–57; J. Yoyotte, *Annuaire du Collège de France* (1991–92), pp. 634–44; ibid. (1993–94), pp. 679–92; ibid. (1994–95), pp. 669–82. Yoyotte has particularly investigated the following three points (to quote him): "1. Was there an Egyptian settlement before the coming of the Greeks? 2. Does the very name 'Naucratis' definitely denote a Greek creation? 3. What would have been the extent and nature of the native Egyptian presence in Naucratis during the periods before and after the Greco-Macedonian control of Egypt?"

48. See P. Briant, *From Cyrus to Alexander: A History of the Persian Empire*, Eng. trans. by P. T. Daniels (Winona Lake, IN, 2002), pp. 340–42.

Later ancient authors took up the same terms. Pausanias (1.6.3) makes Cleomenes a satrap, and that is probably what Dexippus (F. Jacoby, *Die Fragmente der griechischen Historiker* 100 F8) meant too, when he wrote that King Alexander put this individual in charge of the satrapy of Egypt. Arrian (7.23.8) used, as the author of *Against Dionysodoros* did, the verb *arkhein* to define Cleomenes's post.

Debate has divided modern historians on this point. Most think that Cleomenes actually bore the title satrap, but they do not agree on the circumstances of this promotion. For some, Cleomenes appointed himself and presented Alexander with a *fait accompli*. J. Vogt, for example, has vigorously defended this opinion, making the case that Alexander, busied with numerous projects in 324, preferred to accommodate "the powerful satrap of the Nile."[49] For others, notably B. A. Van Groningen[50] and J. Seibert,[51] Alexander of his own volition conferred the title of satrap on Cleomenes at some time or other, thereby violating his own principle of not investing a single individual with the government of Egypt. In so doing, the king wanted to give Cleomenes all the resources necessary for the efficient building of Alexandria.

In my opinion, Alexander treated Cleomenes in such a way that he effectively made him the "strongman" of Egypt. The mission that Alexander entrusted to him, Alexandria, gave absolute priority to all Cleomenes's orders relating to this project. In contemporary eyes, the powers and prerogatives he enjoyed made him seem a satrap, even if he did not possess the title officially. The two verbs *arkhein* and *satrapeuein* came naturally to the lips and pens of people wanting to describe the role he played.

In this context, I am led to believe that neither Alexander nor Cleomenes sought to change the *status quo* established by the sovereign at the time of his Egyptian sojourn. Arrian (7.23.6–8), in mentioning a letter the king wrote to Cleomenes after Hephaestion's death, severely criticizes Cleomenes's conduct, regarding him as an *anēr kakos* ("scoundrel" [WEH]) but making no precise charge. If Cleomenes had usurped the title of satrap, Arrian, it seems to me, would have explicitly noted such a grave act. Likewise, when Egypt was allotted to Ptolemy during the summer of 323, Cleomenes had apparently no difficulty in accepting the role of second-in-command (he was named *hyparkhōn*) to the province's new master. Would he have been so accommodating had he received the title of satrap, either from Alexander or by his own action?[52]

---

49. "Cleomenes von Naucratis, Herr von Ägypten," *Chiron* 1 (1971), pp. 153–57.
50. "De Cleomene Naucratita," *Mnemosyne* 5 (1925), pp. 101–30, esp. pp. 111–13.
51. *Untersuchungen zur Geschichte Ptolemaios' I.*, Münch. Beitr. zur Papyrusforschung und ant. Rechtsgesch. 56 (1969), p. 43.
52. Arrian (7.26.2) mentions a Cleomenes among the individuals surrounding Alexander in his death throes at Babylon. Is this our Cleomenes or someone else? I have summarized the debate, *BCH* 121 (1997), p. 75 (= *Études d'hist. monétaire et financière* III, Athens, 1999, p. 1139).

What Were Cleomenes's Expenses?

In addition to the ongoing expenses required by the normal administration of the country, Cleomenes had to support exceptional costs that were not limited to the building of Alexandria.

For Alexandria, we may assume that the king imposed strict deadlines that Cleomenes made it a point of honor to respect. The author of the *Oeconomica* (2, 33 c) reports that the city plan had already been laid out when Cleomenes had to contend a second time with the priests and property owners of Canopus (a settlement located at the mouth of the Canopic branch of the Nile).[53] Another passage (2, 33 a) gives Cleomenes the ethnic *Alexandreus*, indicating that he had become a citizen of Alexandria. He would not have been given this appellation unless the administrative bodies (council, assembly of the people) had already been established. Alexandria, of course, was still not completely finished, but it already possessed enough buildings, temples, and houses to function as a Greek city.

These undertakings certainly occasioned considerable expense. The local labor force may not have cost very much, but Cleomenes had to recruit qualified craftsmen, technicians, and specialists of every sort in Egypt itself and overseas, whom he had to remunerate at their true worth. He also had to import essential materials (especially marble) and probably to have special equipment built. It is easy to imagine the large sums spent and the incessant activity evident over several years.

I assume, additionally, that Egypt, like the other provinces, participated in Alexander's war effort. Nothing is explicitly said to us about this. Yet Egyptians are mentioned in the royal army in the East (Arrian, *Indica* 18.1). All may not have gone with Alexander in 331; some, perhaps, were sent later, with Cleomenes in charge of their recruitment, training, and equipping.

The demand Alexander made on Cleomenes after Hephaestion's death illustrates the requirements the sovereign could exact at any moment. The oracle at Ammon, when consulted, replied that it was permissible to honor Hephaestion as a demigod (*hērōs*), and Alexander wrote to Cleomenes to build a sanctuary (*hērōon*) for the deceased at Alexandria on the island of Pharos, requiring that this sanctuary be the largest and costliest

---

53. F. Goddio's discoveries in the course of his underwater exploration of the area around the Nile's Canopic mouth have reopened questions about the location of Canopus. My sincere thanks to Jean Yoyotte for the information he kindly communicated to me on this matter. One may consult what he has said in *L'Histoire* 259 (Nov., 2001), pp. 16–17, as well as his study "La découverte de Thônis-Héracléion," *Egypte, Afrique et Orient* 24 (2001). Thônis, the Egyptian *emporion*, and Herakleion were one and the same, at the entry of the Canopic mouth (also called Herakliotic); Greek merchants were taxed there. Canopus was built, perhaps, on the rocky peninsula of Aboukir; the name was extended to the entire district stretching to the west of Alexandria as far as the Nile's Canopic branch.

ever (Arrian 7.23.7). Even if this letter of Alexander is not authentic,[54] I believe we may accept that Cleomenes did receive specific instructions concerning Hephaestion.

What regular revenues would Egypt supply to Cleomenes? To consult Herodotus first (3.91), he gives the following information for the period of Darius I (522–486): "The sixth province was Egypt and the neighboring parts of Libya, and Cyrene and Barca, all being included in the Egyptian province. They paid 700 talents, in addition to the revenue of silver from the fish of Lake Moeris [in the Fayum] and the measure of grain they provided; for 120,000 bushels of grain were also allotted to the Persians quartered at the White Castle of Memphis and to their auxiliaries" (Loeb modified). We know that, in general, numerous and varied taxes, royal and satrapal, added considerably to the tribute properly so called (*phoros*) that marked a country's subjection to the Great King.[55] If we confine ourselves to the text of Arrian already cited (3.5.4), it is the *phoros* amount that the nomarchs had to pay to Cleomenes. One supposes that they needed the income from other taxes for carrying on their own administration. The *phoros* exacted from Egypt in Cleomenes's time was probably higher than under Darius I. Presumably the numbers St. Jerome gives (*In Danielem* 3.11, 5b) for Ptolemy II relate to the *phoros* the latter received: 14,800 talents and 1.5 million *artabai* of wheat.[56] In the first century BC, in the reign of Ptolemy Auletes, the great Cleopatra's father, Cicero (as cited in Strabo 17.1.13, who uses the word *phoros*) says that Egypt rendered to the king 12,500 talents, at a time when the kingdom was probably less prosperous than under the first Ptolemies. It is true that Diodorus speaks, concerning the same period, of just 6,000 talents (17.52.6, using the word *prosodos*, "revenue"); Diodorus was in Egypt during a political crisis, and the figure he mentions possibly reflects a disturbed fiscal situation.[57]

---

54. It is generally supposed that this letter, of which Arrian provides excerpts, is not authentic: cf. J. Seibert, "Nochmals zu Cleomenes von Naucratis," *Chiron* 2 (1972), pp. 99–100 (repeating the opinion expressed in his previous article); K. Polanyi, *The Livelihood of Man* (New York, 1977), pp. 241–42. G. Marasco, *Economia e storia* (Viterbo, 1992), pp. 70–71, inclines towards a forgery, but nonetheless writes: "It is also possible that the letter has at least a basis in fact" [cited in Italian—WEH: "È anche possibile che la lettera contenga almeno un fondo di verità"].

55. See above, pp. 79–80 and p. 81, note 16.

56. Here is St. Jerome's text: "auri quoque et argenti grande pondus, ita ut de Aegypto per singulos annos quattuordecim milia octoginta talenta argenti acciperet . . ."

57. See P. Goukowsky's commentary, *Diodore de Sicile, Livre XVII* (Paris, 1976), p. 76, note 1. Cl. Préaux, *L'économie royale des Lagides* (Brussels, 1939), pp. 425–26, has made the Diodorus passage more obscure than it really is.

Even if Cleomenes received a large number of talents from the nomarchs, the amount was apparently still insufficient to carry out his mission satisfactorily. For he was obliged to resort to extraordinary financial measures that provoked the notice of the *Oeconomica* and the fulminations of *Against Dionysodorus*, whose author bitterly and scathingly describes the commercial system he put into operation.

Cleomenes's Extraordinary Ways to Raise Money

First of all, Cleomenes never hesitated to raise funds where he knew he could find them. One of his moves targeted the priestly caste (*Oeconomica* 2, 33f) by calculating that their excessive expenditures required him to close some temples. The priests, in order to save the temples and their own jobs, provided him money from the sacred treasuries.

Another move concerned the priests of the province who worshipped the crocodile (*Oec.* 2, 33b). When one of these animals carried off a slave of his, Cleomenes ordered open season on crocodiles. The priests offered him all the gold they could gather, and Cleomenes relented of his wrath.

A third move took aim at the priests and property owners of Canopus (*Oec.* 2, 33c). When Cleomenes announced that they were to be transported to Alexandria, they paid money to stay where they were. When Alexandria was built, Cleomenes went after them again, even more threatening and demanding than before. Unable to pay the requisite sum, priests and landowners were forced to move to the new city.

Cleomenes also resorted to a subterfuge (*Oec.* 2, 39) that permitted him to save a month's salary out of what he owed his troops.

The measures just described are not dazzlingly original. I have shown elsewhere[58] that some thirty years previously, also in Egypt, the Athenian Chabrias gave the pharaoh Takhos (or Taos) similar tactical advice, which the same book of the *Oeconomica* (2, 25a–b, 37) also reports. Takhos needed money when he was preparing a campaign against the Great King in 361, and Chabrias encouraged him to siphon off the temples' wealth and to extort funds from rich individuals. In addition, Chabrias was sufficiently devious that he saved two months' worth of maintenance for the crews of sixty ships.

Cleomenes seems to have been less inventive than his predecessor when it came to taxes and new duties. On the other hand, he does demonstrate a special aptitude for taking advantage of the situation (*Oec.* 2, 33a and 33c) when he devised a large-scale manipulation of the wheat (*sitos*) trade.[59]

---

58. *BCH* 121 (1997), pp. 76–79.

59. The word *sitos*, "grain," can designate "wheat" (*pyros*) as well as barley or spelt. Presumably wheat is at issue in these passages of the *Oeconomica*, if we may judge by the quite high price of the *sitos*.

The author of the *Oeconomica* reports that the Greek world at this time was suffering from famine (*limos*)[60] but that Egypt was less affected than neighboring countries.

At first, Cleomenes wanted to prohibit all exports of Egyptian wheat, probably hoping to prevent scarcity in the country. But the officials in charge of the administrative regions (the *nomarchs*) objected that they would be unable to deliver the usual excises to the treasury if they lost the tax base that wheat for export represented. Cleomenes reversed his decision, but he imposed a heavy tax on the wheat (the author of the *Oeconomica* does not indicate the amount). This steep duty, though it lessened the exporters' demand, still brought in a good deal of money to the treasury. The nomarchs could only go along.

Wise provincial management seems to have dictated these early actions of Cleomenes. Careful to avoid the risk of grain scarcity and anxious not to diminish fiscal receipts, he found a satisfying equilibrium while not, we may suppose, profiting personally.

Later, he went much further. Wheat was selling for ten drachms in the countryside. Cleomenes, after having come to an agreement with local merchants (*ergazomenoi*) and dealt with the exporters (*emporoi*),[61] bought all the available wheat in Egypt and sold it for export at thirty-two drachms.

Cleomenes and the Grain Trade

Because the author of the *Oeconomica* writes that ten drachms was the prevailing price "in the countryside" (*en tēi khōrai*), we may accept that he is giving us the price of an Egyptian artaba and not of an Attic medimnos.[62]

---

60. The difficulty in provisioning grain in the Greek world at this period is attested: the stele from Cyrene concerning grains, dated to 330–325, mentions the *sitodeia* [grain scarcity—WEH] prevalent in Greece. Cf. the edition of the inscription, with translation and commentary, in P. J. Rhodes and R. Osborne, *Greek Historical Inscriptions* (Oxford, 2003), No. 96; also A. Laronde, *Cyrène et la Libye hellénistique* (Paris, 1987), pp. 30–34; also G. Marasco, op. cit., p. 73; P. Brun, *Zeitschr. für Papyr. und Epigr.* 99 (1993), pp. 185–96; A. Bresson, "L'attentat d'Hiéron et le commerce grec," *Entretiens d'arch. et d'hist., Saint-Bertrand de Comminges, Économie antique* (1994), pp. 50–52. On the hardships Athens experienced, cf. P. Garnsey, *Famine and Food Supply in the Graeco-Roman World* (Cambridge, UK, 1988), pp. 154–62.

61. A. Wartelle, *Aristote, Economique* (Paris, 1968), p. 31, translates *ergazomenoi* as "*cultivateurs*" ["growers"—WEH]. I do not believe that Cleomenes dealt with the growers themselves; the verb *ergazesthai* designates all sorts of endeavors and can be used in the sense of "engage in commerce," "carry on business." In the text of the *Oeconomica*, I think what is meant is local merchants/dealers, "middlemen" who bought the grain from the peasants and landowners, selling it on to wholesalers, the *emporoi*, who were export specialists.

62. The artaba in Egypt was a measure of capacity amounting to about forty liters; the Athenian medimnos had about a fifty liter capacity.

This price, ten drachms the artaba, is considerable because, in the third century and for some of the second, the average price of the artaba in Ptolemaic Egypt was two silver drachms on the Ptolemaic standard (a drachm weighing ± 3.60 grams).[63] Moreover, in the mind of the author of the *Oeconomica*, the ten drachms in question were probably Attic drachms (one drachm weighing ± 4.30 grams). The difference, in this case, becomes even greater between the ten drachms of Cleomenes's time and the two drachms of the following era.

There are several ways to explain the extremely elevated price of the artaba under Cleomenes. Harvests in Egypt might have been jeopardized after a succession of poor Nile floodings, at the same time as export demand (before severe export restrictions were enacted) became more urgent owing to the scarcity prevalent in the Greek world. Marasco[64] has also suggested that turmoil in Egypt following Alexander's conquest could have upset agricultural life. I might add that Egyptians enlisted in the Macedonian army were no longer present to cultivate the fields. While it is true that a large number of Egyptians were probably professional sailors (cf. Arrian, *Indica* 18.1), we still have to allow for a certain number of farmers among the recruits.

In fixing an export price of thirty-two drachms (Attic) per artaba or medimnos, Cleomenes was charging a sky-high amount. We know from Demosthenes (*Orations* 34.39) that in one instance of serious shortage, perhaps in 330/329,[65] a medimnos of wheat at Athens cost sixteen drachms; two public benefactors, Chrysippus and his brother, generously provided more than 10,000 medimnoi at a price of five drachms. So we may presume Cleomenes's asking price of thirty-two drachms was exceptional. The master of Egypt took advantage of a particularly severe combination of events, which probably lasted only a limited time and affected, perhaps, only some regions of the Mediterranean world. What appears certain is that Cleomenes, in a period of serious famine,[66] did not hesitate to sell wheat at the highest possible price.

The orator who wrote *Against Dionysodorus* vehemently assailed him for having greatly harmed all of Greece by acting this way. He very vividly describes for us the system that, he says, Cleomenes put in place (56.8). The

---

63. H. Cadell and G. Le Rider, *Prix du blé et numéraire dans l'Egypte lagide de 305 à 173* (Papyrologica Bruxellensia 30, Brussels, 1997), pp. 30–31, 59–64.

64. *Economia e storia* (Viterbo, 1992), pp. 56–57.

65. This is the date Garnsey proposes, op. cit., p. 154. On the different prices of the medimnos of wheat at Athens during this period, cf. B. A. Van Groningen, *Aristote et le second livre de l'Economique* (Paris, 1933), p. 190 (referring to A. Jardé, *Les céréales dans l'Antiquité grecque*, Paris, 1925, p. 179).

66. On this point, see Marasco, op. cit., p. 61.

latter had organized a veritable network of agents: "Some of them would dispatch the cargoes from Egypt, others would sail along with the shipments, while still others would remain here in Athens and dispose of the consignments. Then those who remained here would send letters to those abroad, advising them of the prevailing prices, so that if grain was fetching a high price in your market, they would bring it here, while a falling price would prompt them to put in at some other port. This was the chief reason, men of the jury, why the price of grain rose; it was owing to such letters and conspiracies" (Loeb, modified).

Polanyi put a rather novel interpretation on Cleomenes's alleged conduct.[67] In his view, Cleomenes sought to create a "world" market for wheat in the eastern Mediterranean, with Rhodes as its center: "Grain thus was shipped form Egypt to Rhodes, which was kept continually informed of the most recent prices in all Greek cities buying from the syndicate; ... under these conditions, the prices at Rhodes would tend to reflect the average of prices in the Greek cities, i.e., the Rhodian price would tend to be a 'world' market price ... these are *no more than tendencies* (P's italics), it should be noted." According to Polanyi, if one sets aside the brief episode during which the price of wheat was fixed at thirty-two drachms, Cleomenes's action was beneficial to the extent that transporting wheat into areas with insufficient grain could only lower the commodity's average price. Cleomenes would have brought about fair market pricing in the eastern Mediterranean; the deliveries, moreover, were rationally handled according to demand, not at the whim of political influence or military power.

This idealistic interpretation has not gone uncriticized. G. Reger[68] very cogently remarked that the author of *Against Dionysodorus* does not give us at all to understand that Cleomenes tried to normalize prices; on the contrary, he clearly accuses him of having the sale of wheat at the highest possible price as his sole objective and of quite unscrupulously taking advantage of cities in distress. Dionysodorus's associate was Parmeniscus. The Athenian orator presents them both as agents (*hypēretai, synergoi*) of Cleomenes. Parmeniscus had set sail for Egypt, and there bought wheat with the intention of selling it at Athens, where Dionysodorus remained. The latter advised his associate that the arrival of Syracusan wheat had caused the market to fall, and Parmeniscus decided to offload his cargo at Rhodes. Reger emphasizes the modest and pragmatic character of this affair, which does not seem to have transcended the level of individual enterprise.

---

67. *The Livelihood of Man* (New York, 1977), pp. 245–50.
68. *Regionalism and Change in the Economy of Independent Delos* (Berkeley, 1994), pp. 75–80.

H. Kloft also downplayed the novelty of Cleomenes's conduct.[69] Cleomenes, he says, once in possession of the available wheat in Egypt, demanded from exporters a price he fixed based on the available information. The merchant purchasers assumed all the risks of sea transport and sale to interested cities. In order to obtain the information he needed, did Cleomenes set up a large network of agents and associates throughout the Mediterranean, as *Against Dionysodorus* would have us believe? Kloft thinks not: Cleomenes simply employed an information grapevine that all traders had always been using. Xenophon (*Oeconomicus* 20.28) says as follows: grain merchants "don't unload the grain anywhere they happen to be, but rather they take it and sell it wherever they hear that grain sells for the highest price and where men place the highest value on it" (Pomeroy trans.). Cleomenes certainly had no trouble knowing, through the traders stopping at Naucratis and Canopus, where the best prices were to be found and what they were. Kloft adds that the author of the pseudo-Demosthenic speech may say that Parmeniscus and Dionysodorus worked with Cleomenes; in other words, they operated as regular buyers capable of providing pertinent information and were not, strictly speaking, operatives of an intelligence network.

Marasco's analysis[70] agrees with Kloft's on a number of points. He insisted, in fact, on the traditional character of Cleomenes's conduct, showing how the latter, according to *Against Dionysodorus*, was unaware of the expected arrival of Syracusan wheat at Athens, which would not have been the case if he were in control of Mediterranean commerce, as Polanyi supposed. Marasco also questioned the idea that Cleomenes awarded Rhodes a dominant role, for the Rhodians had not waited until this moment to attain leadership in the commodities trade. Finally, Marasco believed he discerned a rhetorical tactic in *Against Dionysodorus*. The oration might have been delivered at the end of 323, when the Lamian War, led by Athens and the Greeks against Macedonia, had just begun. By assailing a high official of the Macedonian administration, who was still fresh in everyone's mind, the speaker was hoping to gain the sympathy of the Athenian judges.

How to Judge Cleomenes as Financial Manager?

The criticisms of Reger, Kloft, and Marasco and the similarities I have noted between certain measures taken by Takhos around 360 and Cleomenes some thirty years later, suggest the latter's action occurred within a financial and commercial tradition that allowed little room for

---

69. "Cleomenes von Naukratis, Probleme eines hellenistischen Wirtschaftsstils," *Grazer Beiträge* 15 (1988), pp. 191–222.

70. Op. cit., pp. 58–72.

genuine innovation. Seibert's evaluation also seems excessive: "On one point we may concur: Cleomenes was a financial and organizational genius."[71] Likewise, Polanyi's grandiose views about Cleomenes do not seem to square with reality.

Nonetheless, Cleomenes was a recognizably capable financier and good manager. He knew how to obtain funds by applying tried and true methods adapted to current circumstances. He was bold enough to profit shamelessly from the grain scarcity that befell the contemporary Mediterranean world. He wisely shifted the risk of maritime commercial transport to others; at least the example of Parmeniscus would suggest that Cleomenes was content to sell (at the best price) without assuming the worries of Mediterranean navigation and the problems of resale.

In acting this way, Cleomenes was conforming to a practice of the pharaohs, which the Ptolemies would later maintain. The pharaohs' administration kept close watch on the internal market and required local products to be sold to foreign traders at Naucratis. The sovereign essentially fixed the prices, while Greek merchants took care of the commodities' export and sale (the individual initiative of Egyptians was not excluded, but it was probably exercised under the same conditions). The Ptolemies acted no differently; they were, as Claire Préaux has indicated,[72] the biggest wheat merchants in Egypt, but nothing attests to their holding a monopoly on foreign commerce. They transferred the inherent risks of this aspect of trading onto others, charging the latter licensing fees and various taxes to boot.

It is to be noted that Cleomenes's involvement in the wheat trade had the laudable aim of not harming the Egyptian population. In his first decision (Ps.-Aristotle, *Oeconomica* 2.33 a), he certainly looked out for his own interests, but he also managed to balance the avoidance of scarcity and the sale of a certain quantity of grain. The size of the duties levied on the producers seems to have been calculated with this situation in mind. The exporters had less grain to buy and a steep tax to pay,[73] but the escalation of prices in the Mediterranean probably compensated them.

The second decision involving wheat (*Oec.* 33 e) treated merchants and exporters fairly: both were called upon to quote the price at which they would sell their stocks to Cleomenes. The latter's purchase of all the available wheat in Egypt has often been interpreted as the establishment of a state monopoly. But we should bear in mind that the operation at issue

---

71. Op. cit., p. 44 [cited in the original German—WEH: "In einem Punkt stimmt man überein: Cleomenes war ein Finanz- und Organisationsgenie."].

72. *L'économie royale des Lagides* (Brussels, 1939), pp. 150–51.

73. Chabrias had advocated that the seller and the buyer, in grain-related transactions, pay a special tax of an obol per artaba (artaba is the term employed in Ps.-Aristotle, *Oec.* 2.25 a); one supposes that Cleomenes's tax was higher.

was born of special circumstances and destined to end when normalcy returned. Moreover, as Kloft showed,[74] the details provided by Pseudo-Aristotle's *Oeconomica* would lead one to think that this monopoly did not actually suppress an internal market ruled by the law of supply and demand.

Cleomenes's conduct was the object of violent criticism in Antiquity. The author of the second book of the *Oeconomica*, truth to tell, does not pass any judgments; he aims only to gather the most well-known examples of financial expedience. Cleomenes's successful sale of his wheat for thirty-two drachms certainly seemed a remarkable *tour de force*, worth passing on to posterity; but the author's role was not to judge the morality of this type of market manipulation.

In contrast, we have noted the animosity of the orator who spoke against Dionysodorus. He described Cleomenes as an unscrupulous exploiter and an evildoer.

Arrian delivered a rough blow to Cleomenes's reputation by describing him as "a scoundrel who had been guilty of many wrongful acts in Egypt" (7.23.6, Loeb, modified) and by reproaching Alexander for treating him too leniently. Arrian mentions in his prologue that his principal sources on Alexander, those he considers most reliable, were the narratives of Ptolemy and Aristobulus. Supposedly, therefore, Ptolemy influenced him about Cleomenes; Ptolemy would not have had any motive to show his predecessor in a favorable light, the predecessor he had had assassinated shortly after taking over Egypt in the summer of 323. Seibert, however, preferred to leave some lingering doubt about the source behind Arrian in this particular case;[75] he declines to accept the letter Alexander allegedly wrote Cleomenes (Arrian 7.23.8) as a complete Ptolemaic forgery.

Cleomenes certainly had his detractors within Egypt as well as in the Greek world. The priests, especially, and a certain number of landowners must have had mixed feelings. Yet Alexander did not disavow him. He was perfectly aware that this man had made exactions from, and behaved harshly toward, starving cities because he wanted to fulfill his mission: to build Alexandria, a task whose financing demanded far more means than the province could normally provide.

Cleomenes was one of those subordinates whose devotion and ingenuity permitted the Conqueror to realize a certain number of grand designs. Chief operating officers, they saw to every essential, by every means possible.

When Ptolemy arrived in Egypt towards the end of summer 323, he found 8,000 talents in the treasury (Diodorus 18.14.1). It is amazing that

---

74. Op. cit., pp. 209–15.

75. *Chiron* 2 (1972), pp. 99–100; Seibert provides a summary of the discussion this passage of Arrian has elicited.

Cleomenes possessed such an ample reserve. How to explain it? In 323, the first phase of construction at Alexandria had been over for some time, it seems, and the large expenditures this effort entailed had probably eased. The sizeable receipts that the treasury collected thanks to the ingenuity of Cleomenes would not, therefore, have been dispensed at the same rate as before. Moreover, we may conjecture that Cleomenes had again made a special effort to amass the necessary funds to build the sumptuous *hērōon* the king ordered for Hephaestion on the island of Pharos. The latter's obsequies at Babylon had alone cost around 10,000 talents (see chapter 7). Cleomenes would certainly have needed considerable sums if the course of events had permitted him to carry out his sovereign's command.

The Problem of Currency in Egypt from 332 to 323

Alexander's stay in Egypt lasted only about five months, from November 332 to April 331. I expressed some reservations above concerning the hypothesis of Price, who suggested that the king had an issue of small bronze coins struck during this period at Memphis showing his portrait. Apart from Price, nobody has so far identified a group of coins produced in Egypt during these five months.

What happened after Alexander's departure? A segment of the Egyptian population had been growing accustomed to the use of coined currency for some decades, it seems. Cleomenes, moreover, could not do without this medium of payment. It is true that some of Alexandria's construction costs did not require the use of signed and minted coinage. Local salaries, for example, were probably paid in the traditional way, in kind and in unminted, weighed metal. In the previous century, the community of Hebrew soldiers from Elephantine (a small island in the Nile in Upper Egypt, near Syene) used this unminted, weighed metal to effect relatively complex transactions, as some papyrological evidence shows.[76] This practice, which is also attested in contemporary bookkeeping records of Persepolis,[77] continued for a number of decades and probably still existed in Egypt during Cleomenes's time. In addition, Cleomenes might sometimes have paid with wheat (or other products) for the materials he ordered from abroad.

Yet coined currency could not be excluded from every transaction. Mediterranean countries in the second half of the fourth century used silver

---

76. See O. Picard, "Les origines du monnayage en Grèce," *L'Histoire*, No. 6 (November, 1978), p. 19; cf. also my *Naissance*, p. 76.
77. P. Naster, "Were the Labourers of Persepolis Paid by Means of Coined Money?" *Ancient Society* 1 (1970), pp. 129–34 (= *Scripta Nummaria*, Louvain-la-Neuve, 1983, pp. 273–77).

and bronze coinage habitually and frequently. Cleomenes had to have such a currency reserve on hand at all times. We may suppose, for example, that he paid in coin the Greek and Phoenician specialists and technicians who worked on building Alexandria. Even within the province's interior, coinage was indispensable; when he bought up all the available wheat in the country from merchants and exporters, he probably settled with them in currency. He also had to pay this way at least some of the salary owed to the Macedonian and Greek soldiers stationed in Egypt.

Modern historians have been right not to doubt Cleomenes's use of actual coins. They have even attributed to him a hardly negligible role in the "monetization" of Egypt. Van Groningen wrote in 1925: "Coins were not struck in Egypt before Cleomenes; he introduced them."[78] In 1925, before the discoveries that have altered our understanding of Egyptian coinage, Van Groningen could even imagine that if some foreign coins had penetrated into the country in the fifth and early fourth centuries, Egypt never possessed any mint of its own (or only occasionally). For him, Cleomenes really was an innovator. In a less specific, but nonetheless suggestive way, Kloft thought that Cleomenes "had stimulated a money-based economy through the striking of coinage."[79] He thought such an economy was attempted in the Thirtieth Dynasty, at the time of Takhos and Chabrias, but it was Cleomenes's action that proved decisive. Kloft's opinion on the coinage of Egypt prior to Alexander needs itself to be reviewed in the light of Buttrey's and Price's observations. This takes nothing away from the action credited to Cleomenes: for most scholars, his activity as coiner promoted the country's "monetization."

The problem, therefore, is to determine which are the coinage issues that go back to him. It quickly becomes apparent, however, that contrary to all expectation, the coinage attributable to him is extremely limited.

Cleomenes and the Coinage with the Name and Types of Alexander

The idea naturally comes to mind that Cleomenes, financial overseer of Egypt, struck coins with the name and types of Alexander, whose production had just begun in Cilicia and Phoenicia.

Indeed, in his publication of the Demanhur hoard, Newell[80] allocated Egypt five issues of Alexander tetradrachms (cf. pl. 7, 1) constituting a rela-

---

78. "De Cleomene Naucratita," *Mnemosyne* 53 (1925), p. 122 (cf. also p. 112). [Le Rider cites Van Groningen's Latin—WEH.]

79. *Grazer Beiträge* 15 (1986), p. 206 (cf. also p. 204). [Le Rider cites the original German—WEH: "hat durch die Münzprägung die Geldwirtschaft angekurbelt."]

80. *Demanhur* (1923), p. 64 and pp. 144–47.

tively substantial portion of the hoard. Newell inventoried 217 specimens; Zervos raised their number to 265.[81] Solid arguments supported Newell's classification. He emphasized that the issues in question formed a homogenous group in style and manufacture, and he observed that they were present in several other deposits found in Egypt while being rare in hoards discovered elsewhere. Finally, Newell drew attention (without further specific comment) to the symbol carried on the reverse of one of the issues, in front of the legs of Zeus (pl. 7, 2–3). This symbol alludes to an Egyptian cult; it consists of a ram's head surmounted by two tall, vertical plumes and bearing a double pair of horns. It is generally taken as a representation of the god Khnum, but that is not the only Egyptian deity one might envisage.[82]

On all the tetradrachms of the group Newell defined, Zeus's right leg is drawn back. This "new style," it will be recalled, had appeared at Sidon in 325/324; Newell suggested that it had started at Alexandria, and he proposed 326/325 for the date of the group's first issue. This dating seemed all the more likely to him because the Demanhur hoard, collected and buried in 318 or the beginning of 317, included only five issues of this mint—five issues whose specimens, as Newell noted in his inventory, were very, or even exceptionally, well preserved.

Newell's analysis won general agreement. Three new issues have come to light: one with the Greek letters OP has been placed somewhat arbitrarily at the head of Newell's sequence, the other two at the end. I refer to Zervos's study and Price's catalogue.[83] One will note that silver was not the only metal coined; in addition to tetradrachms (the silver's only known denomination), gold staters were struck; some among them carry no mint

---

81. See above, p. 147 for a list of the number of specimens attributed to the principal mints represented in the hoard.

82. I owe the description of this often misunderstood symbol to J. Yoyotte; L. Müller, *Numism. d'Alexandre le Grand* (1855), p. 319, wrote: ". . . ram's head with an Egyptian headdress consisting of two goat's horns that carry a disk surmounted by two long plumes or palms; it is the head of the god *Ammon Chnouphis of the Ram's Head.*" This description has become accepted, and the symbol is almost always thought of as an image of Khnum (Price, *Alexander*, 1991, p. 497, adds a variation, "ram-head with Isis-crown"). Yoyotte has pointed out to me that the ram's head is provided with a double pair of horns, horns bent back and horns horizontal and twisted, the latter not being a goat's horns but those of another type of ram. The representation may be that of the god Khnum, but it could also be that of the god Be at Mendes or that of Hershef (Herakles), or that of Ammon (or Amon).

83. O. H. Zervos, "The Early Tetradrachms of Ptolemy I," *Amer. Num. Soc. Museum Notes* 13 (1967), pp. 1–16; M. J. Price, *Alexander* (1991), pp. 496–99. Zervos accepts as a point of departure the date of 326 (I suppose he means the year 326/325). Price has changed Newell's understanding somewhat when he writes that the latter put the opening of the mint "probably after 325"; Newell, in fact, clearly opted for 326/325.

magistrate's mark, while others have the same officials' identifying marks that appear on the silver currency.

Cleomenes, master of Egypt after April 331, supposedly waited, therefore, more than five years before issuing any Alexanders. As I said above, we were rather led to believe that he needed ample quantities of coins to undertake and complete his assigned mission. So his lack of urgency in producing currency is somewhat surprising. But this sense of surprise increases if we rigorously examine Newell's chronology. We will discover, indeed, that Cleomenes very possibly delayed striking Alexanders even longer, and, if pressed, we might say that he did not strike any at all.

Newell postulated that the new style Zeus on the reverse of the tetradrachms (the right leg drawn back) first appeared at Alexandria and that Sidon adopted it the following year, in 325/324 (pl. 4, 6). But the opposite seems just as likely to me: the Egyptian engraver, having to create his first tetradrachm die, could have been inspired by a Sidonian example that he copied because it seemed to him a more up-to-date version of the type on the reverse.

Suppose we examine the content of the Demanhur hoard, assigning it a burial date of the second half of the year 319/318 (October 319 to September 318). The five Egyptian issues that it contains could have been produced from 323/322 to 319/318. Even if the issue with the letters OP preceded them, it might date from the year 324/323 and be placed in the last weeks of that year, after Ptolemy supplanted Cleomenes. The issue's small volume (only one obverse die is known for its tetradrachms) would allow dating it within this timeframe. As for the issue of gold staters without mint magistrate's mark, it could belong to the same period (for now at least, no stater exists displaying the OP signature).[84]

I am not seeking to impose anything extreme. I am willing to accept that the early Alexander staters and tetradrachms from Egypt appeared under Cleomenes. But, in my opinion, nothing requires the date of 326/325 Newell favored. If Cleomenes really produced Alexanders, they are better placed, it seems to me, at the very end of the reign, perhaps not prior to the end of the year 324.

The first phase of the building of Alexandria was over by then. The currency Cleomenes used to bring these works to happy completion, therefore, would not have included Alexanders struck under his direction. In this context, what coins would he have used? Is it conceivable that he produced a coinage with types other than those of Alexander?

---

84. The last two issues of tetradrachms added to Newell's list can be placed after 319/318; they would precede the tetradrachms showing Alexander wearing an elephant skin headdress, whose first specimens were struck around 315.

Would Cleomenes Have Struck Coins Other Than Alexanders?

We have seen that, according to Buttrey's analysis, the pharaohs of the twenty-eighth to thirtieth dynasties struck a number of pseudo-Athenian tetradrachms in the fourth century; but to be certain of this, we must await the complete study of the Fayum hoard now underway. We do know that, after 343/342, Artaxerxes III and (perhaps) Artaxerxes IV, and the later satraps Sabaces and Mazaces struck issues with Athenian types. Might not Cleomenes have continued producing the same coinage?

The question is worth asking because we know that coinages of the preceding period continued to be issued under Alexander. Recall that in Cilicia silver staters of Persian weight displaying Baaltars on the obverse were struck concurrently with Alexander's currency. A little later, in Babylon, Mazaeus, appointed satrap by Alexander, had the right to produce tetradrachms in his own name with types that he had previously used under the Great King (Baaltars/lion). Double darics and darics were also possibly struck in the Babylonian mint during Alexander's lifetime, and it seems that some Athenian imitations appeared at the same time somewhere in Babylonia.[85]

Cleomenes, therefore, following the example of his Egyptian predecessors, could have issued pseudo-Athenian tetradrachms. Judging by the tolerance he showed elsewhere, Alexander would not have objected. An imitation Athenian coinage suited Egypt perfectly and permitted Cleomenes to manage required cash payments because the Athenian types were recognized throughout the Mediterranean world.

But we have yet to find any evidence allowing us to establish that Cleomenes undertook such a coinage. Up to now, it has not been possible to attribute any pseudo-Athenian issue to him. The future, perhaps, will bring new facts for our consideration. At present, all the indications are negative.

Nothing leads us, either, to suppose that he struck coins with personal types. I noted (p. 167, cf. pl 6, 12) the existence in fourth-century Egypt of gold staters showing a leaping horse on the obverse and two hieroglyphs on the reverse that taken together signify "pure gold." Their attribution remains unclear because they have no legend. The best study of them to date is G. K. Jenkins's.[86] The twenty examples he assembled all looked alike, with a single exception, where one of the two hieroglyphic signs was repeated on the obverse. The other specimens were struck from two

---

85. Matters concerning Babylon will be dealt with in the next chapter.
86. "Greek Coins Recently Acquired by the British Museum," *NC* 15 (1955), p. 145, no. 24, and pp. 148–50.

obverse and two reverse dies. Jenkins emphasized the irregularity of the weights (ranging from 8 to 8.9 grams) and asked whether the weight of the daric (±8.4 grams) was not an influence, but he reserved judgment on this point. An attribution to Nektanebo II (359–343) seemed probable to him. Nevertheless, the absence of a legend and the ill-defined character of the hoards containing specimens of this coinage[87] require us to leave the question open. After all, one could also imagine they go back to Cleomenes, who would have issued this currency to pay for his purchases of wheat in the country's interior. But this is pure speculation. It is much more sensible, at the present time, to think that no coinage can be attributed to Cleomenes until around 324, assuming that it was he, and not Ptolemy, who struck the first staters and tetradrachms of Alexander in Egypt.

What Currency Did Cleomenes Use?

If Cleomenes, to all appearances, did not himself issue any coinage during the greater part of his time in office, if ever, it is probably because he thought it normal to reuse the coins he had at hand, whatever they were. Cleomenes was born in Egypt, where the local coinage was not favored over foreign currencies. The coinages produced in the country before Alexander's arrival were basically of Athenian types, a fact that allows us to understand how Athenian tetradrachms preeminently, as well as all the Athenian imitations produced in Asia Minor and in the East, circulated freely on Egyptian soil. Other coins from the Mediterranean world likewise wound up in the Nile valley. The normal practice Cleomenes followed in this monetary situation might explain why he did not think he had to produce his own currency, so long as the influx of foreign coinages satisfied his needs. Presumably the stiff taxes he exacted from grain exporters, not to mention the inflated sale prices he himself charged, resulted in foreign currencies flooding into his treasury. If wheat assumed an even greater than usual importance at this time, owing to the circumstances, we must not forget that Egypt also exported other local products, papyrus for example, and commodities from Arabia and even farther away, all of which would ensure regular revenue streams, thanks especially to the taxes levied. All these were ways for the master of the country to obtain the coined currency his treasury absolutely needed.

The Egyptian hoards that Jenkins dated to around 330 in the *Inventory of Greek Coin Hoards* show, as we would expect for silver coins, a predomi-

---

87. In *IGCH*, Jenkins dates the three hoards (1654, 1657, 1658) containing staters of this type around 330; numbers 1657 and 1658 consist only of this coinage. All three hoards were found in Egypt.

nance of Athenian and pseudo-Athenian tetradrachms.[88] Two hoards reveal the presence at this time in Egypt of Greek gold coins of Philip II, of Lampsacus, and of Cyprus, with which darics of the Great King are associated.[89] The deposits in question do not contain any Phoenician silver coins. This absence, we may surmise, is owing to chance, some hoards, supposedly buried toward the middle of the fourth century, contain coins from Sidon and Tyre,[90] and coins of these two cities probably found their way to Egypt, at least until the 320s. Gold staters and silver tetradrachms of Alexander originating from Cilicia, Phoenicia, Syria, and Macedonia complement these varied coinages after 333/332. The enormous Demanhur hoard, buried in 318 or early 317, probably comprised a certain proportion of coins that wound up in Egypt during the time of Cleomenes.

The latter would therefore have been content, prior to issuing any Alexanders shortly before his sovereign's death (if he actually ever did so), to employ the coinages he found in the Egyptian treasuries when he first took power. Subsequently, he utilized those that the revenues from the province and the commercial grain activities under his direction procured for him. In the monetary realm, his conduct was therefore rather passive. If he did manage a great deal of coinage, one cannot say, in the present state of our evidence, that he initiated a policy of "monetization" in Egypt, as some have asserted. All one can say is that the intense activity provoked by the building of Alexandria probably augmented the volume of the money supply in circulation even as the Egyptians became more familiar, perhaps, with the use of coined currency. But Cleomenes does not seem to have precipitated this evolution deliberately.

Note on the Mint Where the First Egyptian Alexanders Were Struck

Price took up and elaborated the idea that the earliest gold and silver Alexanders in Egypt were struck not at Alexandria, as Newell had supposed, but at Memphis.[91] Ptolemy allegedly used the Memphis mint up to about 314, when Alexandria became the center of Egyptian coinage production.

In defense of this view, Price first of all observed that Memphis was the site of a producing mint in the first part of the fourth century, before Alexander's arrival. This city was, indeed, the administrative center of Lower Egypt for a long time; in Arrian's narrative (3.1.3–4; 5.1; 6.13), it clearly

---

88. *IGCH* 1656, 1659–1663.
89. *IGCH* 1654 and 1656.
90. *IGCH* 1651 and 1653.
91. *Alexander* (1991), p. 496.

appears as the country's "capital." Because the city had a mint, the Macedonian administration would not have changed anything for a while.

Price next mentions the small bronzes found at Saqqara that display, he says, a portrait of Alexander and that he classifies as Egyptian. Based on their findspot and the date he assigns them (332/331), they can only have been struck, he thinks, at Memphis. It is also at Memphis, Price says, that the first Alexanders were produced some years later. The Pegasus appearing as a symbol on one of the issues[92] indicates a continuity with the Pegasus forepart adorning the Saqqara bronzes, while the "Khnum" symbol (a typically Egyptian image, cf. pl. 7, 2–3) was more natural at Memphis than at Alexandria. I have voiced my reservations with Price's interpretation of the small bronzes from Saqqara at the beginning of this chapter. What he says additionally about the "Khnum" strikes me as highly debatable: we are dealing with a mere mint magistrate's mark, of a personal character, present on only one issue—not a mint's own marking.

Finally, Price draws support from the legend on some tetradrachms of Ptolemy, issued around 314. It is known that this satrap struck a coinage with the name and types of Alexander for some years, up until around 315 for the silver tetradrachms and 310 for the gold staters. Around 320 he began simultaneously to issue tetradrachms that, while keeping the type of Zeus and the legend *Alexandrou* on the reverse, replaced the head of Herakles on the obverse with the head of Alexander wearing an elephant skin headdress. From 315–314, Ptolemy gave up striking tetradrachms with the types of Alexander once and for all; moreover, he altered the look of the series that he had been striking concurrently since c. 320 by adding a warrior Athena to the head of the Conqueror wearing the elephant skin headdress. The legend was still *Alexandrou*, and the weight remained an Attic tetradrachm's. Concerning that legend, however, there was a variation: some of the new coins, among the very earliest, carry the inscription *Alexandreion Ptolemaiou* (pl. 7, 4).

After reviewing other interpretations, Price chose the following: it is necessary to understand *argyrokopeion* (mint) and translate "[mint] of Alexandria under Ptolemy"; this legend, according to Price, indicates that the production center had been transferred from Memphis to Alexandria, a decision taken around 314, the date of the tetradrachms in question.

But this interpretation of the legend is grammatically impossible, as Knoepfler has forcefully demonstrated.[93] The adjectival form *alexandreion*

---

92. *Ibid.*, no. 3974.
93. "Tétradrachmes attiques et argent 'alexandrin' chez Diogène Laërce," *Museum Helveticum* 16 (1989), pp. 205–10; cf. also what he has to say in *Topoi* 7, 1 (1997), pp. 39–41. I have already commented on Price's opinion in my review of his book, *Rev. Suisse de num.* 71 (1992), p. 225.

can only derive from "Alexandros" (Alexander) and not from "Alexandreia" (Alexandria). The adjective formed from Alexandreia is *alexandreiōtikos* and later, in Roman times, *alexandrinos*, by analogy with the Latin *alexandrinus*. The only possible interpretation of *alexandreion Ptolemaiou* on our tetradrachms is, therefore, "[coin, *nomisma*, or silver piece, *argyrion*] of Alexander of Ptolemy," "this is an Alexander of Ptolemy." What the satrap of Egypt wanted to communicate is that, despite his complete abandonment of the types of Alexander, these tetradrachms were still "Alexanders" by weight.

Price's arguments, therefore, are not at all convincing, in my opinion at least. Memphis would surely have been the production site of the first Egyptian Alexanders had this currency been struck from 331: Alexandria did not exist at this date. But because this coinage apparently began only c. 324, locating the mint in the new *polis* becomes a serious possibility. According to the author of the second book of the pseudo-Aristotelian *Oeconomica* (2.33 c), Cleomenes had succeeded in making the city livable before his mandate ended in June 323. I think that if he actually struck any Alexanders around this time, he would have organized the production at Alexandria rather than at Memphis. Alexandria was his doing; it was there that he probably spent most of his time. The transfer of administrative activities from one city to the other followed, I presume, the progress of construction. I will also observe that setting up a mint did not require complicated arrangements: imagine, instead, an organization of artisans rather than today's "Bureau of the Mint."

Scholars have asked themselves when Ptolemy established his principal residence at Alexandria and gave the city the status of "capital." Fraser entered the debate[94] opting for an early date, "not later than 320/319." I do not see why Ptolemy would not have installed himself in the new city upon his arrival in Egypt towards the end of summer or the beginning of autumn 323. It is at Alexandria, right from the start, that he struck coinage, whether he was continuing the issues of Cleomenes or was himself inaugurating Alexanders in Egypt.

In addition to the spectacular deeds that marked his brief stay in Egypt (the consultation of the oracle at Ammon and the foundation of Alexandria remain in everyone's memory), Alexander made a series of less

---

94. *Ptolemaic Alexandria* (Oxford, 1972), I, pp. 6–7; II, notes 23–28. Fraser reacts against the assertion of C. B. Welles, according to whom "Memphis clearly long remained the capital." Fraser thinks that Cleomenes, then Ptolemy, struck coinage at Alexandria, not Memphis. To be honest, his reason is no longer acceptable: he writes, in fact, that Egypt, prior to Alexander, had practically no coinage and that, consequently, the choice of Memphis as a mint did not force itself on Cleomenes.

striking but still important decisions. One of them was particularly fortunate: demonstrating his sure judgment, he singled out Cleomenes of Naucratis. Though probably unacquainted with him prior to his arrival in Egypt, Alexander assigned him a critical mission, the building of Alexandria. Cleomenes took up his task in earnest. Because the means put at his disposal proved insufficient, he had recourse to financial expedients and engaged in practices that tarnished his reputation. But he succeeded in completing construction of the city, probably within the allotted deadlines. Unfortunately for him, Alexander passed from the scene prematurely, without having been able to repay him in full. What surprises us from a monetary point of view is that Cleomenes, despite the payments he had to make in coin, does not seem to have struck coinage, unless at the very end of Alexander's reign. He used, therefore, currency that had been struck in Egypt before the end of 332 and whatever foreign trade brought him. Cleomenes's monetary conduct points up a policy gap in Alexander's coinage affairs. Although Alexander created his own currency at the end of 333 and nothing prevented him from having tetradrachms and staters issued with his name and types in Egypt, he apparently did not give any directive to this effect. It is perhaps only in 324 or even later that Alexanders were produced in the land of the Nile.

Chapter 7

Alexander and Coinage in Babylonia and East of the Tigris

Upon leaving Egypt at the beginning of spring 331, Alexander, as we have seen (p. 126), stopped at Tyre. During his stay there, or shortly after he resumed his journey, he punished the Samaritans who had executed the governor of Syria, Andromachus.[1]

Alexander was en route to Thapsacus on the Euphrates. To superintend the treasure accompanying him, Alexander appointed Harpalus, a man who had already held this office, but who had made the mistake of deserting in the months prior to the battle of Issus. Alexander, however, restored him to favor (Arrian 3.6.4–7).

Alexander arrived at Thapsacus in July 331. Mazaeus, whom Darius had set in charge of this area, retreated before Alexander and allowed him to traverse Mesopotamia unharassed. The Macedonian army crossed the Tigris and carried off its third great victory over Darius at Gaugamela. The battle took place on October 1, 331: a Babylonian astronomical tablet confirms the date given by Plutarch.[2] In the first part of the tablet, dealing with the battle,

---

1. Alexander replaced the latter with Menon (Memnon according to Curtius 4.8.10), as I mentioned earlier in chapter 5 apropos of the finds made in a grotto of Wadi-Daliyeh. Cf. the discussion of J. A. Atkinson, *A Commentary on Q. Curtius Rufus' Historiae Alexandri Magni* (Amsterdam, 1980), pp. 370–71.
2. P. Bernard, "Nouvelle contribution de l'épigraphie cunéiforme à l'histoire hellénistique," *BCH* 114 (1990), pp. 515–17. Plutarch, *Life of Camillus* 19.5 and *Life of Alexander* 31.8, provided two concurring pieces of evidence; the astronomical tablet published by A. J. Sachs and H. Hunger, *Astronomical Diaries and Related Texts from Babylonia* (Österreichische Akad. für Wissenshaften, Philos.-hist. Klasse, Denkschriften 195, 1988), no. 330, accords with Plutarch's testimony: the battle occurred on October 1, 331. On the circumstances of this battle and on Alexander's march to Babylon, cf. Bernard, *ibid.*, pp. 517–28. Gaugamela is located northeast of Nineveh and northwest of Arbela.

Darius bears the title "king of the universe"; the title is Alexander's in the second part, which relates his entry into Babylon.

Alexander's Arrival at Babylon

Curtius (5.1.3-9) depicts Darius arriving at Arbela after his defeat and explaining to his friends and soldiers why he decided not to defend Babylon, as his entourage was expecting, but to leave for Media instead, where he would organize the resistance. The Great King's decision left Alexander free access to Babylonia and the region of Susa. After taking possession of the treasures Darius abandoned at Arbela (abundant royal belongings and 4,000 talents; Curtius 5.1.10), the Macedonian headed for Babylon. Along the way, he encountered Mazaeus, who had distinguished himself at Gaugamela where he nearly won the day for the Persians. After having served the Great King loyally and brilliantly, he came to hand over Babylon to Alexander (Curtius 5.1.17). Alexander, the Roman author says, appreciated the defection of such an illustrious individual, and he was enormously relieved because the siege of Babylon would have been a difficult affair. Mazaeus came as a suppliant. Nonetheless, the city's surrender was presumably negotiated, with Mazaeus securing a certain number of guarantees. This is what we understand from the cuneiform text written on the reverse of the tablet just discussed.[3]

Curtius (5.1.19–23) and Arrian (3.16.3–4) report the warm welcome Alexander received from the Babylonian authorities and population. He entered the city on ground strewn with flowers and victory wreaths, and happy throngs bearing all sorts of presents greeted him. At the head of the local notables was Bagophanes, "guardian of the citadel and of the royal funds" (Curtius 5.1.20). Alexander (Arrian 3.16.4) "directed the Babylonians to rebuild the temples Xerxes destroyed, and especially the temple of Baal, whom the Babylonians honor more than any other god." Arrian later remarks that Alexander followed the recommendation of the Chaldaeans concerning the temples and that he sacrificed to Baal according to their instructions.

One might imagine, reading Arrian, that Alexander's conduct towards Babylonian cults differed radically from what the Persians did, and that the promises he lavished were what guaranteed an enthusiastic popular reception and peaceful entry into the city.

But the narratives of Curtius and Arrian demonstably belong to a literary convention, the classic description of a conqueror's entry into a sur-

---

3. Cf. the preceding note and the commentary of Bernard, op. cit., pp. 525–28.

rendered city or a king's entry into one of his own cities. I refer to the convincing studies of A. Kuhrt and P. Briant.[4] Kuhrt recalled the cuneiform texts that relate the entry of Sargon II, king of Assyria, into Babylon in 710, and Cyrus's in 539: the same general acceptance, the same respect for local cults. Concerning the latter, Kuhrt remarks that, contrary to what Arrian says, the Persians respected the religious practices of the Babylonians and that Alexander's order to rebuild the temples "was an ideological desideratum in Babylonian concepts of kingship." Briant also stressed the textual similarities describing the arrivals of victorious kings, emphasizing that "the entry of Alexander into Babylon seems to be modeled after Cyrus's." He also comments that another cuneiform document, belonging to the category of prophecies and entitled the *Dynastic Prophecy*, reveals not the official, propagandistic version of Alexander's arrival, but the viewpoint of at least some Babylonians, who felt the Macedonian conquest was a time of misfortune and who awaited the return of good King Darius bringing prosperity in his train.

Curtius and Arrian report that before he entered Babylon, Alexander drew up his army in battle formation. Curtius adds that armed men surrounded Alexander and that he required the citizen crowd to follow the last ranks of his infantry. Did he fear a change of heart in the populace? Did Mazaeus's reassurances fail to convince completely? Or rather, did Alexander, as Bernard thinks, only want "to display his might by having his army parade right before the eyes of the Babylonians"? It is also conceivable that Alexander was adapting himself to standard operating procedure in this sort of situation.

Alexander's Decisions at Babylon; Officials of Babylon between 331 and 323

The king spent thirty-four days in the city, from the end of October until the end of November 331. The army refreshed itself, according to Diodorus (17.64.4); according to Curtius (5.1.36–39) the army indulged in license, to the detriment of military discipline.

Alexander first drew up an inventory of Darius's goods and chattel and all his fortune, and then proceeded to make government appointments. He named Mazaeus satrap of Babylonia. Alexander probably wanted not

---

4. A. Kuhrt, "Alexander and Babylon," *Achaemenid History* 5 (1990), pp. 121–29; P. Briant, "Alexandre à Babylone: images grecques, images babyloniennes," *Alexandre le Grand dans les littératures occidentales et proche-orientales* (Nanterre, 1999), pp. 23–32; also his *From Cyrus to Alexander: A History of the Persian Empire*, Eng. trans. P. T. Daniels, (Winnona Lake, IN, 2002), pp. 845–50 and 862–64.

only to thank him for surrendering but also to demonstrate his concern for the Persians and to encourage other defections as a result.[5]

Mazaeus's power, however, was circumscribed. Apollodorus of Amphipolis became commander of the troops left with the satrap, Agathon became commandant (*phrourarch*) of the citadel, and Asclepiodorus, son of Philo, was put in charge of tax collection.[6] We encounter the same separation of powers as at Sardis, with one addition: Apollodorus's control of the troops, with the title *stratēgos* ("general").

Mazaeus died towards the end of 328, when Alexander was in Sogdiana. The new satrap of Babylonia was Stamenes, also of Persian origin. Arrian (4.18.3) has transmitted this name to us, while the manuscripts of Curtius (8.3.17) give the following text: *Babylonia demortuo Mazaio Ditameni subiecta est.*[7]

About the same time, at a date impossible to fix precisely, Harpalus appeared in Babylonia. I remarked above that Alexander, at the start of 331, had entrusted him with the management of the military treasury.[8] Goukowsky has convincingly sketched the part this individual played during the king's eastern campaigns.[9] In 330 at Ecbatana, he received custody of the Persian treasures brought from Susa, Persepolis, and Pasargadae. It seems that he quickly rid himself of this latter task; his next assignment was Babylonia. Once in the province, he there became all-powerful. According to Diodorus (17.108.4), the most forthcoming of the ancient sources on this point, he was charged with guarding the treasury of Babylon and the public revenues and was named, moreover, satrap "of a large territory" ("*pollēs khōras*"—WEH),[10] an accumulation of offices totally at odds with the long-standing rule of the Great King which Alexander, apparently, had previously sought to follow. Goukowsky suggests that Harpalus's assump-

---

5. It has been conjectured that Mazaeus defected to Alexander because he was disappointed by Darius's attitude after Gaugamela and because he thought the Great King had seriously compromised his chances. One will note that at the same time as he was putting Mazaeus in charge of Babylonia, Alexander named Mithrenes satrap of Armenia, the man who had surrendered Sardis; cf. P. Briant, *From Cyrus to Alexander*, the section "Darius and his Faithful," pp. 842–52.

6. The evidence of Diodorus (17.64.5), Curtius (5.1.43), and Arrian (3.16.4) does not completely agree on these postings; cf. the commentary of P. Goukowsky, *Diodore de Sicile, Livre XVII* (Paris, 1976), pp. 245–46.

7. ["Babylon was put under the control of Ditamenes when Mazaeus died"—WEH (the Loeb trans. accepts the easy emendation of Zumpt, reading "Stameni" for "Ditameni.")]

8. Arrian (3.6.6) makes clear that Harpalus was physically unfit for military service and that is why he was made overseer of the treasury.

9. *Essai sur les origines du mythe d'Alexandre I: Les origines politiques* (Nancy, 1978), pp. 35–37.

10. Plutarch, *Alex.* 35.8, writes that Harpalus at Babylon exercised the functions of "overseer [*epimelētēs*] of the country."

tion of this key role in the empire, of which Babylon would become the financial capital, explains the expansion of his powers. Harpalus was the liaison between West and East, preparing convoys to the upper satrapies of Asia and recruiting mercenaries. Goukowsky also suggests that Diodorus's expression, satrap "of a large territory," signifies that Harpalus's mandate extended beyond the borders of Babylonia. By the time Alexander returned from India in 325, it might have included Mesopotamia and Syria because the ancient sources do not mention any satrap in these two provinces at that date. If that is so,[11] Harpalus would have possessed exceptional power, without which, perhaps, he might not have proved equal to his responsibilities.

After Harpalus's arrival at Babylon, Stamenes was certainly stripped of his office. The fact that the latter was named satrap in late 328 shows that Harpalus had not yet taken charge of the Babylonian government, whether because he exercised only limited functions for a time or because he was only sent to the province in 327.

What became of Stamenes is unknown. There is no further mention of him in the ancient sources.[12]

Harpalus's conduct in office, according to Diodorus (17.108.4–6), was entirely blameworthy. Persuaded that Alexander would not return from his distant expeditions, he lived entirely for pleasure, surrounding himself with courtesans and demanding delicacies such as fish from the Persian Gulf. One might suppose that Diodorus's account drew from a source hostile to Harpalus, but the latter certainly did not have a clear conscience, because he deemed it prudent to flee upon news of Alexander's return at the end of 325. Harpalus, Diodorus reports (17.108.6), "packed up 5,000 talents of silver, enrolled 6,000 mercenaries, departed from Asia and sailed across to Attica."

Archon probably became the new satrap of Babylonia. Indeed, when Perdiccas proceeded to name satraps shortly after Alexander's death on June 10, 323, it seems he left the dead king's appointments in place as governors of the eastern territories.[13] In the list provided by the ancient sources, the satrap of Babylonia at the end of 323 is Archon, and we may take as fact that his position goes back to Alexander's reign. Because he had accompanied the Conqueror all the way to India, his posting to head Babylonia can only have occurred at the end of 325 at the earliest, when the sovereign, heading west, learned of the serious events taking place in several regions of his

---

11. Goukowsky, *Essai*, p. 37, emphasizes the hypothetical character of his surmises, but they are worth mentioning, nonetheless, and should be kept in mind.

12. Cf. H. Berve, *Das Alexanderreich* II (Munich, 1926), p. 361, no. 718.

13. This is what the texts of Diodorus (18.3.2), Curtius (10.10.4), and Arrian (*Affairs After Alexander* 1.5–8) imply. Still, we cannot rule out the possibility of an exception.

kingdom and the reprehensible conduct of a certain number of his officials.[14] After punishing them appropriately, he had to replace them, and that is probably when Archon was named to head Babylonia.

The author of the second book of the *Oeconomica* informs us of an individual who will engage our attention later on: Antimenes of Rhodes. Judging from the *Oeconomica*, he was in charge of Babylonia's finances and he was in the post at the end of Alexander's reign. We may therefore assume that he was named after Harpalus's departure and almost concurrently with Archon. The king, after the ill-fated exception made for Harpalus, resumed the customary separation of powers.

I: Babylonian Coinages from 331 to 323

Mazaeus's "Lion" Coinage at Babylon and its Posterity

H. Nicolet-Pierre has recently re-examined the coinages struck at Babylon between 331 and 311.[15] She has made an important contribution by providing as complete a survey as possible for two series, namely, the "lion" tetradrachms of Mazaeus and the series comprising the double darics and darics attributable to the Babylonian mint. I will therefore be referring to this study, even as I add some of my own observations.

The Babylonian Coinage of Mazaeus

Among the issues with the name and types of Mazaeus, one group stands out. It was in fact struck on the Attic standard because the coins (tetradrachms) weigh more than 17 grams and not the c. 11 grams of other groups, which use the Persian standard. Apart from this weight difference, the types and inscriptions belong to the repertory dear to Mazaeus: on the obverse, Baaltars seated left, legs parallel, his mantle passing over his left shoulder; in his right hand, he holds a beaded scepter before him; behind him his name is inscribed in Aramaic; on the reverse, a lion advances towards the left; the name Mazaeus is written above in Aramaic. Some specimens carry no mark, while others have a symbol or a letter (in the exergue [below the ground line], on the ground line, or between the lion's paws, cf. pl. 7, 5).

---

14. According to Diodorus (17.106.2), it was in Carmania where Alexander, after having led a Bacchic revel for seven days, learned in late 325 of the troubles erupting in the empire. On the Carmanian bacchanals, see Goukowsky, *Essai II: Alexandre et Dionysos* (Nancy, 1981), pp. 47–64.

15. "Argent et or frappés entre 331 and 311 ou de Mazdai à Séleucos," in *Travaux de numis. grecque offerts à G. Le Rider*, M. Amandry and S. Hurter eds. (London, 1999), pp. 285–299. M. J. Price published a highly interesting group of "lion" coins, "Circulation at Babylon in 323 BC," in *Mnemata, Papers in Memory of N. M. Waggoner*, W. E. Metcalf ed. (New York, 1991), pp. 70–71, nos. 25–133.

It has long been established that these tetradrachms of Attic weight could have only been struck at the time when Mazaeus was serving under Alexander, between autumn 331 (date of his appointment as satrap) and the end of 328 (date of his death), and that they were produced at Babylon, where he held office. F. Imhoof-Blumer had noticed that several "lion" specimens (issued by Mazaeus or posthumously) were reported as having been found in Babylonia and that a certain number of these coins were covered in a dark red oxide common on the coins discovered in this region.

For these tetradrachms, besides the issue without mark I mentioned above, Nicolet-Pierre highlighted six that different signs distinguish: serpent, scallop shell, wreath, club, M, and K; these signs clearly show that, despite the use of Aramaic for the satrap's name, the coins in question were issued at a mint under Greek control.

It is surprising that Alexander permitted his satrap to strike a personal coinage, with the satrap's name and types and evoking the coinage the latter had issued under the Great King. Some will point to a comparable instance in Cilicia, in the mint at Tarsus, which issued silver coins under Alexander similar to those of the Persian regime (more precisely, to those of Mazaeus as Persian satrap) not only in their types but also in their weight (they are Persian staters). Yet serious differences exist between the two series. In Cilicia after 333, the coins do not carry the name of the satrap in office, Balacrus, except in one case that I have tried to explain; moreover, these coins were issued concurrently with Alexander's coins, clearly indicating that they had a limited, strictly local role. At Babylon, in contrast, the tetradrachms are normally in the name of Mazaeus and quite probably constitute the sole currency struck in these years by the Babylonian mint. There are, indeed, good reasons, I believe, for dating the inauguration of Alexander's coinage in this province a little later. So the Babylonian issues of Mazaeus have a status that is not comparable to that of the Cilician staters, and their Attic weight accentuates the difference between the two series.

The explanation Hill advanced, that at Babylon we are dealing with a satrapal coinage, principally meant to pay troops, seems insufficient to me, although attractively argued. Mazaeus, according to Hill, had to repay soldiers whom he had recruited mostly in Cilicia; hence he maintained types with which they were familiar. He took the troops with him to Babylonia, and so the soldiers first fought for Darius and then, with their commander, switched sides to Alexander.

As for the suggestion of Newell, who was tempted to establish a connection between the "lion" coins and the temple of Baal at Babylon, it seems difficult to accept, and I will be content merely to note it.[16]

---

16. G. F. Hill, *BMC Arabia, Mesopotamia, Persia* (London, 1922), p. CXLI; E. T. Newell, *ESM*, p. 106, note 14.

I myself do not interpret this coinage as a one-off affair, the product of a particular circumstance. Rather, I believe that Mazaeus struck coinage by virtue of a prerogative he was granted. I believe that, at the time of the negotiations preceding the surrender of Babylon, this eminent man, who had already been named satrap, sought confirmation for the right to issue a currency with his own name and types—a right he had exercised in this office under the Great King. The six or seven issues constituting his Babylonian coinage seem to indicate that, for the three years he lasted in office, the mint was constantly active.

I also believe that Alexander did not resist this demand, because, at the time, he had no fixed policy in monetary matters. He had, indeed, created his very own coinage in 333 and 332, but we have established that he did not seek to impose it in Egypt even though Cleomenes's responsibilities would have justified the production of Alexanders. Alexander seems to demonstrate in Babylonia, as well, the same propensity to allow the striking, or use, of coins other than his own.

Imitations of Mazaeus's Tetradrachms

In 1991 Price published a (partial) list of coins contained in an extremely interesting hoard found in 1973 not far from Babylon, and perhaps at Babylon itself.[17] I will have to mention this hoard again in the following pages. Among its curiosities, in addition to standard "lion" tetradrachms, are three noteworthy specimens (nos. 67–69 on Price's list). They imitate the coins of Mazaeus but Baaltars and the lion are turned to the right, Baaltars's name is omitted, Mazaeus's has been erased on nos. 68 and 69, and the style is very cursory. Another coin kept in the British Museum[18] and on which Baaltars is turned towards the left but the lion toward the right (no legend is inscribed) is also included among the imitations (pl. 7, 6). The existence of these imitations leads one to conclude that Mazaeus's tetradrachms were widely used; when the satrap's death in late 328 put a temporary halt to the official striking of this coinage, their lack was felt and they were imitated. Aware of this, the Babylonian authorities presumably decided after some delay to resume their production.

Continuation of the Lion Tetradrachms

The new tetradrachms no longer carry legends but only control marks. Nicolet-Pierre highlighted three issues where the legs of Baaltars are

---

17. "Circulation at Babylon in 323 BC," in *Mnemata, Papers . . . Waggoner*, W. E. Metcalf ed. (New York, 1991), pp. 63–72. The hoard has been dispersed. Price stressed how much he owed to N. Dürr and N. M. Waggoner, who both had communicated considerable information to him about this deposit.

18. *BMC*, p. 181, no. 3, pl. XX, 16.

parallel (cf. pl. 7, 7), as in Mazaeus's time. In the following issues, the god's right leg is drawn back (cf. pl. 7, 8–9). Nicolet-Pierre also pointed out some details in the posture of Baaltars that distinguish the new "lion" tetradrachms from the old. This coinage did not break off until the period of Seleucus I and carried on perhaps until Antiochus I, who succeeded his father in 281.

So the types Mazaeus launched at Babylon in 331 had a long posterity. The "lion" coinage constituted the local currency of Babylonia for some fifty years, but its circulation was limited: the discoveries of "lion" coins, whether isolated or grouped together, are mostly situated in this province. One does encounter under Seleucus I (311–281) some specimens with the same types at other mints: perhaps at Seleucia on the Tigris, perhaps at Susa, probably at Ecbatana, perhaps at Carrhae.[19] But these are infrequent, occasional issues, presumably struck to facilitate dealings with Babylonia.

A metrological observation is not without interest. While the tetradrachms of Mazaeus generally had a weight commensurate with the Attic standard, the new "lion" issues were less well standardized. Most of the coins weigh between 16 and 17 grams. Hill estimated that they corresponded to three Persian sigloi (the siglos weighing about 5.5 to 5.6 grams), and that is how he explained the three globules on some specimens.[20] Price thought of double Babylonian shekels as a possibility (the Babylonian shekel having a weight of ± 8.4 grams).[21] Newell, for his part, remarked that denominations typical of the Attic system accompanied these "lion" tetradrachms: didrachms, drachms, half-drachms, and obols.[22] He was of the opinion, which I share, that this coinage was meant for local circulation, which explains the weights' imperfect standardization.

It is also possible that the silver used to make these "lion" coins was inferior in quality to that used in Alexanders. Nicolet-Pierre did some analyses, and while eight Babylonian Alexanders had a 99 percent purity level, eight "lion" coins had levels between 92.3 percent and 97 percent.[23] The difference is small. Yet, if one accepts that at Babylon and throughout Babylonia a "lion" tetradrachm was officially interchangeable with an Attic

---

19. Seleucia on the Tigris: N. M. Waggoner, "The Early Alexander Coinage at Seleucia on the Tigris," *Amer. Num. Soc. Mus. Notes* 16 (1969), p. 25, suggested assigning to Seleucia the issues Newell, *ESM* 272–75, attributed to Babylon. Susa: Price, *Alexander* (1991), p. 451, has put in doubt Newell's attribution of the group *ESM* 318–22 to Susa, proposing Ecbatana or Carrhae; B. Kritt, *The Seleucid Mint at Susa* (Lancaster, 1997), p. 25, retained Newell's Susa attribution. Ecbatana: Newell, *ESM* 461–62.

20. *BMC*, p. CXLVI; cf. Nicolet-Pierre, op. cit., p. 293, no. 10.

21. Price, "Circulation at Babylon," p. 67.

22. *ESM*, pp. 105–6.

23. "Argent et or frappés en Babylonie . . . ," p. 305.

tetradrachm of exact weight and excellent purity, the conclusion emerges that the Babylonian treasury not only extracted the usual profit from this coinage attendant upon striking a local currency (which counted precedence in the market among its advantages), but the treasury also pocketed a gain on the metal, the weight being a little less heavy and the quality slightly less pure.

Finally, it will be noted that the manufacture of the new "lion" tetradrachms differs from that of Mazaeus's. The latter have a relatively thin flan and a lightly rounded edge. The flans on the new specimens are thicker and their edges are often striated and rippled. Two angled burrs directly opposite each other are sometimes evident on the edges, an indication that the flans were poured into molds formed of two ill-fitting hemispheres.[24]

The discernible differences between the old and new "lion" coins in weight and manufacture reinforce the idea (sparked by the imitations of Mazaeus's tetradrachms) that a chronological gap exists between the two series. This supposition remains, of course, highly hypothetical.

If one prefers to suppose that there was no interruption, the new series began in 328/327 (October 328 to September 327), Mazaeus having died in late 328. But I do not completely exclude the possibility that this new series only debuted one or two years later.

Gold Double Darics and Darics (and Possibly Silver Sigloi): Were They Struck in Babylonia during Alexander's Reign?

The large gold coins with the type of the archer Great King and weighing twice as much as a daric, that is, ± 16.8 grams, have never ceased to trouble numismatists. Everyone today agrees that these double darics were struck after the death of the last Great King, Darius III, in 330. But in which mint(s) were they produced, and when? Some darics are stylistically akin to the double darics; some sigloi could also belong to this coinage, but the question remains unresolved.[25]

---

24. Hill made this observation, *BMC*, pp. CXLI–CXLII, as have I, "Tétradrachmes au lion et imitations d'Athènes en Babylonie," *Schweizer Münzblätter* 22 (1972), pp. 1–7, esp. pp. 6–7 (= *Études d'hist. monét. et financ.*, II, Athens, 1999, pp. 735–41).

25. Cf. Hill, *BMC*, p. CXXX, and p. 160, nos. 88–91, pl. XXV, 26. Hill describes in the preceding entries (pp. 159–60), nos. 78–87, a group of darics that he dates to the reign of Darius III and whose relationship to the double darics he emphasizes. Today it is accepted that these darics belong, as do the double darics, to the period of Alexander. Hill associates with these darics the silver sigloi in question, which, he writes, "resemble these darics in the relief and treatment of the obverse"; but the reverse of the specimen that he illustrates has nothing in common with that of the darics under discussion.

Imhoof-Blumer, in 1895, assigned all the specimens that he knew of from this group to the Babylon mint.[26] He thought their production began under Mazaeus and only ended some years after Alexander's death. His conspectus shows that he connected the wreath symbol present on Mazaeus's tetradrachms with the wreath symbol also appearing on the issue of double darics. The latter has a second control mark, the letter M (pl. 7, 10), which some coins of Mazaeus also bear (pl. 7, 5); although Imhoof-Blumer did not know of them, they would have strengthened his conviction that the first double darics were contemporary with Mazaeus's tetradrachms. Imhoof-Blumer also noted the presence of the letters M-ΛY not only on an issue of double darics and darics (pl. 7, 11–12) but also on "lion" tetradrachms (pl. 7, 9), as well as on some Alexanders (cf. pl. 8, 6), confirming in his eyes the Babylonian attribution he proposed.

Nicolet-Pierre, in 1999, reopened the discussion of this coinage's inherent problems.[27] Some years earlier she and M. Amandry had published a hoard of silver coins with Athenian types found in Afghanistan.[28] Three of these coins (nos. 1–3 of the hoard inventory) carry the inscription ΣTA-MNA (pl. 7, 13) on the obverse. Now, these two groups of letters appear on an issue of double darics that also bear another mark, a superimposed Φ and Λ. Because these Athenian imitations under discussion were probably struck in one of the easternmost regions of Alexander's empire, it is appropriate to exclude from Babylon not only the double darics where ΣTA-MNA is read but also several other double darics closely related by the style of their reverse and by the letters Φ-Λ (pl. 7, 14).[29]

The list of those double darics and darics that Nicolet-Pierre continues to attribute to Babylon comprises thirteen issues, which stylistically form a seemingly coherent group. Their assignment to the Babylonian mint rests on the fact that the marks of certain issues (for example, M-ΛY) are the same on the "lion" tetradrachms whose Babylonian origin appears

---

26. "Die Münzstätte Babylon," *Numism. Zeitschrift* 27 (1895), pp. 1–22; cf. also the same author's revisions in *NC* 6 (1906), pp. 17–25.

27. Op. cit., pp. 296–305.

28. "Un nouveau trésor de monnaies d'argent pseudo-athéniennes venu d'Afghanistan (1990)," *RN* 36 (1994), pp. 34–54.

29. With the specimen *BMC*, p. 179, no. 12, pl. XX, 12 (bearing the inscription ΣTA-MNA), I would associate the coins *BMC*, pl. XX, 10, 11, 13 and perhaps 7; cf. also *BMC*, pl. LI, 5. Stylistic traits, like the shapes given the spear's point and quiver (when the engraver did not omit drawing it), can guide classification; on this topic, see the discussion of Amandry and Nicolet-Pierre, op. cit., p. 51. On the inscription ΣTA-MNA and the differing interpretations it has elicited, cf. *ibid.*, pp. 45–54; I cite below the view of these two authors.

incontestable.[30] I might add that the manufacture of these double darics resembles that of the "lion" coins: the flans are thick and the edges carry angled burrs directly opposite one another.[31]

Nicolet-Pierre's metal analyses have led to unexpected consequences. The purity of the gold of the double darics varies, ranging from 90 percent to 71 percent. By contrast, Alexander's staters, especially the Babylonian staters (to be discussed presently), are very pure gold (99 percent, 98 percent). This qualitative difference between the two currencies shows that they were not intended to circulate together or to be used in the same way.

What is the appropriate date for the double darics? Contrary to Imhoof-Blumer and many others, Nicolet-Pierre proposes to put all of this coinage after Alexander's death, that is, after June 323. In her classification, the first issue of double darics bears the marks M-ΛY; these marks also appear not only on the "lion" tetradrachms but also on Alexander's Babylonian tetradrachms that were certainly struck after 323. The interpretation and dating she and Amandry proposed for the ΣTA-MNA legend seem to have influenced her opinion. They thought they were dealing with two abbreviated names, the second being a patronymic. ΣTA, they believed, designates the governor of the province where the double darics and pseudo-Athenian tetradrachms bearing this inscription were issued.

From this perspective, ΣTA could be the beginning of "Stamenes," Mazaeus's successor in Babylonia, but this hypothesis must be excluded because the coins in question were produced in a more easterly region. Amandry and Nicolet-Pierre entertained two other possibilities, Stasanor and Stasander, both Cypriotes. Alexander named Stasanor from Soli satrap of Drangiana in late 328 (Arrian 4.18.3; Curtius 8.3.7). Perdiccas, in summer 323, also gave him Areia (Diodorus 18.3.3), and Antipater named him satrap of Bactria and Sogdiana in 321, while Areia and Drangiana reverted to Stasander (Diodorus 18.39.6). The latter is not heard of after 317, but Stasanor held on to Bactria and Sogdiana a few more years. Amandry and Nicolet-Pierre are very tempted to attribute the coins with ΣTA-MNA to one or the other of these men and, if Stasanor is right, not to place his coinage before 323. This chronology accords with the idea that all the double darics are to be dated to the years following Alexander's death. As for the letters MNA, I note that they appear on the coins in the name of Sophytos, who reigned over a part of central Asia after Alexander died. Is

---

30. See the comparative table Nicolet-Pierre, gives, "Argent et or . . . ," p. 301. I would not assign to Babylon, as I have said (cf. preceding note), the issue with a superimposed Φ and Λ as the mint magistrate's mark (cf. *BMC*, pl. XX, 10).

31. I have noted this point in *Schweizer Münzblätter* 22 (1972), p. 7.

this MNA on the coins of Sophytos the same individual as the MNA of the double darics? Or is this just accidental?[32]

Perhaps Amandry and Nicolet-Pierre's proposed chronology is correct. Some Babylonian issues (those bearing the same marks as some posthumous Alexanders) are certainly later than 323. But is that the case for all the double darics? Were not some of them struck during Alexander's lifetime? If we were to opt for identifying ΣTA and Stasanor, we must not forget that he began his satrapal career at the end of 328 and would have had plenty of time to produce a currency in Drangiana before 323. The inscribing of his (abbreviated) name on a group of gold and silver coins whose types were his sovereign's have a parallel: Balacrus, satrap of Cilicia under Alexander, put his name on silver staters of Persian weight, whose obverse type, Baaltars, harked back to the time of the Great King.[33]

One cannot help recalling here a detail from the history of Harpalus, although its meaning remains unclear. The treasure that this luminary took to Greece consisted of gold and silver in different forms. The offer of a very beautiful gold cup, along with twenty talents, seduced Demosthenes, Plutarch reports(*Life of Demosthenes* 25.3). What especially concerns us is that this same Demosthenes, according to the *Lives of the Ten Orators* (846 A), received 1,000 darics from Harpalus. If we can trust this passage at all, we would conclude that Harpalus in Babylonia dealt in darics, and a question would immediately arise. Were there any double darics among the coins paid out to Demosthenes and would their striking not have begun under Harpalus? On the other hand, perhaps the information given in the *Lives of the Ten Orators* needs to be interpreted. In the fifth century and in a large part of the fourth century, the daric had been the gold coin *par excellence* of the Greek world, and it probably retained a good deal of its prestige in 324. The 1,000 gold coins paid to Demosthenes might be called darics (the term that readily came to mind) even if, in whole or in part, they belonged to other currencies. Moreover, supposing that the Athenian orator actually handled 1,000 gold coins with the type of the Persian king, perhaps all these coins were authentic issues of the Great King, with nary a double daric among them.

I will pose another question about double darics: why was the type of the Great King reused at Babylon and farther east after a gold coinage with

---

32. O. Bopearachchi, *La circulation et la production monétaires en Asie centrale et dans l'Inde du Nord-Ouest*, Indologica Taurinensia 25 (Turin, 1999–2000), p. 26, nos. 59–60 has drawn attention to these coins. On Sophytos, new epigraphical evidence confirms that this is the correct spelling of the name, not the traditional "Sophytes": P. Bernard et al., *Journal des Savants* 2004, pp. 227–332.

33. This coinage of Balacrus has been described and commented on above, chapter 5, pp. 153–54, pl. 6, 6.

the name and types of Alexander had appeared? One cannot argue that these populations were so attached to the Persian coinage that the Macedonian authorities agreed to resume its production. Under the Great King, the eastern regions of the kingdom remained unaccustomed to the use of coined currency; they preserved the habit of closing transactions with the help of uncoined metal, without types, that was cut into as many pieces as needed to obtain the requisite weight.[34] So we must look for another explanation of the monetary recycling of the Persian king's image. I will take up this point again at the end of the chapter.

Coinage with the Types of Athens Struck in Babylonia

In a small work published in 1938, Newell demonstrated that an important group of Athenian imitations was struck in Babylonia at the end of the fourth century.[35] Some of the coins bear the letters AΘE, the Athenians' abbreviated ethnic (cf. pl. 7, 17), while others bear the name of Mazaces in Aramaic (cf. pl. 7, 15), as on the pseudo-Athenian tetradrachms issued by this satrap in Egypt just before Alexander's arrival (the enigmatic sign placed beside his name on the Egyptian tetradrachms sometimes appears in Babylonia too, cf. pl. 7, 16).

Despite the presence of Mazaces's name, Newell argued decisively in favor of a Babylonian attribution for the group under consideration. Its representatives invariably come from this region, in hoards or in isolated finds; their style, without exception, is mediocre, sometimes crude, to be frank, and altogether quite inferior to that of the tetradrachms produced at Memphis (cf. pl. 6, 11). The flans are often thick, so of relatively small diameter; and finally, while the coins made in Egypt sometimes bear some punchmarks on their surface, others do not display these but do show test cuts hammered in by a cutting tool. It is therefore impossible that the two series have the same origin. The findspots are illuminating: as Newell well saw, the group we are concerned with was probably issued in Babylonia but apparently somewhere other than Babylon, where a different currency was produced. Picking up on Newell, I will characterize this group as "Babylonian," without excluding the possibility it could have been struck outside the province's official borders, for example, in Mesopotamia.

---

34. See my *Naissance*, pp. 169–74.

35. *Miscellanea Numismatica: Cyrene to India* (Numism. Notes and Mon. 82, New York, 1938), pp. 82–88. I enlarged upon Newell's remarks in "Tétradrachmes au lion et imitations d'Athènes en Babylonie," *Schweizer Münzblätter* 22 (1972), pp. 1–7 (= *Études d'hist. mon. et finan.* II, Athens, 1999, pp. 735–41). So have Nicolet-Pierre, in *Essays in Honor of Margaret Thompson*, O. Mørkholm et al. eds. (Wetteren, 1979), pp. 229–30; Price, "Circulation in Babylon in 323 BC," in *Mnemata: Papers . . . Waggoner*, W. E. Metcalf ed. (New York, 1991), pp. 67–68 and 71; and P. G. Van Alfen, "The 'owls' from the 1973 Iraq Hoard," *AJN* 12 (2000), pp. 9–58.

In this group, it is not only their presence in the same geographical area and in the same hoards, or their style and general look that connect the tetradrachms bearing the AΘE legend to those bearing Mazaces's name. So do obverse die linkages, of which two examples are currently known; others will probably surface in the future.

Besides the clumsy style, these coins present some rather surprising peculiarities. The owl is occasionally turned towards the left (pl. 7, 18) and the lunar crescent near it assumes a strange shape. The name of Mazaces is often poorly inscribed or incomplete; the "enigmatic" sign mentioned earlier and accompanying the satrap's name in Egypt appears by itself at times on the Babylonian coins, with Mazaces's name omitted. In at least one case, as Nicolet-Pierre observed, the Aramaic legend cannot be read as Mazaces, even allowing for the sloppy inscribing; it is another name, impossible to identify.

P. G. Van Alfen[36] completed an intensive examination of the coins with Athenian types singled out by Price in his list of coins belonging to the Babylon hoard of 1973. Van Alfen illustrated the 163 coins he studied; 58 of them could have been struck, in his opinion, at Athens, 47 are of Babylonian origin and 14 others probably are as well, while 44 (including two drachms) derive from different, non-Babylonian mints.

The Babylonian imitations of Athens raise three major questions. Who was responsible for their issue? What is their chronology? Why was this coinage produced?

As for the "who," because he read the name of Mazaces on a certain number of these imitations, Newell had no doubt that Mazaces himself supervised at least some of these issues. Alexander rewarded this man, who had surrendered Egypt without a fight, with the governorship of a Babylonian city or district. The king had installed Mazaeus in Babylon and put Mithrenes, who handed over Sardis, in charge of Armenia (Arrian 3.16.5). A little later, he gave the satrapy of Parthia and Hyrcania to Amminapes, one of those who had welcomed him warmly with Mazaces in the Nile delta. So there would be nothing surprising in naming Mazaces to a responsible position, a man who, having struck Athenian imitations in Egypt, produced a similar coinage in Babylonia.

Newell's hypothesis has often been regarded as the only possible explanation for the presence of the name Mazaces on these imitations from Babylonia.[37] Price did not express the slightest doubt, writing "Mazaces

---

36. Cf. the preceding note.
37. See, for example, A. R. Bellinger, *Essays on the Coinage of Alexander* (New York, 1963), pp. 65–66; Price, "Circulation at Babylon . . . ," p. 68; Van Alfen, op. cit., pp. 31–32; P. Green, *Alexander of Macedon* (Berkeley, 1991), p. 269, simply says that the surrender of Egypt earned Mazaces an administrative post in the new regime, so one assumes he is alluding to Newell's thesis; Robin Lane Fox, "Text and Image: Alexander the Great, Coins and Elephants," *Bulletin of the Institute for Classical Studies* 41 (1996), pp. 96–97, also approves of Newell (on p. 105, however, he speaks of the "enigmatic" Mazaces in Babylonia).

was rewarded for his surrender of Memphis to Alexander by some official position in Babylonia." There have been skeptics. Badian thinks this is all a myth invented by numismatists; Nicolet-Pierre wondered whether the pseudo-Athenian issues from Babylonia were not copied from coins Mazaces struck in Egypt.[38] Bosworth has been intrigued by the Mazarus whom, according to Arrian (3.16.9), Alexander set over the citadel of Susa, but his suggestions warrant caution.[39]

Several objections can surely be raised against Newell's conjecture. It has been remarked that, after the Egyptian episode in 332, no ancient author mentions Mazaces again. This argument from silence has only a relative value. Another observation has more weight. Mazaces had struck Athenian imitations in Egypt whose style was quite suitable, so one is a bit hesitant to accept that he was behind the issuing of such mediocre coins in Babylonia and that he tolerated his name being sometimes distorted to this extent.

A difficulty arises, however. Suppose the Egyptian tetradrachms of Mazaces were copied in Babylonia. That assumes that many wound up there (brought from Egypt by Alexander's army and its merchant fellow travelers), or in any case a sufficiently large number to invite local imitations. It so happens that the only three Egyptian specimens gathered by Nicolet-Pierre are issued from a single obverse die, suggesting that this coinage was not very plentiful (Sabaces, Mazaces's predecessor, had used at least eleven obverse dies).

As for the style, it is indeed easy to criticize. If Mazaces oversaw these Babylonian issues, their stylistic weakness would show that he had not succeeded in recruiting good engravers (Mazaeus, at Babylon, that great urban center, had access to better artisans). One notes with interest that in a production center also located in the neighborhood of the Euphrates, but rather more to the north, a similar situation lasted for nearly thirty years. I am referring to the famous sanctuary of Membog-Hierapolis, which struck a not negligible series of silver coins from the end of the Persian regime up to the reign of Seleucus I. The types of this coinage throughout its run are very crudely executed and are often borrowed from other mints, like Tarsus,

---

38. E. Badian, "The Administration of the Empire," *Greece and Rome* 12 (1965), p. 173, note 4; Nicolet- Pierre, op. cit., pp. 229–30.

39. "Errors in Arrian," *Classical Quarterly* 26 (1976), pp. 117–19; see also his *Historical Commentary on Arrian's History of Alexander* I (Oxford, 1980), p. 319. Bosworth thought that the poorly engraved legend on the imitation Athenian coins was not perhaps "Mazaces" but "Mazarus," or that Mazarus (one of Alexander's Companions according to Arrian, who is probably mistaken because Mazarus is not, it seems, a Macedonian, but a Persian, name) has to be corrected in Arrian to Mazaces. The Athenian imitations, on both these hypotheses of Bosworth, were struck at Susa, which is improbable.

Nagidos, Aphrodisias in Caria, and Sidon (pl. 7, 19). "All this reveals," Seyrig writes, "an eccentric and short-lived mint without a technical tradition or repertory of types. The few local types ... are clumsily conceived."[40] Yet the sanctuary was not without resources. Despite that, it never managed to secure (or look for?) the services of suitable engravers.

Suppose, as a possibility, that Mazaces was the man in charge of the Athenian imitations we are discussing. Where would he have issued them? All scholars, following Newell, have opted for Babylonia. It is conceivable that the government of southern Babylonia was entrusted to Mazaces; the region, very important economically, prefigures the future province of the Red Sea, attested under the Seleucids and later called Mesene, and finally Characene. This is where Alexander founded an Alexandria, probably after his return from India, in 324.[41] Goukowsky, however, has suggested that Mazaces might have obtained Mesopotamia, whose administrative status after Gaugamela is unknown.[42] This conjecture is not to be dismissed, because many of our Athenian imitations have been seen at Baghdad and could just as well have a northern Iraqi provenance (the old Mesopotamia) as a southern (the old Babylonia). Thus the 1973 hoard Price published is called, perhaps too specifically, "from Babylon," when it was first cited as a hoard found "in Iraq."

Concerning the chronology of these coins, the hoard in question provides a reference point. As I will show at the end of this chapter, I do not think this deposit was buried around 323/322, as Price wanted; rather, I would situate the burial around 320, if not a little later. But this lag of a few years is not hugely important for the dating of our Athenian imitations. The number of coins in the deposit and all their stylistic variations encourage the belief that the issues lasted a while and that they began under Alexander. If Mazaces initiated them, it is conceivable that Alexander's naming him to an important post would have occurred during the king's stay at Babylon

---

40. H. Seyrig, "Le monnayage de Hiérapolis de Syrie à l'époque d'Alexandre," *RN* 13 (1971), pp. 11–21, pl. I–II. On this coinage, see also L. Mildenberg, "A Note on the Coinage of Hierapolis-Bambyce," in *Travaux de numism. grecque offerts à G. Le Rider*, M. Amandry and S. Hurter eds. (London, 1999), pp. 277–84. Membog-Hierapolis is located west of the Euphrates, so in Syria, a little distance from the river, to the north of Thapsacus and south of Zeugma.

41. On this Alexandria, cf. P. M. Fraser, *Cities of Alexander the Great* (Oxford, 1996), pp. 168–69. Arrian 7.21.7 says that Alexander founded a city in this region, but the topographical data he provides are difficult to interpret today (cf. p. 228 below). Pliny the Elder (*Natural History* 6.138) reports that Alexander founded an Alexandria between the mouths of the Tigris and the Eulaeus, on the site where Spasinou Charax must have later arisen. Presumably Arrian and Pliny are speaking of the same foundation.

42. *Essai sur les origines du mythe d'Alexandre I* (Nancy, 1978), p. 181.

in October and November of 331, when Mazaeus and Mithrenes, the two other former high officials of Darius, received promotions. Van Alfen did not hesitate to establish a parallel between Mazaeus and Mazaces, and between the "lion" tetradrachms of the former and the pseudo-Athenian tetradrachms of the latter. Just as Mazaeus's name ceased being inscribed on the "lion" coins after his death, so the name of Mazaces would no longer be engraved on the Athenian imitations after his demise or his transfer to another post. Only the legend AΘE would then be used.

Just as with a certain number of "lion" tetradrachms and double darics, the Athenian imitations in the name of Mazaces or with the AΘE legend sometimes have thick flans and occasionally reveal angled burrs opposite each other on the edges.[43] This similarity in manufacture, added to the fact that the Athenian imitations also sometimes carry control marks, prompted Van Alfen to write that the three coinages (the "lion," double darics, and pseudo-Athenian tetradrachms) "were produced, if not in the same workshops, then workshops that were clearly related to one another by a distinctive, localized production method." In fact, there exists among all these coins a certain technical "family resemblance," which I also find in the series of "Porus" decadrachms to be discussed at the end of this chapter.

Price noted that on those Athenian imitations with a thick flan, the style of the Athena head showed certain idiosyncrasies, and concluded that two mints ("A" and "B") were at work. Van Alfen, without rejecting this opinion, raised the possibility that Group "A" chronologically preceded Group "B" at the same mint.[44] Perhaps one might consider simply that the absence of a coinage tradition (to take up the term Seyrig used apropos of Membog-Hierapolis) caused a lack of uniformity, the artisans acting each in his own fashion, according to his own method.

As to why this money was produced, in examining the plates Van Alfen arranged, one notes that most of the Athenian imitations from Babylonia have test cuts; some users wanted to verify the metal's purity in this way to be certain that the coins were not plated. Their users did not think of these coins as currency but as ingots whose metallic quality had to be ascertained. So the coins circulated in a region either little, or not at all "monetized" and unfamiliar with using coinage whose nominal value was guaranteed by the issuing authority.

One might think that these coins were produced for the new arrivals (Macedonians, Greeks, Phoenicians) whom Alexander left in the region,

---

43. Van Alfen, op. cit., pp. 34–35, remarked that these burrs were not always at an oblique angle but sometimes horizontal, meaning that the flans were poured into molds of different shapes. On different mold shapes, see my *Suse sous les Séleucides et les Parthes* (Paris, 1965), pp. 11–16.

44. Price, "Circulation at Babylon . . . ," pp. 68 and 71; Van Alfen, op. cit., p. 33.

and who were used to employing coined currency. Beyond this relatively narrow circle, the local population would have treated the coins as mere metal. It is normal that the latter population responded in such a way at first and began to act like coinage users only after a certain period of time.

I will add that Mazaces, when he was issuing Athenian imitations in his own name in Egypt, was exercising a right of coinage that the Great King willingly accorded his high officials.[45] Mazaeus, as we saw, exercised it in Cilicia, and I surmised that Alexander confirmed him in the privilege he had enjoyed under Artaxerxes and Darius. Mazaces would not have acted differently, and his new Athenian imitations signaled the permission he obtained, even as they answered to the needs of some "Westerners."

Babylonian Coinage with the Name and Types of Alexander; Newell's Attribution and Price's Objections

Newell in his 1923 publication of the Demanhur hoard attributed a group of 630 tetradrachms with the name and types of Alexander to the Babylonian mint. According to his classification, Babylon held second place on the list of the hoard's imperial mints, after Amphipolis (1,592 specimens) and ahead of Tarsus (462).[46]

[Here, first of all, is a summary description of the first three groups among which the coins Newell assigned to Babylon can be distributed. Some Babylonian Alexanders continued to be issued after Group 3, but, in view of their date (struck after 317), I will not be dealing with them here.

Group 1: the coins carry just the letter M as mint magistrates' marks, or the two letters M and Φ, or Φ, M, and a symbol (of which six are known: ivy leaf, cup [*kylix*], grape cluster, dolphin, trident, laurel branch); the legend is *Alexandrou*, the legs of Zeus are parallel; ten obverse dies have been identified for the tetradrachms of this group (cf. pl. 8, 1), and one for the staters;[47] besides the tetradrachms, there are didrachms, drachms, and half-obols.

Group 2: the marks are M and a monogram; then M, the same monogram, and a symbol (33 are known, 5 of the 6 from Group 1 among them);

---

45. See my *Naissance*, pp. 207–37.

46. Zervos, *NC* 140 (1980), pp. 185–88, raised these figures to 2,005 tetradrachms for Amphipolis, 820 for Babylon, and 549 for Tarsus.

47. Officials of the American Numismatic Society have kindly communicated to me the number of obverse dies, based upon the still unpublished corpus N. M. Waggoner established for the coins of Groups One and Two. Waggoner drew an article from this corpus focused upon Group Two, "Tetradrachms from Babylon," in *Essays in Honor of Margaret Thompson*, O. Mørkholm et al. eds. (Wetteren, 1979), pp. 269–80.

the legs of Zeus are parallel; the legend is *Alexandrou* (pl. 8, 2–4), then *Alexandrou Basileōs* (pl. 8, 5); 77 obverse dies have been counted for the tetradrachms and four for the staters; in addition to tetradrachms, there are decadrachms (all with the simple legend *Alexandrou*; four obverse dies; cf. pl. 8, 3), didrachms, drachms, half-drachms, obols, and half-obols; the Babylon mint was the sole producer of the decadrachm denomination for Alexander's coinage.

Group 3: the marks on the tetradrachm issues in the Demanhur hoard are: M-ΛY (pl. 8, 6); M and a monogram; M and the letter B; M and the letters B and A; a wheel and a monogram (and occasionally a supplementary sign as well); the legend is *Alexandrou Basileōs or Philippou Basileōs*; the right leg of Zeus is drawn behind the left; this group also includes gold staters (pl. 8, 7), drachms, half-drachms, and obols. In the absence of a corpus, Newell furnished information about the tetradrachms: on page 151 of his publication of Demanhur, he informs us that he noted 172 obverse dies for all the coins (Groups 1, 2, and 3) contained in the hoard; we have seen that Waggoner identified 87 dies for Groups 1 and 2, which would therefore leave about 85 dies for the coins of Group 3 Newell counted; because the issues of this group unrepresented in the hoard were apparently not a very copious coinage, we may estimate that about 100 obverse dies were employed for the whole group.]

On what basis did Newell attribute these three groups to Babylon? First, he cited the city's importance and its commercial role. It was situated at the junction of two major routes originating in the Far East, one overland, via Bactra and Ecbatana, the other partially maritime, winding up at the mouths of the Tigris and the Euphrates via the Persian Gulf.

Second, Newell argued that Alexander was taken with Babylon and meant to make it his great capital. Scholars who ascribe such intent to Alexander rely upon a passage in Strabo (15.3.9–10), who wrote that the king did not envisage his palace (*to basileion*) at Susa. He preferred Babylon because of its fame and climate, and it was there that he was going to begin major construction. It may, however, possibly strain Strabo's text to have it say that Alexander wanted to locate his imperial *capital* there.

Third, Newell cited the numismatic evidence itself, referring to Imhoof-Blumer's 1895 study,[48] whose conclusions he approved. Imhoof-Blumer had observed that we encounter the same pair of moneyers, M-ΛY, in the Group 3 Alexanders as on the "lion" tetradrachms (and the double darics and darics); we might add that another monogram and the letter M also appear on these three categories of coins. Because the "lion" tetradrachms were in all probability struck at Babylon, the Group 3 Alexanders could accordingly be considered Babylonian and so, by extension, could Groups 1 and 2, which form an ensemble with Group 3. In approv-

---

48. *Numism. Zeitschrift* 27 (1895), pp. 1–22.

ing Imoof-Blumer's conclusions, Newell promised to publish an in-depth study of the Babylon mint at a more appropriate occasion—a study he did not have the time to see to a successful conclusion.

Waggoner seems to have adopted Imhoof-Blumer's and Newell's opinion without misgiving. Price was much more hesitant by comparison. Although he maintained Newell's classification unequivocally, he set forth numerous reservations in his *Alexander* (1991), which I think are worth recalling.

Price wondered whether Newell had been on the right track in making Babylon the mint *par excellence* for Alexander issues struck in the eastern empire both during Alexander's lifetime and after his death. Indeed, Newell's classifications ended up with no other eastern mint, not Susa, not Ecbatana, as possible rivals to Babylon in the volume of Alexander coinage produced at the end of the fourth century. Alexanders, he argued, were issued during Alexander's lifetime only at Babylon.[49]

And yet, Price objected, Babylon was not a beneficiary of the Persian treasures captured at Susa, Persepolis, and Pasargadae toward the end of 331 and the beginning of 330. Susa seems to have been better treated in this respect because even if these treasures were mostly transferred to Ecbatana in 330, a portion remained in Susa's citadel, as Diodorus says (17.71.2). Price notes that the only generosity Alexander displayed towards Babylon was a sum of 1,000 talents, which he gave in November 331 as he was departing for Susa (Diodorus 17.64.5); but these 1,000 talents were to be shared by Apollodorus, the general at Babylon, and Menes, the general of the satrapies as far as Cilicia (these two men were in charge of recruiting mercenaries).[50] Price also observed that Alexander paid out salaries and bonuses to some Thessalians and other allies at Ecbatana in 330 (Arrian 3.19.5) and that he made large payments at Susa and Opis in 324. So it seems doubtful, according to Price, that Newell was right to accord such preeminence to the Babylon mint and to deprive Susa and Ecbatana of any coinage during Alexander's reign, when the Conqueror distributed large sums of money in these two cities.

In order to shake the reader's confidence even more in Newell's (and Waggoner's) Babylonian attribution of Groups 1, 2, and 3, Price emphasized some details that, in his eyes, weakened such a classification. Over the

---

49. Price, op. cit., pp. 484–89, has the output of Alexanders at Susa begin around 325. Now, the early Susa Alexanders carry the legend *Basileōs Alexandrou*, and there is little likelihood, in my opinion, that this legend was used on coins before the Conqueror's death.

50. Arrian 3.16.10 reports that Alexander at Susa gave 3,000 talents to the same Menes, who was ordered to convey them to Antipater as all the money necessary for the war against the Lacedaemonians. The 1,000 Babylonian talents and the 3,000 from Susa are two separate disbursements, it seems to me, although that apparently is not Price's opinion.

timeframe of Group 2, he observes, the tetradrachms' style becomes quite similar to that of the first series that are conventionally attributed to the Susa mint (after 323). Group 3, moreover, is clearly distinct from Group 2: the style of the Herakles head is different, the position of Zeus's legs is changed, and the reverse field no longer has a variety of symbols. To sum up, Price is very tempted to assign Group 2 (by far the most important of the three) to the Susa mint. Price could also have drawn attention to the relative position of the dies: in Group 1 they are aligned (↑↑), while in Group 2 they are not. This difference would argue for separating the two groups; but because non-alignment also obtains in Group 3, Price did not raise this technical question, his principal aim apparently having been to cast doubt on Groups Two and Three as belonging to one and the same mint.

Arguments in Favor of Newell's Classification

Despite Price's interesting observations, I believe that the attribution to Babylon of Groups 1 through 3 described above remains probable.

To begin with, Groups 1 and 2 have common characteristics linking them to each other. The letter M is such a link, and so is the control system. Two secondary mint officials, whose rotation seems to have been rapid, assist two chief mint magistrates. These secondary officers generally sign themselves by affixing a symbol, more rarely a monogram; and it is noteworthy that of the six symbols known for Group 1, five also appear in Group 2. I wonder whether Group 2 was not struck partly in parallel with Group 1. Both groups, in fact, begin with coins lacking secondary officials, and as I have said, they then have five symbols in common. Conceivably, the need to issue a plentiful coinage in a hurry induced the mint authorities to use another workshop, which would have wound up eclipsing the first and led to its disappearance. The existence of two workshops would explain the technical differences (alignment or not of dies) just pointed out.

Group 1 probably started before Group 2, at least if the Alexanders marked only with the letter M (and not the two letters M and Φ) are to be placed at the head of the series, as Newell thought (the order in which he presents the specimens of the Demanhur hoard is quite clear). Price, to the contrary, places the few coins with just the M at the very end of Group 1. Newell very reasonably interpreted the presence of this single letter on an issue as an indication that the Alexander coinage had just begun and that it did not yet have a highly developed control system. Price disagreed.

This M, we have seen, also figures on some "lion" tetradrachms of Mazaeus. This is surely a common mark, and its appearance on some Alexanders is not a strong argument supporting their attribution to Babylon.

There does exist, however, another, in my eyes more compelling, connection between a series of "lion" tetradrachms struck after Mazaeus's death and the Alexanders of Groups 1 and 2. Nicolet-Pierre's catalogue shows that, strangely enough, nine different symbols accompany the principal mark, Γ, in the series of "lion" coins under discussion, a control system recalling that of the Alexanders. It so happens that eight of these nine symbols also appear on the Alexander tetradrachms,[51] and one of them is quite uncommon, a two-pronged rake (pl. 7, 8 and 8, 2, the latter on an Alexander from Group 2). These numerous similarities indicate, I believe, that the "lion" tetradrachms marked with the letter Γ and the Alexanders of Groups 1 and 2 come from the same mint, which can only be Babylon because the "lion" issues (save for very rare exceptions) are Babylonian.

Some will object that there are serious differences between the Alexanders and the "lion" coins. I have pointed out that the manufacture of the latter was peculiar (thick flans, folded edges) and that the fineness of their metal left something to be desired. Moreover, while the legs of Zeus are parallel on the reverse of the tetradrachms of our two groups, Baal's right leg is drawn back on the "lion" coins. As for this last point, I will observe that the same phenomenon occurs in the Tarsus mint: the silver staters of Persian weight with facing Athena head (one issue of which was signed by the satrap Balacrus, cf. pl. 6, 6) show Baaltars on the reverse with right leg drawn back. On the contemporaneous Alexanders from Tarsus, Zeus's legs are parallel.

Getting back to Babylon, the difference in technique that we have confirmed between the Alexanders of Groups 1 and 2 (dies aligned or not), and the peculiarities of the "lion" coins and the double darics (and darics) raise questions about the organization of currency striking at Babylon under Alexander and his immediate successors. The Babylonian administration does not seem to have cared about introducing any uniformity in this area. Each of the three coinages appears to form a distinct entity; certainly, they neither began nor ended at the same time. Although their issues presumably overlapped for at least a few years, the instances where they carry control marks in common remain exceptions.

In view of this situation, ought we to think of the Babylonian mint as comprising several workshops, independent of each other in technique and generally with their own separate officials? Or, rather, is it appropriate to suppose that coinage striking was entrusted to private artisans who each worked in his own way, supervised most often by different magistrates? We cannot decide.

---

51. I have not distinguished, perhaps wrongly, the symbol described as a drinking cup (*kylix*) on the Alexanders and what is described as a *kantharos*, also a type of drinking cup, on the "lion" tetradrachms. The seven other symbols in common are a rake, a grape cluster, a bee, a sickle, a star, a tight-fitting cap (*pileus*) and an ivy leaf (these last two symbols have not been identified with certainty on the "lion" tetradrachms).

We must still say a word on the attribution of the Group 3 Alexanders. Imhoof-Blumer, we have seen, pointed out that the marks M-ΛY on the Alexanders are also found on the "lion" tetradrachms; a monogram in place of the letters ΛY sometimes accompanies the M on the Alexanders; this M and monogram also appear on the "lion" coins. Short of questioning the Babylonian origin of these two "lion" issues, we ought to consider the Alexanders of Group 3 as Babylonian. The continuity of the letter M is noteworthy, forming a link with Groups 1 and 2.

The Date of the Alexanders of Groups 1, 2, and 3

Newell had no doubts: the Alexander coinage at Babylon began around the end of 331, thus shortly after the Macedonian king captured the city. Group 1, Newell said, dated from 331–329, Group 2 from 329–323; Group 3 began in the aftermath of the Conqueror's death.

Waggoner altered this chronology only slightly. She put the beginning of Group 2 in 329/328 (as Newell had), but she placed its end in 323/322 (not in 324/323, as Newell seemed to suggest). Price shifted the dates a little: Group 1 went from 331 to c. 325, Group 2 from c. 325 to c. 323.[52]

These three authorities agree that the Babylonian mint produced Alexanders from the king's arrival in the city in late 331 or, at any rate, immediately afterwards. The rest of their chronology follows from this starting point, and all three arrive at roughly comparable dates for the end of Group 2, that is, 324/323 or 323/322.

I propose another possibility: the Alexander coinage started at Babylon not in 331/330, but perhaps only in 325/324.

Recall that the legend *Basileōs Alexandrou* characterizes the last phase of Group 2. I have already suggested, following Troxell's conclusions,[53] that the title *Basileōs* was affixed to the coins only after Alexander's death and perhaps not before 322/321. Group 2 might end in late 322/321, to be replaced in 321/320 by Group 3, in which the legend *Basileōs Philippou* is used along with *Basileōs Alexandrou*.

Recall that in Group 1, 1 obverse die was identified for the staters while 10 were identified for the tetradrachms; in Group 2, the stater dies numbered 4, the tetradrachm dies 77, the decadrachm dies 4. Despite these relatively high figures, Price posited a two- or three-year duration for Group 2, while according six years to Group 1. I think he was right to concentrate the issues of Group 2: "This group of issues," he wrote, "with its

---

52. Waggoner, in *Essays in Honor of Margaret Thompson*, O. Mørkholm et al. eds. (Wetteren, 1979), pp. 269–80 (cf. especially the table on p. 276); Price, *Alexander* (1991), pp. 458–59.

53. Cf. above, p. 71 and pp. 93–94.

closely knit interlinking of obverse dies, has every aspect of a large-scale production over a relatively short period of time." One notes, indeed, according to Waggoner's tables, that among the tetradrachms the same obverse die is linked quite often with several reverse dies marked with different secondary officials' symbols. The very multiplicity of these latter symbols creates the impression of intense mint activity.

If Group 2 ended in 321, as I have supposed, and if one assigns it a two- or three-year lifespan, as Price did, one would be led to date its start around 324, perhaps during the year 324/323.

As for Group 1, keeping in mind my proposal that it was struck partly in parallel with Group 2, I think it is necessary to downdate its inauguration considerably. I find it hard to accept a start before c. 325/324. On this point, Price's surprise that the Zeus of Group 1's early tetradrachms was not closer stylistically to the Baaltars of Mazaeus is worth noting. The two series' different opening dates would explain this: Mazaeus struck coins between 331 and 328, while, according to my theory, the Alexanders did not begin before 325/324.

I have focused up to now on Groups 1 and 2. The dating of Group 3 poses fewer problems. It ends with issues in the name of Alexander or Philip (with the title *Basileōs*). Philip III's death in early autumn 317 provides a *terminus ante quem*. Group 3 would stretch therefore from c. 321/320 to 318/317:[54] it would have lasted a little longer than Group 2.

II: Alexander and Babylonia from 325/324. Antimenes of Rhodes

Remarks on Coinage Activity at the Babylonian Mint between 325/324 and Late 317

Accepting the chronology I have just presented makes it clear that the output of the Babylonian mint was significant during the years 325/324 to 318/317. In seven or eight years, around 200 obverse dies were engraved for Alexander tetradrachms.[55] The mint also struck "lion" coins,

---

54. Olympias had Philip III executed at the beginning of autumn in 317; he was perhaps still alive in the first weeks of 317/316, the Macedonian year beginning in October; but, as I have said earlier (p. 115), it is highly unlikely that his name was inscribed on Alexanders during this window, which was, in any event, quite narrow.

55. The four dies for the decadrachms (equivalent to ten tetradrachm dies) are to be added to the ten dies of Group 1, the seventy-seven of Group 2, and the one hundred or so of Group 3. I am unaware of the number of dies used in Group 3 for staters; Groups 1 and 2 have a total of five stater dies. Since a stater is worth five tetradrachms, the money supply produced by five stater dies amounted to as much as that of twenty-five tetradrachm dies (assuming that one stater die struck as many coins as one tetradrachm die).

double darics, and darics. No corpus exists for these two series, making it difficult to estimate their volume.

Babylon's monetary activity is not exceptional in the empire of this period. In Macedonia, at Amphipolis, the number of obverse dies put into service for Alexander tetradrachms during the same time surpassed 700, and issues of staters and distaters accompanied those of tetradrachms.[56] At Aradus, in Phoenicia, between c. 322/321 and c. 319/ 318, almost 200 obverse dies were employed to strike Alexander tetradrachms.

So the size of the Babylonian mint's production is not distinctive. Yet it was voluminous enough, and we must ask why the Babylonian authorities felt the need to have on hand such a large quantity of currency in the last years and following of the reign.

Price, in expressing his doubts about locating a major Alexander mint at Babylon, emphasized the large expenditures Alexander made at Susa and Opis in 324. In fact, perhaps all the payments in question occurred at Susa, because, as we have seen,[57] Arrian is the only ancient author to mention Opis. Consequently, Price suggested a major Alexander mint was needed at Susa, not at Babylon.

Yet Price did not observe that the evidence of the ancient authors shows that large sums also had to be paid at Babylon and in Babylonia during the same period, that is, after Alexander returned from India in late 325. Presumably a portion of these sums was paid out in coinage, and for certain settlements coins with the name and types of Alexander were essential. After Alexander, Babylonia became the scene of events that similarly required a well-stocked treasury. So the existence of an active mint at Babylon seems to me completely plausible.

We can easily gauge the financial resources which the Babylonian officials needed in 324 and 323 from the demands Alexander addressed to them and from the actions he undertook during his brief sojourn in the satrapy in 323. They also become clear in the conduct of Antimenes of Rhodes, whom the king appointed chief financial officer of Babylonia at the start of 324. The schemes which the author of the second book of the *Oeconomica* attributed to him highlight how insistently the public purse laid claim to sizeable assets.

---

56. See above, chapter 3, p. 55; shortly before 317, tetradrachms in the name, types and weight of Philip II were likewise struck at Amphipolis: more than one hundred obverse dies were used.

57. Chapter 2, p. 20, note 6.

Alexander's Expenditures in Babylon and Babylonia at the End of His Reign

First of all, the preparations and rites for Hephaestion's funeral involved enormous expense. Alexander's childhood friend, companion, and confidant, Hephaestion died at Ecbatana during the summer of 324. A convoy under Perdiccas's command was entrusted with transporting the body to Babylon, where the deceased hero's pyre was to be built. The king gave orders for a grand ceremony: "He showed such zeal about the funeral that it not only surpassed all those previously celebrated on earth but also left no possibility for anything greater in later ages" (Diodorus 17.114.1). Diodorus has described in detail (17.115) the superbly decorated pyre of six levels, reaching a height of almost sixty meters. The sovereign gave *carte blanche* to Stasicrates, the individual who once suggested to Alexander transforming Mt. Athos into the king's statue (Plutarch, *Alex*. 72.5–8).

The pyre's construction and the various spectacles accompanying the obsequies cost 10,000 talents according to Plutarch (*Alex*. 72.3), 10,000 or more according to Arrian (7.14.8), 12,000 according to Justin (12.12.12), and more than 12,000 according to Diodorus (17.115.5). Has the tradition corrupted the reality and exaggerated the sum spent? We cannot say for sure because Alexander, to honor Hephaestion, seems to have stopped at nothing. The orders he gave to Cleomenes in Egypt concerning his friend show how carried away he was (Arrian 7.23.6, cf. above, p. 182). As for the ceremonies at Babylon, it seems to me highly likely that, one way or another, the Babylonian treasury was forced to contribute.

In addition, during the few weeks he spent in Babylonia during the spring of 323, Alexander was enormously busy, initiating enterprises and making preparations that surely cost a great deal. This time, too, the Babylonian authorities were undoubtedly obliged to share in the expenses. According to Arrian, Alexander decided to rebuild the temple of Baal and set his army to the task (7.17.3). He had the Phoenician fleet come to Babylon: the ships were disassembled and transported to Thapsacus, and from there, after re-assembly, they went down the Euphrates to Babylonia. The king ordered the construction of another fleet, made with Babylonian cypress; recruits for the ships and the different naval services were organized in Phoenicia and the other coastal regions. For these two fleets and that of Nearchus, who arrived from India by way of the Persian Gulf,[58] a port capable of handling 1,000 war vessels was dug at Babylon and dockyards were built (Arrian 7.19.3–4). Miccalus of Clazomenae left for Phoenicia and Syria, provided with 500 talents, his mission to

---

58. Nearchus did not come to Babylon directly upon his arrival at the mouths of the Tigris and Euphrates; he made a detour to meet Alexander near Susa (Arrian, *Indica* 42).

enroll seafarers who would help to colonize the shores of the Persian Gulf (Arrian 7.19.5). Alexander was also interested in the Pallakopas canal, and he "sailed down [the Pallakopas River] to the lakes in the direction of Arabia. There, having seen a good site, he built and fortified a city[59] and settled in it some of the Greek mercenaries, volunteers and men unfit for service through age or wounds" (Arrian 7.21.6–7). He sent navigators to explore the Gulf: one reached the island of Tylos (Bahrain), another made it to the tip of Arabia, and a third went even farther (Arrian 7.20.7–8). Alexander decided to undertake an expedition against the Arabs because they had not shown him sufficient deference and also because they possessed prosperous oases and a vast territory (Arrian 7.19.6; 20.1–2). The preparations for the expedition were, it seems, rather advanced when Alexander died.

These diverse activities, even if some were only in the planning stages, occasioned expenses additional to those for Hephaestion's funeral. The conduct of Antimenes of Rhodes further confirms, I think, that Alexander tapped the Babylonian treasury.

Antimenes of Rhodes

I have recently devoted an essay to this individual, so I will not go into all the details here.[60]

We know of Antimenes solely through the second book of the *Oeconomica* (2.34a, 34b, 38). None of the Alexander historians mentions him. Yet his role at Babylon was not negligible, as we shall see.

Although the anonymous author does not tarry over chronological information, what he says about Antimenes is sufficiently explicit to enable us to place his activity in Babylonia at the end of Alexander's reign. As I have remarked at the beginning of this chapter, it seems likely that after Harpalus's flight in late 325, the king named Archon as satrap of the province and put Antimenes at his side as chief financial officer. The manuscript readings identify Antimenes as *hēmiodios*, a word appearing nowhere else, possibly meaning "half-way," a perplexing term when applied to our individual. So the text has been emended to *hēmiolios*, an adjective describing a soldier whose bravery was rewarded with a salary one and one-half times ordinary pay.[61] Van Groningen thought that this correction (paleographically irreproachable) was undoubtedly right.[62] Yet it is not the only

---

59. See above, p. 217.
60. "Antimène de Rhodes à Babylone," in *Alexander's Legacy in the East, Studies in Honor of Paul Bernard, Bulletin of the Asia Institute* 12 (1998), pp. 121–40.
61. See above, p. 75, note 4.
62. *Aristote, le second livre de l'Economique* (Leiden, 1933); Van Groningen's comments on Antimenes are found on pp. 193–97 and 203–4.

emendation possible. Amidst this uncertainty, it is better to avoid endowing Antimenes's career with a distinction he perhaps did not receive.

When he assumed his duties at Babylon in the waning days of 325 or in early 324, the treasury was probably in critical condition. His predecessor Harpalus had certainly not wanted for revenues, chiefly the tribute (*phoros*) the province paid and the taxes of every sort to which the inhabitants were subjected.[63] Moreover, if it is true that Harpalus received special powers encompassing all the imperial finances, the satraps were probably required to remit to him at least a portion of the sums they collected as *phoros* (following a system, we may suppose, the Persians practiced). On the other hand, however, Harpalus had to deal with heavy financial burdens. As chief treasurer, he had to have money to respond to Alexander's potential demands; additionally, because, as we have seen, he was centrally situated between the empire's east and west, he played a leading role in readying troops and matériel all the way from Macedonia to Bactria and India. This activity would have entailed onerous costs because there can be no doubt that Alexander's requirements during these years were particularly numerous and unrelenting. We also know, as I have said, that Harpalus led a luxurious life, and, to quote Diodorus (17.108.4), "squandered much of the treasure under his control on unbridled pleasure" (Loeb modified). When he fled, absconding with 5,000 talents, he may have appropriated everything in the Babylonian treasury. Antimenes, in any case, had to take the situation in hand.

In normal times, he probably could have righted affairs without too much difficulty. The treasury continued to receive the usual taxes and proceeds, which permitted balancing income and expenses. But the fact that Antimenes was forced to have recourse to three expedients that the author of *Oeconomica II* thought worthy of mention, shows, I think, that the Babylonian authorities had to finance expenses well beyond the means of their operating budget.

---

63. Herodotus (1.192) reports that the satrap of Babylonia collected a Babylonian artaba of silver daily, that is, as Herodotus specifies, an Attic medimnos and three choinixes, corresponding to c. 56 liters. Silver has a density of 10.5, so the weight of silver received daily was around 590 kilograms; by the end of a year, more than 212,000 kilos of silver, about 8,000 Attic talents, were raised. The information Herodotus later provides (3.92), under the heading of his ninth tax zone, on the tribute paid to Darius I (522–486) does not permit us to determine the portion that came from Babylonia strictly defined. He says the king received 1,000 talents annually in tribute from "Babylon and the rest of Assyria", to which were added 500 young eunuchs; "Assyria" is taken in this passage in a broad sense to designate the territories the kings of Nineveh and Ashur ruled at the height of their power. On the later meaning of "Assyria," see A. Maricq, "La province d'Assyrie créée par Trajan," *Syria* 36 (1959), pp. 254–63. If these texts of Herodotus are reliable, note that the amount of tribute (which can be considered as the king's personal property) represented only a small fraction of the province's total revenue.

Here are the extraordinary measures Antimenes undertook. First (*Oec.* 2. 34a),

> An old law on the books at Babylon, but no longer observed, imposed a tax of 10% on all imports. Antimenes seized upon the moment when all the satraps with soldiers in large numbers were expected, as well as ambassadors and artisans, and . . . [textual corruption] individuals on private business and delegations bearing numerous gifts to the king. He exacted the 10% tax in accordance with the law which was, in fact, still in force.[64]

This passage gives a valuable piece of chronological information. The influx of countless visitors to Babylon can only be placed in the early months of 323, when Alexander's own advent was proclaimed and he decided to organize the funeral ceremonies honoring Hephaestion there. Diodorus (17.113.1–2) and Arrian (7.15.4–6) report the immense assemblage from Asia, Europe, and Africa that occurred then in Babylon, not only ambassadorial delegations but visitors of all sorts.[65]

A 10 percent import tax (*dekatē*) is attested in some other parts of the Persian Empire as well as in the Greek world.[66] Levied by Antimenes in Babylonia at a time when so many different items were entering the province (materials for Hephaestion's funeral pyre, gifts brought to the king, goods to support a huge crowd, etc.), it undoubtedly garnered the treasury appreciable revenue.

Next (*Oec.* 2, 34 b),

> In supplying the army with slaves for its use, [Antimenes] invited the slaves' owners who so desired to list them at whatever value they wanted and to pay an annual premium of eight drachms per slave. If the slave ran away, the owner would be reimbursed for the listed value. Many slaves were thus registered, and Antimenes profited

---

64. [Le Rider uses the French translation of A. Wartelle in the Budé edition of the *Oec.* Because it deals with the textual crux in the MS and other variant readings differently from the Loeb translation, I have preferred to offer an English version based upon Wartelle's French, after consulting the Greek text—WEH.]

65. Here is Diodorus: "Now from practically all the inhabited world came envoys on various missions, some congratulating Alexander on his victories, some bringing him crowns, others concluding treaties of friendship and alliance, many bringing handsome presents, and some prepared to defend themselves against accusations. Apart from the tribes and cities as well as the local rulers of Asia, many of their counterparts in Europe and Libya put in an appearance . . ."

66. On this and the other points raised below concerning Antimenes's expedients, cf. the details I have provided in the previously cited article, "Antimène de Rhodes . . . ," *Bull. Asia Institute* 12 (1998), pp. 124–26.

the treasury considerably. And when a slave ran away, Antimenes ordered the satrap of the province where the army was located to recover the fugitive or to pay the value to his master.

Antimenes's measure is generally viewed as the oldest known example "of an insurance system organized and guaranteed by the State," to quote a note of A. Wartelle apropos of this text. But there is one difficulty: it is strange that the owners paid a fixed premium, given their broad latitude to declare whatever value they liked for their slaves.

Hence, several commentators have attempted to emend the text, whose principal manuscripts, moreover, are not without flaws. One of the proposed emendations, which is logical and also paleographically possible, in effect establishes a percentage: the owner would have to pay eight drachms per mina, that is, 8 percent of the declared value, the Attic mina having 100 drachms. By way of information, we point out that P. Ducrey, in his book on the treatment of prisoners of war, has set forth what we know on the price of slaves in the fourth century.[67] Based on indications in Xenophon and the orators, and excluding the statistical outliers, a slave was usually worth between 100 and 200 drachms (between one and two minas).

Other scholars have prudently foresworn textual emendation and have sought to explain the text instead. A. Andreades, in 1929, suggested that Antimenes, launching a new system and anxious for its success, sought to attract owners by offering them advantageous terms: such a scheme could certainly only function if the number of subscribers was sufficiently high.[68] Van Groningen, judging that the slaves of the army were generally not very valuable, concluded that Antimenes was not assuming too much risk because, in the latter's opinion, the stated price was not apt to reach an excessive amount.[69] Van Groningen's view seems questionable to me. I should have thought that a certain number of these slaves were chosen for their technical skill, for their ability to maintain equipment and to fashion weaponry and machines, so they might come with high price tags.

It will be noted, according to the *Oeconomica*, that Antimenes's initiative was crowned with success. That would imply that successful runaways were numerous enough to worry owners. The army traversed foreign regions whose populations were not always trustworthy, conditions probably favoring escape attempts. So Antimenes had to find a way to shore up

---

67. *Le traitement des prisonniers de guerre dans la Grèce antique des origines à la conquête romaine* (Paris, 1999), pp. 240–54.

68. "Antimène de Rhodes et Cléomène de Naucratis," *BCH* 53 (1929); pp. 5–10 of this article are devoted to Antimenes.

69. Op. cit., p. 197.

his system, which would not have earned the expected profit if runaways multiplied. The satraps in the provinces where the army marched were ordered to spare no effort in capturing any possible fugitives. In this way, Antimenes was in a sweet spot: he insured his clients against a risk that he had the foresight to render almost non-existent. The text also says that, in the case where a slave managed to escape in spite of everything, it was the satrap concerned who had to reimburse the owner. The satrap then probably deducted this amount from what he owed the central treasury, but in the meantime Antimenes had to pay nothing.

According to the *Oeconomica*, the instructions sent to the satraps came directly from Antimenes. If this was actually the case, one sees what a powerful position he occupied in the administrative hierarchy.

Although some obscure points remain in the measure Antimenes devised, we have to acknowledge that he showed an inventive mind, bold and ingenious. If he really was the first to establish an officially guaranteed insurance system, he merits rescue from the shadows of oblivion and recognition as one of the great financiers of history.

Finally (*Oec.* 2.38),

> Antimenes ordered the satraps to replenish, according to the custom of the country, the magazines along the royal highways. Whenever an army or some other force passed through the country unaccompanied by the King, he sent an officer to sell them what was stored in the magazines. (Loeb, modified)

Andreades, Van Groningen, and Wartelle have elucidated this passage well. Briant in his recent comments has set it within the Achaemenid context.[70] The "magazines" in question were repositories or storehouses that together with postal relays and caravansaries were a typical and valued aspect of the Persian royal highways. Herodotus (5.52) praised the installations along the major route linking Sardis and Susa. Those in charge of the magazines, before handing over any items to customers, required them to present a satrap's authorization. The satrap, for his part, saw to the provisioning of the stores. This efficient system continued to function under Alexander, and Antimenes, as often as he could, used it to the advantage of the treasury he had to manage. The writer of *Oeconomica II* once again attributes broad authority to Antimenes, for, he says, Antimenes could not only order satraps to refill the storehouses, but he was also powerful enough to send one of his men to organize the sale of goods to the army forces (which he probably required to replenish their needs only in these depots). This was certainly a lucrative practice. Between late 325 and mid-323, many

---

70. *From Cyrus to Alexander: A History of the Persian Empire*, Eng. trans. by P. T. Daniels (Winona Lake, IN, 2002), pp. 364–65.

troops moved among Susa, Opis, Ecbatana, and Babylon under, effectively, Alexander's leadership, and in these instances Antimenes could not profit from the situation. But numerous military convoys circulated in the west of the empire apart from the royal presence. Some of them wound up in Babylon to attend the obsequies of Hephaestion and also to be at the sovereign's disposal; others departed for the Mediterranean and the Aegean. Craterus, for example, was in charge of escorting the Macedonian veterans back home.

Presumably some of the travelers received food supplies *gratis* in the official storehouses we are discussing, while others were authorized to help themselves only if they could pay. Goukowsky suggests to me that, in the former case, the satrap could deduct the value of the resources he had distributed against his province's required *phoros,* while in the latter case the receipts reverted to the satrap's account. It seems Antimenes favored sales and appropriated what they yielded. It was probably intended that the satrap would eventually receive compensation, but Antimenes profited nicely in the meantime.

He can therefore be described as a highly talented, albeit unscrupulous, financier. I judged Cleomenes in Egypt similarly. I repeat that, in my opinion, these men were not driven to act as they did out of greed or malevolence but because they received orders which required large sums of money to execute. Building Alexandria in Egypt and meeting Alexander's needs in Babylonia all required financing that the usual budgets of these two satrapies were incapable of providing. In order to obey their king, Antimenes and Cleomenes displayed real ingenuity, which was not always compatible with noble sentiments.

Alexander's Treasury in 324/323

But, someone will say, why suppose that the Babylonian treasury was tapped to the point that Antimenes was forced to dream up the expedients described in the *Oeconomica*? In 324, Alexander was in the vicinity of Babylonia and, in 323, he resided in the province for a few weeks. Was he unable to finance the funeral rites of Hephaestion and his various other initiatives entirely on his own? Did he not have enormous reserves at his disposal on which he could draw unstintingly? The treasure deposited at Ecbatana in 330 comprised the riches taken from the Great King, which amounted to 180,000 talents (the capture of Persepolis yielding 120,000 of that!). Concerning the Ecbatana treasure and the events of 330, Arrian's narrative differs from that of the other Alexander historians. Goukowsky has proposed a plausible reconstruction of events:[71] oversight of the treasure, which Parmenio

---

71. *Essai sur les origines du mythe d'Alexandre* I (Nancy, 1978), pp. 35–40; see also Bosworth's judicious remarks in *A Historical Commentary* I (Oxford, 1980), pp. 333–38.

conveyed to Ecbatana, was first entrusted to Harpalus and 6,000 Macedonians; then, contrary to the original plan, which was revoked, Parmenio replaced Harpalus; it was after Parmenio's assassination that, still in 330, the 6,000 Macedonians left to rejoin the royal army, which they met in Arachosia in early 329. Presumably the 6,000 Macedonians took custody of the treasure, or at least most of it, because that was their mission.

The 180,000 talents in question were not ordinary revenue. They constituted war winnings, booty. So we need not be surprised that Alexander kept this enormous reserve nearby, at his immediate disposal. Curtius mentions its presence with the king. In relating the "Pages' Conspiracy" (in 327, on the eve of Alexander's passage to India), he has the ringleader Hermolaus say that for Alexander "30,000 mules carry captured gold, while your soldiers will bring home nothing save scars got without reward" (8.7.11). Although Hermolaus might have been inclined to exaggerate out of anger, the figure of 30,000 mules is not pure fantasy. Indeed, Plutarch (*Alex.* 37.4) reports that 10,000 pairs of mules and 5,000 camels were needed to transport the booty captured at Susa and in Persia, that is, at Persepolis and Pasargadae,[72] in short, the 180,000 talents Parmenio had conveyed as far as Ecbatana.[73] The agreement on the number of animals in Curtius and Plutarch is interesting. If we were to accept the two authors' evidence, we would infer that between 329 and 327 the quantity of military treasure had remained almost constant. We also note that Alexander's Companions did not part with their acquisitions: Curtius (6.11.3) speaks of Philotas's chariots of gold and silver (implying that the inner circle kept these chariots permanently).

During the Conqueror's victorious march, the royal treasury surely received abundant spoils and numerous gifts. In 326, on the Indus, the local prince Taxiles showed exceptional kindness, furnishing grain to the soldiers, presents to Alexander and his friends, and adding eighty talents of coined silver. The king, charmed, returned Taxiles's presents and gave him 1,000 talents "from the booty which he was carrying," as well as precious objects and horses (Curtius 8.12.15–16). In this partic-

---

72. On the transport of silver by single or hitched mules, see the interesting remarks of F. de Callataÿ, "Les trésors achéménides et les monnayages d'Alexandre," *REA* 91 (1989), p. 263, who calculated the weight a single mule could carry or two hitched mules could draw. He concluded that Plutarch's information is reasonable.

73. As I have said above, a small part of the treasure was left in the citadel at Susa (Diodorus 17.71.2); the 180,000 talents transported to Ecbatana included not only the riches captured in Susiana and Persia, but also, probably, the booty previously acquired, for example, at Damascus and Arbela. Clearly, what was found at Susa and especially Persepolis constituted the core of the 180,000 talents.

ular case, Alexander was the donor. But we may suppose that in other circumstances he accepted what was offered him without attempting to outrival in generosity. He probably did not reciprocate the rich gifts the Sambastai made him, for example (Diodorus 17.102.4). Upon his return from India, Aboulites, satrap of Susiana, brought Alexander 3,000 talents in coin. This still did not prevent his arrest and execution along with his son: Alexander blamed him for not having prepared food supplies (Plutarch, *Alex.* 68.6).

Booty and gifts resulted from the vagaries of war, but did not Alexander receive regular transfers of money as well? Earlier, I noted and discussed Justin's information that the empire's revenue at the end of the reign came to 30,000 talents.[74] Did not a part of this revert to Alexander? Or rather, in view of the exceptional effort asked of the satraps during these years, did all this money go to finance not only the different provinces' operating expenses but also the reinforcements of every kind that the Conqueror needed?

Be that as it may, one has the feeling that the 180,000 talents seized in the Persian treasuries, as well as the booty and the gifts that the king collected during his victorious advance, allowed him to meet the expenses he encountered without trouble. These expenses were considerable.

His army, to begin with, cost him more and more as his troop strength grew. Arrian (*Indica* 19.5) indicates that in the conquest's last phase, there were 120,000 men in arms. Salaries and bonuses must have increased proportionately. Matériel, increasingly numerous, had to be maintained or replaced. By late 326, Alexander ordered a fleet prepared to go down the Hydaspes (a tributary of the Indus) as far as the Indian Ocean. Arrian (6.2.4) writes on this topic: "The entire number of ships, according to Ptolemy son of Lagus, my chief source, was eighty thirty-oared galleys, while all the boats including the horse transports, light vessels, and all the other craft that had been long plying on the rivers or that had been constructed at the time came to nearly 2,000" (Loeb, modified).

Founding cities, defending and reinforcing strategic points, restoring ruined sites all occasioned further huge outlays. Fraser has provided a detailed study of the Conqueror's foundations.[75] Up to 330, Alexander undertook such an initiative only in Egypt. From early 329, city foundations became frequent. Almost all were named after Alexander, which geographers have distinguished from one another by adding some descriptive

---

74. See chapter 4, p. 79: "Note on the Revenues of the Great King and Alexander."

75. *Cities of Alexander the Great* (Oxford, 1996), pp. 65–74, where Fraser presents an overview of these foundations, on which Arrian provides ample data; on pp. 240–42 there is an impressive list of fifty-seven names.

geographical feature (like Alexandria of the Caucasus, Alexandria of Arachosia, Alexandria of Carmania). One foundation was called Bucephala, after the sovereign's dead horse; a Nicaea was founded in Bactria, another in India on the left bank of the Hydaspes, almost opposite Bucephala, which was built on the same river's right bank. These foundations or refoundations entailed public works (construction of buildings and ramparts) and organizing civic life; each time Alexander had to expend considerable funds. Similarly, he had to contribute financially to the furbishing of sites where he left garrisons as a rearguard, and naturally the soldiers of these garrisons continued to receive their salary. The foundation of cities in the eastern regions responded to necessity. Alexander could only defend and maintain his conquests by installing outposts entrusted to loyal troops. Over these vast stretches, with relatively little urbanization, free and conspicuous settlements worked. Alexander, moreover, probably had fewer local sensibilities to deal with than previously.

Another financial drain was the king's extreme generosity, which the tradition has celebrated and maybe exaggerated. I refer especially to a chapter in Plutarch (*Alex.* 39), where he reports several examples of Alexander's benefactions, which were always made, the author is clear, with just the right touch. One of Plutarch's anecdotes is worth citing because it concerns the funds that accompanied the Conqueror on his campaigns. A Macedonian was driving a mule laden with royal gold before him; the animal was exhausted, so the man removed the burden and put it on his own shoulders. When Alexander saw him at the end of the day's march completely done in, he encouraged the man to go a few more steps with the gold to the man's own quarters; the gold would henceforth be his. Curtius (9.1.6) writes that the king, after his victory over Porus and his founding of Bucephala and Nicaea, offered crowns to each of his generals, along with 1,000 gold coins. Bellinger thought that this was all a literary topos, not to be taken too seriously.[76] Yet these gifts accord well with Alexander's temperament as the ancient sources describe it. Plutarch (*Alex.* 70.3) and Arrian (7.4.8) relate the largesse that marked his passage to Susa in 324. After he had his Companions and soldiers marry eastern women, he organized a magnificent banquet for 9,000 invited guests, according to Plutarch, and he gave each of them a golden cup. Arrian specifies that he gave a gift to each of the young wives and that he gave a wedding present to each of the more than 10,000 Macedonian men who were wed. He then decided (Plutarch, *Alex.* 70.3; Arrian 7.5.1–3) to pay off his soldiers' debts, which amounted, according to Arrian, to 20,000 talents, or, according to Plutarch (and Curtius 10.2.9-11; cf. Diodorus 17.109.1–2), 9,870 talents. He also distributed favors to sundry others, "varying in proportion to the honour that rank

---

76. *Essays on the Coinage of Alexander the Great* (New York, 1963), p. 77.

conferred or to conspicuous courage displayed in dangers" (Arrian 7.5.4). A little later, at Susa or Opis, each of the 10,000 Macedonians mustered out received a bonus of one talent, in addition to his salary (Arrian 7.12.1–2).

Alexander also lived well.[77] Athenaeus (4, 146c) reports the evidence of Ephippus of Olynthus: every time the king had friends to dinner, he distributed 100 silver minas, that is, 2,500 tetradrachms (nearly two talents) for sixty to seventy guests. For comparison's sake, recall that an infantryman's normal annual salary did not equal 100 tetradrachms (one-fifteenth of a talent). Athenaeus adds that the king of Persia typically laid out 400 talents for a banquet of 15,000 participants; so Alexander was spending roughly the same amount per banqueter. The Conqueror also surrounded his audiences with sumptuous display. He sat upon a golden throne and beneath an immense pavilion supported by fifty gold-plated columns (Athenaeus 12, 539d, e, citing Phylarchus; Polyaenus 4.9.24). Goukowsky rightly observes that all this ostentation carried on the Achaemenid tradition: certain precise details show that the Macedonian conqueror had taken over the trappings of the Great King. But, by the same token, such conduct was in some sense inherent to the royal state. Lavishness and extravagant fetes had already distinguished Philip II.[78] A sovereign, in order to raise himself above mere mortals, is wont to dazzle his subjects with his munificence. What is certain is that Alexander discovered refinements of luxury in Achaemenid pomp, which he was quick to adopt.

So we may assume that by late 324 the king had seriously depleted the treasure he had taken with him on his eastern campaigns. Despite that, he probably still had decent reserves. According to Justin (13.1.9), the royal treasure contained 50,000 talents at the time of Alexander's death. That is a far cry from the 180,000 talents of 330. But presuming Justin's information is correct, the royal treasury still enjoyed a nice cushion in 323.

One would think that Alexander wanted to keep these funds for the new expeditions he had planned and that this is what forced Antimenes to establish the financial regime I have commented on. I will observe, taking the example of Cleomenes in Egypt, that the king was not averse to entrusting selected men with missions whose financing was only partially in place. It was up to them to find the means to complete their assigned tasks successfully. Cleomenes of Naucratis, as we saw, was obliged to resort to some occasionally shady dealings in the performance of his duty. In Macedonia, Antipater was also sorely tested. If, early on, a certain number of

---

77. Cf. P. Goukowsky, *Essai sur les origines du mythe d'Alexandre* I (Nancy, 1978), pp. 191–92, "Le luxe royal d'Alexandre."

78. See my article, "Philippe II de Macédoine jugé par Théopompe," *NAC* 30 (2001), pp. 87–99.

talents were dispatched to him, there is no further mention of Alexander's sending him comparable aid between 331 and 324, despite Antipater's constant requests for assistance. It is only at the end of the reign that, according to Diodorus, a fleet brought considerable sums to Macedonia.[79] Financial requirements beyond their means also probably confronted the Babylonian authorities in 324/323.

Antimenes and Coinage in the Name of Alexander

The chronological uncertainties we have encountered in dating the various coinages that began in Babylonia after 331 prevent an exact appreciation of the role Antimenes played in monetary affairs.

Mazaeus inaugurated the silver "lion" coins in 331/330. I have conjectured that the issues ceased for a time upon the satrap's death (end of 328): the imitations that subsequently appeared seem to argue in favor of such an interruption. If that is so, at what date did the official striking of this coinage recommence? Was it Harpalus who resumed production of these coins? Would he have realized the fiscal advantages that the existence of a local currency provided, whose weight might be substandard? Only a corpus could possibly answer these questions and permit, perhaps, an estimate of how much of the coinage was issued during Antimenes's time in office.

These same uncertainties recur with the double darics and their associated darics. Nicolet-Pierre, it will be recalled, came to think that these coins were not issued before Alexander's death. That is very possible. If, however, some issues were to be placed prior to 323, we would then have to determine what the reason was for striking such a coinage.

As for the silver tetradrachms imitating the types of Athens and sometimes bearing the name of Mazaces, I will put them aside because they were struck independently of the Babylon mint and because Antimenes, in all probability, was not involved in their production.

On the other hand, if the ideas I have set forth above concerning Alexander's coinage at Babylon are acceptable, Antimenes's role in the issuing of these coins is easier to clarify. Indeed, it seemed to me that the earliest among them can be placed around 325/324 and that the rate of production immediately accelerated. Possibly the Babylonian mint did not begin producing Alexanders before Archon and Antimenes were appointed to lead the province. Antimenes's activity would have been important. While in theory subordinate to the satrap, his position as chief financial officer involved him with coinage, and it was he who had to furnish the metal necessary for projected issues.

---

79. On this information of Diodorus (18.12.2), see above, p. 50.

The need to strike Alexanders must have imposed itself quite quickly on the Babylonian officials. I have no doubt that some of the sovereign's desired outlays could not have been met without recourse to this currency. To be sure, there were the "lion" coins, which were used in some local payments (many of the latter continuing to be settled in kind or in uncoined metal, as under the Persian regime). But to build the pyre of Hephaestion and celebrate his funeral rites probably required materials from western suppliers. The call went out to numerous artists and technicians from the West, and the contests organized for the occasion attracted foreign athletes and virtuosi. These people demanded remuneration in a universally recognized coinage. Alexanders recommended themselves as a means of payment: they were the king's coinage and he guaranteed their value throughout his immense empire. The issues of Cilicia, Phoenicia, Syria, and Macedonia had familiarized the Mediterranean world with this currency. The large public works the king undertook at Babylon were also probably partly paid for with Alexanders (especially where non-Babylonian experts and imported products were involved). So, too, were the Phoenician seafarers whom he recruited and the mercenaries he enlisted for his intended Arabian expedition.

These circumstances could explain the sudden activity I believe discernible in the striking of Alexanders at the Babylon mint during this time. This currency was clearly meant for international circulation, as Price's list of hoards shows: the chief among them, unearthed from the late fourth and third centuries in Phoenicia, Egypt, Asia Minor, and Greece, contain Babylonian Alexanders.[80] The difference between these coins and the "lion" coins is clear: the latter left Babylonia only rarely.

Note that the money supply represented by the Alexanders issued at Babylon around the time of the king's death, on my chronology, amounted to only a modest part of the costs that the provincial administration had to assume. I propose accepting that Groups 1 and 2 were used to pay the expenses Alexander incurred. Group 2 extends beyond 323, but sums probably still remained to be settled after this date for Hephaestion's funeral rites and the sovereign's pet projects. Surely other expenses accrued after June 323. But in any case, examining Groups 1 and 2 more closely is not without interest.

[We have seen that obverse dies for the tetradrachms totaled about 87; there are 4 obverse dies for the decadrachms, the equivalent of 10 tetradrachm dies. The dies used for smaller denominations, according to information I have from the American Numismatic Society, equal in all about 1 tetradrachm die. In addition to silver coins, gold staters were produced, for which 5 obverse dies are known. Supposing that c. 323 the ratio between gold and silver was 1:10, and that one gold stater of 8.60 grams was accordingly worth 5 silver tetradrachms of 17.20 grams, the 5 stater

---

80. *Alexander* (1991), pp. 57ff.

dies counted could be equated with 25 tetradrachm dies. In all, the value of the metal employed for striking Groups 1 and 2 would correspond to the value of silver necessary for the production of tetradrachms deriving from about 123 obverse dies. This is a somewhat arbitrary figure: it is hardly likely, in fact, that a stater die or a drachm die produced the same number of coins as a tetradrachm die and that each tetradrachm die produced the same number of coins. But because I only want to provide an order of magnitude, I think that the sum proposed can be regarded as acceptable.

The question now arising has already been broached in chapter 3:[81] how many coins on average could an obverse die strike? I repeat the figure of 20,000 that I favored earlier. Multiplying 123 dies by 20,000 specimens gives 2,460,000 tetradrachms, equivalent to 1,640 talents. The result speaks for itself: if we believe the tradition, Hephaestion's pyre alone cost around 10,000 talents, and the Macedonian authority incurred other hefty expenses at the same time in Babylonia. Only a small portion, therefore, of the payments was concluded in Alexanders; the rest were settled by the other means I have mentioned above. Even if a die yielded a larger number of coins (30,000 to 40,000), the proportion of Alexanders in the payments would remain relatively modest. And we must not exclude the possibility that one obverse die actually produced, on average, only 10,000 or 15,000 coins.]

In mentioning the other conceivable means of payment ("lion" coins, uncoined metal, settlements in kind), I left out the double darics and the darics associated with them: their chronology is actually too uncertain. Assume that some issues were struck before 323. This currency did not circulate in the western regions of the empire: it does not appear in hoards discovered west of the Euphrates. Moreover, its uncertain metallic composition prevented it from having a wide distribution. It was used, without any doubt, in local trading. So if its striking began before Alexander's death, it would have served with the "lion" coins to cover local outlays. The gold double darics and the silver "lion" coins would contrast with Alexander's gold staters and silver tetradrachms, which had the status of international currencies.

III: Alexander's Coinage East of the Tigris

Mediums of Exchange in the East

Alexander's Currency Requirements

It is almost taken for granted that no series of coins with the name and types of Alexander was struck east of the Tigris during the sovereign's

---

81. On p. 65, note 43, I recalled the debate between Buttrey and F. de Callataÿ, and Marchetti's correction concerning the Amphictyonic coinage at Delphi.

reign. It has also been noted that finds of Alexanders are quite rare in these regions and that they almost always consist of coins struck after the king's death.[82] Price in his collection left some doubt about Susa, whose first group of Alexanders falls, according to him, between c. 325 and c. 320.[83] But as I have already indicated, all the issues of this group carry the legend *Alexandrou Basileōs* and so are probably later than 323.

Most of the territories where Alexander campaigned from 330 did not yet practice the western use of signed and struck coinage. People employed traditional mediums of exchange, barter, payments in kind, weighed metal. One area, however, possessed a more developed system, I mean the regions located to the south of the Hindu-Kush, that is, Arachosia in northwest India.[84] "Bent-bars" succeeded roughly circular silver disks, with round coins accompanying the bars as smaller denominations. These items came into use rather early, because specimens are found in the Kabul hoard, whose burial Schlumberger dated to c. 380.[85]

According to Bopearachchi's classification, the silver disks divide into three groups. The earliest among them reveal an impression on the two sides; the rest carry one or several marks on one face while the other face of the disk remains smooth. The bent-bars are likewise smooth on one side and stamped on the other; the round coin fractions are stamped with a single punch.

Bopearachchi thinks the eighty talents of *signati argenti* ["coined silver"—WEH] that the Indian king of Taxila presented to Alexander in 327 consisted of these stamped bars, whose production was therefore under way by this time.

These disks and bars can be compared, to some extent, to the coins of the western world. In each case, we are dealing with marked metal, distinct from raw and completely anonymous metal. In both cases as well, each series has a uniform aspect and the weights are standardized. Yet differences do exist. The stamps probably guarantee the metal's quality, but who applied them? Considering how enigmatic these marks remain to us, were the actual users able to identify the stamping authority? In contrast, the types on Greek coins (with, quite soon, an accompanying legend) permitted clear recognition of the issuer, who made himself known in this way as both the

---

82. See, for example, Bellinger's remarks, op. cit., p. 70 and, for Bactria, pp. 75–76. O. Bopearachchi's observations tend in the same direction, *La circulation et la production monétaires en Asie centrale et dans l'Inde du Nord-Ouest*, Indologica Taurinensia 25 (Turin, 1999–2000), pp. 73–76.

83. *Alexander* (1991), p. 485.

84. I base myself on Bopearachchi's extensive study, pp. 69–73, cited in note 82.

85. *Trésors monétaires d'Afghanistan* (Mém. Délég. Arch. Franç. en Afghanistan, Paris, 1953), pp. 31–45; cf. *IGCH* 1830. Schlumberger named this hoard's silver disks "coins of a new kind."

master and guarantor of his currency. The king or the city could take various advantages of their coinage,[86] but at least they considered themselves obliged to exchange it at face value. I doubt that the stamps on the disks and bars played such an extended role. For Alexander and his soldiers, King Taxiles's money must have seemed something different from coinage as they knew it.

Alexander was therefore in a world where Greek coinage practices had not penetrated. One might ask if he did not think it more useful, in this situation, to adapt himself to the region's habits by adopting its methods of exchange. This would explain the absence of any mint east of the Tigris.

I am convinced that he did precisely that in a number of cases. To settle his financial problems with rulers and different officials met en route, he employed, I believe, raw metal or other forms of payment (finely wrought objects and merchandise of every sort). In these areas, the booty he gathered, the gifts he received, the tribute he collected, all normally came in this form, so why would he not have re-used them as such?

Yet apparently Alexander's army could not completely forsake signed and minted coins. The Macedonians and Greeks were accustomed to receiving their pay in coined currency. Within the camp, purchases in the markets traveling with the expeditionary force were probably concluded in cash. When Alexander founded cities and fortified strategic positions, the settlers and soldiers stationed there were not without coined currency, or so we are lead to believe. It made sense that these men, left in a strange environment and threatened literally with feelings of complete bewilderment, not be deprived of their customs and especially the coinage to which they were attached. Bernard has provided a psychological explanation for the revolt, in 323, of the Hellenic mercenaries in the upper satrapies, and reasonably so.[87] Signed and minted coinage was a part of the Greek way of life; it could not disappear just like that.

But, in this case, what currency did Alexander have on hand?

We have seen that finds of his own coins east of the Tigris are rare. Probably the soldiers who arrived as reinforcements possessed some Alexanders issued in Macedonia, Cilicia, or Phoenicia (I think that Babylon did not produce currency with the name and types of the king before c. 325/324), but we are talking here of small sums that played only a minor part in the general movement of buying and selling within and around the army.

In these conditions, the first idea that comes to mind is that Alexander employed the coined metal that he carried in his baggage train amongst his other possessions. During the first part of his expedition, coins were

---

86. See the thoughts I have set forth in my *Naissance*, pp. 79–83.
87. *Fouilles d'Aï Khanoum IV, Les monnaies hors trésors. Questions d'histoire gréco-bactrienne* (Paris, 1985), pp. 127–28.

certainly present in the booty, gifts, and tribute that came his way. The seizure of Persian riches was particularly profitable in this regard: recall the 2,600 talents in coin that were captured at Damascus with other valuables; the royal treasure of Susa contained 50,000 talents, 9,000 of them darics. For other treasures, no distinction is made between coined and uncoined metal. But we cannot doubt that the 3,000 or 4,000 talents found at Arbela, the Babylonian funds, the 120,000 Persepolis talents and the 6,000 from Pasargadae included relatively large amounts of coins.

Arbela, Babylon, Susa, Persepolis, and Pasargadae were located in areas where coined money, in theory, did not circulate. But the treasures deposited in these cities constituted special cases. They were the reserves of the Great King, who, at any moment, might need coins to handle the affairs of his empire's western regions. Moreover, he liked to make presents of currency to his distinguished foreign visitors, and he occasionally delighted his eastern subjects with a purse of darics, coins that, owing to their metal and type, could only foster the sovereign's prestige (the subjects in question using them as metal ingots according to local practices).[88]

The Daric: Alexander's Gold Coinage in the East?

So Alexander possibly became the owner of a vast amount of gold darics, the Great King's coinage of choice, which he preferred to keep at the ready and near at hand.[89] The daric might have constituted Alexander's gold currency *par excellence* during his eastern campaigns, from the end of 331 until late 325.

The incident at the Rock of Sogdiana may provide evidence supporting the Conqueror's use of darics. Arrian (4.18.7) relates that, in 329, Alexander arrived at this lofty fastness, reputed to be impregnable, and where, accordingly, many Sogdianians, and even the wife and daughters of Oxyartes from Bactria, had taken refuge. The Macedonian king had a herald proclaim that he would award twelve prizes, decreasing from twelve talents to one, to the first twelve soldiers who scaled the cliff. Arrian, instead of saying "a talent" for the last prize, writes "300 darics," a sum tantamount to a talent in the Persian system. We might deduce from this information that the daric was then in current use, that all the prizes were paid in this coinage (so an outlay of seventy-eight talents), and that the use of the daric

---

88. See my *Naissance,* pp. 71–72; on the prestige Darius I won from his gold coinage, see pp. 167–69.

89. Athenaeus 12, 514e–f, cites Chares of Mytilene, who said that the Great King kept a personal reserve of 5,000 gold talents by his bedside; Athenaeus's narrative leads one to think that these 5,000 talents were darics.

entailed the use of the Persian weight standard.[90] Bosworth, without discounting this possibility, wondered whether the term "daric" in this passage did not have the broader sense of "gold stater"[91]: Arrian employed the expression "300 darics" to avoid repeating the word "talent." Accepting Bosworth's hypothesis, what staters are we talking about? The most natural response would be that Alexander used his own gold coinage, which, at this time, was being struck in Cilicia and Phoenicia and perhaps in Macedonia. But the output of Cilician and Phoenician staters probably did not begin before 332/331. It is difficult to calculate exactly the number of obverse dies engraved in these mints up to the second half of 329, the date of the Rock of Sogdiana episode: between ten and twenty? Such an output would not have sufficed, it seems, for Alexander's needs, even if it had all been earmarked for the army treasury.[92] But this was not the case: one constantly encounters staters from Cilicia and Phoenicia in western hoards.[93] I personally am quite tempted to accept that Arrian's darics were actually Persian coins, and I would imagine that Alexander had such a sizeable number of these coins at his disposal that he was never short of them during his eastern campaigns. The 9,000 talents in darics found at Susa would represent 2.7 million coins; I have no hesitation in assuming that this was only a portion of the Persian gold coins that fell into the Conqueror's hands.

Goukowsky, referring to the present passage in Arrian, also thought that Alexander used darics in the East; he has reasonably posited the existence from 330 "of a mobile mint, basically for striking" this coinage.[94] Bellinger, as well, commented that the issuing of double darics supposed the use of the daric, and that the Macedonian king, therefore, employed the latter.[95] But was the double daric created before 323? This is not certain. In any case, no matter the date of its first appearance, it would probably not have come about unless the daric had been circulating at that time, and on this point I am inclined to agree with Bellinger.

He also reminds us of Berve's proposal that Harpalus's mission at Ecbatana, where he was appointed in 330, was to coin the Persian treasures

---

90. One daric was worth twenty silver sigloi; the Persian talent therefore contained 6,000 sigloi of ±5.60 grams and weighed ±33.60 kilos. The Attic talent also contained 6,000 drachms, but weighed ± 25.8 kilos, the drachm weighing ± 4.30 grams.

91. *A Historical Commentary on Arrian's History of Alexander* II (Oxford, 1995), p. 129.

92. Assuming one obverse die struck 20,000 specimens, 20 dies would have produced 400,000 staters. The rewards for the capture of the Rock, if all paid in gold coins, would alone have cost nearly 25,000 coins.

93. Cf. Price, *Alexander* (1991), pp. 47ff.

94. *Essai sur les origines du mythe d'Alexandre* I (Nancy, 1978), p. 259, note 72.

95. *Essays on the Coinage of Alexander* (New York, 1963), pp. 68–73.

transported there.[96] Bellinger asked himself what currency might have been produced. Would Harpalus have had Alexanders struck? But no issue of Alexanders can be attributed to this mint before c. 310.[97] Rather, would not Harpalus have issued darics? Bellinger thought this a fetching idea and suggested that double darics (especially the specimens of "oriental" aspect, which do not fall within the Babylonian series) were also manufactured at Ecbatana. He would include the group of silver sigloi that Hill distinguished from other Persian sigloi.[98] Bellinger points out, in favor of this theory, that Newell reasonably attributed to Ecbatana the sole gold issue of Seleucus I that had the weight of a double daric (its types the head of Alexander wearing an elephant skin, and Nike with a *stylis*).[99]

Bellinger, however, wondered about the problem of transporting funds. Ecbatana was quite far from the theatre of operations, particularly when Alexander was fighting in Bactria, Sogdiana, or India. The repeated dispatch of coin-laden convoys over this long a route would not have been very easy (or very sensible, I might add, because each convoy would require a heavy guard). Might Alexander have had, Bellinger asked, other mints, farther to the east? This suggestion is not very different from Goukowsky's, who speculated that a mobile mint could conceivably have accompanied the army.

I myself would say, supposing Alexander used darics, that this currency would not have been his only means of payment. He probably also had silver coins at his disposal and, as I have indicated, he resorted to raw metal and exchanges in kind as the situation demanded. Within the army, a certain number of rewards took the form of precious objects, including golden cups and crowns made by craftsmen in the king's retinue. I would imagine, therefore, that the darics seized in Persian treasures arguably sufficed to meet his gold outlays during the Conqueror's five years of eastern campaigning, obviating the need to strike any himself. If that is so, if the daric really became Alexander's gold coinage *par excellence* at this time, his relative indifference to the staters he had created in 332 is understandable.

Note that few darics have been discovered east of the Tigris. I. Carradice has thoroughly researched the hoards containing Persian coins: he found only one group of seven darics, from Iran, to which eight darics from

---

96. *Das Alexanderreich* II (Munich, 1926), pp. 76–77.
97. Price, *Alexander* (1991), pp. 489–90.
98. I have mentioned this group of sigloi earlier in this chapter, p. 210, note 25, where I expressed some reservations about Hill's thesis.
99. *ESM*, p. 171, no. 460, pl. 35, 6. These coins are without legend. The symbol of a horned horse's head and the letters ΔI allowed Newell to attribute them to Seleucus I and assign them to the Ecbatana mint.

the Oxus deposit must be added.[100] This deposit, whose composition is confused and somewhat disconcerting, included items dating from the second century BC; besides darics, it contained double darics and sigloi.[101]

The Other Coins Alexander Would Have Used in the East

In addition to gold coins, Alexander's coffers surely contained sizeable quantities of silver coins. This silver currency would have come his way through outright seizure or payments he received. It was presumably composed of coins of diverse origins, reflecting the variety of currencies produced at this period in Greece, Asia Minor, and the Near East. Persian sigloi, whose issuance is to be situated in western Asia Minor, were probably not absent from the royal treasury, which also undoubtedly contained some examples of Alexander's own coinage, coming from Macedonia, Cilicia, and Phoenicia. But in all likelihood the most well-represented coins were Athenian and pseudo-Athenian tetradrachms. These coins, prior to Alexander, had already penetrated deep into the East (the Kabul hoard, buried c. 380, included a large group), where they were treated as simple metal ingots and readily cut up. Granting that Alexander employed coined metal within his army and that he deposited it among the settlers and garrisons whom he charged with guarding conquered territories, we may suppose that coins with Athenian types were a major component of this money supply, with Alexander tetradrachms playing only a minor role.

This hypothesis is all the more likely because it seems certain that Athenian imitations were struck even in central Asia at the end of the fourth century: I refer to the remarks of Bernard[102] and the suggestions of Amandry and Nicolet-Pierre in their 1994 publication of the Afghanistan hoard. Additionally, a group of "eagle" drachms and diobols from this period carry an image of Athena of Athenian inspiration on the obverse (except for some diobols that show a head of Zeus), as do certain coins in the name of Sophytos. Seleucus I's royal coinage, inaugurated at the beginning of the third century, put an end to these local productions.

Bernard, studying the manpower of the Greco-Macedonian settlers whom the Conqueror established in the north and south of the Hindu Kush, has rightly highlighted this population's important role in developing

---

100. "The 'regal' coinage of the Persian Empire," *Coinage and Administration in the Athenian and Persian Empires*, BAR International Series 343 (1987), p. 87.

101. Cf. A. R. Bellinger, "The Coins from the Treasure of the Oxus," *Amer. Num. Soc. Museum Notes* 10 (1962), pp. 51–67; IGCH 1822. I have already mentioned this hoard above, chapter 4, p. 105, note 72.

102. *Fouilles d'Aï Khanoum IV: Les monnaies hors trésors* (Paris, 1985), pp. 20ff.

coinage practices in these regions. Apropos of Bactria, he says: "There is therefore nothing improbable in supposing that in Bactria, one of the richest provinces, where the number of settlers must have remained high despite the drain in 323, the authorities were concerned about coinage problems and opened one or several mints. The preponderance of small denominations [in the "eagle" series and that in the name of Sophytos] shows that these issues were meant not for large-scale international commerce, which the political circumstances scarcely permitted at the time, but for local business and more, undoubtedly, for the Greek than the indigenous populations whose trading must have remained based upon barter."[103]

IV: A Mysterious Group of Silver Coins: The Coinage Memorializing Alexander's Combat with King Porus in India

On several occasions, I have mentioned the "Babylon hoard," whose coins first appeared on the market in 1973. Price provided a partial list of its contents in the 1991 volume dedicated to Waggoner's memory. He counted 300 coins, and I have already commented on the 106 "lion" specimens struck at Babylon, as well as on the tetradrachms and the 2 drachms with Athenian types (163, among which at least 61 have every likelihood of being "Babylonian").

The lot also included a large number of specimens with the types of Alexander. Price described eight Babylonian decadrachms (belonging to my Group 2), but in the absence of sufficiently precise information, he provided very few details on the tetradrachms. He merely noted that some of them carried the letters M-ΛY, my Group 3 from Babylon; apparently none was in the name of Philip III.

The "Porus" Decadrachms and Related Tetradrachms

Besides various other coins, the hoard contained an extremely interesting series: a) seven decadrachms called "Porus," marked with two monograms, one in the form of Greek *xi* with a vertical central bar, the other combining the letters A and B (pl. 8, 8 and 11); b) eleven tetradrachms, similarly marked (pl. 8, 9); c) three tetradrachms without marks but whose types connect them to the preceding decadrachms and tetradrachms (pl. 8, 10)

---

103. *Ibid.*, pp. 28–32.

I will not rehearse in its entirety the scholarly literature relating to this group of coins. Bernard[104] and R. J. Lane Fox[105] have done recent and thorough studies. The discussion has focused on two principal points: explication of the types and determining the date and place of issue. Price raised another problem: on what standard was this currency struck?

I will begin with the question of weight standard. The eight Alexander decadrachms that the hoard contained fall between 41.72 grams and 43.23 grams, clearly the Attic standard. Yet the seven "Porus" decadrachms range between 38.73 grams and 40.96 grams, and Price preferred to regard them as Babylonian five-shekel coins (a shekel weighing ± 8.4 grams). Likewise, the weight of the tetradrachms ranges between 14.72 grams and 16.30 grams, so they could be two-shekel coins. One of the two decadrachms kept in the British Museum, however, weighs 42.20 grams, which would accord with the Attic standard.[106] Recall that Price thought the "lion" coins struck after 328 were also double shekels. I am more inclined to view them as slightly underweight coins of Attic standard meant for local use, and I would be tempted to propose the same explanation for the "Porus" coins.

As for the types, Bernard has decisively advanced their interpretation. I provide a brief description.

The decadrachms (pl. 8, 8 and 11) on the obverse show Alexander astride a horse attacking Porus perched on an elephant, with someone else beside him; on the reverse, Alexander is shown standing, crowned by Nike, and holding a scepter and thunderbolt; his helmet has a curved point on top and is decorated with a crest and two large plumes on the sides; he wears a breastplate and mantle, and he is armed with a sword (note that his head covering is the same on both sides of the coin).

The tetradrachms, whose monograms connect them with the decadrachms (pl. 8, 9), have a standing archer drawing a bow on the obverse and an elephant on the reverse. The remaining tetradrachms, on one side, show the same elephant, carrying two individuals, as the decadrachms; the other side has a charging four-horse chariot (*quadriga*) carrying an archer similar to the archer of the aforementioned tetradrachms (pl. 8, 10).

These coins have no legends inscribed.

Bernard clearly established that the "the types, with only one exception (the depiction of Alexander with thunderbolt) reproduce the facts of

---

104. "Le monnayage d'Eudamos, satrape grec du Pandjab et maître des éléphants," *Orientalia Josephi Tucci memoriae dicata*, G. Gnoli and L. Lanciotti eds. (Rome, ISMEO, 1985), pp. 65–94.
105. "Text and Image: Alexander the Great, Coins and Elephants," *Bulletin of the Institute of Classical Studies* 41 (1996), pp. 87–108.
106. *BMC*, p. 191, no. 61.

war in the Indian world with such realism that we have to think the engraver knew them first hand." He demonstrated that none other than Porus is the elephant driver on the decadrachms (and second group of tetradrachms). He emphasized that the standing or *quadriga*-mounted archer was Indian, as his bow, his clothing, and his hairstyle prove. Bernard showed that the war chariot "also fits quite naturally within the Indian context." As for the elephants, they symbolize India and the country's customary methods of combat.[107]

The representation of the Nike-crowned Alexander in helmet and breastplate and holding a thunderbolt creates a problem. One is tempted with Bernard to see the image as Alexander, the demigod son of Zeus. Lane Fox has downplayed this interpretation. Alexander, he says, is depicted on both sides of the decadrachms, on the obverse as a warrior attacking a valiant enemy, and on the reverse as a victorious king. "This clear context of human victory," he writes, "limits the scope of the thunderbolt: it need only signify that Alexander conquered barbarian India with the special aid of Zeus."

When and where these coins were issued is controversial. For Price the hoard was "almost certainly" buried in 323/322. He argued that the majority of Alexander specimens he inventoried belonged to Groups 1 and 2 of the Babylon mint. Group 3 (with the marks M-ΛY) was also represented, but only, it seems, by the very earliest issues because none of the coins that appeared on the numismatic market carried the legend *Basileōs Philippou*. The "Porus" decadrachms and their associated tetradrachms were therefore struck during Alexander's lifetime. Price is clearly tempted to attribute them to the Babylon mint, where they would rejoin the "lion" coins and double darics.

Lane Fox shares Price's view on the date of the hoard's burial but not on our coins' place of issue, Susa in his opinion. The monogram formed by the letters A and B accordingly designates Aboulites, still satrap of Susiana in 324, while the other monogram belongs to Xenophilus, commander of the citadel (Curtius 5.2.16) and guardian of the treasury (*thēsaurophylax*, Diodorus 19.18.1). Aboulites, it is argued, had these coins struck before the arrival of Alexander (who came to Susa in early 324), at a time when the Conqueror's Indian exploits had already begun to assume legendary status. The 3,000 talents of coined silver, which Plutarch says (*Alex.* 68.6) he remitted to the king, consisted partly of this currency (which did nothing to prevent Aboulites's punishment for dereliction of duty).

Bernard thought that the hoard was buried not in 323/322, but only in 317 or a little later. Such a date is not impossible, because the Alexanders belonging to the find have only been described rather vaguely and we cannot

---

107. Goukowsky also perceived the Indian characteristics of these images, *Essai sur les origines du mythe d'Alexandre* II (Nancy, 1981), p. 3.

be completely confident about the information Price assembled on the subject. Bernard argued that Eudamus issued the "Porus" decadrachms and their related tetradrachms in 317. Eudamos had held an important command in the Punjab up to 318/317. In that year he left for Iran with 500 horsemen, 300 foot soldiers, and 120 elephants captured from Porus after he assassinated him. He took part in the coalition against Peitho, the satrap of Media, then switched sides to Eumenes (Antigonus's opponent), whom he met in Susiana in early 317. It was in Susa that Eudamus, "master (*hēgemōn*) of the elephants" as Plutarch calls him (*Life of Eumenes* 16.2), would have struck the series we are examining, because he needed currency.

Although this interpretation merits consideration, and despite our uncertainty over the deposit's exact composition, I prefer, for the time being, to stick with the list Price presented and to think that the treasure was not buried as late as Bernard wants. I will, however, somewhat alter Price's proposed dating. Group 3 from Babylon, which does appear in the hoard, did not begin, in my opinion, before 322/321 and, in that case, the burial could have occurred in 321 or in 320, taking into account the fact that no specimen with the legend *Basileōs Philippou* has been identified.

Bernard dated the "Porus" decadrachms after Alexander's death, considering it hardly likely that their remarkable reverse type (Alexander in full panoply and wielding a thunderbolt) was engraved during the king's lifetime. I share this opinion. Bernard's suggestion that this image was the expression of a military cult seems to me pertinent. This cult could have been fostered, for political ends, within the army that was stationed at the time along the Tigris and the Euphrates. Alexander's hearse, built at Babylon and described by Diodorus (18.26–27, commenting on its high cost), shows the veneration surrounding the dead king's memory. We note that one of the tableaux decorating the hearse "showed the elephants arrayed for war who followed the bodyguard. They carried Indian mahouts in front, with Macedonians fully armed in their regular equipment behind them." We may well imagine that Perdiccas, then all-powerful in Babylon and full of ambition, oversaw the hearse's decorative scheme. Its Indian references recall the types on the "Porus" coins. Could there be a connection between hearse and coins?

Objectively speaking, an attribution of the "Porus" coinage to Babylonia is feasible. The presence of several specimens of this exceedingly rare series (the decadrachms previously numbered three, the tetradrachms were unknown) in a hoard found in Iraq is not, I think, without significance. It has been emphasized, moreover, that these coins demonstrate peculiarities in manufacture also found in the "lion" coinage, the double darics, and the Athenian imitations.[108] In addition, a

---

108. Bernard, op. cit., pp. 81–82.

certain stylistic awkwardness recalls the clumsiness of the engravers of the pseudo-Athenian tetradrachms.[109]

More recently, F. L. Holt has conducted a richly documented investigation of the Porus coins.[110] He thinks we are dealing with commemorative medallions distributed to officers and soldiers as rewards for valor (*aristeia* in Greek). They would have been struck in India, shortly after Alexander's victory over Porus, hence in 326, and the circumstances of their issue would explain their varying weights and occasionally slapdash style (even if the engravers themselves were not unskillful). The coins might have been used as a means of payment, and soldiers so recompensed took some of them from India to Babylonia.

In 2005, O. Bopearachchi and P. Flandrin published a hoard discovered only a short while ago at Mir Zakah (in Afghanistan, southeast of Kabul, in the mountainous region separating ancient Bactria from the Indus basin).[111] Mir Zakah never ceases to provide ancient coins in impressive quantities. The hoard just unearthed seems to have been buried at the beginning of the third century BC. I refer for its contents to the work of the previously mentioned scholars, and I deal here only with the coins concerning Alexander and Porus.

The two authors described a new gold coin weighing 16.75 grams. Alexander's head, wearing an elephant skin, is on the obverse; the horn of Zeus Ammon envelopes his ear, and the aegis is tied around his neck. On the reverse, an elephant advances towards the right, and the two monograms above and below the elephant are the same as on the "Porus" decadrachms and the group of related tetradrachms (note that the two monograms appear on the reverse of the gold coin; on the decadrachms and the tetradrachms, one is on the obverse, the other on the reverse).

One wishes that this gold coin, with all its peculiarities, were made easily accessible to scholars, who would like to satisfy their legitimate curiosity by a close examination.[112]

---

109. The "Porus" decadrachm put up for the Leu 13 sale, April 29–30, 1975, no. 130, seems to have been an overstrike (cf. pl. 8, 11), as the author of the sale catalogue notes; traces distinguishable on the reverse, to the left, recall the mane of the lion whose skin encircles Herakles's head on Alexanders. But this is probably an illusion; it would be helpful to examine the coin itself, whose current whereabouts I do not know.

110. *Alexander the Great and the Mystery of the Elephant Medallions* (Berkeley, 2003). The mystery, Holt says, is comparable to the mysteries it took the logic and cleverness of Sherlock Holmes to solve. Holt invites us to think that his own investigation is conducted along the lines of the celebrated detective.

111. *Le portrait d'Alexandre le Grand. Histoire d'une découverte pour l'humanité* (Paris, 2005).

112. W. Fisher-Bosserl, *Amer. Num. Soc. Magazine*, 5, 2 (Summer 2006), pp. 62–65, and S. Mani Hurter, *Schweizerische Numismatische Rundschau* 85 (2006), pp. 185–95, doubt this gold coin's authenticity. Other scholars, however, think it genuine. The future, one hopes, will settle the issue.

The hoard contains at least fifteen decadrachm specimens, whereas previously only ten or so coins had been identified.

Bopearachchi and Flandrin favor, like Holt, an Indian production shortly after Alexander's victory in 326. They note that the presence of at least fifteen decadrachms in the Mir Zakah hoard weakens the case for the coinage's being struck at Babylon (there were seven decadrachms in Price's partial listing of the Babylon hoard).

The coinages produced in the eastern empire in the time of Alexander present multiple problems. Their chronology remains often doubtful (beginning with that of the Alexanders), the site of their production remains uncertain in a number of cases, and their interpretation is not always easy. The question of which currency the sovereign used in the upper satrapies and in India cannot be answered confidently, either. What is certain is that these territories, which the Great King had not attempted to convert to the use of coins, found themselves suddenly in contact with a new form of exchange. Babylonia was given mints. A population (military and civilian) accustomed to using coinage traversed the East, as far as Sogdiana and the Indus. Yet we cannot doubt that local practices still endured for quite some time. Nevertheless, Alexander's arrival marked the beginning of an evolution whose effects will become clear, especially in Bactria, under the Seleucids and the Greek kings who succeeded them. Throughout this chapter we have tried to gauge how much historical information coins provide. They teach us that the famous Babylonian "lion" coinage began with Mazaeus, the Persian grandee whom Alexander named satrap of Babylon. They encourage us to think that Mazaces, Darius III's last satrap in Egypt, was later politically active on the banks of the Euphrates. They make us aware, to our surprise, that a gold currency with the type of the Great King was maintained after the last of the Achaemenids. As for the "Porus" coinage, it probably owes its existence to an episode of some importance. At present, we cannot locate the incident exactly in time and place. Nonetheless, engraving of particularly original types commemorated it.

Conclusion

Having now completed the analyses I undertook in chapters 1 through 7, I can sum up and comment as follows on Alexander's conduct of monetary affairs.

In Macedonia, the young king *may* have heralded his accession by issuing a group of so-called "eagle" silver tetradrachms. This coinage, whose dating is open to discussion, had only limited volume and a short life. If it actually belongs to the early part of the reign, we have to believe that Alexander abandoned it quite quickly. Might he have thought, as his ambitions grew, that the types and weight of the "eagle" coins were too strictly Macedonian? What appears certain is that he struck gold staters and silver tetradrachms of Philip II at this time, and they were produced in sizeable quantities for several years. It seems that Alexander, dissatisfied with the "eagle" coins, preferred to wait for something better and to use Philips, which had the advantages of familiarity and esteem.

The conquest of western Asia Minor, starting in April 334, apparently did not alter the sovereign's monetary conduct. In Macedonia, Antipater continued, most probably, to strike Philips. In western Asia Minor, it seems that no royal mint was opened at that time, and we assume that a certain number of cities continued to issue their own coinage. Curiously enough, when Alexander did create his silver tetradrachms and gold staters, he judged it neither useful nor opportune to organize their striking in western Asia Minor immediately: on the chronology I have presented, his own production did not begin there until the very end of the reign.

The victory at Issus in the autumn of 333 is probably the key event that influenced coinage affairs in the decades to come. Several indications, in fact, lead us to think that silver tetradrachms with the Herakles head and Zeus types were inaugurated in the battle's aftermath at Tarsus. A little later, upon the fall of Tyre (July 332), the Conqueror initiated his gold staters with Athena head and Nike holding a stylis. If my conclusions are correct, the Tarsus mint had the honor of issuing not only the first tetradrachms of Alexander but also his first staters. Sidon, and then Tyre, followed Tarsus's lead. Antipater, for his part, did not tarry in producing the new royal coinage in Macedonia. The Conqueror's homeland was bound to make it known and expand its usage.

It would not have surprised us at all if, from 332–330, the already conquered territories and those Alexander was soon to subject were granted one, or several, royal mints. They would have been responsible for furnishing, in the form of Alexander's coins, the funds necessary for any payments requiring coined currency.

Yet nothing of the sort occurred. At the end of 332, Alexander took control of Egypt and entrusted its governance to Cleomenes of Naucratis. No coinage of any kind seems to have been issued in this country between 332 and c. 325/324. It is even possible that the issuing of Alexander's coinage, whose inception I have cautiously dated prior to his death, did not take place in Egypt until after June 323.

Babylonia also holds a surprise in store. Alexander became master of this satrapy in October 331. In marked contrast to Egypt, it, indeed, proceeded to issue coinage immediately after the Macedonians' arrival. But the Babylon mint did not begin by producing coins with the name and types of Alexander. It struck tetradrachms in the name of the satrap Mazaeus and with his chosen types, types that continued after his death in 328; this is the coinage we call "lion." Moreover, it is not out of the question that before 323 the Babylon mint undertook to issue gold double darics and darics, showing the image of the Achaemenids' Great King as an archer. Finally, somewhere in Babylonia Athenian imitations (certain among them in the name of the former Persian satrap of Egypt, Mazaces) appeared during Alexander's lifetime. Alexander coinage, in this setting, seems to have been a little overlooked: I would place the start of its issue at Babylon only towards the end of the reign, perhaps in the early months of 324.

No evidence entitles us to suppose that Alexander opened a mint in the immense territories that submitted to him east of the Tigris. It has been suggested that a mobile mint accompanied him and moved along with the army. This remains hypothetical because no group of coins presents any characteristics in which the work of itinerant moneyers may be discerned. The apparent absence of Alexander mints in these regions is to be emphasized: the king waged war there for six years, and he probably could not forgo coined currency for handling some of his expenses.

Thus, during most of the reign, in the areas of the empire west of the Tigris, apparently only two regions, Cilicia, Phoenicia, and Syria on the one hand and Macedonia on the other, produced the coinage that Alexander created after his victories at Issus and Tyre. The other areas, namely, western

Asia Minor, Egypt, and Babylonia, waited several years before undertaking its production. As for the eastern satrapies, from Susiana and Media to Bactria and India (satrapies covering a territory more vast than the rest of the empire), we have so far been unable to locate any mint of Alexander there.

One conclusion is, therefore, compelling: Alexander did not mandate exclusive use of his coinage throughout all of his possessions. He took no all-encompassing measures. It follows that, in some regions, mints antedating Alexander's arrival continued to function, and that coins of local origin continued to be used almost everywhere, a point of view that the contents of coin hoards confirm. Cilicia provides interesting testimony: local silver staters were struck there contemporaneously with Alexander tetradrachms and received the Macedonian satrap's guarantee. As for Babylonia, I stressed above the diversity of coinages that were produced there after 331 under the aegis of the Macedonian administration.

The philosophic vision found in Plutarch, according to the most reliable manuscript tradition, is also not based on reality. We cannot say that the Conqueror (with a civilizing intent, Plutarch writes) sought to replace "barbarian" coinage with his own. Likewise, examination of the evidence belies the idea, often accepted today, that Alexander desired an "imperial coinage." The silver tetradrachms with Herakles head and the gold staters with Athena head did not, during Alexander's lifetime, eclipse, let alone supplant the other currencies within the empire.

Yet one might object that the Conqueror does seem to have paid more attention to his coinage at the end of his reign and that he did intend to make it the one true currency of his realm. Indeed, it is precisely then that Alexander mints opened in western Asia Minor, perhaps in Egypt, and probably in Babylonia, on a plausible chronology. Could we not interpret this development as the opening salvo in the sovereign's new monetary policy?

I keep asking myself if this extension in the production of Alexander's own coins was not, rather, the result of a process whose occurrence required no royal intervention.

Indeed, unless I am mistaken, although the issuing of Herakles head tetradrachms and Athena head staters was limited to two regions during the early part of the reign, this coinage was circulating and had begun to spread. It was the only coinage that bore Alexander's name and that users could think he guaranteed. When, at the end of his reign, the sovereign's decisions required him to make large outlays to beneficiaries hailing from very varied regions, the most suitable currency was that which bore the royal seal and which was universally accepted for that very reason. Take Babylon as an example. The Babylonian authorities in 324 and 323 had to pay all sorts of non-Babylonians who demanded payment in cash: soldiers, technical experts, artists, local suppliers from the Mediterranean world. The "lion" tetradrachms were too parochial in character: their types and the absence of inscription restricted their use to Babylonia. In contrast, the currency with the name and types of the king was entirely designed to become the inter-regional coinage *par excellence*.

The favor, completely understandable, which Alexander's coins enjoyed in this category of transactions would probably not have sufficed to make them the international coinage of the Hellenistic Age. Here the Conqueror's successors played a decisive role. They needed large quantities of coined metal to finance their incessant military campaigning. Finding themselves in the years following 323 under the (nominal) authority of Alexander IV and Philip III, they had no other choice but to strike Alexander tetradrachms and staters. This coinage so dominated non-local cash settlements that it continued to be produced from the third to the first centuries BC, with cities eventually taking over from the kings.

It does not seem that its creator purposely intended this universal use of his coinage. On the contrary, Alexander gives the impression of being somewhat detached with regard to his own currency. Such an attitude gives us pause because we cannot help but ask ourselves what drove Alexander to act like that.

Would he have lacked the time, owing to his brief, ephemeral reign taken up with soldiering, to consummate the monetary reform he had conceived, if only in rough outline? Some authors have advanced this view, but I am not convinced. Withdrawing coins from circulation and replacing them with the king's coinage required two measures: this coinage had to be struck in sufficiently large quantities to meet currency payments throughout the empire, and the treasury had to decree that henceforth the king's coinage was the only acceptable tender for official transactions. These two measures were easy to take. The governors of the different satrapies would not have had any trouble in organizing the striking of the royal coinage, if so ordered. Coins other than Alexanders would have disappeared quite rapidly once the imperial treasury refused to accept them.

A state is undoubtedly led to strike coinage, first and foremost, to pay the expenses for which it is obligated. But beyond that, coinage presents advantages that the issuing authority tends not to ignore. Currency production immediately provides the state with a fiscal resource, the tax derived from coinage manufacturing (what we call "seigniorage"). This resource increases if the state in question imposes exclusive use of its coinage within its borders, because foreign money has to be converted into local currency, and this exchange tax constitutes a substantial source of revenue. Additionally, issuing a coinage can foster the prestige of the king or the city striking it. The coins promote the name and types of the sovereign or civic entity and in some cases represent effective tools of propaganda.

Alexander does not seem to have made a priority of these different aspects of coinage. Perhaps, however, when he created his silver tetradrachms after Issus, and his gold staters after the capture of Tyre, he was anxious to use coinage as a means to assert his power and manifest his supremacy, the viewpoint I set forth in chapter 5. In any case, if he had the idea to institute an "imperial coinage" at that time, it was only a wish, as succeeding events showed.

In fact, when it comes to monetary affairs, motives born either of expedience (whether we call it pragmatism or realism) or psychology (about which we can only have the vaguest sense) seem to have guided Alexander most. It is a really difficult and delicate task to try and unravel the part each of these motives played in the Conqueror's monetary behavior, such as I have believed it could be described.

Political motivation can explain in large part his non-intervention in the coinage of the cities in western Asia Minor and the absence there, for several years, of any issue with his name and types. Alexander was concerned, in my opinion, not to appear less liberal than the Great King, at a time when he was portraying himself as liberator. Because the treasures he seized, the spoils of war, and the cities' contributions provided him with ready means of payment, he could quite easily defer the question of his personal coinage to another day.

Nothing prevented him, in Egypt, from having his own currency struck. But there, too, the financial empowerment provided by local resources possibly freed him from all monetary worry. Egypt offered more engrossing projects: the consultation of the oracle of Ammon and the building of Alexandria.

What we observe in Babylon allows us to say with some confidence that he had made an arrangement with Mazaeus and that, here as well, he deferred the question of his own coinage out of political expedience.

The idea that the daric was the Conqueror's gold coinage east of the Tigris is seductive. If it is correct, we could accept that Alexander had drawn enough darics from the Persian treasures of Susa, Persepolis, and Passargadae to cover his gold currency outlays during his eastern campaigns and that he did not have to trouble himself, therefore, with producing his own coins in this metal. But another factor may have intervened: after Darius III died in 330, the Macedonian sovereign became the Great King and might have thought of the Persian darics (and sigloi) as henceforth his own coinage. He had acted somewhat similarly at the start of his reign vis-à-vis the staters and tetradrachms of Philip II, which he employed as his currency too.

In the midst of all this, the silver coins with Herakles head and the gold coins with Athena head were rather neglected. The confluence of events, not Alexander's deliberate desire, explains the key role they played after a certain date.

Fernand Braudel in *Memory and the Mediterranean* has a chapter entitled "Alexander's Mistake."[1] In his judgment, the Macedonian king "failed

---

1. *Les Mémoires de la Méditerranée* (Paris, 1998), English translation by S. Reynolds (New York, 2001), pp. 244ff.

to recognize the value of the western Mediterranean," and Hellenism would have been better off turning its energies "against Carthage, the Italic peoples and Rome." Braudel realizes that his chapter title is a little "condescending," but he cannot help imagining that a triumphant Hellenism could have "pre-empted the destiny of Rome."

If, following Braudel's lead, we indulge ourselves in remaking Alexander's monetary history, we might ask what his coinage would have been if the Macedonian king had chosen to conquer the West and what place that coinage would have assumed in the western world. We might say that there, too, Alexander would probably have made pacts with cities, but that his currency would have been the one to prevail in transactions beyond the local context. As for the types, they would have been the same: Herakles and Zeus spoke to all minds, and the stylis would have been quite appropriate after the fall of Carthage.

The fact remains, that if Alexander had turned toward the West, the Great King would have kept his throne and continued to strike his own gold coinage, the daric, whose fame in the fourth century is well-known. Would Alexander's gold stater have coexisted with the daric? Would one have won out over the other? On this topic, one could open up an interesting chapter in coinage's fictional history.

Notes to Plates

Plate 1

1. Silver tetradrachm of Alexander struck at Tarsus; on the reverse, Zeus's footstool is clear; under the chair, a *globule*.
2. Gold stater of Alexander struck, in my opinion, at Tarsus; the helmet of Athena is decorated with a serpent; on the reverse, the legend is placed in the left part of the field; on the right, beneath Nike's wing, a *wreath*.
3. Silver stater struck by Mazaeus at Tarsus.
4. Same as no. 3, but the footstool is now discernible.
5. Silver didrachm of Philip II struck at Pella, in my opinion; on the reverse, beneath the horse, a *thunderbolt*; in the exergue, the letter N.
6. Alexander tetradrachm struck at Amphipolis; on the reverse, a *prow* turned to the right; this issue probably inaugurated Alexander's coinage under Antipater in Macedonia.
7. Silver tetradrachm of Philip II struck at Pella in the second half of his reign, with victorious jockey as type; the reverse has no mint magistrate's mark.
8. Silver tetradrachm of Philip II struck at Amphipolis in the first half of the reign, with the mounted king as type; between the horse's forelegs, a *bow*.
9. A one-fifth tetradrachm struck at Pella; beneath the horse, a *thunderbolt*; in the exergue (area below the ground line), the letter N.
10. Gold stater of Philip II, perhaps struck at Pella (symbol: *thunderbolt*).
11. Gold stater of Philip II, struck at Amphipolis (symbol: *caduceus*).

12. "Eagle" tetradrachm of Alexander; on the reverse, *oriental headdress* and *club*.

13. "Eagle" tetradrachm of Alexander; on the reverse, *oriental headdress* and *olive branch*.

14. Tetradrachm of Philip II, struck at Pella; on the reverse, beneath the horse, a *kantharos* (stemmed, two-handled goblet); the style of Zeus's head has been compared to that of the head on nos. 12 and 13.

Plate 2

1.–3. Tetradrachms of Philip II, struck at Amphipolis; symbols: *prow* (1), *stern* (2), *Janus head* (3).

4.–6. Tetradrachms of Alexander, struck at Amphipolis; same symbols.

7.–8. Alexander tetradrachms, struck at Amphipolis and bearing the legend *Basileōs Alexandrou*; on the reverse of no. 7, a *Macedonian helmet*; on the reverse of no. 8, a *laurel branch* to the left and, between the chair legs, the letter Π.

9.–10. Alexander tetradrachms, struck at Amphipolis; on the reverse of no. 9, a *crescent moon* and the letter *pi*, with, between its downstrokes, a tiny *omicron* that often looks like a globule; on the reverse of no. 10, to the left, the letter Λ above a *relay race torch*; between the chair legs, a *dolphin*.

11. Alexander tetradrachm, struck in Macedonia; on the reverse, to the left, a *broad jump athlete*.

12. Distater of Alexander, struck in the same mint as no. 11; on the reverse, to the left, a *comic actor* (?).

Plate 3

1.–8. Gold staters of Alexander, struck in Macedonia; symbols: *kantharos*, *trident*, or *thunderbolt*.

9. Distater of Alexander, struck in Macedonia; symbol: *thunderbolt*.

10. Distater of Alexander, struck in Macedonia; symbol: *kantharos*.

11. Alexander drachm, attributed to Lampsacus; symbol: *Pegasus forepart*; monogram between the chair legs.

12. Gold stater of Lampsacus, struck during the Persian period; on the obverse, beardless head of Herakles; on the reverse, Pegasus forepart.

13. Alexander drachm, attributed to Abydus; symbol: *Pegasus forepart*; above, monogram.

14. Alexander drachm, struck at Miletus; on the reverse, monogram of Miletus.

15. Alexander tetradrachm, struck at Miletus; on the reverse, the monogram of Miletus above a *lion turning back its head* and with a *star* above; a monogram between the chair legs.

16. Alexander drachm, attributed to Magnesia on the Maeander; on the reverse, to the left, a monogram; between the chair legs, *ram's head facing*.

17. Alexander drachm, attributed to Miletus; on the reverse, to the left, a monogram.

18. Alexander gold stater, attributed to Sardis; on the reverse, to the left, *griffin head*.

19. Alexander drachm, attributed to Lampsacus; on the reverse, to the left, *Artemis facing, holding a torch in each hand*; between the chair legs, a monogram.

20. Alexander tetradrachm, attributed to southwest Asia Minor (Side mint?); on the reverse, to the left, a *wreath*; between the chair legs, the letters ΔI: the legend is *Alexandrou Basileōs*.

21. Gold stater with the types of Philip II, struck in western Asia Minor; attributed to Lampsacus (beneath the horses, *facing head* and monogram).

22. Gold stater with the types of Philip II, struck in western Asia Minor; attributed to Magnesia on the Maeander (beneath the horses, a *bee*).

Plate 4

1.–10. Tetradrachms and staters of Alexander, struck at Sidon.

1. Obverse of a tetradrachm from year 1 of Sidon (333/332), kept in New York (American Numismatic Society).

2. Reverse of another tetradrachm from year 1 of Sidon, also in New York; to the left, the letter *sade* (Sidon's initial); beneath the chair, the letter *aleph* (i.e., year 1, 333/332).

3. On this stater, the legend *Alexandrou* is inscribed to the left; beneath the Nike's right wing, ΣI beneath the left wing, a *palm branch* bedecked with a fillet.

4. Beneath Zeus's chair, Σ.

5. On the reverse, to the left, the letter *teth* (year 9, 325/324) and *palm branch* bedecked with a fillet; beneath Nike's right wing, ΣI.

6. For the first time, Zeus has the right leg drawn back; to the left, the letter *teth* (Year 9, 325/324); beneath the chair, ΣI.

7. On the reverse, to the left, the letter *yod* (year 10, 324/323); beneath the throne, ΣI.

8. On the reverse, to the left, K (year 10, but this letter could have been mistakenly inscribed instead of Λ, year 11).

9. The legend is *Philippou*; to the left, O (year 15, 319/318); beneath the throne, ΣI.

10. On the reverse, to the left, A (*alpha*, year 1, i.e., probably 309/308) above the letter M; beneath the throne, ΣI.

11. Tetradrachm of Alexander, struck at Tarsus; on the reverse, A beneath Zeus's chair.

12. Tetradrachm of Alexander, struck at Tarsus; on the reverse, *globule* above the letter B.

13. Tetradrachm of Alexander, struck at Tyre; on the reverse, between the chair legs, M and, underneath, a *globule*.

14. Tetradrachm of Alexander, struck at Tyre; on the reverse, o (the letter *ayn*, probably the initial of Azēmilkos) between the chair legs.

Plate 5

1. Alexander stater, struck at Tyre; the legend *Alexandrou* is inscribed left of Nike; beneath her left wing, o (i.e., *ayn*).

2.–4. Tetradrachms of Alexander, struck at Tyre; on no. 2, left of Zeus, the letters *ayn/kaph*; on nos. 3–4, the same letters, and, below them, the dates 26 (322/321) and 28 (320/319); also, between the chair legs, the letter *aleph*.

5. Bronze Alexander, struck at Tyre; on the obverse, beardless Herakles head; on the reverse, a bow in its case and a club; between the bow and club, *Alexandrou*; beneath the club, TY and the letters *ayn/kaph*.

6. Alexander tetradrachm, struck at Tyre; the letters *ayn/kaph* and year 11 (306/305).

7. Alexander tetradrachm, struck at Tyre; two monograms in circles.

8. Tyrian shekel; on the obverse, Melkart (?) astride a winged hippocamp upon the sea (waves and fish); on the reverse, owl with a scepter and a flail; in front of the owl, the letter o (*ayn*) and a date: year 15.

9.–11. Alexander staters, struck, in my opinion, at Tarsus; the legend is inscribed left of Nike; on no. 9, Athena's helmet is decorated with a serpent, on nos. 10 and 11 with a griffin or lion-griffin; the symbol of no. 9 is a *wreath* (beneath Nike's left wing); the symbols of nos. 10 and 11 are a *caduceus* and a *star*; the *stylis* on nos. 10 and 11 bears a small Nike at each end of the transverse bar.

12.–13. Alexander staters, struck at Tarsus; Athena's helmet is decorated with a griffin or lion-griffin; on the reverse of no. 12, the marks are a *plow* and a *thunderbolt*; on the reverse of no. 13, a *caduceus* and a monogram; the transverse bar of the *stylis* on no. 12 seems to be decorated with two little Nikes, who are clearly discernible on no. 13.

14. Alexander tetradrachm, struck at Aradus; the legend is *Alexandrou Basileōs*; in front of Zeus, a *caduceus*; beneath the chair, the monogram of Aradus.

Plate 6

1. Tetradrachm of Alexander, struck at Byblos, according to Newell, who interpreted the monogram on the reverse as that of king Adramelek.
2. Alexander tetradrachm, struck at Damascus; beneath the throne, ΔA.
3. Gold stater of Alexander, attributed to Salamis on Cyprus, but maybe struck in western Asia Minor; an *eagle* at Nike's feet.
4. Silver stater struck by Mazaeus at Tarsus; on the obverse, Baaltars; behind him, his name in Aramaic; on the reverse, a lion attacking a bull above two rows of battlemented wall; Aramaic legend indicating that Mazaeus is governor of Transeuphrates and Cilicia.
5. Silver stater, struck at Tarsus under Alexander; on the obverse, Baaltars; behind him, his name in Aramaic; beneath the chair, T; on the reverse, same type as on no. 4 but without legend; a *club* is placed in the field; the coin has a test cut.
6. Silver stater, struck at Tarsus; on the obverse, Baaltars as before, but his name in Aramaic is replaced by that of Balacrus (*Balakrou*); in front of Baaltars, a *grape cluster*; beneath the chair, T; on the reverse, bust of Athena almost facing; the coin has a test cut.
7. Like no. 6 but on the obverse the letter B above an *ivy leaf* replaces the name of Balacrus.
8. Gold stater of the pharaoh Taos (Takhos), with Athenian types, with one peculiarity, however: a *papyrus stalk* is placed behind the owl instead of an olive branch; the pharaoh's name is written in Greek.
9. Tetradrachm with Athenian types, but in the name of "Pharaoh Artaxerxes," written in demotic Egyptian; two test cuts on the obverse, one on the reverse.
10. Tetradrachm with Athenian types, but in the name of the satrap Sabaces written in Aramaic; in front of the owl, a mark resembling a stylized thunderbolt surmounted by a crescent moon; on the obverse, on Athena's cheek, the coin has a punchmark.
11. Tetradrachm with Athenian types, but in the name of the satrap Mazaces written in Aramaic; in front of the owl, a somewhat puzzling mark.
12. Gold stater without legend; on the obverse, bounding horse; on the reverse, two hieroglyphs signifying "pure gold."
13. Small bronze coin of Sabaces; on the obverse, the head of Sabaces; on the reverse, a Persian archer; behind him, the satrap's name in Aramaic.

14. Small bronze coin of Mazaces; on the obverse, the head of Mazaces and, in front of it, the satrap's name in Aramaic; on the reverse, prow of a galley; above, the sign accompanying Mazaces's name on no. 11.

15.–17. Small bronze coins showing, on the obverse, a juvenile head, wearing a headdress ending on top in a more or less curved point (rather upright on no. 17); on the reverse, forepart of Pegasus; no marks are discernible on the reverse; on one of the bronzes of Saqqara that he published, Price recognized a *wreath* and the letter A.

18. Bronze coin of Naucratis from a sketch; on one side, a female head and the letters NAY; on the other side, a male head and the letters AΛE; it is difficult to determine which side is the obverse and which the reverse.

19. Alexander tetradrachm, attributed to Sardis; in front of Zeus, a *juvenile head* wearing an oriental headdress with curved point; under the chair, a *triskeles*.

20. Alexander drachm, attributed to Abydus; on the reverse, beneath the chair, a *juvenile head* as on no. 19; before Zeus's legs, a monogram.

21. Bronze coin of Teuthrania (Mysia); on the obverse, laureate head of Apollo; on the reverse, juvenile head wearing the same headdress as on preceding coins; behind the head, the letters TEY are legible.

Plate 7

1. Alexander tetrdrachm, struck at Alexandria, Egypt; marks on the reverse: *ear of wheat* and A.

2.–3. Alexander stater and tetradrachm (only the reverse of the latter is shown), both of Alexandria, having a *ram's head* with a double pair of horns and surmounted by two tall plumes as a symbol; beneath Zeus's chair, a monogram.

4. Tetradrachm of Ptolemy, with the legend *Alexandreion Ptolemaiou*; on the obverse, head of Alexander wearing an elephant skin; on the reverse, a warrior Athena; at her feet, an *eagle* perched on a thunderbolt; behind her, ΔI.

5. Tetradrachm struck by Mazaeus, satrap of Alexander at Babylon; on the obverse, Baaltars; his name to the right in Aramaic; on the reverse, a lion; above, the name of Mazaeus in Aramaic; between the lion's paws, M; the coin has a test cut on the reverse.

6. Imitation of a tetradrachm of Mazaeus: the lion advances towards the right.

7. "Lion" tetradrachm, without legend; Baaltars's legs are parallel, as on no. 5; above the lion, a *spear point*.

8. "Lion" tetradrachm, without legend; Baaltars's right leg is drawn back; in front of the god, a *two-pronged rake*; above the lion, Γ.

9. "Lion" tetradrachm, like no. 8; in front of Baaltars, M; above the lion, ΛY.

10. Gold double daric; behind the archer, a *wreath*; in front of his left leg, M.

11. Double daric; behind the archer, ΛY; before his left leg, M.

12. Daric: same description as no. 11.

13. Double daric; behind the archer ΣTA; under his right leg, MNA; in front of his left leg, a monogram formed by Λ surmounted by Φ.

14. Double daric; behind the archer, same monogram as on no. 13.

15. Babylonian imitation of Athens coinage; on the reverse, to the right, Aramaic inscription where the name of Mazaces is found.

16. Reverse of a Babylonian imitation of Athens; in front of the owl, the enigmatic sign is recognizable that accompanies Mazaces's name on the tetradrachms he struck at Memphis in Egypt (cf. pl. 6, 11); to the right, traces of an Aramaic inscription (Mazaces's name).

17. Babylonian imitation of Athens; the letters AΘE are poorly engraved; the coin has a test cut.

18. Babylonian imitation of Athens; the owl is turned towards the left.

19. Silver stater, struck at Membog-Hierapolis; on the obverse, bust of Atargatis facing left; in the field, *star, crescent moon,* and *ring*; to the left, name of the goddess in Aramaic; on the reverse, imitation of a Sidonian type: a *biga* [two-horse chariot] driven by a charioteer and carrying a bearded individual lifting his right arm; the exergue has a checkerboard pattern; above, an Aramaic inscription.

Plate 8

1. Tetradrachm of Alexander, struck at Babylon; on the reverse, beneath the chair, Φ above M (Group 1).

2. Similar tetradrachm; beneath the chair, a monogram above the M; to the left, a *two-pronged rake* (Group 2).

3. Babylonian decadrachm of Alexander; beneath the chair, the same monogram and M as on no. 2; the field has no symbol (Group 2).

4. Tetradrachm like nos. 1 and 2; beneath Zeus's chair, the same monogram; to the left, M and, above, a *star* (Group 2).

5. Similar tetradrachm, but the legend is *Alexandrou Basileōs*; beneath the chair, the same monogram; to the left, M and, above, a *Nike* (Group 2).

6.–7. Babylonian tetradrachm and stater with the types of Alexander and the legend *Philippou Basileōs*; the markings are LY and M (Group 3).

8. and 11. "Porus" coinage, none with legend. Nos. 8 and 11: decadrachms; on the obverse, Alexander on horseback attacking Porus and his

aide who are mounted on an elephant; above, visible on no. 11, Ξ; on the reverse, Alexander in military garb, holding a thunderbolt in his right hand and crowned by Nike; in front of his right leg, a monogram (visible on no. 8) formed by A and B. No. 11 is an overstrike: on the reverse, traces of an earlier type are discernible (cf. p. 251, note 109).

  9. Tetradrachm; on the obverse, an Indian archer armed with his large bow; to the left, the same monogram, formed of A and B, as on nos. 8 and 11; on the reverse, an elephant; below, Ξ, as on nos. 8 and 11.

  10. Tetradrachm; on the obverse, an elephant carrying two individuals; on the reverse, a charging *quadriga* [four-horse chariot] with driver, at whose side there is an Indian archer with a large bow.

Index

Aboulites, 235, 249
Abydos, 85, 88, 90, 128
Achilles, 10–11
Agis III, 46
Aigeai, 1, 17, 35, 53
Ake, 5, 62, 113–116, 126–128, 130–131, 135–138, 144
Alexander and Babylonia from 325/324, 225–240
    Alexander's arrival at Babylon, 202–203
    Alexander's expenditures in Babylon and Babylonia at the end of his reign, 227–228
    Alexander's treasury in 324/323, 233–238
    coinage activity at the Babylonian mint between 325/324 and late 317, 225–227
Alexander and coinage in Babylonia and East of the Tigris, 201–252
Alexander and coinage in Cilicia, Phoenicia, Syria, and Cyprus, 111–160
    financial and monetary questions, 112–113
Alexander and coinage in Egypt, 161–201
Alexander and coinage in Macedonia from October 336 to April 334, 17–44
Alexander and coinage in Western Asia Minor, 73–110
Alexander and local coinages, 7, 109, 152–160
Alexander and the coinage of Philip II, 41–43
Alexander and Tyre, 125–126
    Alexander's mint, location of, 126–130
    Beginning and end of Alexanders from Tyre, 130–134
Alexander at Tarsus, 117–120
    Alexander's tetradrachms from Tarsus, 119–120
Alexander Drachms of Asia Minor issued at the end of the 4th Century, remarks on the, 95–99

Alexander in Egypt, 162–165
Alexander's coinage East of the Tigris, 240–247
    other coins Alexander would have used in the East, 246–247
Alexander's coinage in Macedonia from October 336 to April 334, 31–37
Alexander's financial situation during summer 334, 80–84
Alexander's financial situation, evolution of, 77–78
Alexander's issuance of his own silver coinage with the types of Herakles head and seated Zeus, 120–123
Alexander's monetary practice in Asia Minor, 84
Alexander's striking of bronze coins in Egypt between November 332 and April 331 with his portrait on the obverse, 171–173
Alexander's struck in Western Asia Minor years after the Macedonian conquest, chronology of, 88
    Alexander coinages from Western Asia Minor and Thompson's theory on the paying of demobilized mercenaries, 92–94
        hoard of Alexander Drachms, 88–92
Alexander IV, 6
Alexandria (Egypt), 60, 162–163, 165, 175, 180–182, 184, 190–194, 197, 198–200, 217, 233, 236
Ammon, 163, 164, 182
Amphipolis, 19, 22, 32, 34–36, 38, 40–41, 52–57, 59, 61–62, 64–68, 70, 71, 72, 117, 137, 147–149, 204, 219, 226
Antigonus, 23, 48, 57, 116, 130–131, 152, 216, 250
Antimenes of Rhodes, 206, 225–226, 228
Antipater and coinage production in Macedonia from April 334, 50–57
    Antipater and the coinage of Alexander, 51–57
    Antipater and the coinage of Philip II, 50–51
Antipater's financial burdens from 334 to 323, 45
    Antipater's campaigns, 46–47
    reinforcements sent to Alexander, 48–50
Aradus, 140, 146
Archon, 205–206, 228, 238
Army (of Alexander), 28, 30, 48, 63, 66, 242
    manpower, 28ff., 76, 235
    cost, 30, 76, 235
    decommissioning, 60, 66, 237
    rates of march, 66, 162
    convoys, 62, 233, 245
Athenian "imitations", 195–196, 211, 214–219, 246, 250
Azemilkos, 111, 125, 129–131, 133–134, 157

Babylonian coinages from 331 to 323, 206–224
    Babylonian coinage of Mazaeus, 206–208

Babylonian coinage with the name and types of Alexander, 219–222
  coinage with the types of Athens struck in Babylonia, 214–219
  Gold double darics and darics, 210–214
  imitations of Mazaeus's tetradrachms, 208
  lion tetradrachms, continuation of the, 208–210
  Newell's classification, arguments in favor of, 222–225
Balacrus 153–155, 207, 213, 223
Basileus, date of appearance on Alexanders, 71, 93, 139, 224
Byblos 111, 129–130, 135, 141, 147, 151, 157–159

Cilicia 16, 48, 54, 62, 66–67, 69, 87, 103, 110–113, 115, 117–119, 121, 123, 125, 127, 129, 131, 133, 135, 137, 139, 141, 143, 145, 147–157, 159, 170, 192, 195, 197, 207, 213, 219, 221, 239, 242, 244, 246
Citium, 142–143, 147, 149, 151
Cleomenes of Naucratis, 179–197
  Cleomenes and the coinage with the name and types of Alexander, 192–195
  Cleomenes as financial manager, 188–191
  currency used, 196–197
  expenses, 182–184
  extraordinary ways to raise money, 184–185
  grain trade, 185–188
  striking of coins other than Alexanders, 195–196
Coinage, gold, 134, 135, 138, 143, 149, 159
Coinage in Macedonia under Antipater from April 334 to June 323, 45–72
Coinage production in Alexander's mints and the return of demobilized soldiers, 60–62
Coinage with name and type of Alexander, 1–17
Coinage with the name and types of Alexander in Western Asia Minor, Attribution of a, 85–87
Coinage with the name of Alexander, traditional interpretation of the, 6–8
Coinages of Cilicia, Phoenicia, Syria and Cyprus in the last two years of Alexander's reign, 149–152
Coins of Philip II after Alexander's accession, the continued striking of, 37–41
  gold stater hoards, evidence of, 38–39
  Philips struck under Alexander, the, 40–41
Colophon, 60, 85–86, 88, 90, 92–93, 97–98, 107
Craterus, 49, 61, 63, 66–67, 69–70, 94, 151, 233
Currency used in Asia Minor from 334 to the end of Alexander's reign, 105–110
  coins used in Asia Minor between 334 and 323, 109–110

did Alexander leave with a supply of Macedonian coins?, 105–106
gold staters of Philip II struck in Asia minor after 323, remarks on, 107–109

Damascus, 112, 136, 141, 143, 147, 149, 151–152, 157, 161, 234, 243
Darics, 8, 109, 134, 210–213, 238, 243–245
Dascylium, 77, 96, 104, 118
Debord, P., 173ff., 174–175, 177–178
Decadrachms, 3, 220, 247
Demanhur, 5
Dies, production capacity, 65, 240
Drachms, 3, 8, 10, 95–97

"Eagle" tetradrachms, 32, 105, 123
Ecbatana, 68, 204, 209, 220–221, 227, 233–234, 244, 245
Egyptian coinage before 332, 165–167
Egyptian coinage before Alexander, 167–168
Ephesus, 81, 86, 92, 101, 104, 142, 169

Fleet, of Alexander, 29–30, 235

Gaugamela, 2

Harpalus, 46–47, 50, 57, 68, 99, 109, 126, 201, 204–206, 213, 228, 229, 234, 238, 244–245
Hephaestion, 67, 129, 181–183, 191, 227–228, 230, 233, 239–240

Issus, 2, 8, 12, 13

Lamian War, 49, 67, 70, 94, 188
Late striking date of the first Alexanders from Asia Minor, reasons for, 99–105
    Alexander and the Greek cities of Asia Minor, 100–101
    Alexander, successor of the Great King, 101–105
Lemaire, André, 126, 128–130, 132–134, 169
Leosthenes, 67, 69
"Liberation" of Greeks, Asia Minor, 102–103
"Lion" coinage, 8, 206–210, 218, 223, 238–239

Macedonian finances under Alexander, 24–31
    Alexander's resources, 26–27
    evidence of ancient authors, 24–26
    expenses of the Macedonian king, 27–31

Magnesia on the Maeander, 85, 86, 88, 90, 93, 107
Mazaces, 162, 166–170, 172, 177, 195, 214–219, 238, 252
Mazaeus, 8, 11, 14, 117, 118, 202, 203, 206
Membog-Hierapolis, 169, 174, 216–218
Memnon, 46, 47, 49, 77, 81, 83, 201
Memphis, 162–163, 165, 168, 170–173, 175–176, 179, 183, 191, 197–199, 214, 216
Miletus, 30, 60–61, 82–83, 85–86, 88–93, 95–96, 103, 107–108, 140
Mithrenes, 77–78, 104, 204, 215, 218
Myriandrus, 119, 141–144, 146–147, 149, 151

Naucratis, 165, 173, 177, 179–181, 183, 188–189, 200, 231, 237

Patraus, 33–34, 36
Pella, 17, 19, 22, 27, 34–36, 38, 40–41, 52–53, 55–56, 63, 71–72, 138, 139
Perdiccas, 6, 117, 123, 152, 154, 205, 212, 227, 250
Philip II, 1, 2, 6, 9–10, 12–13, 115–116, 123, 226, 237
    Monetary situation Philip II bequeathed in October 336, 18–21
Philip III (Arrhidaeus), 5–6, 115–117
Phoros, 81, 101, 183, 229, 233
Porus, 247ff.
Price, M. J., 2, 5, 8, 10, 13, 15, 113, 126, 128, 143
Priene, 81–82, 101

Salamis (Cyprus), 15, 131, 142–143, 147, 149, 151
Sardis, 77–78, 80–82, 85–86, 88–93, 95, 96, 99, 102, 104–105, 107, 109, 118, 204, 215, 232
Side, 60, 75, 85, 87, 93, 95
Sidon mint's striking of Alexander tetradrachms, 113–117
Silver coinage issued by Antipater with Alexander's name, chronology of, 57–60
Sogdiana, 204, 212, 243–245, 252
Soli, 143, 146
Stylis, 3, 10, 12, 15–16, 113, 134, 136, 138, 159, 245
Susa, 2, 150, 202, 204, 209, 216, 220–222, 226–227, 232–234, 236–237, 241, 243–244, 249–250
Syrian hoard, The, 168–170

Tarsus, 8, 11–14, 111–113, 117–124, 131, 134, 137–139, 142–144, 147–156, 159, 207, 216, 219, 223
Taxiles, 234, 242
Teos, 85–86, 88–90, 92–93, 107

Tetradrachms with Herakles head and seated Zeus, 8–16
    E.T. Newell's "high" chronology, 9
    G. Kleiner and O.H. Zervos, the "low" chronology of, 9–13
    M.J. Price, reassertion of the "high" chronology, 13
    new arguments favoring the "low" chronology, 13–15
    the first gold coins of Alexander, 15–16
Thompson, M., 8, 38, 60, 86, 178
Thompson thesis, a critique of, 62–72
Types of Alexander's tetradrachms, comments on, 123–125
Tyre, 5, 11–13, 16, 48, 50, 111–114, 116–117, 122, 124–140, 144–147,
    149, 151–152, 154, 157–159, 161–162, 169, 197, 201

Plate 1

Plate 2

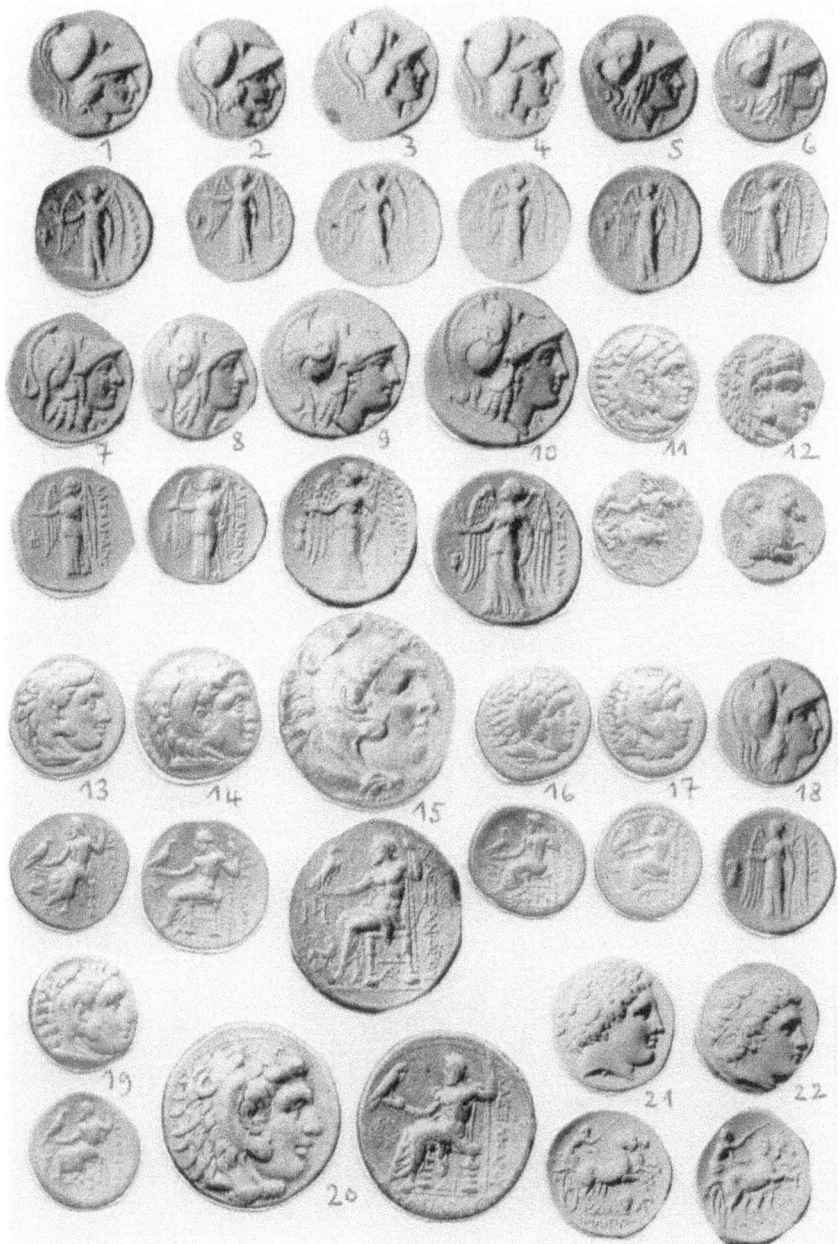

Plate 3

Plate 4

Plate 5

Plate 6

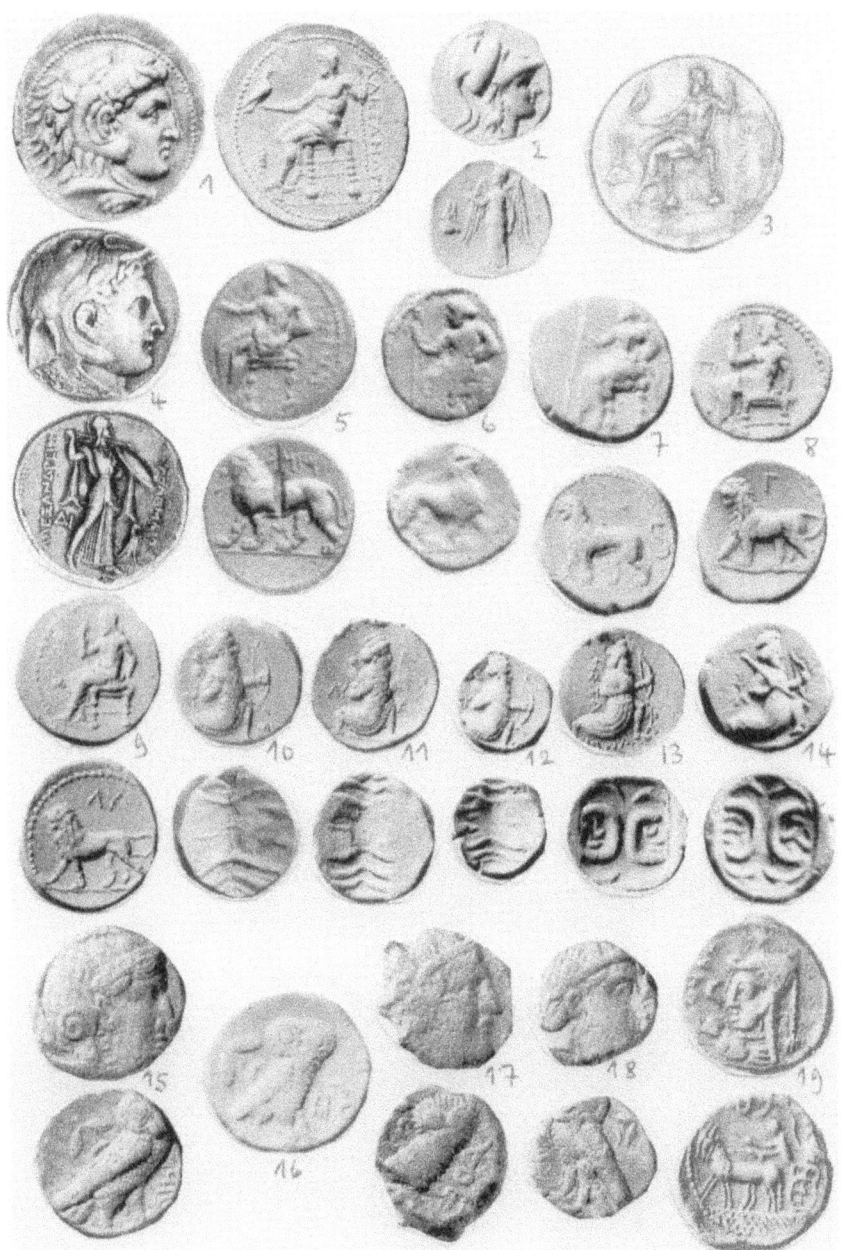

Plate 7

Plate 8